P9-CRR-650

"ELOQUENT . . . THE BOOK IS GLOBAL IN ITS REACH. . . . [A] COMPELLING AND INSPIRATIONAL ACCOUNT."
—*Charleston Post & Courier*

"Compelling and surprisingly easy to read . . . Freedman's emphasis on global experiences and progress, and her use of examples and stories of individual women from villages in Africa to urban areas in the United States, brings concepts to life. . . . Freedman's skill in making complex material readable is evident, as is her passion for the subject."
—*St. Louis Post-Dispatch*

"[A] rigorous work that not only stands as an excellent primer on the current state of feminism, but also includes a historical perspective for content. . . . With an accessible writing style and obvious love for her subject, Freedman has penned a major work that fits well both in the classroom and on the bedside table."
—*Publishers Weekly*

"A welcome and stimulating overview that connects the modern feminist movement not only to its own past, but to global struggles for economic and social justice."
—*Kirkus Reviews*

"*No Turning Back* is a model of how to write global history."
—*Women's Review of Books*

NO TURNING BACK

THE HISTORY OF FEMINISM
AND THE FUTURE OF WOMEN

ESTELLE B. FREEDMAN

BALLANTINE BOOKS • NEW YORK

For my students

A Ballantine Book
Published by The Random House Publishing Group

Copyright © 2002 by Estelle B. Freedman

Grateful acknowledgment is made to the following for permission to reprint
previously published material:
HarperCollins Publishers, Inc.: excerpt from "Lilith, we are your children . . ." from *She
Who Dwells Within* by Lynn Gottlieb. Copyright © 1995 by Lynn Gottlieb. Reprinted
by permission of HarperCollins Publishers Inc.
Alfred A. Knopf, a division of Random House, Inc., and the Wallace Literary Agency:
excerpt from "In the Men's Room(s)" from *Circles on the Water* by Marge Piercy.
Copyright © 1972, 1973 by Marge Piercy and Middlemarsh, Inc. First appeared in
APHRA Magazine. Reprinted by permission of Alfred A. Knopf, a division of Random
House, Inc., and the Wallace Literary Agency.
Bernice Johnson Reagon: excerpt from "Oughta Be a Woman," June Jordan (lyrics)
and Bernice Johnson Reagon (music), copyright © 1980, Songtalk Publishing Co.,
recorded by Sweet Honey in the Rock on Good News (Flying Fish Records, 1981).
Reprinted by permission of Bernice Johnson Reagon.
Thunder's Mouth Press: excerpt from "I Give You Back" from *She Had Some Horses*
by Joy Harjo. Copyright © 1983, 1997 by Thunder's Mouth Press. Reprinted
by permission of the publisher, Thunder's Mouth Press.
International Creative Management, Inc.: "Myth" from *The Collected Poems* by Muriel
Rukeyser (New York: McGraw Hill 1978). Copyright © 1973 by Muriel Rukeyser. Used
by permission of International Creative Management, Inc.

www.ballantinebooks.com

Library of Congress Control Number: 2002095016

ISBN 0-345-45053-1

Cover design by Lynn Buckley

Manufactured in the United States of America

First Edition: March 2002
First Trade Paperback Edition: January 2003

3 5 7 9 10 8 6 4

CONTENTS

PART V FEMINIST VISIONS AND STRATEGIES

PREFACE

Like each of the books I have written, this one began with a question that I could not answer. Several years ago a woman whom I admire asked me to recommend one book that she could read to learn about feminist scholarship. At first it seemed like an easy enough request. I had been reading widely in the interdisciplinary women's studies literature since 1970, the year I entered graduate school in U.S. history and first defined myself as a feminist. Now I taught a course called Introduction to Feminist Studies and chaired the Program in Feminist Studies at Stanford University. As I began to name my favorite books, though, I realized that no one selection fit the bill. My choices tended to be studies of women's history or important theoretical works in other disciplines that would not necessarily appeal to a nonacademic reader. Neither a textbook nor an anthology of short essays, such as those I assign in class, would do the trick either. I eliminated one possibility after another until I realized that no single book brought together the interdisciplinary literature that the past generation of feminist scholars has produced. Unable to fulfill her request, I jokingly said that I would have to write that book myself.

Our conversation that evening and my mental review of the literature stuck in the back of my mind as I finished another book and continued to teach Introduction to Feminist Studies. The course has been an education for me, not only because I must reach beyond my training as a historian to incorporate other disciplines but also because the material can have such a profound impact on students and teacher alike. Each time I enter the classroom, and whenever I witness the intellectual and personal growth that takes place there, I recall a definition I heard in the late 1970s that women's studies is "the educational arm of the feminist movement." My classroom is neither polemical nor overtly political, but by providing a space for rethinking how we treat women, teaching represents my personal contribution to feminism. I began to wonder if I could transpose this educational experience from the classroom to a book that would reach a wider audience.

I had a personal stake in writing about the history of feminism and its contemporary impact, for it allowed me to think back on my own education, particularly the way my consciousness as a woman has changed over the decades. Working with college students, I often recall myself as a sophomore at Barnard College in 1966. I wanted nothing to do with women's movements or women's history. When my advisor, Annette Baxter, suggested that I enroll in her course on U.S. women's history, I had the nerve to reply that I would rather study "real" history. How swiftly times changed during that decade. Just two years later, my values shaken by the antiwar and student movements, I was questioning all of my old priorities. Working in Japan for a summer, I gained a more critical perspective on my own culture. Determined to apply my education to social change, I saw few clear paths beyond the then limited conventional expectations for young women. I was ripe for feminist analysis. As a senior, I was disappointed to learn that women's history would not be offered that year, but as I wrote my honors thesis on African American history I also began reading about Emma Goldman and other radical women.

After graduation, a job in a social justice project that held few opportunities for women contributed to my growing feminist consciousness. It was 1970, and someone gave me a set of mimeographed radical feminist essays that would become *Notes from the Second Year*. They began to change my life. I eagerly sought ideas that could explain the contradictions between my aspirations and my options, between my generation's goals of peace and love and the violence that pervaded our culture. Reading books such as Doris Lessing's *The Golden Notebook*, Simone de

Beauvoir's *The Second Sex*, and Kate Millett's *Sexual Politics* threw open to debate all of my prior training as a nice Jewish girl. I was taking myself seriously in new ways and expecting others to do the same. By the time I started graduate school I needed to know why feminism had taken so long to reach me and how it could be sustained in the future.

Feminism unleashed my intellectual energies. It also made me appreciate the women in my life in new ways, valuing their friendship and love, respecting their choices, and admiring their struggles. Women's caucuses at Columbia University, the early Berkshire Conferences on women's history, and local women's studies gatherings sustained me as I pursued a doctorate at a university that remained unwelcoming to women. Reading Gerda Lerner's early historical writing, Angela Davis on slave women, and later Susan Brownmiller's analysis of the history of rape supplemented my formal graduate training. In the burgeoning women's culture of the 1970s I found music, poetry, and theater that fed my soul as well as my intellect. By the time I finished graduate school, women's history had become a passion as well as a profession.

Once I began teaching, undergraduates asked me to offer my first feminist courses, on U.S. women's history and on women in Third World revolutions. With other women faculty I formed reading groups on interdisciplinary feminist scholarship and worked to launch women's studies programs at Princeton and then at Stanford. In the San Francisco Bay Area after 1976, local study groups on sexuality and on socialist feminism, the grassroots Lesbian and Gay History Project, and the creative and political writing by diverse women of color all transformed my own feminism from its middle-class, East Coast origins to a broader and more diverse political entity. My historical research on women's social reform movements would reflect these concerns. I wrote my dissertation and first book, *Their Sisters' Keepers* (1981), in response to a question about the origins of separate prisons for women in the United States, and I pursued the subject in *Maternal Justice* (1996), a biography of Miriam Van Waters. Writing about the history of sexuality with John D'Emilio in *Intimate Matters* (1988), and in my own essays on lesbian history, I repeatedly asked how gender, race, and class hierarchies have shaped sexual meanings. All of these experiences eventually led me to take on the introductory course in feminist studies.

Teaching FS101 has been as challenging and rewarding an experience as I can imagine. I have watched students change before my eyes, shedding their fears of feminism as they recognize their own power to make choices about their reproductive, economic, and sexual lives. I have seen a subtle shift over time as more students, some of them the children of feminist parents, come into the classroom already comfortable with the feminist label. It has been heartening to watch young women and men forge new political paths, linking gender to the environment or the economics of globalization. At the same time, I have hated being the messenger whose lectures evoke in students a sad recognition of the personal costs of persistent injustice. It disturbs me deeply to learn each year how many young women still struggle to find their voice, to accept their bodies, and to recover from sexual assault. I try to give all of these students the analytical tools to help them make sense of gender in their lives and in the world around them.

Looking back on the personal history that brought me to teaching FS101, remembering how important a book could be to my own development, I determined to write broadly about the history of feminism, largely based on my teaching. Seven years later, having completed the final version of this book, I realize how naive I was to think I could simply write what I teach. Although many of the ideas and examples in the following pages come directly from my lectures or the questions my students have asked, almost half is new material that I learned in the process of working on this book. Along with the historical approach that has structured my teaching, I incorporate more about economics, politics, the arts, and the world beyond my national and disciplinary borders. The task has been both exhilarating and humbling. My perspectives on both gender and feminism have grown enormously, but I remain acutely aware of how much I do not know. Early on, however, I made a conscious decision that I would rather risk making mistakes than ignore entire topics that I believe are critical to understanding feminist history.

In this book, I dwell on what I know best, reiterating throughout how historical changes shape both gender systems and feminist politics. I hope that my framework will allow readers to explore further both the topics I address and those I could not incorporate here. The bibliographical essays at the end of the book offer a guide to both wider and deeper literatures on women, gender, and feminism. They also hint at my debt to the many scholars and writers whose work supplied the building blocks for this synthesis. I have tried to credit everyone who has influenced my interpretations, and I regret any oversights.

I hope that this book can do for others what early feminist writing did for me. At a time of profound changes in women's lives throughout the world, we need tools to probe more deeply into the meaning of gender. At a time when it would be easy to dwell on resistance to feminism, we need a longer historical perspective. Based on the vibrant scholarship surveyed here, I find that the prospects for women have never been brighter. We have much reason to hope that there will be no turning back from a feminist future.

ACKNOWLEDGMENTS

From its inception, this book has been shaped by faculty and students in the Program in Feminist Studies at Stanford University. By claiming the label *feminist*, we announced our interest in understanding and undermining gender inequality, the very goals of this book. The faculty seminars and workshops we have held since 1980 have guided me through scholarly literatures across the disciplines. I will always be indebted to Michelle Zimbalist Rosaldo, with whom I first cochaired the program. The memory of her wisdom continues to shape my academic life. A grant to internationalize women's studies, secured by program chair Sylvia Yanagisako, allowed me to expand the scope of my introductory course. An Associates Faculty Research Fellowship from the Institute for Research on Women and Gender, where the program originated, enabled me to start turning my teaching into a book. During my terms as program chair, administrator Cathy Jensen offered me the same valuable encouragement for my book that she lavished on our students.

Since 1988, teaching FS101 has taught me more than I ever expected to learn about how to confront power and inequality without becoming cynical or immobilized. Every student's question or story has in some way contributed to this process. In addition, it has been a pleasure to share pedagogical tasks with outstanding graduate student teaching assistants: Oona Ceder, Alicia Chavez, Susan Christopher, Antonia

Fore, Jeanne Fraise, Susana Gallardo, Martha Mabie Gardner, Amber Garza, Shawn Gerth, Lisa Hogeland, Diana Khor, Wendy Lynch, Nina Menendez, Kevin Mumford, Daniel Rivers, Lynn Schler, Cari Sietstra, Wilmetta Toliver, Cecilia Tsu, Aviva Tuffield, Karin Wahl-Jorgensen, Kim Warren, and Judy Wu. Diana Khor and Martha Mabie Gardner also provided excellent research assistance.

The quarter before I decided to write this book, I gave permission to Stephanie Enyart, a student in the class, to tape my lectures. She both provided a timely introduction to the importance of accessibility for people with low vision and generously donated her tapes to me. Oona Ceder and Rita Abraldes painstakingly transcribed the tapes, and Susan Christopher tried to decipher my expansive interchanges with students during lectures. I learned from reading these transcripts how much I did not know. I began to track down references and data with the able assistance of Shana Bernstein and Kim Davis. Paul Herman and Susan Lindsay each contributed tasks as well. During the final year and a half of drafting this book, I relied heavily on the extraordinary detective, technological, and statistical skills of Susana Gallardo. I gratefully acknowledge her expert and reliable research, as well as her persistence and wonderful humor. As I completed the manuscript, history majors Caley Horan and Sarah Grossman-Swenson meticulously filled in bibliographic references.

I could not have undertaken this ambitious project without the generous contributions of a legion of Stanford colleagues. Tara VanDerveer deserves credit for asking the initial question that inspired this book. During two history department workshops, graduate student and faculty colleagues gave me astute feedback on early drafts of the chapters on the history of feminism. I am particularly grateful for written comments from Shana Bernstein, Carolyn Lougee Chappell, Gabriela Gonzalez, Gina Marie Pitti, and Kim Warren and for references provided by Peter Duus and Peter Stansky. Two of my faculty comrades, Joel Beinin and Richard Roberts, gave special attention to the material on the Middle East and Africa, and I am indebted to them for teaching me so much. My friend and colleague Hal Kahn has long offered a window onto the history of China, as well as more rides than I can count.

Feedback from colleagues in the Program in Feminist Studies has been crucial to my thinking and has saved me from many an embarrassing error in this book. I benefited greatly from the thoughtful comments on chapter drafts and suggestions for further reading offered by Jane Collier, Hill Gates, Sharon Holland, Purnima Mankekar, Diane Middlebrook, Paula Moya, Susan Okin, and Debra Satz. Visiting faculty members also contributed generously to my interdisciplinary education: Peggy Phelan offered a much needed tutorial on feminist art, and Ann Stoler gave a valuable reading of several chapters. Feminist studies librarian Kathy Kerns has been a patient and knowledgeable resource. In addition, my interdisciplinary and historical range has been expanded over the years through dialogue with the following Stanford colleagues and visitors: Barbara Allen Babcock, Alice Bach, Renate Bridenthal, Judith C. Brown, Laura Carstensen, Carol Delaney, Penny Eckert, Barbara Gelpi, Nancy Hartsock, Carol Jacklin, Terry Karl, Patricia Karlin-Neumann, Shulamit Magnus, Gerda Neyer, Mary Pratt, Cecilia Ridgeway, Paul Robinson, Deborah Rhode, Joan Roughgarden, Kathryn Strachota, Myra Strober, and Yvonne Yarbo-Bejarano.

Outside Stanford, many people contributed to improving this book. Andrew Franklin's detailed commentary on the first draft proved very useful for my revisions. I thank Sue Warga for her careful copyediting. Both my agent, Sydelle Kramer, and my editor, Elisabeth Kallick Dyssegaard, replenished my confidence when I wondered if I could do justice to this challenging project. I thank each of them for believing in it and in me. Elisabeth's comments on several versions of the manuscript drew out the best in me and taught me a great deal about getting to the point.

Several of my friends and colleagues helped sustain my writing at crucial moments. I gained important perspective on teaching and writing from conversations with Ricki Boden. Katherine Callen King offered literary references and much-needed recreation. Mary Felstiner, Joe Gurkoff, Ilene Levitt, Jenna Moskowitz, Peggy Pascoe, Elizabeth Hafkin Pleck, Esther Rothblum, Leila Rupp, Penny Sablove, Carol Seajay, and Nancy Stoller deserve thanks for their insights on chapter drafts, their ongoing encouragement, and their friendship. I am especially appreciative of those who gave close and discerning readings of the entire first draft: Margaret L. Andersen, Nancy Cott, Sue Lynn, Elaine Tyler May, Barrie Thorne, and Susan Christopher each had an important influence on the final shape of the book. John D'Emilio read the entire manuscript early and often and talked me through some of the roughest spots. It is hard to find words that are adequate to express my appreciation for the intellectual insight and personal sustenance he has given me over the past thirty years.

My close family members deserve special mention, for we have spent much time together while I wrote this book. My mother, Martha H. Freedman, has patiently awaited its completion; she started me on the path of critical thinking and has cheered me on throughout this effort. Both my sister, Mickey Zemon, and my niece, Jenna Moskowitz, have understood its importance at every stage. Above all, I want to thank my partner, Susan Krieger, who has lived with me and with this project from the early lecture preparations to the final, intense months of polishing the manuscript. Our twenty years of daily conversations about women and feminism, along with her close readings of chapters, have made the analysis in this book clearer and more honest. Her love and support mean all the world to me.

Because it originated in the classroom, and because they have taught me so much, I dedicate this book to my students, from those who initiated my first women's history seminars at Princeton a quarter century ago to the Stanford history graduate students in whom I take such pride, the generations of Stanford undergraduates who have taken my classes, and especially those who have majored in feminist studies. To all of them I offer here what I have learned so far.

-ONE-

THE HISTORICAL CASE FOR FEMINISM

In the past two centuries, a revolution has transformed women's lives. Unlike national revolutions, this social upheaval crosses continents, decades, and ideologies. In place of armed struggle it gradually sows seeds of change, infiltrating our consciousness with the simple premise that women are as capable and valuable as men. To measure the breadth of this ongoing upheaval of old patterns, consider the way feminist movements have transformed law and politics, from divorce reforms in Egypt and sexual harassment cases in Japan and the United States to the nomination of equal numbers of male and female candidates by French political parties. Or note the change in leadership: During the 1990s, 90 percent of the world's nations elected women to national office, and women served as heads of state in more than twenty countries. Just as important, consider the thousands of grassroots organizations such as Women in Law and Development in Africa, the National Black Women's Health Project in the United States, and the Self-Employed Women's Association in India. Women's movements have never been so widespread.

In *No Turning Back* I explain why and how a feminist revolution has occurred. I argue that two related historical transitions have propelled feminist politics. First, the rise of capitalism disrupted older, reciprocal relations within families in ways that initially enhanced men's economic opportunities and defined women as their dependents. Second, new political theories of individual rights and representative government that developed alongside capitalism extended privileges to men only. In response, feminist movements named these disparities as unjust, insisting on the value of women's economic contributions and the justice of political rights for women. In short, the market economies and democratic systems that now dominate the world create both the need for feminism and the means to sustain it.

Feminist politics originated where capitalism, industrial growth, democratic theory, and socialist critiques converged, as they did in Europe and North America after 1800. Women and their male allies began to agitate for equal educational, economic, and political opportunities, a struggle that continues to the present. By 1900 an international women's movement advanced these goals in urban areas of Latin America, the Middle East, and Asia. Since 1970 feminism has spread globally, in both industrialized nations and in the developing regions where agriculture remains an economic mainstay.

Given their specific historical origins, the feminist politics initially forged in Europe and North America have not simply expanded throughout the world. Elsewhere, abundant forms of women's resistance to men's patriarchal authority predated Western democratic theories; they continue to influence feminist movements today. Socialist responses to capitalism invite quite different women's politics than where free markets prevail. Both the term *feminism* and the politics it represents have been continually transformed by the evolving responses of women and men from a variety of cultures. Indeed, women's politics have developed organically in settings so diverse that the plural *feminisms* more accurately describes them.

By the year 2000 these growing international movements to improve women's lives increasingly influenced each other, due in part to the forum provided by the United Nations Decade for Women from 1975 to 1985 and the follow-up conference in Beijing in 1995. While they share the conviction that women deserve full human rights, international feminisms often diverge in their emphases. Only some concentrate solely on women, while others recognize complex links to the politics of race, class, religion, and nationality. Despite these differences, most Western feminists have learned that global economic and political justice are prerequisites to securing women's rights. Women in the developing world have found that transnational feminist movements can help establish strategic international support for their efforts at home.

None of these feminist movements has proceeded without opposition, including formidable backlash in every era in which women have gained public authority. Nonetheless, at the beginning of the twenty-first century the historical conditions that promote feminism can be found in much of the world. Whether through the influence of Western economic and political systems, the refashioning of earlier practices, or both, an impressive array of movements now attempts to empower women. At present, economic globalization, along with international efforts to create stable democratic governments, suggests that new forms of feminism will continue to surface. Because of their flexibility and adaptability, women's political movements, whether explicitly labeled feminist or not, have set much of the world's agenda for the twenty-first century.

THE HISTORY OF A TERM

Since I use *feminism* to describe movements whose participants do not necessarily apply that label themselves, I want to acknowledge at the outset the specific historical origins of this term. *Feminism* is a relatively recent word. First coined in France in the 1880s as *féminisme*, it spread through European countries in the 1890s and to North and South America by 1910. The term combined the French word for woman, *femme*, and *-isme*, which referred to a social movement or political ideology. At a time when many other "isms" originated, including socialism and communism, *féminisme* connoted that women's issues belonged to the vanguard of change. The term was always controversial, in part because of its association with radicalism and in part because proponents themselves disagreed about the label. Although self-defined *socialist feminists* appeared in Europe as early as 1900, many socialists who supported women's emancipation rejected the label *feminist*. They believed that middle-class demands for suffrage and property rights did not necessarily speak to working women's needs for a living wage and job security. Middle-class women also hesitated to call themselves feminists, especially when the term implied a claim to universal rights as citizens rather than particular rights as mothers.

In the United States this conflict over the political meaning of feminism split the women's movement for almost half a century. In the 1800s the usual label for first-wave activism was simply "the woman movement." Along with educational and property rights, many of its participants linked authority for women to motherhood. After 1910, however, a younger generation consciously rejected the maternal argument in favor of women's common human identity with men as a basis for equal rights. They claimed a *feminist* political identity and staged dramatic public protests during the suffrage movement. After U.S. women won the vote in 1920, the feminists' single-minded campaign to pass an equal-rights amendment to the U.S. Constitution further cemented the association of feminism, extremism, and a rejection of the concept of female difference. For decades, most women social reformers opposed the amendment and rejected the feminist label.

From its origins through the social upheavals of the 1960s, *feminist* remained a pejorative term among most progressive reformers, suffragists, and socialists around the world. Even as universal adult suffrage gradually extended to women—in England in 1928, in countries such as France, Japan, Mexico, and China by the late 1940s—few politically engaged women called themselves feminists. Within the international women's movement, participants debated whether the term *humanist* rather than *feminist* best applied to them. Nations ruled by communist parties, such as China and later Cuba, officially pronounced the emancipation of women as workers, but their state-sanctioned women's organizations rejected the feminist label and their suppression of oppositional political discourse precluded feminist politics.

A critical turning point in the history of feminisms occurred during the politically tumultuous 1960s. Women's politics revived in the West, at first under the banner of "women's liberation." Although the press quickly derided adherents by calling them "women's libbers," this second wave proved quite tenacious. By this time, both capitalist and socialist economies had drawn millions of women into the paid labor force, and civil rights and anticolonial movements had revived the politics of democratization. In Europe and the United States, millions of women expected to earn wages as well as raise children. The old feminist calls for economic and political equality, and a new emphasis on control over reproduction, resonated deeply across generations, classes, and races.

Western women's movements also significantly expanded their agendas after the 1960s. Along with demands for economic and political rights, women's liberation revived a politics of difference through its critique of interpersonal relations. Women's liberation championed both women's *equality* with men in work and politics and women's *difference* from men within the arenas of reproduction and sexuality. In this way the two competing strains of equality and difference began to converge. Within a decade, the older term *feminist* began to be used to refer to the politics of this new movement, deepening its radical connotation but potentially widening its appeal. At about the same time, the introduction of the term *gender*, rather than *sex*, signaled feminists' growing belief that social practices, and not only biology, have constructed our notions of male and female.

By 1980 an umbrella usage of the term *feminism* took hold in Western cultures. Anyone who challenged prevailing gender relations might now be called a feminist, whether or not they lived long before the coining of the term *feminism*, agreed with all the tenets of women's liberation, or claimed the label. A generation of Western women came of age influenced by feminism to expect equal opportunities. The majority of this generation often proclaimed, "I'm not a feminist, but . . . ," even as they insisted on equal pay, sexual and reproductive choice, parental leave, and political representation. The children they raised, both male and female, grew up influenced by these feminist expectations but not necessarily comfortable with the term. Outside the West, the term *feminism* could still evoke a narrow focus on equal rights. Thus a 1991 essay in the influential Indian women's journal *Manushi*, titled "Why I Do Not Call Myself a Feminist," contrasted Western concerns about women's rights with broader human rights and social justice campaigns that address the needs of both men and women in developing countries.[1]

The term *feminism*, in short, has never been widely popular. Yet the political goals of feminism have survived—despite continuing discomfort with the term, a hostile political climate, and heated internal criticism—largely because feminism has continually redefined itself.

Over the past twenty-five years, for example, activists have amended the term to make it more compatible with their unique perspectives. Self-naming by black feminists, Asian American feminists, Third World feminists, lesbian feminists, male feminists, ecofeminists, Christian feminists, Jewish feminists, Islamic feminists, and others attests to the malleability of the label and to the seemingly contradictory politics it can embrace. To make the movement more racially inclusive, the African American writer Alice Walker once coined *womanist* to refer to a "Black feminist or feminist of color." In the 1990s young women in the United States such as Walker's daughter promised to go beyond the second wave of feminism by forging a more racially and sexually diverse movement that emphasized female empowerment rather than male oppression. "I'm not post-feminist," Rebecca Walker explained in 1992, "I'm the Third Wave."[2] Significantly, this generation reclaims rather than rejects the term *feminist*. Internationally as well, more women's organizations incorporate the word, such as the Feminist League in Central Asia, the Center for Feminist Legal Research in New Delhi, and the Working Group Toward a Feminist Europe.

By the 1990s the cumulative contributions of working-class women, lesbians, women of color, and activists from the developing world had transformed an initially white, European, middle-class politics into a more diverse and mature feminist movement. Taking into account the range of women's experiences, feminists have increasingly recognized the validity of arguments that once seemed contradictory. Instead of debating whether women are similar to or different from men, most feminists now recognize that both statements are true. Instead of asking which is more important, gender or race, most feminists now acknowledge the indivisibility and interaction of these social categories. Along with demanding the right to work, feminists have redefined work to include caring as well as earning. Along with calling for women's independence, feminists have recognized the interdependence of all people, as well as the interconnection of gender equality with broader social justice movements.

DEFINING FEMINISM TODAY

Given its changing historical meanings, is there any coherence to *feminism* as a term? Can we define it in a way that will embrace its variety of adherents and ideas? For my purposes, a four-part definition contains the critical elements of feminisms, including views that may be shared by those who claim the label as well as many who reject it.

> Feminism is a belief that women and men are inherently of equal worth. Because most societies privilege men as a group, social movements are necessary to achieve equality between women and men, with the understanding that gender always intersects with other social hierarchies.

Each of the four components of this working definition—equal worth, male privilege, social movements, and intersecting hierarchies—requires some clarification. I use "equal worth" rather than *equality* because the latter term often assumes that men's historical experience—whether economic, political, or sexual—is the standard to which women should aspire. The concept of equal worth values traditional female tasks, such as childbearing and child care, as highly as other kinds of work historically performed by men. It also allows us to recognize that women's different experiences can transform, and not simply integrate, political life.

The term *privilege* can refer to formal political rights such as suffrage or the right to hold office, but privilege can also include more personal entitlements, such as the greater social value placed on male children as expressed by strong parental preference for boys across cultures. Privilege also ensues when societies have a sexual double standard that allows male heterosexual autonomy, punishing women but not men who seek nonmarital sexual expression.

To refer to feminism in terms of *social movements* may conjure images of people marching in the streets or rallying around political candidates, but it may also mean individual participation, such as enrolling in a women's studies class or engaging in artistic or literary creativity that fosters social change. While women may participate in a variety of social movements—civil rights, ecology, socialism, even fundamentalism—those movements cannot be feminist unless they explicitly address justice for women as a primary concern. Thus human rights or nationalist movements that insist on women's human rights and women's full citizenship may be feminist, while those that overlook or affirm patriarchal authority cannot.

Similarly, feminism must recognize the integral relationship of gender to other forms of *social hierarchy*, especially those based on class, race, sexuality, and culture. Despite the prevalence of hierarchies that privilege men, in every culture some women (such as elites or citizens) enjoy greater opportunities than many other women (such as workers or immigrants). Some women always have higher status than many men. If we ignore these intersecting hierarchies and create a feminism that serves only the interests of women who have more privilege, we reinforce other social inequalities that disadvantage both women and men in the name of improving women's opportunities.

The overlapping identities of women as members of classes, races, and nations raises questions about the usefulness of the category *woman* itself. I use the term but with the recognition that there is no single, universal female identity, for gender has been constructed differently across place and time. Because of historical, social, national, and personal differences, women cannot assume a sisterhood, even though we can find common ground on particular issues. At the same time, feminism cannot deny the significance of gender in a world in which 70 percent of those living in poverty and two-thirds of those who are illiterate are female.

Feminists must continually criticize two kinds of false universals. We must always ask not only "What about women?" (what difference does gender make?) but also "Which women?" (what difference do ideas about race, class, or nationality make?). Taking these concerns into account, a dual revisioning lies at the heart of this book. I believe that we must question both the assumption that the term *man* includes woman as well and the assumption that the term *woman* represents the diversity of female experience.

The American poet Muriel Rukeyser provides a compelling illustration of the first critique. In 1973 Rukeyser imagined a second conversation between Oedipus and the Sphinx, long after the legendary Greek king had saved his city by answering a riddle that the Sphinx once posed. Since that first meeting, Oedipus had unwittingly killed his father and married his mother; he then tore out his eyes and wandered the world in exile. In "Myth" Rukeyser has Oedipus ask the Sphinx, "Why didn't I recognize my mother?" The poem continues:

> "You gave the
> wrong answer," said the Sphinx. "But, that was what
> made everything possible," said Oedipus. "No," she said.
> "When I asked: 'What walks on four legs in the morning,
> two at noon, and three in the evening,' you answered,
> 'Man.' You didn't say anything about woman."
> "When you say 'man,' " said Oedipus, "you include women
> too. Everyone knows that." She said, "That's what
> you think."[3]

Viewing the world through male eyes, the poem suggests, can misconstrue the female, with tragic consequences.

Similarly, however, assuming that all women experience the world alike can blur the power of feminist vision. A South Asian woman who attended the UN-sponsored Fourth World Conference on Women in Beijing in 1995 brought home this point. The signs publicizing the Non-Governmental Organization (NGO) Forum on Women held just outside the city proclaimed "Look at the World Through Women's Eyes." In response, Suneeta Dhar asked participants to think about the question "Which women's eyes?"[4] Just as "That's what you think" exposes the false male universal, "Which women's eyes?" reminds us that we cannot universalize the female, given our national and cultural differences. As feminism has expanded, sometimes through difficult intercultural conflict, it has embraced both of these critical positions—asking "What about women?" and "Which women?" In the process it has become more powerful and more broadly based.

WHY FEAR FEMINISM?

Some readers of this book may be initially uncomfortable with my choice of the word *feminism* to describe diverse women's movements. Ask most people in Europe or the United States if they believe that women should have equal rights, and they will answer in the affirmative, as did 85 percent of Americans in an opinion poll taken in 2000. Ask them if they are feminists, however, and most reject the label; the same year, only 29 percent of Americans in another poll claimed it.[5] Ask others what they think of feminists, and you may hear a string of negative associations: radical, man-hating, bra-burning, and worse. Women may be acceptable as equals, but feminists are often seen as frightening, threatening, or simply unnecessary. This hostility to feminists and feminism cannot be dismissed simply by avoiding the terms, for these harsh stereotypes can always be used to discredit women activists, whether they call themselves feminists or not.

The media have contributed to this discomfort by treating feminism as a thing of the past. In the United States, for example, ever since its revival in the 1960s journalists have proclaimed the death of feminism. In 1976 *Harper's* declared a "requiem for the women's movement"; in 1980 the *New York Times* assured readers that the "radical days of feminism are gone"; in 1990 *Newsweek* trumpeted "the failure of feminism." Unconvinced by two decades of obituaries, in 1998 *Time* asked readers to respond online to the question "Is feminism dead?" So ubiquitous is this story that a feminist journalist recently labeled it "False Feminist Death Syndrome."[6] Perhaps these writers notice feminism only during periods of mass public protest and overlook its quieter but more pervasive forms. Or perhaps they are engaging in a form of wishful thinking, for given the power of the media, declaring the death of feminism could become a self-fulfilling prophecy.

If feminism, as I will argue, is so deeply rooted historically and so expansive in the present, why the contradictory claims in the press that it is near death? Why is feminism highly unpopular, even vilified, when first articulated? I suspect that the answers to these questions lie in part in what might be called "fear of feminism." No matter how insightful its politics, feminism feels deeply threatening to many people, both women and men. By providing a powerful critique of the idea of a timeless social hierarchy, in which God or nature preordained women's dependence on men, feminism exposes the historical construction, and potential deconstruction, of categories such as gender, race, and sexuality. Fears that feminism will unleash changes in familiar family, sexual, and racial relationships can produce antifeminist politics among those who wish to conserve older forms of social hierarchy.

Those who do not oppose change may still fear certain connotations of feminism. The recurrent caricatures of feminists as "mannish" reveal an anxiety that feminism is somehow antithetical to femininity, that to embrace its politics is to reject a gender identity that many women and men wish to preserve. For women of color, feminism has often seemed competitive with movements for racial justice. In former colonies and developing countries, suspicion, if not fear, of feminism may result from its association with Western colonialism. In some cultures, feminism connotes a form of rampant individualism associated with the worst features of contemporary Western societies.

Even in countries with strong women's movements, feminism forces all women and men to think about social inequalities and about their own relationships to systems of power. For some, it conjures the fear of losing taken-for-granted privileges; for others, it brings up the pain of acknowledging lack of privilege. Neither is a very pleasant prospect, especially if feminism is presented in the oversimplified language of male oppression and female victimization. Portraying a movement as blaming one group (white men) and denying the resilience of another (all women) will keep it unpopular, even though, as I will argue, feminism at its best offers much more complex interpretations of the dynamics of gender, race, and power. For those of us raised in the United States, a related antipathy sometimes operates, since acknowledging any kind of structural inequality challenges the deeply held myth of equal opportunity. The myth professes that in America anybody can succeed, as if there were no obstacles based on gender, class, or race. To raise questions about fairness implicitly asks whether those who have succeeded are in fact the most deserving. Little wonder they are left fearful of feminism.

NO TURNING BACK

I believe that a better historical understanding of feminism can assuage some of these fears and illuminate the impact that this revolutionary movement continues to have on all of our lives. In the following chapters I draw on a generation of interdisciplinary scholarship to show that despite recurrent opposition, feminism has passed the historical test of time, largely because it has redefined itself in response to a variety of local and global politics. Because my own expertise is U.S. women's history, I provide fuller analysis of this locale, but I attempt to place it within the broader framework of world history that is essential to understanding feminism. The arguments I make throughout this book respond to four basic questions that I hope readers will keep asking:

- What difference does gender make? That is, how do women's experiences change our understanding of social life and politics, and how do women differ from each other?
- Why did feminist politics emerge historically, and how have they changed over time and place?
- What do feminists want? That is, how do feminist interpretations of inequality lead to new ways of thinking and acting?
- Where is feminism going, and what strategies best advance gender justice?

Although the title of this book suggests historical progress, I do not present a story with inevitable outcomes. Only with great struggle on the part of both women and men have feminist ideas remained part of our political landscape. Nor does this book tell a single, unified history of revolutionary triumph. Feminism has survived only through multiple, complex responses to economic and political change, through adaptation to diverse cultural settings, and through incremental shifts in popular thought. The future of women depends on how we continue to redefine and implement feminist goals.

To date, feminists from around the world have challenged the hierarchies of male and female, public and private, citizens and mothers. Millions of women and their male allies now engage in the serious political task of transforming gender relations and gender conventions. They struggle as grassroots leaders in peasant villages, as candidates for national office, in international agencies that challenge discrimination. Wherever democratization occurs, women's groups seek to extend it to the fullest. Given the momentum that feminism has built thus far, combined with ongoing global economic and democratic movements, the quest for universal recognition of women's equal worth is not likely to be reversed. To understand the future of women, we must appreciate the history of feminism that has brought us to this revolutionary moment.

PART I

BEFORE
FEMINISM

–TWO–

GENDER AND POWER

*The history of mankind is a history of repeated injuries and
usurpations on the part of man toward woman, having in direct
object the establishment of an absolute tyranny over her.*
— ELIZABETH CADY STANTON, UNITED STATES, 1848

*Patriarchy as a system is historical: it has a beginning in
history . . . it can be ended by historical process.*
—GERDA LERNER, UNITED STATES, 1986

At the first U.S. women's rights convention, held in 1848 in the
town of Seneca Falls, New York, three hundred women and men
launched a major social movement. As convention organizer Elizabeth
Cady Stanton read the Declaration of Sentiments, these early feminists
heard a litany of complaints about the unjust laws and practices that
denied women education, property rights, and self-esteem. Echoing
the revolutionary generation that had overthrown British colonial rulers,
the declaration boldly called for women to overthrow the male rulers who
denied them liberty. Stanton introduced women's grievances with a rhetorical flourish worthy of her rebellious predecessors. She pronounced a
sweeping historical generalization: "The history of mankind is a history
of repeated injuries and usurpations on the part of man toward woman,
having in direct object the establishment of an absolute tyranny over
her." Only a movement to empower women legally and politically could
correct this injustice.

If the Declaration of Sentiments was right, and men had been
tyrants throughout world history, why did it take so long for women to
rebel? What could have enforced such total, unrelenting patriarchal
power throughout past millennia? Had patriarchy robbed women of their
very ability to question male authority? Elizabeth Cady Stanton would

have answered yes, women had been deprived of liberty throughout history. They did not rebel because the denial of education and self-respect had contributed to their becoming "willing to lead a dependent and abject life."[1]

Such downtrodden creatures seemed unlikely to foment a revolution. Surely Stanton knew that history was full of resilient women who defied tyranny, whether queens such as Nefertiti, warriors such as Joan of Arc, or simply clever wives and mothers who bowed to no man's will. What distinguished these earlier, strong women from Stanton and later feminists was a new political view of the world. The future society envisioned at Seneca Falls in 1848 incorporated the concept of equality, a relatively recent political ideal that had already helped motivate the American and French revolutions. For most of world history, however, few people questioned the inequality of social hierarchies, including the rule of men over women, or patriarchy. Because they accepted supernatural (theological) and natural (biological) explanations of male dominance, women and men rarely questioned their inherited gender systems—until feminism, that is.

Inspired by democratic ideals of equal rights, when Stanton and her colleagues turned a feminist eye to women's history, they vastly oversimplified the patriarchal past. True, most human societies value men more highly than women. Fortunately for the future of feminism, however, women have not been so tyrannized that they have no usable history. Even a brief review of the past refines the Declaration of Sentiments to show how patriarchy itself has changed over time in response to changing economic systems, family structures, and religious beliefs. In historian Gerda Lerner's words, "Patriarchy as a system is historical: it has a beginning in history . . . it can be ended by historical process."[2] Understanding that history and women's resistance to it is critical to the feminist political project.

THE EVIDENCE FOR PATRIARCHY

The world before feminism offers ample evidence that men had more power than women. If we simply listen to folk wisdom or read sacred texts, we learn about the virtues of sons and the lesser value of daughters.

A girl is "merely a weed," in a Zulu saying. According to the Old Testament, "The Lord said to Moses, 'Set the value of a male between ages of twenty and sixty at fifty shekels . . . and if it is a female, set the value at thirty shekels.' " A Dutch proverb declares that "a house full of daughters is like a cellar full of sour beer," while Koreans learn that "a girl lets you down twice, once at birth and the second time when she marries." Even contemporary parents usually prefer male children; a 1983 survey of forty countries found only two with daughter preference and only thirteen with equal preference for boys or girls. Where strong son preferences persist, parents may selectively abort female fetuses and neglect girls, leading to higher mortality rates for female infants in parts of the world, such as India and China.[3]

So widespread is the greater privilege, opportunity, and value attached to boys and men that anthropologist Michelle Zimbalist Rosaldo once referred to its occurrence as "universal sexual asymmetry." Almost all societies, Rosaldo wrote in 1974, not only differentiate by gender but, more important, they value the male more highly than the female. She provided a vivid illustration of this phenomenon in the case of a New Guinea culture that cultivated both yams and sweet potatoes. Although they were quite similar foods, the yams, raised by men, were reserved for festival consumption, while the sweet potatoes, raised by women, provided daily sustenance. In this case, as in so many features of social life, seemingly neutral traits or activities take on greater symbolic value simply by their association with the male gender.

Stories of human origins help support these beliefs in male superiority. Most of the supernatural theories of how humans came to be assert that a higher power—a God, gods, or other spiritual force beyond human reason—ordained that men should rule over women. When anthropologist Peggy Reeves Sanday surveyed stories of human origins she found that most cultures imagine a male divine force as the origin of life. Fewer than one-fifth of all creation stories include a female deity (usually in less patriarchal societies). The major Western monotheistic religions, which originated around five thousand years ago in the ancient Middle East, provide a good example of the use of supernatural theories to support patriarchy. In this settled agricultural region, fathers exercised extensive authority over wives and children, who had few if any rights. The Judeo-Christian

Bible reflected this patriarchal gender system, as did later commentaries on the Islamic Qu'ran. Each cited the story of Adam and Eve to justify the rule of men: God created Adam to rule over the earth and the animal kingdom, while Eve, a physical outgrowth from Adam's rib, brought sin into the world.

Aside from origin stories, religious institutions have often enforced patriarchy. In Judaism and Christianity, a male symbol for God the Father set the standard for earthly rule. The elevation of male prophets and male priests showed that only men were worthy of hearing or speaking the word of God. Both traditions denigrated women as mere flesh, closer to nature and less capable of spiritual growth than men. Like traditional Judaism, Islam segregated women during worship. An exclusively male priesthood in Catholicism reproduced patriarchy by treating women like subordinate members of the spiritual family. Even Buddhism, which began with a gender-neutral ideal of enlightenment, came to emphasize male qualities of the Buddha and mandated female obedience to men. As one Japanese Buddhist sect explains, "The husband is the lord and the wife is the servant."4

The evidence for patriarchy is not universal, however. Prehistoric artifacts suggest that men and women have at times shared spiritual prestige. Ancient female deities, such as the Middle Eastern fertility goddess Astarte and the Greek earth goddess Gaia, attest to women's powerful role in pantheistic religions. Historically, we know that women have sometimes held other powerful social positions. Women ruled as queens in ancient Egypt and among Bedouins in pre-Islamic Arabia. In ancient Japan, female emperors ruled as often as men. Jewish women, such as the biblical Deborah, played important public roles as judges in the era after the Exodus from Egypt.

Short of formal power, some women have enjoyed rights similar to men, as they did in pastoral, nomadic cultures in Asia and the Middle East, such as the Mongols. In ancient Sumer and Egypt, adult women could own property, serve as clergy, and play active roles in public marketplaces. Women in ancient Japan could also own property. In precolonial Latin America, some native cultures practiced what anthropologists term "gender parallelism," valuing highly the distinct and overlapping tasks performed by men and women. Women traders sold goods in the marketplace, but even their household labors ranked as highly as men's military exploits. In the Andes, girls learned to use brooms and looms—the latter called "weaving swords"—as if they were weapons of war; giving birth was equivalent to taking a prisoner of war, and death in childbirth was as honorable as death in battle.

The Seneca of North America provide another example of the influence women wielded in communal, agricultural societies. Well into the 1800s, Seneca women cultivated the land and shared child rearing with men. Because women controlled the food supply, Seneca men could not hunt or wage war unless elder women agreed to allocate food for these purposes. These elders knew they held political authority. During the American Revolutionary War, they explained to American army officers that "you ought to hear and listen to what we, women shall speak, as well as to the sachems [chiefs]; for *we are the owners of this land,—and it is ours.*"[5]

Exceptions to patriarchal rule persist in more recent history. In the 1930s, Margaret Mead shook up our notions of "natural" male dominance when she described three New Guinea cultures, one in which men and women were equally parental, one in which men and women were equally aggressive, and one in which women were businesslike and men were decorative. Male tyranny was far from universal, even in this one region. Sanday too noted that on the Pacific Island of Bali, male and female social roles are highly interchangeable. Another contemporary case is Vanatinai (the name means "motherland") Island, also in the South Pacific. Both women and men share in child care and decision making and use gender-neutral language. Significantly, both sexes can officiate during the public yam-planting ritual.

What Happened to Women's Power?

At the time Elizabeth Cady Stanton called for a female independence movement, she seemed unaware of the Seneca women who lived just a few dozen miles from her Seneca Falls home. In 1848, the year of the women's rights convention, the Seneca formed a constitution that granted both men and women voting rights. Had Stanton taken notice, the early feminists might have couched their demands for equality in less universal terms; perhaps they would have called for a *return* of women's power. Unlike the subsistence farming villages of the Seneca, however, in the middle-class, commercial, and increasingly urban world that Stanton inhabited, women no longer shared formal authority, nor did they control economic life, although they certainly contributed to it. The democratic governments of the United States denied women voting rights and legitimated a husband's control of his wife's property. For her own culture, Stanton correctly observed that legal inequalities denied women the rights enjoyed by men. Unaware of the alternative histories around her, she failed to ask how a patriarchal world had emerged, given the more egalitarian potential of human cultures.

That question is worth contemplating, even if we can never answer it definitively. The short answer is that as human societies became more complex, they became less egalitarian. Among the early hunter-gatherers, men and women had distinct but complementary tasks and shared important economic and religious duties. Though women never ruled over men, as the term *matriarchy* implies, they once enjoyed more equal footing. When these egalitarian societies shifted to settled agriculture (around 3100 to 600 BCE), they developed complicated class and gender relations. More-specialized farming, the barter of surplus goods, and an emerging class hierarchy contributed to patriarchal families in which only male children inherited property and wives became subjects in their husbands' homes. Around the same time, female deities seemed to disappear, replaced by a single male god. In Western cultures, by the time of the Hebrew Bible and Greek and Roman civilizations, only men exercised political power. Women retained some authority in the home but little in the public realm. Gone, for example, were the temple priestesses of earlier civilizations. By the time of Christianity the Virgin Mary had become an intermediary to God rather than a goddess in her own right.

Two influential theories of the emergence of patriarchy help explain this process. The first appeared in an 1884 essay, "On the Origin of the Family, Private Property and the State," by Friedrich Engels (the coauthor, with Karl Marx, of *The Communist Manifesto*). Engels argued that the subjugation of women began only when economic surpluses accumulated; thus private property, which leads to class hierarchy and the formation of states, is the source of women's oppression. When individual families replaced larger clan and communal living groups, women lost their reciprocal roles. In short, Engels argued, private property was the source of "the *world historical defeat of the female sex*."[6] In the second, more recent account, *The Creation of Patriarchy* (1986), feminist historian Gerda Lerner revised Engels's theory. She agreed that male control over women gradually formed during the long transition to settled agriculture. A new farming system in the Middle East, based on private land ownership and domesticated farm animals, coincided with the emergence of a hierarchical state led by military elites and based on the rule of fathers in the family. Male gods and ultimately monotheism replaced earlier female deities. To this story Lerner added a critical point: Reproductive labor was key to men's subordination of women.

In Lerner's view, children helped a family produce more crops, allowing the accumulation of surpluses that created family wealth. Since women's reproductive labor provided these workers, reproduction itself became a commodity, something purchased from a father when a young man's family paid a bride-price to a young woman's family. In order to ensure the husband's paternity, and with it his ownership of the wealth produced by children, women had to be chaste before marriage and faithful within it. Another source of reproductive labor was the theft of women during war raids. By acquiring captive female slaves as additional wives, men could increase the number of children they fathered, adding to the family's workforce and its ability to accumulate surpluses. According to Lerner, women were the first slaves, and all other forms of enslavement built upon female reproductive slavery. "Economic oppression and exploitation," Lerner wrote, "are based as much on the commodification of female sexuality and the appropriation by men of women's labor power and her reproductive power as on the direct economic acquisition of resources and persons."[7] In this way she turned Engels upside down by arguing that the appropriation of women's labor led to the possibility of accumulating surplus private property, rather than private property giving rise to women's subjugation.

Historical theories that emphasize the economic and reproductive origins of patriarchy do not dismiss the role of culture. For Lerner, denying access to education played a key role in the patriarchal control of women, whether as slaves or as wives. Myth, folktales, and religious precepts helped deepen the hold of patriarchy; thus knowledge could enable women to question their status.

Limits of Patriarchy

Whatever its precise origins, the history of patriarchy cannot be understood in isolation from a larger matrix of social relations. Aside from the power of mythology and religion to enforce male dominance, women did not rebel in the past because gender was only one of many power relations affecting their lives. In short, not all men exercised control over all women. The privileges of age or family status could mediate patriarchal power. In simple societies, for example, older women command service from younger men, who are obligated to provide food for both male and female elders. In many patriarchal cultures, the wives of elite men enjoy privileges, and women often exercise authority as mothers. Indeed, as long as they do not challenge the legitimacy of the patriarchal ideal, women could find ways to advance their own interests and those of their children. Allowing some female authority also helped prevent disloyalty to patriarchy.

Given the interconnection of gender and other social hierarchies, the simple fact of being born female was not necessarily the most important one in a woman's life. Consciousness of gender identity, a precondition for feminism, surfaced only rarely when caste, class, and family defined one's social position. Take, for example, the Hindu caste system, which mandates what tasks each group may perform; women and men of a common caste share more than women of different castes. Or consider those African women who as slave owners once benefited from the labor of captive women. In either case, thinking about oneself primarily as a "woman" did not always make sense. The Chinese language illustrates how distinct, age-related kinship identities could be more important than a broader gender identity. The terms for daughter, wife, mother, or mother-in-law once sufficed to name most women. Only after 1900 did terms such as *funü* and *nuxing* define "women as a political category," apart from their family relations.[8]

A final problem with Stanton's assertion of absolute male tyranny is that it presents a static picture. As economic practices, family relations, and religious beliefs change over time, they shift the balance of gender and power. Although the pace of change is uneven across cultures, in each phase of economic development—from settled agriculture to urban trade to early world capitalism—we find evidence of a female resilience that strongly contradicts Stanton's claim of unrelenting sexual oppression.

COMPARATIVE PATRIARCHIES: AGRICULTURAL LIFE IN AFRICA, CHINA, AND EUROPE

Patriarchy took unique forms once humans moved from a nomadic life to the cultivation of crops in settled communities. Men exercised most formal authority, and a sexual division of labor organized the production and exchange of food and child care. But the particular tasks performed by each sex and the political balance of power varied widely across regions and eras. In parts of West Africa, for example, men cleared fields, but women planted and harvested the crops; women bore children, but fathers and uncles maintained strong ties to children who would one day support them. In China and Europe, men dominated agricultural field labor while women primarily raised children and often produced textiles. Depending on the systems of farming, kinship, and religion, both patriarchal power and women's influence could be relatively stronger or weaker.

Female Farming in Africa

Women's agricultural labor provided a critical source of social authority in certain parts of sub-Saharan Africa. In regions where small populations lived on abundant land, crops tended to be raised collectively rather than on individual plots. Whoever planted and harvested on a piece of land had rights to the food they raised. In parts of the Congo region and in West Africa, wives and children raised most of the crops, leading Dutch economist Ester Boserup to label this system "female farming."

Even though men officiated in farming villages, both sexes played important economic and political roles. Young men engaged in tasks such as herding, hunting, and clearing land; adult men practiced medicine and diplomacy or waged war. Wives prepared daily meals and cared for children, but they also hoed, planted, and harvested in fields to which they had usage rights. If women produced more than they needed to meet their family obligations, they might barter the surplus at a local market. Through trade women could accumulate wealth and enjoy physical freedom of movement.

Because women produced food, they represented a form of wealth, whether in matrilineal groups, in which men inherited rights to land use through maternal relatives (uncles), or the more common patrilineal practice of sons inheriting from their fathers. In polygynous societies, as a man grew older he gained prestige by acquiring more wives who could cultivate more land and produce more children. As long as her family returned the bridewealth given by the husband or his family, usually in the form of animals or household goods, a woman could leave her husband. Senior and junior wives worked together, sometimes cooperatively and sometimes with intense rivalry. The senior wife might welcome other wives because they shared domestic work and child care and provided female companionship, but her authority could also feel oppressive.

The male elders who had the most wealth usually arranged these marriages, and they held most—but not all—of the formal political leadership within the village. Women in some parts of Africa could wield significant political authority. In a few ancient African kingdoms mothers shared royal power with their sons; in an exceptional case, during the 1600s the former slave Nzinga became the ruler of a region in what is now Angola. Even in recent history, Nigerian villages included both male and female rulers, each of whom had their own advisers. The female ruler, called "mother," headed a social hierarchy with authority over village women. Acting as local judges, the female ruler and women's network regulated the market, set prices, settled disputes, maintained order, meted out justice, and represented women's interests. These women's organizations might take collective action against husbands who behaved badly toward their wives, ridiculing the men publicly to force them to change their behavior.

Village women often cooperated with each other through mutual aid associations, such as those made up of a cohort that came of age together.

In some cultures a group of young women who underwent ritual genital cutting in a particular season pledged to help each other throughout their lives in times of financial or family troubles. This mutual support, as well as the importance placed on genital cutting for marriage, helps explain why mothers insisted on the painful ritual for their daughters.

In West African cultures, motherhood carried great weight, both economically and spiritually. Land represented Mother Earth, as illustrated by an Igbo annual prayer that asked Mother Earth for permission to cultivate her. For both women and men, children served as farm labor, ensured support in old age, and created a link from the ancestors to the future. Therefore, women derived prestige from producing children. In art and poetry, the Yoruba celebrated the Great Mother, and one of their proverbs proclaimed that "mother is gold." But a barren woman could be divorced and socially stigmatized. Even a fertile woman experienced pressure to bear sons and to sacrifice her own well-being for them. "Her love and duty for her children were like her chains of slavery," wrote the contemporary Nigerian novelist Buchi Emecheta.[9]

Male Farming in China

The dominant form of agriculture in China provides a fairly stark contrast to those areas of sub-Saharan Africa where women worked the land. In much of Southeast and East Asia, the high population pressure on available land required intensive cultivation of crops. Men utilized the plow on individual land holdings. Although they might help in the fields, especially in rice-producing areas, women usually remained in or near the home. In what Boserup called "male farming" areas, women were more economically dependent on their husbands than in cultures where women raised most of the food.

The major form of Chinese kinship required female subservience. Although the practice varied regionally, a majority of rural Chinese women left their parental homes following arranged marriages to reside within their husbands' families (patrilocality). A woman's family had to provide a dowry—a certain amount of wealth—to obligate the man she married to support her. In her new home a wife worked within the household under the strict, sometimes harsh, supervision of her mother-in-law. Family life for most Chinese women involved extremely hard domestic labor, centered around preparing food and caring for children. Women's work also included processing silk and weaving textiles in the home. During centuries of early Imperial Chinese history (before 1000 CE), women's domestic cloth production contributed significantly to both family and state economies.

Until the revolutions of the twentieth century, the family system regulated gender relations in rural China. If a woman bore sons, they would marry and bring their wives into the family to be subservient to the now powerful mother-in-law. Because daughters left their parental homes, while sons brought wives into the household to work, families strongly preferred sons. In addition, male descendants ensured the worship of ancestors. The birth of a male child was cause for celebration, while the birth of a female child was considered only a "small happiness." As an early Chinese poet, Fu Xuan, explained, "No one is glad when a girl is born / By *her* the family sets no store." In rural China, a barren woman, or a woman who bore only daughters, could be divorced by her husband; a wife rarely had recourse to divorce, even in cases of abuse. Once divorced, she could support herself only as a house servant, prostitute, concubine, or beggar. "How sad it is to be a woman!" wrote Fu Xuan. "Nothing on earth is held so cheap."[10]

Along with male farming, the moral principles established by Confucius (551–479 BCE) shaped the patriarchal Chinese family system, especially for elite women. As the foundation of the larger state, the family provided a model and training ground for a world in which women provided an "inner space" to balance men's public lives. These ideals encouraged gender segregation and female subordination. In elite households, women ideally remained in an inner area that only male family members could enter. Confucian ideology also required obedience of children to elders and wives to husbands. The ideal woman worked hard in the home, remained meek and modest around others, and achieved status through her sons. If widowed, an ideal woman remained "faithful" to her husband by not remarrying; in some eras, widows who committed suicide won great respect. In peasant families, of course, girls and women engaged in hard labor, whether spinning cloth or processing foods. Even among elites, women's manual labor contributed to the household economy.

Despite the constraints of the Chinese family system, women could circumvent strict patriarchal control. Elite women often maintained some property rights. In areas such as Taiwan, some wives made decisions about family formation when they adopted girls who would later marry their sons. Other mothers ensured that they would achieve authority in later years by forging close ties with their sons, a practice labeled "uterine politics" by anthropologist Margery Wolf. Drawing on the Confucian requirement of obedience to elders, the aging mother-in-law could expect power over her daughters-in-law as well as her sons. For women in poorer families, however, the very lack of property mediated patriarchy; if a father did not have land to leave his sons, they might strike out on their own with wives who would head their own households rather than work under the rule of their mother-in-law.

Other women avoided the patriarchal marriage system entirely. Some insisted on remaining within their family of origin instead of accepting an arranged marriage. Others turned to Buddhist or Taoist monastic life. As nuns, they could study and live in a community of women; widows sometimes joined convents as well. Buddhist nuns lived together in common houses, renouncing sexuality and pledging not to marry or eat meat. Some single women who did not become nuns simply joined one of these vegetarian halls. These Buddhist women could adopt daughters to raise so that they would have aid in their old age. Though convent celibacy rested upon negative views of female sexuality, women used the institution to their best advantage as an alternative to patriarchal marriage.

European Peasant Life

As in Africa and China, elite women in Western European history occasionally shared power or owned property within ruling families, but for most women agricultural life predominated for centuries. Before 1500, and in some regions until the 1800s, the self-sufficient rural household produced much of the food and clothing needed by the peasant farm family. Women's productive labor was essential to this endeavor. "One woman in the house will always be working," an Irish proverb explained.[11] Women helped cultivate and prepare food; they raised chickens and cows; they also produced textiles and made clothing, served as both midwives and healers to the sick, and engaged in a number of domestic crafts. In this preindustrial world, the work lives of men and women often overlapped, although each had primary responsibility for different tasks. Peasant women joined in planting and harvesting, as they would well into the contemporary era, while male labor in agriculture or crafts took place close to the home. Only sons usually inherited anything owned by the peasant family, but at marriage a daughter received goods to establish her home. (In the case of serfs, who owed labor to their lords, neither men nor women could own or leave the land they worked.)

European religions, like African and Chinese beliefs, emphasized the cultural importance of maternity. In the Judeo-Christian Bible, women's prestige typically came through motherhood. Bearing children in old age redeemed Sarah, the wife of the Hebrew patriarch Abraham, making her "a mother of nations." Judaism praised women for raising children in religious homes, while men officiated at public worship. Popular Christian views of women supported the patriarchal rule of men. In contrast to earlier interpretations of Eve as a spiritually powerful figure, by the fourth century CE St. Augustine emphasized Eve as the source of "original sin." Christian thinkers now justified patriarchy by blaming Eve for the troubles of the world, adding biblical authority to the older Greek myth of Pandora. Over time, the roles available to women within Christianity narrowed to the maternal, with Mary as the ideal. The church structure itself reinforced gender hierarchy, since only men could become priests.

Both religion and law required that peasant women obey their husbands as superiors, and men expected to rule within their households. At the wedding of his daughter, a father transferred to her new husband both the responsibility for protecting her and the right to her labor. Wives who disobeyed could be chastised physically, and women who fought back were exceptional. Summarizing the European case, historians Bonnie S. Anderson and Judith P. Zinsser explain that, exceptional women aside, the "majority of peasant women throughout the centuries accepted the circumstances, the attitudes, and the necessities of survival even though they were left vulnerable and subordinate."[12]

TOWNS, TRADE, AND MARKETS: NARROWING AND WIDENING SPHERES

At different historical moments, a shift from subsistence agriculture to trade fostered urban commercial life and with it more highly stratified societies. In towns and cities, women's experience of patriarchy became more varied as a widening gap separated classes. Elite women enjoyed greater privileges, including some education. A far greater number of urban women, however, shared poverty, and some shared enslavement. In each group, women faced constraints based on their gender, and in each they found ways to resist those limitations.

The growth of market towns in Africa illustrates these divergent female experiences. Women participated in the long-distance trade that increased after 1400, when Europeans arrived to exchange goods and procure slaves. By serving as intermediaries to European traders, some African women on the Atlantic coast gained new prestige. Elsewhere women traders acquired wealth and with it higher status. Among the Igbo, in a region that is now part of Nigeria, a wealthy woman could buy a wife to work for her, becoming what was called a "female husband" (although she herself might be the wife of a man). Trade required legal institutions to settle disputes; among groups such as the Yoruba women elected their own female representatives to hold court and protect their trading interests.

Trade, however, also involved the exchange of humans. Well before the arrival of Europeans, an internal slave trade operated in parts of Africa. Female slaves captured in war performed agricultural labor and also provided household help, including child rearing for elite African families, such as local rulers or traders. As concubines, they often bore children, who could eventually become free. In contrast, the European slave trade would transplant Africans to distant cultures without the possibility of social integration; their offspring would remain slaves. While male captives were more likely to be sold overseas, Africans valued slave women for their agricultural, domestic, and reproductive labor. In

African towns, female slaves increasingly relieved elite women of manual labor.

We can see how growing class stratification affected women's lives in China as well. After 700 CE, an economic revolution expanded trade, the production of goods, the growth of cities, and a commercial class. This small-scale (petty) capitalism created new opportunities for some women to travel when they brought goods to market towns. Growing commercialization, however, diminished the importance of women's home weaving. Once partners in domestic production, women found their roles narrowed to reproductive labor. In cities, the trade in women expanded. Poor families devastated by famine or war might sell a daughter in order to bring in money to buy food. These daughters worked as servants in other homes, as concubines for elite married men, or as prostitutes in cities in China (and during the nineteenth century in the United States). Girls sold to brothels in China represented the low end of a trade that also encompassed highly educated courtesans who entertained men with poetry and dramatics.

Commercial growth afforded some elite urban Chinese women greater leisure and even access to education. Although families usually educated only boys, tutors sometimes taught girls within their households. A few educated women became scholars, and many produced highly admired poetry. In the 1600s, for example, elite Chinese women in cities such as Beijing could become "teachers of the inner chambers," sharing their art and literature and sometimes engaging in scholarship. Only exceptional women defied the limits on their sex by traveling and living independently. Most educated elites embraced Confucian values of women's obedience. As one woman writer, Gu Ruopu, explained, "Bring girls together, let them study / . . . the Four Virtues, the Three Obediences." Another poet, Fang Weiyi, exulted maternal influence when she advised her widowed niece that "when your son completes his studies / Your day of honor and glory will come / . . . Generations will emulate your motherly virtues."[13]

Despite these educational opportunities, elite urban women experienced greater seclusion in their families over time. The neo-Confucian thought that flourished after 1000 CE renewed ideals of female obedience and chastity. In addition, foot binding enforced women's dependence and helped limit their mobility to the inner quarters of the family home. The practice originated among elites after 1300 CE but ultimately spread to other classes as well. It severely deformed the toes by binding them from childhood to lie under the foot, making movement slow and difficult. Foot binding and the desire for diminutive feet may have reflected a concern about controlling women's sexuality to ensure virtuous mothers. Initially it also served as an indicator that a family could afford to remove a woman from active labor, although bound girls could perform light labor at home, such as spinning. As compensation for enduring foot binding, a girl could expect a good marriage rather than life as a servant. Because it became so fashionable, even peasant women who worked in rice fields aspired to the small, painfully achieved feet of the ideal in order to ensure their marriage prospects. Foot binding spread through much of China, lasting into the twentieth century.

In addition to convents, some Chinese women devised alternatives to marriage. Where daughters continued to produce textiles at home, they might delay moving to their husbands' homes for several years after they married. In addition, after 1800 women in coastal boomtowns began to renounce marriage without taking religious vows. They lived independently with other women, a practice known as "combing your own hair." When silk manufacturers hired female workers in areas such as the Canton Delta, young women who knew they could earn wages pledged spinsterhood to avoid marriage. They paid for a "celibacy ceremony" equivalent to a wedding, and some worshiped the goddess of mercy, Guan Yin, because she had been unmarried. When women migrated out of the Canton area to take jobs as domestic servants in cities, they took the practice with them. Anthropologist Janice Stockard considers these forms of marriage resistance the loopholes in gender hierarchy in China. As in other cultures, both productive labor and female solidarity softened the harshest features of patriarchy.

European Cities and the Ideal of Separate Spheres

Where urban life and trade flourished in Europe, as in Africa and China, class greatly affected the experience of gender. As early as the ancient city-states of Greece, when urban wealth allowed some European women to cease agricultural labor, new ideals for elite women emerged. Because these ideals became highly influential in western European thought, they deserve close attention. Beginning with the ancient Greeks, Western political theory divided life into the *polis*, or public arena, a male domain of politics, and the *oikos*, a private female sphere of the home. These spaces were not simply different; they were differently valued. Because the ancient Greeks and later Europeans associated the *polis* with male rationality and the *oikos* with female irrationality, they excluded women from politics. Their weaker natures, Plato argued in *The Republic*, meant that women endangered the state. As Aristotle put it in the fourth century BCE, "The courage of a man is shown in commanding, of a woman in obeying."[14] Exceptional women transcended the limitations of gender, as did the Greek poet Sappho or the wives of Sparta's military elite, who accumulated wealth while their husbands fought foreign wars. But the ideological framework of separate spheres remained influential for centuries.

Class differences affected women's experience of these ideas. In medieval Europe, wealthy urban women could enjoy the privileges of servants and the possibility of some education, and those who ran feudal manors could exercise significant authority. Like their Chinese Buddhist counterparts, Christian women could choose religion over marriage by becoming nuns, especially if they had the wealth to join a convent. Female abbesses exercised authority over large religious institutions during the Middle Ages. Some ran convents with up to eight hundred nuns, far removed from male church authorities. The exceptional twelfth-century nun Hildegard of Bingen established several convents, preached widely, and wrote medical treatises, books, and music inspired by divine revelations.

Outside of convents, urban women exercised religious authority in the public sphere when they cared for the needy, healed the sick, or organized charities. This model of women's charitable role continued to provide a source of public female authority in later eras of western European history. Servants, serfs, and poor urban women had no such opportunities. Most of these women continued to contribute productive labor in the home, where husbands retained authority over their wives and daughters. Outside the home, women could earn wages as servants, a very important source of income that also delayed marriage. When women engaged in skilled crafts, they could expect to be paid one-half to two-thirds of what men earned.

The decline of feudalism and the birth of a "modern" worldview in Europe seemed to accentuate gender asymmetry rather than undermine it. Intellectual and cultural life reflected this distinction, as the historian Joan Kelly once suggested in an essay titled "Did Women Have a Renaissance?" The Renaissance era, roughly from 1400 to 1600, witnessed an important flowering of the arts and literature, but Kelly pointed out the greater distinctions between male and female modes of authority. In intellectual life, woman represented the antithesis and inferior of man. According to Thomas Aquinas, men were created in the image of God, while women came later as the subordinates of men. Men were active but women passive; as perpetrators of original sin, women were not capable of perfection. Reviving classical notions about women's irrationality, Renaissance depictions viewed woman as the flesh, sexually uncontrollable and liable to temptation by the devil. This association of women, sin, and the devil laid the groundwork for the accusations of witchcraft that targeted women during the Inquisition and the later witch hunts. From 1500 to 1800 four times more women than men were persecuted as witches, with estimates of those killed ranging from a hundred thousand to more than a million.

The narrowing of European women's sphere affected their public influence. For centuries nuns had ministered to the poor and sick in their communities. Increasingly, however, the church required nuns to remain in the convent rather than the world at large. Once-powerful abbesses came under the oversight of the male church hierarchy, losing their administrative independence. As universities formed to expand higher education outside the Church, only elite men could benefit from the new knowledge of the Renaissance. Exceptional women might still succeed at trade or in the arts. Christine de Pizan overcame opposition to her writing in the 1400s by arguing that God had created men and women with equal potential. The Jewish merchant Glikl of Hameln left a memoir of her life in the 1600s that included travel, trade, and business as well as piety and motherhood. Nonetheless, influential women in public life remained on the margins of European society as both religion and the law prescribed a stronger domestic ideal for women and a stricter gender division of labor.

CAPITALISM AND COLONIALISM

Capitalism intensified the growth of markets, the specialization of labor, and the belief in separate male and female spheres. In China, the petty capitalism of family shops and trading expanded, but state economic policies precluded large-scale capitalism from taking root. In contrast, after 1600 a predominantly capitalist mode transformed the western European economy, setting the stage for an industrial revolution that would take off after 1800. Based on the unlimited accumulation of wealth, investment for profit, and expanding commercial markets, capitalism affected all features of European life. In addition, it encouraged the colonial enterprise and the slave trade, which would in turn disrupt gender relations in Africa and the Americas.

With its merchants, shops, and the putting-out system of production, capitalism encouraged a new economic division between women and men by separating wage labor from the household. Early capitalism narrowed women's opportunities for work outside the home. The guild system, through which apprentices advanced in rank as they learned crafts and trades, excluded women workers, who could engage only in certain types of labor, such as laundry or clothing production. By the 1500s, only one professional role remained for women, that of midwife. As wage labor spread, the value of women's traditional work in the home diminished. Women's home production helped fuel economic expansion (spinning provided the basis for textile production, for example), but factories and shops would soon supplant the old domestic economy. Whether as laborers or merchants, men increasingly earned money, the measure of worth under capitalism. Limited by child-rearing tasks to the home, women had less access to wages and thus became more dependent on men in the family.

Separate Spheres Revisited

Along with these economic changes, ideas about gender increasingly relegated many European women to a more dependent, domestic role. Although the Protestant Reformation inspired a few radical sects that preached gender equality, in England and northern Europe, Protestantism eliminated the option of the convent and emphasized woman's piety as wife and mother within the home. Women who did not fit into the family, such as spinsters and widows, became more economically vulnerable. They were more likely to be accused as witches in the trials that lasted into the early 1700s. European legal thought reinforced women's subordinate status in the family. Influential commentaries on English common law emphasized that in marriage the husband and wife became one legal entity, represented solely by the man. According to William Blackstone, "The very being or legal existence of the woman is suspended during the marriage."[15] A married woman had no right to her own property or her own wages. This concept of "coverture" enforced patriarchy within the middle and upper classes. For propertyless families, it had less direct impact.

During the 1800s, the ideology of separate sexual spheres intensified. "Man for the field and woman for hearth . . . Man to command and woman to obey; all else confusion" was how Alfred Lord Tennyson characterized the British point of view in an 1849 poem.[16] In England and the United States, the mark of middle-class status became a wife who remained in the home while her husband earned money in trade, commerce, or the professions. In contrast to this private ideal, a woman who turned to prostitution became a "public woman," stigmatized for her fall from chastity. Although working-class women had to help support their families, the domestic ideal shaped the occupations available to them—mostly servant or seamstress—and their low wages.

In the nineteenth century, new scientific ideas bolstered earlier religious precepts in support of women's dependence on men. According to Charles Darwin's evolutionary theory of sexual selection, reproductive strategies produced different male and female natures, his much stronger than hers. In order to compete for mates, Darwin proposed, male animals had more variations (the colorful peacock, for example) and were more advanced than females. Generalizing to humans, Darwin wrote, "Man is more courageous, pugnacious, and energetic than woman, and has a more inventive genius." Man thus attained "a higher eminence, in whatever he takes up, than woman can attain."[17] A product of his own time, Darwin's ideas and his language rested upon Victorian views of proper female and male behavior. His examples from animal life overlooked or ignored the many species that do not fit a Western cultural ideal of aggressive males and passive, nurturant females. (Had Darwin considered the red queen and black widow spiders, who destroy the male after mating, or those polyandrous shore birds with larger and more brightly feathered females who leave males to sit on their eggs and feed hatchlings while they mate with a few other males, he might have revised his view of the female sex.)

Darwin's views of women's weaker intellect came to justify male privilege. Influential nineteenth-century scholars invoked evolutionary theory to discourage women from seeking higher education or entering male professions. Herbert Spencer in England and G. Stanley Hall in the United States warned that using their brains made women unfit for motherhood because it would "enfeeble their bodies."[18] Similarly, these social Darwinists believed that natural selection had endowed Europeans (particularly Anglo-Saxons) with greater mental and moral capacity than "primitive" peoples. Because they associated higher civilization with the elaboration of gender difference, they denigrated cultures in which male and female tasks overlapped.

Gender and Colonialism

As capitalism expanded, the colonial conquest of native peoples in North America, Asia, Africa, and Latin America exported European technologies and values throughout the world. Beginning around 1500 Christian missionaries proselytized their patriarchal religion, converting pantheistic cultures by force or persuasion. By 1900 Great Britain, France, Germany, Belgium, and the United States had established global economic and political outposts. Together, missionaries, merchants, and colonial officials brought Christianity and capitalism to much of the world.

Europeans justified colonialism in part by the belief that they could bring the benefits of civilization, progress, and technology to the peoples they deemed to be primitive. In fact, the colonized included highly developed cultures, such as the Maya and Inca in Central and South America and the Arabs, Persians, and Chinese in Asia, who had developed advanced technologies long before the Europeans. Nonetheless, colonialists viewed all of them as uncivilized heathens, more primitive and less modern than Europeans. Since colonialists themselves produced the opposition between the "traditional" and the "modern" (as well as between "heathen" and "Christian," and later "First World" and "Third World"), these terms must be used with caution. They provide insight into the European worldview but not an accurate description of the rest of the world.

Colonialism transported many ideas about gender that both reinforced existing inequalities and introduced new ones. European colonial rulers assumed the natural superiority of the separate male and female spheres idealized in their own societies. To missionaries and colonial officials, all other gender systems oppressed women. Separate spheres, however, did not fit gender relations among the Seneca, the Inca, or, for that matter, working-class or peasant families within Europe. Yet missionaries attempted to impose a strict gender distinction. In North America, Protestants encouraged Seneca women to give up agriculture and spin cloth in private households. During the Spanish conquest of Latin America, Catholic priests persecuted as witches those women who worshiped female deities, while colonial officials recognized only male political leaders.

Colonialism and Gender: The Case of Africa

From the mid-1400s to the mid-1800s colonial economic projects profoundly affected African life. Aside from the extraordinary human costs of the slave trade, the accumulation of capital altered the balance of gender relations. Europeans encouraged cash crops, trade, and the individual ownership of land. Where women had once controlled home production, the marketing of goods for sale in other parts of the world upset their reciprocal family relations. Cloth production in the western Sudan provides a good example. Maraka women had produced most family clothing, which enabled them to maintain rights to their own wealth and authority within their families. During the era of slave labor, however, production for a regional market expanded. Men, rather than women, controlled this process. Although their families became wealthy, wives lost their customary rights and the balance of power in families shifted toward men.

In the past, farm life in Africa had imposed obligations and constraints on both genders. Although men enjoyed greater privileges, women could earn wealth and status by providing food, trading surpluses, and bearing children. In the colonial era, Europeans encouraged only male cultivation of land, preferring to import men from other parts of Africa rather than hire female farmworkers. Men, but not women, learned to use the plow and other farming innovations, creating a technological gap between male and female productivity. Among the Igbo, the British government not only gave new technology solely to men but also banned the custom of "female husbands." Colonial policies eroded Igbo women's customary land use rights as well.

A range of colonial practices further weakened women's social authority. Most missionaries in Africa proselytized for patriarchy when they emphasized the biblical image of God the father as a model for the family. In addition, colonial administrators, such as the British in Nigeria, ignored women's local political power by recognizing only male rulers. Even though colonial courts often ruled in favor of women, the courts themselves supplanted the women's tribunals that once had jurisdiction over women's local disputes. The colonial economy encouraged migration, particularly by sons who sought work for wages on plantations and in cities. In the early 1900s, male migrants to cities had access to education and thus to more desirable jobs, such as those in the civil service. Women who migrated to cities usually became domestic servants or prostitutes. When men's wages could not support their families, wives entered the informal sectors of the urban economy, bartering or selling goods such as matches and cigarettes on city streets.

African women recognized their loss of economic and political leverage and tried to preserve their customary rights. A major resistance movement, the 1929 "women's war" in Nigeria (the British called it the Aba riots), was a response to rumors among Igbo women's trading networks that the British were going to impose a new tax on women's property. Long-seething resentments erupted as tens of thousands of women participated in mass protests. In an effort to prevent men from enforcing these new policies, the chanting women ridiculed and attacked both African chiefs and colonial officials. Women went to the jails en masse and released prisoners. They burned down the very courts that had usurped female juridical power in the villages. To try to quell the women's revolt, the British first sent police, then soldiers, and finally even the Boy Scouts. Eventually shooting into crowds, the British killed fifty women and injured fifty others, ending the "women's war" for the moment.

Elsewhere in Africa group resistance occurred sporadically. In 1959, about two thousand eastern Nigerian women protested their declining status by marching into a neighboring town, occupying the market, and setting fire to it. They negotiated a resolution that eliminated all foreign courts and schools in their area and expelled all foreigners. The movement spread to neighboring ethnic groups, especially where new farming techniques had been introduced. Resistance occurred within the family as well. In the Cameroon, men given land by European law consulted with their wives before making decisions (in part so their wives wouldn't desert them). Some wives refused to help their husbands produce cash crops or perform household labor unless they were paid for their labor or at least consulted about decisions.

The colonial encounter in West Africa illustrates the historical complexity of patriarchy. Long before feminism called for political equality, African women had enjoyed forms of authority as farmers, traders, or mothers. Capitalism and colonialism weakened their base of power and increased women's dependence within the family. Resting firmly on an ideology of separate spheres, colonialism failed to value sufficiently women's labor in the family, and it did not view women's economic dependence on men as problematic. In their acts of resistance, African women recognized their historical losses.

As the examples in this chapter suggest, even if we acknowledge the ubiquity of male privilege in African, Chinese, and western European history, the wide ranges in both patriarchal practices and women's resistance are equally striking. Women's power in relation to men could be reciprocal or subordinate, depending on economic structure and cultural beliefs. Certain practices have historically heightened gender asymmetry: patrilineal, patrilocal families, such as those in rural China; the removal of women from productive labor when early capitalism reshaped European and African economies; or the imposition of external gender systems, as during the colonial encounter in Latin America and Africa. History reveals as well common themes in the empowerment of women under patriarchy. The status that women achieve through bearing children, along with the cultural celebration of motherhood, recurs across cultures. So does the importance of solidarity with other women. "Even if you girls are not sons," wrote the Chinese poet Zhang Shulian, ". . . develop together, support and do not impede each other."[19] Women supported each other in alternatives to the family, such as convents and the women's trading networks that regulated markets and intervened in family conflicts.

Finally, this cross-cultural review reveals the importance of labor as a critical source of women's power in the past. When women's labor entitled them to use or sell products such as food or cloth, they enjoyed greater leverage in the family and were more likely to hold public authority. When the labor of wives and children enhanced men's prestige, as among African farmers, women might have greater influence, even if they were culturally devalued. Capitalism produced sharper contrasts between men's and women's labor in Europe and its colonies. When women's economic dependence in the family deepened and new ideas questioned inequality, the stage was set for feminist politics.

PART II

THE
HISTORICAL
EMERGENCE OF
FEMINISMS

THREE

WOMEN'S RIGHTS, WOMEN'S WORK, AND WOMEN'S SPHERE

Why cannot a woman profit by the privilege of enlightenment?
—SOR JUANA INÉS DE LA CRUZ, MEXICO, 1691

We are not contending here for the rights of the women of New England, or of old England, but of the world.
—ERNESTINE ROSE, UNITED STATES, 1851

In July 1848, when feminists gathered in the United States to demand equal rights for women, they joined a much larger revolutionary force that erupted across Europe that year. In the words of feminists Jeanne Deroin of France and Anne Knight of England, the crusade sought no less than "the complete, radical abolition of all the privileges of sex, of race, of birth, of rank, and of fortune."[1] In England, France, Germany, and Italy, women marched along with workers and the poor; in the United States they fought for the abolition of slavery. Inspired by this social ferment, politicized women began to publish feminist journals, such as the French *La Voix des Femmes* (Voice of Women). Announcing its radicalism in the first issue in March 1848, the editors insisted that "men are no longer permitted to say 'We are humanity.' Liberty for all men *is* liberty for all women."[2] Within a year a half dozen other feminist journals published in France, Germany, and the United States circulated news of women's politics, including the momentous convention at Seneca Falls, New York.

In the course of one remarkable generation, feminism burst onto the Western political stage with demands for education, property rights, suffrage, and much more. This critique of Western gender relations did not erupt full-blown, however. Like other social movements, feminism required both a perception of social injustice and the resources for political mobilization. Patriarchy remained quite stable where traditional elites continued to control markets and political authority, as they did in China. But where a capitalist market revolution encouraged new labor systems, the older patriarchal equilibrium lost its grip. The era of industrialization fostered both a sense of injustice and the resources to protest, first in western Europe and North America and later through much of the world.

When factories replaced home-based, artisanal production, the gap between men's paid and women's unpaid labor widened. Women became more economically dependent on men, enjoying less leverage within marriage and fewer opportunities outside it. Equally important, capitalism encouraged political theories of individual rights and a social contract between the people and their rulers. This new definition of citizenship drew sharp exclusionary lines. In place of older, divinely ordained hierarchies, the concept of "natural" rights distinguished between rational white men, who could be independent citizens, and the irrational, dependent, or less human categories of women, servants, and nonwhite races, who could not.

In short, both industrial capitalism and democratic revolutions disadvantaged women in relation to men. But they also provided critical new resources that allowed women to question gender inequality. Within the middle class, education exposed more women to new ideas about citizenship. When families accumulated wealth under capitalism, some women who gained new leisure used it to write or organize. Even the ideology of separate spheres provided a resource for women who rejected older views of female inferiority and claimed that their maternal calling required education and citizenship.

Building on a century of intellectual ferment and responding to the initial throes of industrialization, women in England, France, Germany, and the United States were the first to organize for their political rights. But wherever capitalist economic relations took hold, whether in Japan, Brazil, or Mexico, middle-class women sought education and property rights. Simultaneously, working-class women who joined utopian and Marxian labor movements demanded higher wages and better working conditions. Women of all classes continued to embrace motherhood as a route to citizenship. Early feminist politics offered a rich toolbox of arguments for change, often combining claims of women's equality to men with an insistence that gender difference carried its own entitlements.

LIBERAL FEMINISM: EXTENDING THE RIGHTS OF MAN TO THE RIGHTS OF WOMEN

After 1800, a democratizing process replaced rule by the arbitrary powers of hereditary elites with individual rights for citizens through the law. The subsequent rise of the "common man" was as gender-specific as the phrase implies. Rooted firmly in the needs of capitalist economies, liberal political theory applied initially to those male economic actors who owned private property and engaged in trade. Wherever capitalism spread during the nineteenth century, political rights such as suffrage gradually extended from the upper and middle classes to wage-earning but propertyless men.

But what did the rights of man mean to women? The ideal of a woman as mother in the home, removed from productive labor and dependent on her husband's income, defined middle-class family status. Although women's unpaid labor within families provided critical economic services, the ideology of separate spheres reserved economic and political rights for men. The legal precedent of coverture made husbands the guardians of dependent wives. Education, however, would provide middle-class women with an initial wedge into the public sphere, from which they launched movements for equal legal and political rights.

Claims for Women's Education

The European Enlightenment spawned a debate about women's education that engaged writers of both sexes and produced the first arguments for female equality in the West, as it would throughout the world. Education was becoming far more critical than in the past, and ultimately too important to withhold from women. Before the invention of the printing press in the 1400s, only a few scribes could write and copy manuscripts, and only monastics and court officials might be literate. Most men and women could not read and write. In an age of print, however, literacy opened access to money, jobs, prestige, and political rights. Ever since the Renaissance, the extension of education primarily to men had widened the knowledge gap between the sexes. During the 1700s, when Enlightenment thinkers heralded rational thinking as a prerequisite of citizenship, they had in mind the education of men.

The French writer Jean-Jacques Rousseau justified women's exclusion from education by idealizing a separate maternal and domestic realm. Like other Enlightenment writers of the 1700s, Rousseau believed that formal education was essential to representative government because it ensured that citizens would be reasonable, virtuous, and independent, rather than vulnerable to manipulation by others. But women, he explained, were neither citizens nor independent; they relied on their powers of manipulation to gain men's support. Reflecting ancient Greek medical notions that bodily functions ruled women while the rational mind ruled men, Rousseau characterized women as highly irrational but also highly manipulative. In his book *Emile* (1762) he wrote that theirs was "the empire of softness, of address, of complacency; her commands are caresses; her menaces are tears." For Rousseau, women's place was "to oblige us, to do us service, to gain our love and esteem, these are the duties of the sex at all times, and what they ought to learn from their infancy. Woman is framed particularly for the delight and pleasure of man."[3] Not only was education an unnecessary luxury for women; far worse, it could unsex a woman by taking her outside of the domestic sphere. Women only needed to learn how to please and manipulate men, who in turn would take care of them.

Though influential, Rousseau's views on women's education would not prevail in the long run. As early as the 1670s European women had begun to demand access to formal education; some of them even broached the subject of political rights. Most early proponents of educating women argued that if a mother was going to raise sons, she had to be able to teach young children at home so that they would be prepared to enter a literate world. In the United States, this argument would be termed "republican motherhood," because mothers raised future male citizens. Even single women who did not have children had a reason to become literate. In Protestant countries such as England and the United States, where personal, rather than priestly, interpretations of the scripture prevailed, women needed literacy in order to study the Bible. In addition, the religious principle of the equality of souls before God inspired arguments for women's education. Beginning in the 1690s, Western women articulated both views to justify the education of their sex.

Two early advocates of women's education, one Catholic and one Protestant, illustrate the arguments that foreshadowed liberal feminism. Sor Juana Inés de la Cruz, a seventeenth-century Mexican nun, presented one of the first defenses of women's education based on the equality of women's souls. Because she did not wish to marry, at age eighteen she entered a convent, where she wrote both religious and secular poetry. By the time she was thirty years old Sor Juana was defending herself eloquently to her Jesuit confessor, Father Núñez, who complained about her writing. Rejecting many of the traditional Catholic views that women were too irrational and passionate to undertake learning, she wrote in 1691: "Have they [women] not a rational soul as men do? Well then, why cannot a woman profit by the privilege of enlightenment if they do? Is her soul not as able to receive the grace and glory of God as that of a man?" In response to her confessor's criticisms, Sor Juana cited earlier church women as models and invoked her "God-given free will" as a higher authority than his.[4]

In the same decade but unknown to Sor Juana, a Protestant Englishwoman made similar arguments. In 1692, Mary Astell published *A Serious Proposal to the Ladies*, in which she protested that men blamed women for being irrational but prevented them from learning. Assumptions about the natural inferiority of women, she suggested, might not stand the test of education. To improve women's character and morality, Astell called for a kind of Protestant convent, a retreat where women could turn away from the trivial affairs of the world and engage in the serious study of books, the better to understand Christianity. Echoing Sor Juana's thoughts, Astell wrote: "For since God has given Women as well as Men intelligent Souls, why should they be forbidden to improve them?"[5] She reassured her readers that women would not preach in church or usurp men's authority, a promise repeated whenever women first sought the right to formal education.

In other parts of the world, exceptional, usually elite women have sometimes had access to education, from late Ming Dynasty Chinese poets to Renaissance "learned ladies." With the spread of literacy and the increasing importance of education, however, more women flourished intellectually. In the 1700s literate French, German, and Italian women held salons in their homes, while in England the bluestockings discussed political affairs with influential men. Recalling her Berlin salon, Henrietta Herz described women who "have thrown all the conventions overboard and are indulging in an exuberant freedom of spirit."[6] Over the next centuries educated middle-class women read, wrote, and discussed the world around them. Some of them extended Enlightenment political ideas to gender relations.

From Education to Women's Rights

A century after Sor Juana and Mary Astell wrote, the public debate about women's education grew more heated as a language of political rights gradually replaced the polite requests of earlier thinkers. Toward the end of the eighteenth century, two major world revolutions put into practice the critique of social hierarchy initiated during the Enlightenment: the American revolution against British colonial rule, begun in 1776, and the French revolution against aristocratic rule, begun in 1789. An older social order visibly collapsed as common people, both male and female, insisted on their rights to political representation. By undermining colonial rule in America and inherited status in France, these revolutions legitimated the concept of equality and inspired broader critiques of unequal power relations, including abolitionism and feminism. "Can man be free, if woman be a slave?" asked the British poet Percy Shelley in 1818.[7] Increasingly, European women answered no.

The call for liberty, equality, and fraternity echoed throughout Europe over the next century, even as the limitations on a politics of equal rights became clear. In France, for example, the revolution mobilized working women, who marched on Versailles and demanded bread. It also inspired a reconceptualization of gender. In 1791 the French playwright

Olympe de Gouges issued *The Declaration of the Rights of Woman and the Female Citizen*, in which she called on women to "discover your rights." A champion of educational and marital equality for women, as well as the abolition of slavery and the emancipation of the Jews, de Gouges died by the guillotine as the French revolutionaries rejected demands for equal rights. The French revolution never extended universal citizenship to include women. In its aftermath, the legal code introduced by Napoleon Bonaparte in 1804 gave formal power to husbands over wives. Reflecting a renewed emphasis on women's domestic roles, in nineteenth-century France, calls for female education typically invoked maternal duties to justify learning. Although some radical French women did continue to demand equal rights as citizens, especially after the introduction of universal manhood suffrage in 1848, their goal of woman suffrage would not be achieved until 1944.

After the French Revolution, the intellectual attack on gender inequality flourished in England, where Mary Wollstonecraft, Harriet Taylor, and John Stuart Mill laid the groundwork not only for education but also for property rights and voting rights for women. A former governess and a writer, Wollstonecraft traveled within a radical British intellectual circle that supported the French Revolution and the rights of man. She rejected not only aristocratic hierarchies but also conventional family authority. Wollstonecraft bore a child out of wedlock, survived her lover's rejection, and later engaged in an open affair with the radical editor William Godwin before they married. (The couple's daughter, Mary Godwin, who later married the poet Shelley, wrote the classic science fiction novel *Frankenstein*.) Until her death in childbirth in 1797, Wollstonecraft championed the new values of economic individualism and political liberty. One of her earliest essays, "A Vindication of the Rights of Man," applied Enlightenment ideals of equal opportunity to justify the French Revolution. In 1792 she extended those ideals to women in her work *A Vindication of the Rights of Woman*. Just as Enlightenment thinkers rejected the divine rights of kings in favor of the rights of man, Wollstonecraft opposed the divine rights of husbands over their wives, adding gender to the politics of democratic revolution. As kings are tyrants over the people, she argued, husbands can be tyrants over wives. Speaking of women, she explained, "I do not wish them to have power over men, but over themselves."

A sharp critic of Rousseau, Wollstonecraft believed in education for both men and women. She challenged long-standing assumptions about female inferiority, especially in terms of intellect, and insisted that women should learn skills rather than rely on beauty or emotional influence to survive. Even for Wollstonecraft, however, the justification for women's education remained closely linked to family roles. Education would produce "sensible mothers" and rational wives. Between the births of their children, she assured her readers, women could find the time to strengthen their minds and cultivate the fine arts, rather than pursue fashion. Wollstonecraft did allow that exceptional women could do more than marry and have children. They might "be physicians as well as nurses. . . . They might also study politics." Expecting to "excite laughter," she even suggested that "women ought to have representatives, instead of being arbitrarily governed without having any direct share allowed them in the deliberations of government."[8]

Wollstonecraft wrote almost entirely about the lives of middle-class or elite women, those who had the leisure for education and servants to help with their domestic labor. During the nineteenth century, some of these women put her theories into practice in England and the United States. They created academies for girls, teacher training schools, and later colleges for women. Not all proponents of women's education shared Wollstonecraft's desire for political rights, however. In the United States, for example, Catharine Beecher devoted her life to establishing schools to train women teachers. Because she believed firmly that the home, and not politics, was woman's proper sphere, Beecher opposed woman suffrage.

In contrast to Beecher, the British liberals Harriet Taylor and John Stuart Mill extended the argument for the rights of woman to include property and suffrage as well as education. Harriet Taylor published the essay "Enfranchisement of Women" in 1851, the year she and Mill married. Drawing on the language of the abolitionist movement, she compared women to slaves and called for their emancipation through education and legal reform. After his wife's death from tuberculosis in 1858, John Stuart Mill, who was already an eminent liberal theorist, continued to write about women's rights. His important political treatise on *The Subjection of Women* (1869) credited Harriet Taylor for inspiring his beliefs. As a member of Parliament and a champion of liberalism, Mill had earlier supported the extension of education and suffrage to adult men who did not own property; now he sought these rights for women as well.

Harriet Taylor and John Stuart Mill accepted Enlightenment arguments about the rights of man and the need for personal liberty. Like other classical liberals, they believed that giving more opportunity to individuals would correct all social inequalities. In place of a world of fixed social position, they supported what has been called the "unfettered choice of individuals." Citing the contradictions within liberalism of privileges based on gender, race, and class, Mill extended the philosopher John Locke's critique of absolute authority. As Mill wrote in *The Subjection of Women*, "If the principle of equal opportunity is true, we ought to act as if we believed it, and not ordain that to be born a girl instead of a boy, any more than to be born black instead of white, or commoner instead of a nobleman shall decide the person's position through all life."[9] Influenced by his wife, Mill explained that women's "choice" to be wives and mothers was not yet a free choice because it was based on limited opportunities. With education, though, instead of becoming "willing slaves," women would act independently and be freed from subordination in emotional relationships.

Politically John Stuart Mill acted on his beliefs. After 1865 he fought for woman suffrage in the House of Commons. Mill objected to the British common-law principle of coverture, which held that in marriage the husband and wife became one legal entity, represented by the husband, who had the rights to his wife's property and person. One could not assume, Mill argued, that a husband's vote necessarily represented his wife's interests, the theory generally held at the time. In a statement that presaged later feminist concerns about domestic violence, he told his fellow members of Parliament that "I should like to have a return laid before this house, of the numbers of women who are annually beaten to death, kicked to death, or trampled to death, by their male protectors."[10] Like Wollstonecraft's work, however, Mill's writings assumed that most women, given the choice, would marry and remain at home raising children, rather than work for wages. Also like Wollstonecraft, he largely ignored the condition of working-class women, although he too allowed that exceptional women could become professionals rather than marry.

National Movements

In the 1790s Mary Wollstonecraft stood nearly alone in proposing women's rights; by the time Harriet Taylor and John Stuart Mill wrote, a growing audience supported the cause. As more middle-class women attended schools, they gained skills for questioning the status quo. As antislavery ideas, religious liberalization, and utopianism swept across Europe and the United States, they provided seedbeds for feminist organizing. From the 1820s through the 1850s educated women in Germany, England, and the United States corresponded and sometimes met to demand their own rights. Their journals carried news of activism across national boundaries. As Polish-Jewish immigrant Ernestine Rose told a U.S. women's rights convention in 1851, "We are not contending here for the rights of the women of New England, or of old England, but of the world."[11]

In the United States, women's rights conventions met locally throughout the northern states during the 1850s. Through speeches, reform newspapers, and petitions to legislatures they demanded, in Elizabeth Cady Stanton's words, "the equal station to which they are entitled." These early feminists inspired vicious attacks from hostile journalists, who insisted on the impropriety of women in political life. Caricatures portrayed them as pants-wearing, cigar-smoking, unfeminine, bossy shrews. Nonetheless, persistent pressure from feminists achieved moderate successes. Along with new educational opportunities, the U.S. movement chipped away at restrictive state laws, gaining married women the right to own their own property and control their own wages. They were far more successful in extending these rights than in winning support for woman suffrage.

Although no dramatic event like the Seneca Falls convention marked the onset of the British women's movement, in the 1850s middle-class British women petitioned Parliament to allow married women to own property. Defeated in their first efforts, they continued to organize. In the 1860s liberal feminists such as Barbara Bodichon and

Emily Davis campaigned for university education, divorce reform, and woman suffrage. The feminist *Englishwomen's Journal* furthered the cause, while organizations such as the Ladies' Institute provided classrooms for women. By the 1880s British women won control over their own property through the Married Women's Property Act (1870) and gained access to university education, laying the groundwork for the militant suffrage movement of the early twentieth century.

In England and the United States the antislavery movement and universal male suffrage provided important political frameworks for the liberal feminist call for women's rights. Elsewhere, other liberal movements also inspired feminism. In Russia, the emancipation of the serfs in 1861 raised women's expectations for equality. When Russia limited its universities to men, many women traveled to western Europe to pursue higher and medical educations. In mid-nineteenth-century Germany, liberal reformers such as Hélène Lange and Bertha Pappenheim pressed for equal education and careers for women; rarer was the campaign for women's votes waged by the Judischer Frauenbund (Jewish Women's League). In the 1870s and 1880s political liberalism in Scandinavia encouraged both women's societies in support of education and the Swedish Society for Married Women's Property Rights. In 1910 Norway granted women voting rights in local elections. By then New Zealand, Australia, and Finland had also enacted woman suffrage. Few other countries followed this step toward full citizenship before the close of World War I. By that time, masses of women in Europe and North America had achieved educational and property rights. (See Appendix A.)

In other parts of the world, liberal feminist critiques appeared wherever reform movements pressed for democratic government. In Brazil (which gained independence from Portugal in 1822), a series of urban women's newspapers championed female emancipation. In the 1850s *O Jornal das Senhoras* (The Ladies Journal) complained that men considered women solely as "a *propagation machine*" and that marriage meant "unbearable tyranny." Women deserved "the just enjoyment of their rights." In the 1870s *O Sexo Feminino* (The Female Sex) supported the emancipation of slaves along with women's rights to education, property, and legal equality. Brazilian feminists recalled the heritage of the "French Revolution, this enormous human epic event" that had established the principles of the rights of man but "did not expand the civic capacity of women." Now, Francisca Diniz wrote in 1890, "we Brazilians, Portuguese, French, English, Italian, German, etc., women . . . are asking for what is due us and what, by natural right, cannot be denied us."[12]

Latin American women invoked ideas about national progress to advance the reform of marriage laws and women's entry into higher education. They contended that new American nations should prove their democratic spirit by educating women. Universities in Chile, Brazil, Mexico, and Argentina began to admit female students in the late 1800s. Soon middle-class Latin American women called for rights to property and wages as well. When a political revolution erupted in Mexico after 1910, a Mexican women's movement held regional congresses that introduced the question of woman suffrage, which would be debated for decades. In Chile, Amanda Labarca downplayed suffrage at first, but by 1920 her *Concejo Nacional de Mujeres* (National Women's Council) supported the vote, as did the Woman's Progressive Party. Most Latin American women would gain voting rights between 1930 and 1960.

The theory of individual rights influenced the founding of a Japanese women's movement soon after Japan opened its doors to Westerners in 1868. Male reformers supported schooling for girls on the grounds that, as mothers, they would raise brave sons. These men did not necessarily support political rights for women, but in the 1870s and 1880s feminists argued that women who owned property ought to be allowed to vote. Kishida Toshiko and others also criticized the limited opportunities for girls within families. Once a lady-in-waiting to the empress, Kishida rejected life at court for being "far from the real world." In 1882, when she was just twenty years old, she gave her first public speech, "The Way for Women," in which she criticized the Japanese family. Like Wollstonecraft, Kishida stressed the compatibility of education and marriage, but she also hoped to reform marriage to give women more choices. When she toured the country, women flocked to her talks and formed women's groups to effect her goals. One speech in which she called for expanding women's horizons to be "as large and free as the world itself" earned her a week in jail.[13]

For most Japanese, educating women to be moral mothers meant keeping them away from the world of politics. The government banned women's political participation during the 1890s. Nonetheless, women's magazines, schools, and workers' societies sustained the movement. Once Japanese women could legally organize in the 1920s, the Suffrage League petitioned the national legislature for voting rights for women. The militarization of Japan after 1930 delayed the process, but woman suffrage finally passed in 1945 as part of the postwar effort to foster democracy in place of authoritarianism.

Whether in Japan, Brazil, Chile, England, France, or the United States, where liberal ideas about the rights of man circulated, both women and men called for the extension of these rights to women. Yet the liberal feminist emphasis on education, property, and suffrage largely ignored the ways that the historical changes wrought by capitalism affected women in the propertyless working class. Nor did it persuade the majority of women or men who believed firmly in the power of women's domestic and maternal roles.

MARXISM AND SOCIALIST FEMINISM: THE ORGANIZATION OF WORKING WOMEN

In response to the rise of capitalism in Europe, classical liberal political theory celebrated the individualism that was essential to middle-class economic success. In contrast, socialist political ideologies criticized the new economic system from the perspective of artisans and unskilled workers. Artisans had once controlled their own tools and labor, but increasingly they worked for wages. During the 1800s, while owners profited, work conditions deteriorated in agriculture, mining, and manufacturing. Workdays of up to fifteen hours, under unsanitary and dangerous conditions, resulted in frequent injury and disease; overseers often exercised uncontrolled power over workers. Many working families could not survive without the labor of children as well as of women.

Dismayed by the "proletarianization" of work, many laborers sought an alternative to capitalist economic and social organization. In contrast to the unfettered individualism of liberalism, socialist theories emphasized cooperation among workers and collective ownership of the means of production. From the 1830s through the 1850s utopian socialists experimented with collective living that included alternative gender relations. After 1848, when Marx and Engels published *The Communist Manifesto*, Marxian socialists called for proletarian revolutions that would replace capitalism with worker-run state socialism.

Viewed through the history of feminism, utopian socialists seem more radical than the later Marxists. The followers of French writers Henri de Saint-Simon and Charles Fourier believed in women's emancipation within the family as well as workers' control of production. Fourier's 1808 scheme for social reorganization included one of the earliest articulations of *féminisme*: "The extension of women's privileges is the general principle for all social progress," he wrote. Similarly, women among the Saint-Simonians, who in the 1830s published a newspaper called *La femme libre* (The Free Woman) insisted that "with the emancipation of woman / Will come the emancipation of the worker."[14] Other utopian socialists compared the status of married women to that of slaves, protesting the legal and economic domination of men. Jeanne Deroin later applied these principles to her feminist paper, *La Voix des Femmes*.

Both Saint-Simonian and Fourierist communities attempted to socialize not only craft production but also housework. Theoretically, if not in practice, they insisted that both men and women help prepare food and care for children. This socialization of housework could restore the proximity of men's and women's tasks, reversing the stricter separation of spheres encouraged when wage labor drew male workers outside the home. Freed from doing all the cooking, cleaning, and child care in individual households, women could then engage in productive labor alongside men. Socialized housework and child care also meant that all adults took responsibility for all children. Some Saint-Simonians took the collective theory even further to socialize sexuality and reproduction; they accepted "free love," or open marriage, which eliminated the private family.

Other communities attempted to practice many of these principles. The British utopian Robert Owen inspired several communities in England and the United States. Scottish-born radical Frances Wright created an interracial, abolitionist utopia at Nashoba, Tennessee, in the 1820s. Because she espoused free love and allowed interracial relationships, Wright became a symbol of immorality, and her community ultimately failed. The taint of free love, open marriage, and sexual scandal attached to other utopianists as well, especially the Saint-Simonians. In the popular mind, socialism and sexual immorality went hand in hand, a link that would haunt radical women's movements for generations.

In contrast to the isolated and short-lived utopian socialist communities, Marxian socialism inspired a lasting mass political movement in Europe. From the labor organizing in the 1850s to socialist parties and then the communist states of the twentieth century, Marxism captured the allegiance of workers and intellectuals. The utopians had tried to socialize both production and the reproductive tasks of child care and housework. The central Marxian strategy to emancipate women was to undermine female dependence within the family. Bringing women into the paid workforce and organizing them into trade unions would accomplish this goal.

Marx and Engels acknowledged that women in the working class faced a dual exploitation, in both the family and the workplace. Women's low wages kept them economically dependent on husbands, who could exploit female labor in the home. While liberal feminists compared the rule of husbands to the tyranny of kings, in Engels' metaphor the husband represented the bourgeois and the wife the proletarian. Despite this insight, Marxism discounted the economic worth of women's work in the home. Since housework did not produce surplus value (profit), it did not count as productive labor. Only as workers in a proletarian revolution against exploitation by capitalists would women become emancipated.

Like liberal feminism, Marxism failed to resolve the dilemma of women's dual labors. Moreover, the strategy of mobilizing women as paid workers did not win immediate support among European socialists. For one, male workers feared that women would compete for their jobs. In addition, when male workers felt exploited by capitalists they still had authority over their wives in the household. If wives could earn as much as men, they might challenge that authority.

Nonetheless, Marxism inspired feminist organizing in socialist movements throughout the world. Across Europe vocal socialist women addressed the "woman question" from the perspectives of both class and gender. In France, Flora Tristan drew on her personal experience to write passionately about the plight of working-class wives. In 1843 she compared their status to that of slaves, since women were vulnerable to the abuse of husbands and forced to bear their children. Women held the key to solving the working-class woes of poverty and ignorance, she argued, but only if they had access to education. Paralleling liberal feminists, Tristan championed education for working women, explaining that "because women have the responsibility for educating male and female children" they would raise future generations to respect women equally.[15]

The German radical Clara Zetkin epitomized a strategy of socialist feminism, combining concern for workers with a focus on women's work conditions and organizing women politically. While studying to become a teacher, she had met exiled Russian revolutionaries and converted to socialism. In a pamphlet she published in 1889, Zetkin insisted that "woman would remain in subjugation until she is economically independent."[16] In the socialist movements she justified the organization of women workers by insisting that the working class would never succeed without them. Only by bringing women into unions would the wage scale rise for all; excluding women created a low-paid and unorganized labor force that only increased the profits of owners. In the 1890s Zetkin successfully incorporated women into the German Social Democratic Party by establishing a separate Women's Bureau. She also founded the Socialist Women's International in the decade before World War I. Although she and other socialist women shunned the middle-class women's rights movement, Zetkin supported woman suffrage as long as it applied universally, across classes, and she urged the socialist movement to do so as well. She even renamed the socialist women's newspaper *Gleichheit* (Equality).

A Russian protégé of Zetkin, Alexandra Kollontai, achieved the formal political authority to advance socialist feminism. Kollontai served as commissar for social welfare in the early Soviet Union. Like German socialists, she rejected "bourgeois feminism" because it failed to address working women's problems. "For the majority of the women of the proletariat," Kollontai wrote in 1908, "equal rights with men would mean only an equal share in inequality." Only "in a world of socialized labor, of harmony and justice" would equal rights make women "truly free."[17] Unlike Zetkin, who concentrated on labor organizing, Kollontai also paid close attention to personal issues. She championed birth control, public child care, and women's sexual liberation. To support women as both mothers and workers, the state would have to take on family responsibilities such as health care, education, and child rearing. After the Bolshevik Revolution of 1917, Kollontai tried to implement these policies. As commisar she decreed free maternity care as well as equal work responsibilities for women in the early Soviet Union. Hospitals, schools, and nurseries represented a step toward communal child rearing and housekeeping. She also rejected the sexual double standard, by which only men could have sex outside of marriage, and she supported both abortion and divorce. Opponents labeled her a libertine.

Although she had the early support of Lenin, Kollontai's insistence on addressing familial as well as labor force inequalities stood at odds with the communist government, and her influence was short-lived. Reassigned to diplomatic posts, she continued to write about women's issues, but after 1926 the Soviets reversed her policies in favor of strengthening individual families. During the Great Depression and the Stalinist repression of the 1930s, almost all of the reforms Kollontai had enacted in the 1920s disappeared. Most Soviet women worked outside the home, some in professional jobs such as medicine, but like women elsewhere, they worked a double day—first for pay and then for their families—with minimal social support.

The case of China further illustrates the problems communist states had in implementing Marx's vision of women's emancipation. As in European socialism, feminist critiques predated the communist revolution. During the 1890s Chinese liberal reformers, like those in Japan, called for women's education for proper motherhood. By the early 1900s Chinese feminists were demanding laws to ensure equal rights to property, marriage, and divorce and an end to foot binding. The political space for a liberal feminist critique ended abruptly in 1949 when the Communist Party triumphed after a long civil war.

The Chinese Communist Party adopted the Marxian strategy of organizing women into productive labor. Women's emancipation, the state insisted, would follow from the workers' revolution. The People's Republic of China (PRC) collectivized production, encouraged women to enter the state-run labor force, and tried to socialize child care. Public policy included a new marriage law in 1950 that granted women equal rights to property and divorce, a potentially revolutionary alternative to the traditional patriarchal family. Through a state-run women's organization, the All China Women's Federation, the government sponsored local efforts to mobilize women as workers and educate them about their oppression within the family.

The PRC successfully mobilized women as laborers, but it did not necessarily emancipate women in the family. With little capital to invest in national economic growth, using women workers increased production by freeing men to engage in new rural industries and advanced technologies. In contrast, women's work training consisted largely of unskilled agricultural tasks, such as planting and harvesting on rural communes. The strategy succeeded, for during the Great Leap Forward of the 1950s, women's labor accounted for 50 percent of the increase in agricultural production in some rural areas. In cities, women entered factories as unskilled labor, freeing men for higher-skilled jobs in heavy industries.

In the family, however, much of the old patriarchal order survived. Despite the marriage law, women found it hard to divorce their husbands. Women laborers faced heavy domestic duties when they returned home from work. Labor policies did recognize women's reproductive roles by allowing maternity leave and the right to take breaks from work to nurse an infant (although only female and not male workers could take time from their jobs to attend to housework). The government tried to socialize child care through state-run nurseries, but since women rather than men filled these jobs, the system reinforced the gender-based division of labor. Moreover, in times of economic retrenchment, communal facilities closed and state propaganda claimed that "Women Should Do More Family Duties."[18]

The Socialist Feminist Legacy

Despite the limitations of communist state policies, socialist women have contributed a wide and important spectrum of political strategies to the history of feminism. Flora Tristan emphasized education; Clara Zetkin called for organizing women as workers as well as woman suffrage; Alexandra Kollontai insisted on the centrality of reproduction, sexuality, and child care to the mobilization of women workers. Although communist states rejected feminism as "bourgeois," socialist women first imagined many of the policies that the world's social democracies would eventually enact to reconcile the work and family responsibilities of laboring women.

Socialist women also influenced trade union movements in liberal democracies such as England and the United States. From the 1870s onward, when labor unions failed to organize the increasing numbers of women who worked for wages, female activists reached out to do so. When British match girls, cigar makers, or laundresses protested wage cuts, socialist women publicized their cause in speeches and books. Inspired by the populist and socialist revolutionaries in Russia, young working-class women who emigrated to the United States helped mobilize female garment workers on New York's Lower East Side. Inspirational organizers such as Fannia Cohn and Clara Lemlich brought tens of thousands into unions. In 1909 the young Lemlich passionately implored her sister New York City shirtwaist makers in Yiddish to walk off their jobs; ultimately over twenty thousand joined the strike for better wages. Emma Goldman, another Russian Jewish immigrant, proselytized an anarchist version of socialism that defended "free motherhood," or women's sexual and reproductive emancipation from marriage. Goldman's speeches on prostitution, free love, and socialism thrilled radicals but enraged the U.S. government, which in 1919 deported her to Russia.

Throughout the twentieth century, the socialist critique inspired not only labor activists but also women novelists, theorists, and scholars. Indeed, writers with socialist backgrounds would help to reignite the woman question after the 1940s: novelists Simone de Beauvoir in France and Doris Lessing in England, historians Eleanor Flexner and Gerda Lerner in the United States, and even the liberal feminist Betty Friedan all had strong roots in communist, labor, or leftist movements. Each one expanded on socialism to question further the dilemmas of gender inequality. As de Beauvoir explained in 1972, a generation after the publication of her 1949 treatise *The Second Sex*, "We must fight for an improvement in woman's actual situation before achieving the socialism we hope for."[19]

In 1911 socialists began to observe March 8 as a day to honor the women who had walked out on strike for better working conditions in the nineteenth and early twentieth centuries. International Working Women's Day became a national holiday in socialist countries, although Western nations largely ignored the occasion. In the 1960s, however, both liberal and socialist feminists in the West revived it under the name International Women's Day by staging marches and demonstrations for women's rights. In the United States, a movement to declare March as Women's History Month gained congressional support, and today schools throughout the country teach some women's history that month. Few who celebrate, however, recognize the holiday's origins in early socialist commemorations of the strikes waged by working women.

WOMAN'S SPHERE: MATERNALISM, GENDER DIFFERENCE, AND RADICAL FEMINISM

The Enlightenment and revolutionary political thought that gave birth to women's longings for emancipation rested upon contradictory views. New beliefs in universal rights promised emancipation from the old regime of inherited status; simultaneously, however, the principle of natural law drew biological distinctions between the sexes and among races. The flip side of natural rights was natural sex and natural race. Thus when women or Africans or Asians claimed universal rights, critics could respond that their biological difference disqualified them from inclusion as citizens. The very contradiction within modern political thought, historian Joan Scott argues, required a dual strategy on the part of feminists. On one hand they emphasized universalism and demanded inclusion in the language of rights; on the other hand they pointed to particularistic, biologically rooted female claims to political authority.

It is not surprising that early feminists often valorized, rather than rejected, the ideal of motherhood. Both middle-class and socialist women's arguments for education frequently invoked their roles as mothers. Whether in Africa, China, Europe, or Latin America, motherhood had long endowed women with social power. With industrialization and urbanization, it acquired new historical meanings. At a time of growing urban poverty and crime, and when politics generated scandals that tested the virtues of democracy, the private home symbolized a haven from corruption. It also provided a sacrosanct pulpit for middle-class women. From their domestic base they waged public campaigns to bring the allegedly superior moral values of the home to bear on the world.

Historians have applied a variety of labels to women's efforts to transform social policy in the name of family protection. These labels range from "female consciousness" and "difference feminism" to the Latin American concept of *marianismo* and the idea of "social motherhood." Although it is an imperfect term, *maternalism* covers a wide range of women's public activism, either as mothers or for the sake of children and families. But maternalism could be a double-edged sword. Women might mobilize as mothers to gain rights, but they could also be confined as mothers to a dependent economic and political role. Opponents of suffrage invoked maternalism when they insisted that women exercised more authority as mothers than they would as voters. By setting up an opposition between motherhood and citizenship, antisuffragists retained both the ideology of separate spheres and the principle of coverture, in which a husband represented the economic and political interests of his wife. Feminists had to walk a thin line, balancing their identities as mothers with their demands for equality. In the process, they articulated a powerful defense of female difference as a source of political authority.

Maternalism in the Americas

In the nineteenth century, women seized public authority as mothers in both the temperance and antiprostitution movements. In the United States, efforts to oppose intemperate drinking turned into a women's crusade during the 1870s. Women poured out of the churches and into saloons, destroyed the liquor supply, and began preaching to men on the streets. They even convinced some saloon owners to sign on to temperance and close their businesses. By 1900 millions of women had mobilized to oppose men's drinking. The Woman's Christian Temperance

Union (WCTU) became the largest women's organization in the United States. Rather than rejecting women's domestic identities, the WCTU tried to protect women and children in the home. Since drunken husbands abused wives and children and failed to support their families, women mobilized to achieve temperance.

Similarly, because prostitution corrupted their children, moral reformers in the United States stationed themselves outside brothels and recorded the names of male patrons to publish in local newspapers. At least one astonished mother yanked her own son out of a house of ill repute. The WCTU waged a "social purity" campaign to protect young women from sexual ruin and prevent prostitution. Borrowing temperance techniques, they enjoined male relatives to take the pledge of sexual purity and wear a white ribbon to announce their adherence to a single, female standard of sexual morality.

The social purity campaign reached widely, mobilizing African American churches and the British women's movement. In the southern United States, the Women's Convention of the black Baptist Church insisted on sobriety and social purity, calling upon mothers of all classes to uplift the race. As Nannie Burroughs wrote in 1903, "Every mother can become a benefactor to the race. It matters not how poor the mother if she possesses a character in which sobriety, honor and integrity, and every other wholesome virtue hold sway."[20] In England, Josephine Butler spearheaded a campaign to help raise women's legal age of consent so that sexual relations with girls under age sixteen constituted statutory rape. Purity reformers also convinced several American states to raise the age of consent as a means of protecting young women from sexual relations that might lead to prostitution or social ruin.

Although some social purity activists, such as suffragist Susan B. Anthony, recognized that low wages and lack of job opportunities drove many to prostitution, most early moral reformers emphasized the sexual, rather than economic, exploitation of women. Eventually, however, maternalist reformers did turn to the plight of working women, even as they continued to emphasize motherhood. In the early 1900s U.S. reformers campaigned for laws that would protect working women from low wages and long hours, explicitly invoking the need to preserve the health of future mothers. Maternalists also supported the establishment of the U.S. Children's Bureau in 1912. Gradually many maternalists adopted suffrage as a means for achieving their reforms. Women in the United States won the vote in 1920 in part by claiming that morally superior women would serve as the mothers of civilization.

In Latin America, where the Catholic Church strongly influenced social thought, reformers frequently invoked maternalism to support liberal feminist demands for education and equal rights. After Mexican independence in 1823, male reformers criticized women's subordination in the family, but rather than embracing equal political rights, they glorified motherhood and the new ideal of women as moral guardians. The concept of *marianismo* identified women with the powerful figure of the Virgin Mary. According to historian Silvia Arrom, marianismo contributed to improved education for women but also served socially conservative goals of domestic stability and excluded women from full citizenship. In Brazil, feminist Francisca Diniz wrote in 1890 that women "as mothers represent the sanctity of infinite love. . . . As wives, immortal fidelity." But she continued that these qualities, "prove their superiority, not their inferiority, and show that equality of action should be put into practice by those men who proclaim the principle of equality."[21]

When the term *feminism* circulated in the early twentieth century, some Latin American women redefined it to reflect the maternalist strain of their own politics. Amanda Labarca of Chile, who had studied at the Sorbonne and in New York, reported to a U.S. women's group in 1922 that she expected "a new feminist creed" to arise on the southern continent, one "more domestic, more closely linked to the future of the home, the family, and the children" than that marked by the "exaggerated individualism" of what she called "Saxon feminism." Labarca endorsed women's efforts to "forge peace, tranquility, well-being, and the greatness of our country" before she accepted suffrage as a means to those ends.[22] Even when maternalism did not converge with liberal demands for equal education and suffrage, it helped authorize women's public life. In Mexico, middle-class women engaged in charitable work, became teachers, and pressed for maternal health care. The Mexico City newspaper

La Mujer Méxicana (The Mexican Woman) called on educated women to come to the aid of the thousands of women migrants who became prostitutes.

Maternalism represented a political consciousness that could either reinforce the ideal of separate spheres or subvert it to oppose certain forms of inequality. Like the radical feminism that would emerge after the 1960s, maternalism called attention to personal life, including moral issues such as drinking and prostitution. Also like later radical feminisms, it rested upon essentialist notions of a common womanhood that ignored class differences and presumed female moral superiority. The seemingly paradoxical beliefs in gender equality and gender difference would continue to characterize modern feminism, politicizing women who might otherwise reject the movement.

The Legacy of Difference: Charlotte Perkins Gilman and Virginia Woolf

In the twentieth century, feminist theorists built upon the maternalist legacy of extending women's moral authority beyond the family into public reform. They articulated a politics that simultaneously criticized the domestic realm for limiting women and celebrated the superior values attached to women because of their maternal and domestic roles. Both Charlotte Perkins Gilman in the United States and Virginia Woolf in England wrote passionately about the ways in which gender difference provided women with a uniquely critical perspective. Each writer combined liberalism, socialism, and maternalism, and each foreshadowed the radical feminist politics of a later generation. While Gilman based her theories in evolutionary biology, Woolf turned to history to explain how gender affected moral values.

At the turn of the twentieth century Charlotte Perkins Stetson Gilman was the most important feminist theorist in the United States. Her books *Women and Economics* (1898) and *The Home* (1903), as well as her short story "The Yellow Wallpaper" (1892) and her utopian novel *Herland* (1915), have all become classic feminist texts. In the 1880s Gilman had cured her serious depression by leaving an unhappy marriage, giving up her child, and becoming a writer, lecturer, and "humanitarian socialist." Although she later remarried happily, she recognized that domestic life alone could never fulfill her. She supported woman suffrage, but economic independence seemed even more important to her than the vote. Gilman's plan to end women's economic dependence on men involved not only jobs and careers but also the kind of structural changes that utopian socialists and Alexandra Kollontai had imagined. Instead of the demanding unpaid labor women performed in private homes, Gilman envisioned centralized nurseries to raise children and cooperative neighborhood kitchens and residential hotels to provide domestic services for couples or individuals.

Alongside her liberal and socialist policies, however, Gilman also celebrated female difference and strongly criticized the "man-made world" for its aggression, competition, and destruction of female values of peace, cooperation, and life giving. Her utopian fantasy, *Herland*, depicted an all-female world that was close to nature, balanced, and nurturing, in contrast to men's violence, competition, and jealousy. Appropriating Darwinian ideas in the service of women's rights, Gilman argued from biology that life-giving women were naturally superior to men, whose behavior reflected a primitive aggression. By crediting women with the advancement of civilization, she reversed evolutionary theories of natural male dominance. Yet she retained evolutionary racial hierarchies by charging African civilizations with primitive barbarism toward women while praising Teutonic cultures for the strength of their women.

Gilman's gender analysis attempted to transcend the limitations of separate spheres ideology and resolve the paradox of difference. In addition to "sharply defined and quite different" spheres for woman and man, she added that "there remains a common sphere—that of humanity, which belongs to both alike."[23] That common sphere, however, often resembled a female rather than male model. For example, Gilman wanted to minimize sex differences by having men evolve to the higher standards of women. Unlike Kollontai, she did not consider sexual freedom very important to women's emancipation. Reproductive sexuality served the race by contributing to evolution, Gilman felt, but overemphasizing female sexuality signified a primitive rather than civilized state. In the 1920s, as young women in the United States sought sexual expression equal to men's, Gilman feared that sex would become a means of keeping women in their place. Rather, she called on the mothers of the world to utilize their special "transcendent power to remake humanity."[24] Like suffragists who claimed that empowering women would improve politics, Gilman hoped that superior female values could bring a more peaceful and just world.

The British novelist Virginia Woolf also invoked women's unique values, forged in the private sphere of the home, as a source of world peace. Although her best-known feminist essay, *A Room of One's Own* (1929), called for access to education, income, and the professions, her equally brilliant later essay, *Three Guineas* (1938), recognized the limits of these liberal goals. Written as Nazi militarism loomed on the horizon, Woolf contemplated how women could respond to fascism and prevent war. She imagined requests for donations from three societies: one to prevent war, one to promote women's education, and one to advance women in the professions. In granting each a small contribution, Woolf insisted that as women entered the public sphere, they should not forget the lessons forged within the private home, where they had learned to fight patriarchy. The feminists of the nineteenth century, she wrote, were the "advance guard" in the struggle against fascism. "They were fighting the tyranny of the patriarchal state," she told the Society to Prevent War, "as you are fighting the tyranny of the Fascist state."

Although she criticized the home and viewed higher education as a path to self-sufficiency and political rights for women, Woolf did not want educated women to join the "procession of the sons of educated men" in perpetuating a society that promulgated social inequalities and waged war. Better, she thought, to maintain "the cheap college," modeled on the modest home, than to emulate the pomp and circumstance of universities that prepared men to perpetuate social hierarchy. Similarly, even though she recognized that women's entry into the professions eliminated historical barriers to full citizenship, Woolf insisted on the importance of women's traditional, unpaid profession of motherhood.

To prevent women from simply joining the existing system, Virginia Woolf extracted several stipulations in exchange for donating her three guineas. In order to undermine gender or racial hierarchies, she insisted that "any woman who enters any profession shall in no way hinder any other human being, whether man or woman, white or black, provided that he or she is qualified to enter that profession, from entering it; but shall do all in her power to help them." Furthermore, educated professional women must refuse to give up the virtues formed in the private sphere in earlier centuries. These virtues included "poverty" (earning no more than needed to live independently), chastity (refusing to "sell your brain for the sake of money"), and freedom from "unreal loyalties to nation, religion, school, or family." Above all, Woolf warned women to sustain a separate feminist consciousness. By remaining outsiders to the establishment, women could criticize its inequalities, press for a living wage for all workers, and eschew the patriotism that bred war. "As a woman," Woolf wrote, "I have no country. . . . As a woman my country is the whole world."[25]

Neither Charlotte Perkins Gilman nor Virginia Woolf inspired mass feminist organizing within their lifetimes. Both the onset of World War II and their respective suicides—Gilman's in response to terminal cancer, Woolf's because of recurrent depression—undercut their immediate influence. When a younger generation of women engaged in social activism in the 1960s, however, radical feminists would echo these earlier critiques of male dominance. Like Gilman, they would often adopt essentialist theories that suggested the biological superiority of women. Like Woolf, they would point to the links between patriarchy in the home and tyranny in national and international politics. Like both of these foremothers, they would speak largely to white, middle-class, educated women, assuming that the problems of working women and women of color would be addressed by opposing patriarchy.

Distinguishing among types of feminisms always risks overstating their differences. Maternalism was not incompatible with liberal or socialist feminism. From a domestic power base, for example, maternalists ultimately called for woman suffrage as one means to achieve their goals. While support for workers emanated from socialist feminists, liberal and maternalist feminists in England and the United States joined the Women's Trade Union League to support strikers. In turn, most European and American socialists supported woman suffrage. Each approach contributed to the momentum for change; each added a political strategy that could be used in different settings.

Distinctions can also be instructive, however. Philosopher Allison Jaggar offers a different and useful contrast of feminist theories. Liberal and traditional Marxist feminisms, she explains, have a human ideal based on male experience into which women can be integrated, whether into the middle class or the working class. Radical feminism, in contrast, has a human ideal based on female experience, which then becomes the basis for separate political organizing. It includes women's experience of reproduction and sexuality, in particular, which liberal and Marxist feminisms usually exclude. She sees socialist feminism as a distinct approach that has neither a male nor a female human ideal but rather the vision that women and men "will disappear as socially constituted categories."[26]

However one portrays these different strains of Western feminism, they have never been entirely distinct, and over time they have interacted with each other to blur some of their differences. Later generations of feminists redefined these political strategies to address middle-class women's rights, working-class women's labors, and all women's potential for maternity. Two kinds of alliances, however, remained most elusive: those between women of different races and nations. In response to challenges from women throughout the world, Western feminists have had to reconsider their partial visions of justice in light of a history of racial and cultural inequalities. In the long run, these challenges would redefine feminism and make it more flexible, more heterogeneous, and more durable.

-FOUR-

RACE AND THE POLITICS OF IDENTITY IN U.S. FEMINISM

The investigation of the rights of slaves has led me to a better understanding of my own.
—ANGELINA GRIMKÉ, UNITED STATES, 1838

Feminism is the political theory and practice that struggles to free all women. . . . Anything less than this vision of total freedom is not feminism, but merely female self-aggrandizement.
—BARBARA SMITH, UNITED STATES, 1979

In the spring of 1920 a group of African American women met to discuss how they could integrate white organizations. In the words of Lugenia Burns Hope, black women wanted to "stand side by side with women of the white race and work for full emancipation of all women." For such interracial cooperation to take place in the United States at this time would be highly unusual. American society divided the world into black and white, whether in neighborhoods, schools, churches, or cemeteries. So did the U.S. women's movement, despite its founding by antislavery activists. For a generation African American women had tried unsuccessfully to gain white women's support for their efforts to end racial hatred and its most virulent act, the murder of innocent blacks by lynching. Now a small opening appeared. A group of southern white women from churches, clubs, and the Young Women's Christian Association

(YWCA) invited four distinguished African American women to speak to their conference in Memphis, Tennessee, in October 1920.

On the last day of the Memphis conference, North Carolina educator Charlotte Hawkins Brown reached across a wide chasm of racial distrust to deliver a talk that gave white women a firsthand account of the daily insults borne by African Americans. On the train ride to Memphis, Brown revealed, a dozen white men had forced her to leave her seat in the overnight sleeping car and ride in the segregated day coach for blacks only. Humiliated and angry, she told the audience that "the thing that grieved me most is that there were women in the car and there wasn't a dissenting voice." She asked the white women that day to put themselves in her place, to "just be colored for a few minutes." In closing her speech about the terrors of lynching and the daily insults to black womanhood, Brown reminded her white, Christian audience that "in the final analysis" they would all reach out a hand to the same God, "but I know that the dear Lord will not receive it if you are crushing me beneath your feet."[1]

In her speech that day Charlotte Hawkins Brown illustrated two critical themes in women's history: the power of personal testimony to reach across social boundaries and the role of women of color in expanding the feminist agenda. By revealing her experience of both racial insult and racial pride, Brown forced white women to think outside their own experience, to reconceptualize womanhood as a more complicated entity, and to build a politics of coalition across the racial divide. Their dialogue provided an opportunity to "pivot the center," that is, to learn from the experience of others how to question the dominant culture.[2] By doing so, women's movements can incorporate difference, not merely for the sake of inclusion or diversity but also to change their fundamental goals for social justice.

Questioning the dominant meaning of womanhood can occur in any culture where racial or class divisions complicate feminism. The particularly troubled history of race relations in the United States has compelled women's movements to grapple with the complexities of women's identities. Race became central to national politics during the same period that feminism called for women's rights. While similar issues arose in Europe, until well into the twentieth century race remained largely at the distance of empire. In the United States, in contrast, the colonized lived among the colonizers. In a nation that simultaneously championed freedom, exterminated native people, and enslaved Africans, it is not surprising that issues of race would become so central to women's movements.

Beginning in the 1830s and continuing to the present, the crucible of race has forced U.S. feminists into a dialogue about difference and dominance. In each wave of the movement, women of color have insisted upon pivoting the center so that feminism addresses the needs of all women. During the first wave, when American laws enforced white dominance over blacks, African American women led the way in formulating this critique. After the 1960s, when the U.S. population had become more diverse, women who identified as Chicana, Native American, or Asian American, as well as lesbian or disabled, insisted on the significance of their experiences to second-wave feminism. The repeated process of naming difference, organizing separately, and building political coalitions has ultimately strengthened feminism in the United States by extending its critique of inequality to all women and recognizing its historical connection to all movements for social justice.

RACE AND FEMINISM, 1830–1930

The rejection of inherited privilege that nurtured European feminisms also called into question other social hierarchies such as those of age, class, and religion, but none more vigorously than those based on the concept of race. In the era of democratic revolutions, when republican political ideas justified self-rule, racial slavery represented a stark contradiction to both the liberal principle of unfettered individualism and the socialist principle of worker control over production. Yet the expansion of capitalism that enriched democratic nations rested in part on enslavement. While the Spanish seized land and labor in Mexico and Peru, the Dutch, English, and other Europeans transported twelve million African men and women to the Americas between 1500 and 1800 to raise sugar cane, cotton, and tobacco. The profits earned by slave traders, slave owners, and merchants helped finance the industrial revolution in England and the United States.

The very notion of race served to mark the slave's subordinate status.

Popular beliefs in a biological, as well as theological, basis for racial hierarchy justified both slavery and colonialism. Scientists who investigated brain size and structure relegated both women and "lower races," such as Africans, to the bottom rungs of the human hierarchy. In North America theories of white (northern and western European) racial superiority also justified the appropriation of land inhabited by Native Americans and Mexicans and fostered hostility toward immigrants from Ireland, Asia, and southern or eastern Europe.

For white feminists, race presented a particularly vexing dilemma. Just as the principle of natural rights could exclude women on biological grounds of natural sex, the concept of natural race excluded Africans, Asians, and other non-Europeans as less fully human than Europeans. White feminists could claim race privilege by insisting that they were more intelligent and deserving of rights than other demeaned groups, but doing so both negated the idea of a common womanhood and reinforced the subordination of African, Asian, Native American, and Mexican women as well as men. Would claims of universal womanhood extend to these racial others? Did the identity "woman" include all women, or only those entitled to rights based on their race or class? Just how profoundly would feminists challenge social hierarchies?

The Antislavery Movement and Women's Rights

The political birthplace of feminism in the United States was the antislavery movement. After independence, northern states gradually eliminated slave labor but the South increasingly relied upon it. Slavery politicized northern women for several reasons. Some white women opposed the system because the dispersal of slave families and the rape of female slaves offended their ideals of womanhood. Both religious principles and beliefs in female moral authority inspired them to form dozens of Female Anti-Slavery societies in the 1830s. Through pamphlets and talks they exhorted women to exercise their indirect political influence by praying to convert Americans to antislavery. Women gathered the bulk of the signatures asking legislators to abolish slavery. Taking direct action, northern women who supported the Underground Railroad hung special quilts on their clotheslines to mark safe houses for fugitives from slavery.

Yet opposition to slavery did not necessarily translate into a belief in racial equality. Some antislavery societies admitted only white women. In response, northern free black women formed their own groups and became activists on three fronts: to free the slaves, to end the race barrier within the female antislavery movement, and to gain rights as women. Their personal testimony about race initiated the dialogue on the complexities of womanhood. In 1837, for example, Sarah Forten circulated a poem at the first Anti-Slavery Convention of American Women asking white women to abandon their own race prejudice and in the name of sisterhood welcome all women to a common Christian cause. The convention admitted black women and called for the racial integration of churches.

In the free black community, women activists faced other obstacles. When Maria Stewart spoke in public against slavery, she was effectively ostracized by other northern free blacks who objected to her unwomanly behavior. "What if I am a woman[?]" she asked in 1833. "Is not the God of ancient times the God of these modern days[?]" Citing biblical and historical women, from Deborah and Mary Magdalene to medieval nuns, Stewart justified her right to speak out politically, whatever her race or sex. Although she withdrew from public speaking under pressure, in her farewell address she chastised African American reformers: "Let us no longer talk of prejudice till prejudice becomes extinct at home. Let us no longer talk of opposition till we cease to oppose our own."[3]

White women's determination to speak out against slavery initiated a crisis over women's rights in the abolition movement. Two southern white women, Sarah and Angelina Grimké, forced the issue. Raised in a southern, slaveholding family, the sisters converted to the Quaker faith and rejected slavery as a moral sin. They attempted to subvert the institution by illegally teaching their slaves to read. The Grimké sisters' views were so unpopular that they left the South for Philadelphia, where they joined the Female Anti-Slavery Society. At first they urged women to use their influence to extend natural rights to blacks. "Try to persuade your husband, father, brothers and sons that slavery is a crime against God and man," Angelina Grimké urged in *An Appeal to the Christian Women of the Southern States* (1836). But when she spoke out in public to audiences of men and women, she shared the fate of Maria Stewart.

Northern white clergy condemned her for disobediently stepping outside the female sphere. "How monstrous, how anti-Christian is the doctrine that woman is dependent on man!" she responded. "The investigation of the rights of slaves has led me to a better understanding of my own."[4]

In the process of opposing slavery the Grimké sisters recognized the broader implications of political rights. In 1838, a decade before the Seneca Falls convention, they published *Letters on the Equality of the Sexes*, which analyzed women's inferior status, refuted biblical injunctions against women's activism, and rejected female subservience to men. Abolition, Angelina Grimké recognized, had "opened the way for the discussion of other rights, and the ultimate result will most certainly be the breaking of *every* yoke, the letting the oppressed of every grade and description go free."[5] Most abolitionists did not want to dilute their movement by adding women's rights, however. Only a handful of male allies, such as William Lloyd Garrison, protested when organizers of the 1840 World Anti-Slavery Convention in London refused to seat female delegates. Two of those women, Lucretia Mott and Elizabeth Cady Stanton, pledged to respond one day. With the support of abolitionists such as former slave Frederick Douglass, they organized the first women's rights convention in 1848.

Free African American women stood at the intersection of abolitionism and women's rights. Most concentrated on antislavery. A few, such as former slave and itinerant preacher Sojourner Truth, testified from their own experience that race and gender were inseparable. At one of the women's rights conventions held throughout the northern states in the 1850s, Truth defied clergymen who claimed that women needed to be supported and protected by men. "I have as much muscle as any man, and can do as much work as any man," she told the crowd. "I have plowed and reaped and husked and chopped and mowed, and can any man do more than that?"[6] Years later the white feminist Matilda Joselyn Gage reconstructed Truth's speech with a rhetorical flourish that became legendary: "Nobody ever helps me into carriages, or over mud puddles, or gives me any best place! And ain't I a woman?"[7] Apocryphal as the precise phrases may be, Sojourner Truth's message echoed for generations, reminding feminists that middle-class white women's experiences do not encompass the full range of women's subordination. By listening to other voices the movement could refute the argument that women should be satisfied with the privileges that only a few enjoy.

After the Civil War and the emancipation of slaves, the U.S. women's movement split over a constitutional amendment to enfranchise former slaves that did not include woman suffrage. When Frederick Douglass proclaimed, "This is the Negro's hour," Sojourner Truth, then eighty years old, predicted that "if colored men get their rights, and not colored women theirs, you see the colored men will be masters over the women, and it will be just as bad as it was before." But Truth recognized that she was "about the only colored woman that goes about to speak of the rights of the colored women."[8] In 1869 Douglass, along with Lucy Stone and others, supported the black suffrage amendment through the American Woman Suffrage Association (AWSA). Elizabeth Cady Stanton and her colleague Susan B. Anthony formed the National Woman Suffrage Association (NWSA) to press for black and woman suffrage. In 1870 the Fifteenth Amendment to the U.S. Constitution enfranchised black males only. The breach among black and women's rights advocates remained bitter.

Suffrage and Segregation

Over the next generation the U.S. women's movement reflected the increasingly racist national political climate. Jim Crow policies of segregation spread through the southern states, enforced by the white supremacist Ku Klux Klan (KKK), which terrorized blacks through vigilante violence and murder by lynch mobs. Northern support for reform diminished, while the economic and political plight of former slaves deteriorated. From the 1890s onward southern states found ways to disfranchise black male voters, depriving them of the power to challenge discriminatory practices.

The women's rights movement, blocked in its campaign for the vote, ignored these growing racial injustices. Some suffragists even tried to bolster their unpopular cause by exploiting racial stereotypes directed at both African Americans and the masses of Catholic and Jewish immigrants arriving from Europe. If ignorant black and immigrant men could

vote, they argued, why not educated white women? They were not alone
in their rhetorical tactic. In South Africa as well, English and Afrikaner
women's suffrage associations were arguing that white women needed to
vote to counter the political power of black Africans. In the United
States, suffrage organizations agreed to exclude black women from leadership at conventions or visibility at demonstrations, partly to accommodate their southern members. The maternalist white women's club
movement segregated African American women. The YWCA had separate African American (as well as Chinese American) branches. Only rare
exceptions, such as white missionary teachers in the South, worked in a
common cause across race, united by a belief in "woman's work for
woman."9

Once again, African American women struggled on several fronts:
for suffrage, to improve conditions for their race, and to achieve equality
with white women. Black women wanted the vote not only for themselves but also as a way to represent their race in those northern states
where blacks could exercise the franchise. Mary Church Terrell rejoiced
"not only in the prospective enfranchisement of my sex but in the emancipation of my race."10 In addition, middle-class African Americans tried
to uplift former slaves through education and temperance. To avoid the
condescension of white women, they formed separate black chapters of
the maternalist Woman's Christian Temperance Union (WCTU). They
also risked their lives to oppose racial discrimination. In the 1880s, for
example, Memphis newspaper editor and former slave Ida B. Wells was
run out of town when she tried to expose the trumped-up charges of rape
used to justify the lynching of innocent African American men by white
mobs. Wells turned to northern black women for support and inspired
the first African American women's clubs. By 1909 the National Association of Colored Women had established branches in twenty states. Locals
concentrated on community self-help by establishing day care facilities,
hospitals, and mothers groups. They also turned their attention to the
most pressing problem facing African Americans, lynching.

The black women's clubs attempted to dispel several myths about
race and sexuality. Racial stereotypes cast all black women as sexually im-
moral and available to men, a legacy of black women's vulnerability to
assault during slavery. As Anna Julia Cooper pointed out in the 1890s,

American prejudice "cynically assumes 'A Negro woman cannot be a lady.' "[11] White women's reluctance to work with black women rested in part on this supposed moral divide between white female purity and black female depravity. Organized black womanhood insisted that women of their race were as chaste as white women and equally offended by unwanted sexual advances. Few white women's clubs took heed of this message. Along with excluding African Americans they ignored the call to help abolish lynching. When Wells called for support in her campaign, the leader of the influential WCTU, Frances Willard, failed to speak out and even seemed to condone lynching as necessary to protect white women's virtue.

Ignoring the voices of African American women did not advance the white women's movement. In 1890, when AWSA and NWSA united as the National American Woman Suffrage Association (NAWSA), to appease southern members they permitted chapters to exclude African American women. But this strategy won little support for suffrage in the South. Only northern state legislatures, and few of them, granted the vote to women. As the suffrage movement finally gathered momentum after 1910, African American women participated but did not feel welcome. The huge suffrage parades placed them at the back, but with the help of some white allies the black women literally forced their way into the mainstream of the marches. After Congress finally passed the suffrage amendment in 1919, only one southern state joined those ratifying the measure. Although the law now extended the vote to both black and white women after ratification in 1920, Jim Crow legislation effectively disenfranchised most black women, along with black men, in southern states.

Whose Equal Rights?

In the aftermath of suffrage, white women's racial attitudes ranged from intolerance to neglect to engagement. At one extreme, the resurgent Ku Klux Klan established a Women's KKK, which in 1924 claimed a membership of a quarter million. More typical was the dismissal of race by younger radicals such as Alice Paul, the charismatic leader of the self-identified feminists, who had helped revive the U.S. suffrage movement. Borrowing the militant tactics of the British suffragettes, they had chained themselves to the White House fence and survived hunger strikes in jail. In 1923 these militant feminists, now called the National Woman's Party, introduced the Equal Rights Amendment (ERA) to the U.S. Constitution to mandate that "equality of rights under the law shall not be denied or abridged by the United States or any state on account of sex." With a single focus on sex, however, they refused to discuss racial injustice, even when African American women raised the subject at their meetings.

This refusal to acknowledge racism recurred in the anti-Semitism of the women's movement. Like African Americans, Jewish women had formed their own clubs in response to exclusion from white Christian organizations. Although Jewish women supported suffrage more often than other groups, the suffrage movement had ignored their cultural life when it scheduled conventions and parades on the Jewish sabbath. Historian Elinor Lerner refers to these acts as "anti-Semitism by neglect."[12] After suffrage, Jewish women called on their Christian allies to protest anti-Semitism at home and in the growing Nazi movement in Germany in the 1920s and 1930s. The National Council of Jewish Women sought political support for amending restrictive immigration laws that prevented persecuted Jews from emigrating to the United States. They also hoped that the National Consumers League would join a boycott of German-made goods. Just as the National Woman's Party did not consider lynching a "woman's issue," most women reformers did not see anti-Semitism as part of their agenda. Former NAWSA president Carrie Chapman Catt did circulate a petition among non-Jewish feminists calling for an end to the persecution of German Jews, but neither the boycott nor the efforts to lift immigration quotas won feminist support.

Despite the legacy of racism and neglect, some postsuffrage activists began to sow the seeds of interracial cooperation. In 1924 the League of Women Voters, which had formed after suffrage to help educate women for politics, established a Committee on Negro Problems. The YWCA had begun to hold interracial conferences in 1915; in the 1920s its college branches confronted the organization's policy of segregated facilities. Charlotte Brown's 1920 Memphis speech contributed to this incipient interracial cooperation. By the 1930s the antilynching movement gained the support of several liberal white women's groups, including the

Women's Trade Union League, the Women's Joint Congressional Committee (which was the major women's lobbying group in Washington), and the YWCA, which in the 1940s fully integrated and adopted the goals of racial equality and civil rights for minorities.

In the 1930s white southerner Jessie Daniel Ames responded to pleas by black churchwomen by spearheading the Association of Southern Women for the Prevention of Lynching (ASWPL). The members decided to take responsibility for preventing or exposing the murders carried out by men who claimed to be protecting the purity of white womanhood when they lynched alleged black male rapists. Echoing the earlier ideas of Ida B. Wells, Ames recognized the deep connections between race and gender subordination. Ames reported that after reviewing the history of lynching, the ASWPL resolved "no longer to remain silent in the face of this crime done in their name."[13] By rejecting the pedestal of sexual protection, the ASWPL undermined the hold of white supremacy. The group collected forty thousand signatures from southern white women pledged to stop lynching in their localities.

After 1930, both interracial and interfaith cooperation found a foothold within the U.S. women's movement. First Lady Eleanor Roosevelt's gradual rejection of the racism and anti-Semitism she had learned growing up foreshadowed a later trend. The tentative connections made across race and religious lines would nurture the rebirth of feminism in the 1960s. As in the past, African American women in particular provided a critical perspective for white women, alerting them to the integral connections between race and gender. By articulating their personal experience of race, African American women contributed the knowledge that enfranchisement alone could not ensure equality; that the female pedestal was a myth; that sexual stereotypes, whether of purity or immorality, exerted forceful social controls; that power relations always rested upon both race and gender hierarchies; that alliance across race and gender could challenge these hierarchies; and that dignified resistance in the face of seeming powerlessness could be a mighty weapon for change.

RACIAL JUSTICE, 1930–1970:
SEEDBED FOR SECOND-WAVE
FEMINISM

Viewed from the perspectives of race, class, and gender, the U.S. women's movement experienced significant growing pains in the decades after the suffrage victory. During the 1930s women organized as consumers, pacifists, professionals, and workers. The radical wing of the American labor movement spoke to the needs of working-class women, such as Mexican American cannery and field workers. In 1939, for example, labor organizer Luisa Moreno called on the Congress of Spanish-Speaking Peoples to form a women's committee to support the "education of the Mexican woman" and equality in wages and civil rights.[14] Women mobilized to support the war effort in the 1940s, and they did not necessarily demobilize afterward. With more women working for wages, female union membership expanded. A new generation of labor feminists revived socialist feminist goals and initiated a campaign for "equal pay for equal work." Above all, a movement for racial justice insisted that white supremacy had no place in the postwar democratic world. When the U.S. Supreme Court struck down the legality of public school segregation in 1954, it ushered in a revolution in race relations in which women played a central role.

Ella Baker, an organizer for the Southern Christian Leadership Conference (SCLC) and a founder of the Student Non-Violent Coordinating Committee (SNCC), recalled that "the movement of the 50s and 60s was carried largely by women, since it came out of church groups."[15] African American churchwomen fed, housed, clothed, and prayed for the black and white civil rights workers who mobilized throughout the South. They also helped organize and lead the movement. College professor Jo Ann Gibson Robinson and the Women's Political Council of Montgomery, Alabama, instigated and sustained the inspirational bus boycott of 1955–56 after Rosa Parks refused to move to the back of the bus. In 1964 former sharecropper Fannie Lou Hamer took the cause of black political representation to the floor of the Democratic National Convention to demand seating of popularly chosen black delegates. College students such as Anne Moody and Diane Nash bravely demonstrated at lunch counters, participated in the racially integrated Freedom Rides, and went to jail for challenging segregation.

The politics of racial justice directly inspired a revival of feminism from two political perspectives, one liberal and one radical. The Civil Rights Act of 1964 outlawed racial discrimination but also banned sex discrimination, partly at the urging of lobbyists from the aging National Woman's Party. The act established the Equal Employment Opportunity Commission (EEOC) to hear complaints about discrimination based on either race or gender. When the EEOC failed to respond to sex discrimination complaints, feminists decided they needed a political lobby akin to the National Association for the Advancement of Colored People. In 1966 three hundred charter members signed on to the National Organization for Women (NOW). They included black civil rights lawyer Pauli Murray, union leaders, professional women and men, and white feminists like Betty Friedan, whose 1963 book *The Feminine Mystique* had touched a nerve among educated suburban white women. The organization pledged "to bring women into full participation in the mainstream of American society, now, assuming all the privileges and responsibilities thereof in truly equal partnership with men."[16]

This liberal branch of the second wave of U.S. feminism emphasized antidiscrimination law, supporting court cases to achieve equal pay and promotion for women workers at all levels. The feminist magazine *Ms.*, founded in 1972 by journalist Gloria Steinem, promoted these and other goals in its pages. Along with the National Women's Political Caucus, NOW encouraged the election of women to public office. It also rallied behind the ERA, which Congress passed in 1972. Although the amendment failed to be ratified by enough states to become law, the equal-rights strategy ultimately prevailed. Legislation such as the Women's Educational Equity Act and the Equal Credit Opportunity Act (1974) banned discrimination in schools and lending, and the EEOC filed suits on behalf of workers who complained of sex discrimination in hiring, training, and promotion.

Though predominantly white, the ranks of liberal feminists included politically active women of color such as Shirley Chisholm, Patsy
Mink, and Aileen Hernandez, a former labor organizer who in 1971 became NOW's second president. The National Black Feminist Organization reached out to African American women to embrace liberal
feminism. One of its founders, Eleanor Holmes Norton, recognized that
"every problem raised by white feminists has a disproportionately heavy
impact on blacks." She also knew that the white feminist movement
would "only take on the color line if we who are black join it."[17]

The second, radical wing of the feminist revival grew out of both the
civil rights and student movements of the 1960s. During the voter registration and community organizing drives in the southern states, young
white female volunteers met strong black women activists. "For the first
time," one young white woman stated, "I had role models I could really
respect."[18] Working with black leaders such as Ella Baker or Septima
Clark taught these white students about women's potential for activism
and leadership.

Radicalized in New Left organizations such as SNCC, idealistic activists soon objected to the limitations placed on them as women. Like
Maria Stewart and Sarah and Angelina Grimké more than a century earlier, they hoped to be full participants in the quest for racial justice.
When men in the movement relegated them to serving coffee, cooking,
and having sex, these young women applied their political analysis to
gender. Ruby Doris Smith Robinson, a black activist, inspired Casey
Hayden and Mary King to write a position paper on women in the movement. The contradiction of sexual subordination in a liberation movement also inspired protest from women in Students for a Democratic
Society (SDS). "Having learned from the Movement to think radically
about the personal worth and abilities of people whose role in society had
gone unchallenged before," they wrote in 1965, "a lot of women in the
movement have begun trying to apply those lessons to their relations
with men."[19]

Neither white nor black men responded with much enthusiasm, and
some blatantly ridiculed women for raising these issues. The rhetoric es-
calated. In 1967 SDS women prepared the Women's Manifesto, which

compared women to Third World people—colonized by white males. They called on SDS to work for communal child care, rights to birth control and abortion, and equality within the home. "[W]e demand that our brothers recognize that they must deal with their own problems of male chauvinism in their personal, social and political relationships," they wrote.[20]

Women's Liberation

Radical women began to extend the politics of self-determination to gender. Just as a call for Black Power purged whites from some interracial organizations and separate movements formed to empower Chicanos and Native Americans, some feminists articulated separatist politics. These radical, or cultural, feminists considered gender the most important aspect of all liberation struggles. To Shulamith Firestone, for example, injustices of class and race would end only when women achieved equality. Not surprisingly, the majority of those who adopted this strategy were white and middle-class.

Breaking away from the male-dominated New Left, the women's liberation movement created a network of predominantly white, women-only organizations. In Chicago, New York, Berkeley, Boston, and smaller cities, radical feminists formed groups such as the Redstockings, the Feminists, the Furies, and Radical Women. In private consciousness-raising sessions members revealed their personal struggles as women, including stories of rape, unwanted pregnancies, lesbian desires, illegal abortions, and the dilemmas of child care and housework. In mimeographed pamphlets they insisted that "the personal is political," rejecting the ideological division of public and private spheres that dismissed women's claims of injustice as merely personal. Power, these feminists realized, operated within and through personal relations, including sexuality and the family. In addition, they questioned the liberal feminist goal of integrating women into male power structures. "We in this segment of the movement," Bonnie Kreps explained in 1968, "do not believe that the oppression of women will be ended by giving them a bigger piece of the pie as Betty Friedan would have it. We believe that the pie itself is rotten."[21]

Through direct action, radical feminists challenged cherished beliefs about women's place. They gained publicity for women's liberation when they demonstrated against the Miss America pageant, occupied the offices of the *Ladies Home Journal*, and held speak-outs about once-unmentionable topics such as abortion, rape, and prostitution. They created woman-only spaces to heal from the daily wounds of patriarchy. To replace the demeaning images of women in the media they celebrated a positive "women's culture" through alternative bookstores, publishing firms, coffeehouses, record companies, concerts, spiritual retreats, exhibit spaces, and back-to-the-land cooperatives and communes.

Explorations of sexuality contributed to a new politics of identity. Second-wave radical feminists shared with first-wave moral reformers a critique of men's sexual exploitation of women. But they differed in their exploration of an explicitly sexual bond among women as an alternative to heterosexual relations. A group called Radicalesbians drew connections between the rejection of male dominance and the assertion of sexual love for other women. Their 1970 essay "The Woman-identified Woman" began by defining a lesbian as "the rage of all women condensed to the point of explosion." Because women's "self-hate and the lack of real self are rooted in our male-given identity," they reasoned, "only women can give to each other a new sense of self."[22] By embracing lesbianism as a positive identity, they rejected the stigma of mental illness that had previously been attached to love between women.

While not all radical feminists became lesbians, the message of putting women first pervaded separatist organizing. Much of the women's culture of the 1970s was largely lesbian culture, and lesbians provided a great deal of the woman power to run feminist bookstores, concerts, and conferences. In response to attempts to exclude or closet them in mainstream feminist organizations, lesbians formed separate consciousness-raising groups and caucuses. In essays, songs, and art they expressed their alternative experience of sexuality and insisted on its legitimacy. Along with the fledgling gay liberation movement, lesbian feminists helped forge an influential concept of sexual identity.

THE LIMITS OF SISTERHOOD AND THE COMPLEXITIES OF IDENTITY, 1970–2000

Both liberal and radical feminists hoped to achieve gender solidarity through the politics of identity. Poet Robin Morgan called the anthology of feminist essays she edited in 1970 *Sisterhood Is Powerful*. As women of color pointed out from the beginning of the movement, sisterhood was also complicated. Many women of color felt excluded from a theory that elevated gender at the expense of race or class identity. By making white women's experience their standard, both liberal and radical feminists overlooked the perspectives of women of color. For example, when Betty Friedan called for liberating women from the home through employment, women of color who had always worked knew that joining the men of their race on the job meant they would still encounter discrimination. Or when the radical feminist theologian Mary Daly spoke about reclaiming women's spirituality through rituals honoring the goddess, African American poet Audre Lorde asked, "What color is your goddess?" A white female deity matched the white male deity, ignoring the heritage of African spirituality. Separatist politics troubled other women of color. For many Chicanas, the extended family represented both economic and cultural survival. "When a family is involved in a human rights movement, as is the Mexican-American family," Enriqueta Longeaux y Vásquez wrote in 1972, "there is little room for a woman's liberation movement alone."[23] Other women of color echoed the pervasive homophobia of the society when they rejected radical feminism because of its inclusion of lesbians.

Despite these tensions, women of color in the United States clearly recognized that gender as well as race affected their lives. A 1972 poll showed that two-thirds of black women, compared to only one-third of white women, were sympathetic to the women's movement. A 1976 survey of Chicana students found agreement with the goals of feminism as well as the view that the white women's movement was elitist and too focused on men as the oppressors. Many women of color longed for a more inclusive feminism. Former SNCC worker Elizabeth Martinez recalled that after the assassination of Martin Luther King Jr. in 1968 she realized "that if the struggle against sexism did not see itself as profoundly entwined with the fight against racism, I was gone." At the same time, though, she "looked hard at the sexism in the [Chicano] *movimiento*, and knew a Chicana feminism needed to be born."[24]

Women of color who shared feminist goals faced dual obstacles, from their own communities and from women's movements. Black nationalists, for example, urged women to align with racial rather than sexual politics, primarily by supporting men through women's roles as wives and mothers. Asian American feminists were criticized as traitors to their race for threatening ethnic identity, just as Chicana feminists risked being labeled "*vendidas*," or sellouts, in the Chicano movement, especially if they accepted lesbianism. Yet when women of color did join the women's movement, they encountered overt and subtle racial bias. Given their small numbers, they often felt the discomfort of being treated as tokens, expected to represent their race but not to bring their own issues to the table. "Inclusion without influence," Lynet Uttal called it, or as Bernice Johnson Reagon explained, "You don't really want Black folks, you are just looking for yourself with a little color in it."[25]

The title of one collection of African American women's writing captured well the quandary of exclusion: *All the Women Are White, All the Blacks Are Men, but Some of Us Are Brave* (1982). In response to this dilemma, women of color initiated a redefinition of identity politics. They refused the pressures from both men of color who would subsume women's issues and white women who would subsume race issues. As Pauli Murray poignantly explained her "equal stake" in women's liberation and black liberation: "I have one foot in each camp and cannot split myself apart."[26] When the Chicano movement called on the women of La Raza (the race) to reject feminism, Adelaida del Castillo insisted that "true freedom for our people can come about only if prefaced by the equality of individuals within La Raza."[27]

Just as women had separated from men within the New Left, women of color established their own groups. One of these, the Combahee River Collective, issued a "black feminist statement" in 1974 that pledged to "struggle together with black men against racism, while we also struggle with black men about sexism."[28] Asian American Women United, Women of All Red Nations, and the National Black Women's Health Project served specific groups. Women from a variety of racial backgrounds formed Kitchen Table/Women of Color Press to present diverse women's stories. In 1981 they published an influential anthology, *This Bridge Called My Back: Writings by Radical Women of Color* (1981), edited by Chicana feminists Cherríe Moraga and Gloria Anzaldúa, which opened a cultural space for further explorations of multiple personal identities.

The theme of bridging different female identities recurred in other personal writing that expanded beyond the historically dominant categories of black and white. Jewish and Asian American feminists wrote passionately about the two worlds they bridged. Lesbians insisted on the inclusion of sexuality as another component of identity. Disabled women called for access to feminist events and acknowledgment of their sexual and reproductive capacities. Latinas explored how language represented both a link to family and community and a potential barrier to understanding across ethnicities. In *Borderlands/La Frontera: The New Mestiza* (1987) Gloria Anzaldúa captured well the empowering effect of articulating a mixed, or mestizo, identity: "I will have my voice: Indian, Spanish, white. I will have my serpent's tongue—my woman's voice, my sexual voice, my poet's voice. I will overcome the tradition of silence."[29]

Of all these identity groups, women of color stood at a particularly critical intersection. Frustrated by racial exclusion in the women's movement and tired of being asked to educate white women, writers such as Moraga asked, "How can we—this time—not use our bodies to be thrown over a river of tormented history to bridge the gap?"[30] Only if white women took race into account would the burden be shared. Indeed, the work of radical women of color profoundly affected white feminists. Combahee River Collective member Barbara Smith, who led antiracism workshops for white women in Boston, felt that white feminists had to "take responsibility for their racism," and she believed they were learning to do so. As she told a predominantly white audience at the National Women's Studies Association meeting in 1979, "The reason racism is a feminist issue is easily explained by the inherent definition of feminism." In Smith's view, the struggle to free *all* women had to include "women of color, working-class women, poor women, disabled women, Jewish women, lesbians, old women—as well as white, economically privileged, heterosexual women. Anything less than this vision of total freedom is not feminism, but merely female self-aggrandizement."[31]

White women contributed to the redefinition of feminism that made alliance across races, religions, and sexual identities a possibility. By recognizing cultural difference, including their own fragmented identities, many rejected the primacy of gender that characterized early radical feminism. By acknowledging their own racism, they also began to question whiteness as a source of privilege. As Ruth Frankenberg put it in 1993, "Racism shapes white people's lives and identities in a way that is inseparable from other facets of daily life."[32] Recognizing white privilege did not have to be a source of immobilizing guilt; rather it could be a productive step toward applying that privilege to combating racism. Realizing that racial categories had been historically constructed—that whiteness, like any color, could change its meaning—opened an effort to "unlearn" the internalized racism that affected all women. As Gloria Yamato cautioned white women, "Work on racism for your sake, not 'their' sake."[33]

The intense conversations on identity and privilege encouraged some U.S. feminists to form coalitions across lines of race, ethnicity, gender, and sexuality. So did the political conservatism of the 1980s, which put feminists on the defensive. Whether addressing reproductive rights, the AIDS crisis, or welfare reform, feminists from diverse backgrounds built cross-cultural political support, sometimes painfully but also productively. Bernice Johnson Reagon captured the importance of this effort in a speech she gave at a women-only music festival. Separatism, she recognized, offered a safe space for groups who felt threatened by the outside world—lesbians, for example, or minorities—but it could be reactionary as well as healing. In the real world, she explained, "There is nowhere you can go and only be with people who are like you." Reagon challenged women to move from that safe space of separatism into the streets to engage in the difficult work of coalition politics.[34] Thus white women learned to protest race discrimination, heterosexual women of color to support lesbian rights, and feminist men to defend women's reproductive rights. Facing common opposition and learning to trust across difference, though never an easy task, helped sustain grassroots feminism in the face of opposition.

THE FUTURE OF IDENTITY POLITICS

For two centuries, women of color in the United States have stood in the vanguard of redefining feminism to ask not only what difference gender makes but how also women experience gender differently because of their access to or lack of social privilege. In defining a "multiracial feminism," social scientists Maxine Baca Zinn and Bonnie Thornton Dill point to the importance of going "beyond a mere recognition of diversity and difference among women to examine structures of domination." Sociologist Patricia Hill Collins refers to these structures as a "matrix of domination" in which gender is but one source of power, always connected to other forms. To recognize that matrix, to pivot the center, feminists have turned repeatedly to the lived experiences of women from diverse backgrounds.[35]

In the past two decades, some feminists have questioned whether the categories of gender and race continue to matter. For one, recognizing the multiplicity of identities within us reveals the limits of single labels. We need long strings of adjectives to locate our complex selves by race, religion, sexuality, physical ability, ethnicity, and the like. In addition, postmodern critics point out that Enlightenment ideas about fixed race and sex rest upon biological definitions that have often been used to restrict the rights of women and minorities. To Donna Haraway, who calls all identities "fabricated hybrids," our consciousness of gender, race, or class "is an achievement forced on us by the terrible historical experiences of . . . patriarchy, colonialism, and capitalism."[36] If so, refusing to be categorized by race or gender can become an act of political resistance. Claiming interracial or transgendered identities, for example, shakes up our beliefs about fixed biological categories. In her influential book *Gender Trouble* (1990), philosopher Judith Butler proposed that playing with the way we "perform" gender can also disrupt the category. In this view, exaggerated parodies of clothing and speech styles, such as the performances of drag queens or drag kings, could undermine the constraints of gender.

In contrast to those who emphasize the reactionary implications of our inherited categories, feminist critics such as Chela Sandoval and Paula Moya want to retain identity politics but refine them as well. Sandoval has insisted that identities are not necessarily imposed on us but that we may self-consciously choose among them, switching at times from an emphasis on our gender to an emphasis on our race or sexuality. Such "differential consciousness," she argues, can help forge political alliances among women. Paula Moya takes the argument further by calling for what she terms a "realist" account of identity. Since the social facts of race and gender continue to affect our personal experiences, to deny these categories overlooks "the fact that some people are more oppressed than others." Only by acknowledging this structural reality can we undermine it.[37]

The lived realities of race and sex remain as powerful in contemporary U.S. society as in the past. What has changed, however, is the political meaning of these categories. Instead of dismissing race, feminists have learned to confront its effects on all women. The acknowledgment of racial injustice has led to further explorations of personal identities that now empower many groups once relegated to the margins of women's movements. Listening to personal testimony has contributed to the feminist goal of extending the rights of women to all. The poet Audre Lorde recognized the importance of this historical process when she wrote that "those of us who have been forged in crucibles of difference—those of us who are poor, who are lesbians, who are Black, who are older," know that survival means "learning how to take our differences and make them strengths."[38] Nowhere would this lesson prove more challenging than when Western feminism reached beyond its cultural base and confronted gender inequality in the global arena.

-FIVE-

THE GLOBAL STAGE AND THE POLITICS OF LOCATION

To talk feminism to a woman who has no water, no food and no home is to talk nonsense.
—NGO FORUM '80, DENMARK, 1980

Everything is a woman's issue.
—CHARLOTTE BUNCH, UNITED STATES, 1985

In her 1984 essay "Notes Toward a Politics of Location," the American poet Adrienne Rich reevaluated her earlier use of the category "woman" in light of the writings of women of color. Acknowledging her own "politics of location" as a North American, white, Jewish lesbian, Rich named "the faceless, raceless classless category of all women as a creation of white, western, self-centered women." Because national and political location affected women throughout the world, Rich reconsidered Virginia Woolf's statement that "as a woman I have no country; as a woman my country is the whole world." One's country, she suggested, deeply influenced one's view of the world and of womanhood.[1]

Other Western feminists, stimulated by women of color and women outside the West, were also recognizing the "politics of location." In 1978, for example, a special issue of the radical feminist journal *Quest* on international feminism asked readers, "Can we talk about the global oppression of women—its causes and lives—in any universal terms?" In an influential 1988 essay, sociologist Chandra Mohanty argued persuasively

against the Western feminist assumption of "a commonality of the category of women."[2] Mohanty called on Western feminists to understand
how local contexts created gender relations that differed from those in the
West. Neither oppression nor liberation looked the same from the perspective of women in Asia, Africa, Latin America, and the Middle East.
Just as women of color transformed U.S. feminism, so too exchanges
across nations placed Western women's rights movements within the contexts of racial and social justice as well as national sovereignty.

More than an extension of Western feminisms, international
women's movements have had varied origins. In one pattern, elite women
or men exposed to European political ideas brought demands for education and suffrage to their countries; these reforms did not necessarily
reach far beyond urban areas. Colonialism set the stage for most global
encounters among women, leaving a powerful legacy of unequal relations
across regions. In some countries, such as India and Egypt, anticolonial
and nationalist politics mobilized women.

In addition, international organizations provided a forum for both
communication and conflict among diverse women's movements. A key
locus of these discussions was the Decade for Women, declared by the
United Nations from 1975 to 1985. Subsequent regional and international gatherings, including the UN's Fourth World Conference on
Women, held in Beijing in 1995, facilitated transnational feminist organizing across regions. By the end of the twentieth century, women's
movements had expanded to all parts of the world—in rural and urban
settings, in liberal or conservative states. From a history of colonial encounters to a growing transnational movement, the politics of location
have taken both common and diverse paths to gender equality.

HISTORICAL LEGACIES:
COLONIALISM AND NATIONALISM

The emergence of Western feminisms during the 1800s coincided with
the expansion of European empires in Africa, the Middle East, and Asia.
Just as race slavery stood in stark contrast to the Western ideal of individual rights, so too colonial rule seemed to contradict the political ide-

ology of democratic self-government. Like slavery, colonialism served the economic interests of western Europe and the United States. In both cases an ideology of white, European superiority served to justify the denial of individual rights and self-government. Gender played a central role in this theory of European superiority. A key measure of "civilization," colonialists argued, was the treatment of women: the more women's lives resembled those in western Europe, the more civilized the culture. Native practices such as foot binding in China, polygyny in Africa, and the veil in the Middle East provided evidence that so-called primitive peoples needed guidance to elevate women's status. While each of these practices did enforce patriarchal authority, so did European customs. When colonialists argued that they should rule over the less civilized peoples of the world because of their superior treatment of women, they ignored their own comparable practices, including child labor, wife beating, tight-laced corsets, and child prostitution.

Through law and education, colonial powers claimed to bring enlightened attitudes toward women. Yet their criticisms of natives did not necessarily improve women's lives. Imposing male farming in West Africa, for example, undermined women's economic authority. Some interventions unintentionally reinforced the very practices that they decried. In India, the British were appalled by the custom of *sati*, in which a widow threw herself on the funeral pyre of her husband. Many Indians also opposed widow suicide but worried that imposing legislation would foster resistance. Indeed, when the British did outlaw *sati* in 1829 they condemned the custom as "barbaric" and used soldiers to enforce the law. Offended Indians defended *sati* in reaction to British rule. Permitted but not required by religious texts, and formerly limited to upper-caste Hindu Brahmins largely in the Bengal region, the practice spread further as a means of defying British authority. Similarly, female genital cutting became a nationalist issue in Kenya only after the British outlawed the practice. In both of these cases, men argued across national cultures about how to protect women, without consulting the women themselves.

European feminists contributed to this colonialist discourse. Liberals such as Mary Wollstonecraft and John Stuart Mill supported their call for extending education and political rights to women by comparing civilized British people to the "savages" of Africa. Later writers depicted

African and Indian women as the helpless victims of men, in need of rescue by Christianity and European civilization. Like missionaries before them, these feminists employed images of victimized foreign women and brutish foreign men to justify their activism as part of the "white woman's burden." At the same time, just as American women called for suffrage to counteract African American and immigrant male voters, British suffragettes incorporated the language of white racial superiority. As "mothers of the race," they argued, white women needed the vote to support the work of imperialism.

Not all observers stereotyped women outside the West as helpless victims of patriarchy. Although most Europeans condemned the veiling of women as a sign of barbarism, some women appreciated this clothing. To Lady Mary Wortley Montagu, the veiled Turkish women she observed "have more liberty than we have." Since it was impossible for a man to know if a heavily veiled woman was his kin, a slave, or a "great lady," "no man dare either touch or follow a woman in the street." Similarly, French feminist Flora Tristan praised the hooded garment worn by Peruvian women on the streets because it made any woman "eminently respectable, so nobody ever accosts her."[3] At the same time antifeminists produced some of the harshest stereotypes of colonial subjects. In *Mother India* (1927) a conservative American woman, Katherine Mayo, condemned child marriage and portrayed Hindus as sex-obsessed and thus incapable of home rule. U.S. feminists criticized Mayo's arguments, as did women in India, although later radical feminists uncritically incorporated parts of her flawed interpretations of Indian culture. Feminists would have to learn to distinguish legitimate critiques of discriminatory practices from incendiary, often racist, rhetoric that demonized colonized men and denied moral authority to colonized women.

Self-Determination for Nations and Women: India, Egypt, and South Africa

Colonial subjects questioned both foreign rule and gender hierarchy during the long period of contact with Europeans. Drawing on both local and Western ideas, they rejected some older practices and revised others. In India both Sufism and British writers such as Mary Wollstonecraft influenced the reformer Rammohun Roy, who in 1815 published a critique of *sati* in which he argued that Hindu texts did not require widows to die. Roy was an early advocate of women's education as well as their property rights. A widowed scholar in Bombay, Pandita Ramabai, also drew on Wollstonecraft's ideas about education. Ramabai started a training institute for teachers and called for women's medical schools. In the case of Rokeya Sakhawat Hossain, a personal quest for education inspired her establishment of a school for girls in Calcutta in 1911. A Bengali Muslim, Hossain expressed her hopes for women's contributions in "Sultana's Dream," a feminist utopian story she published in 1905. The women's universities of the future, she imagined, would carry out major scientific advances, including control of the climate and the use of solar power to avert war.

Building on a century of reform efforts, the men who led the Indian independence movement in the twentieth century adopted a variety of feminist strategies. Themes of maternal power influenced some nationalists, who invoked the image of the mother goddess Kali to personify India as a mother whose sons would protect her from foreign rule. Mahatma Gandhi, who led the independence movement from 1917 until its victory in 1947, expressed strong opposition to male domination of women. Gandhi embraced an essentialist ideal of gender difference in which women's unique nature embodied virtue, sacrifice, and humility, in contrast to male aggression. These qualities suited women for his nonviolence movement, but Gandhi believed that gender differences required unique education for women. In contrast, Jawaharlal Nehru, who in 1947 became the first prime minister of an independent India, rejected separate spheres and claimed that women had no monopoly on nonviolence. More concerned with women's economic independence, Nehru called for equal educational and work opportunities for women and men. For different reasons, many Indian nationalists adopted the slogan "India cannot be free until its women are free and women cannot be free until India is free."

During the long movement to end British rule, Indian women mobilized politically on several fronts. Elite women such as the feminist Pandita Ramabai had participated actively in the early independence movement, while thousands of women joined the Gandhian effort in the twentieth century. Women were essential to the boycotts of British goods. They engaged in domestic craft production as an alternative to imports, and many were arrested for picketing shops that sold foreign cloth. National independence and women's rights went hand in hand for some activists. Sarojini Naidu, who worked with Gandhi and in 1925 served as the first woman president of the Indian National Congress, campaigned for the right of widows to remarry and for woman suffrage. During the 1920s Indian women achieved local suffrage and created the All India Women's Conference, which joined Muslim and Hindu women. The members took the lead in arguing for legislation to abolish child marriage by raising the age of consent.

Like Western feminists, Indian women faced the paradox of gender by employing multiple strategies. According to the historian Radha Kumar, "Pre-Independence feminists clung with one hand to gender-based definitions of themselves while reaching with the other for an existence based on equality and sameness, rather than complementarity and difference."4 The 1947 Indian constitution guaranteed equality between the sexes, but huge gaps in economic and political opportunities prevented Indian women from realizing this possibility. Some women called for a uniform civil code that would abolish both *sati* and the prohibition on widow remarriage, while others favored religious rather than state regulation of family practices. In Pakistan, which became a separate state in 1947, religious authority would eventually prevail.

Women's rights also coincided with the anticolonial movement in Egypt, where the British ruled from 1882 until 1923. In the late 1800s men involved in progressive intellectual movements invoked Islam to justify the education of women, a cause supported by women writers as well. In 1910 Bahithat al-Badiyah collected her writings in a book, *Feminist Pieces*. "The division of labour," she insisted, "is merely a human creation."5 Now that machines lightened household labors, women should be able to attend school and train for professions. She repeated this message to the Egyptian National Congress in 1911, calling on the mobilization of women to serve the nation. When the independence movement strengthened after World War I, Egyptian women such as Huda Sha'arawi championed it.

For Sha'arawi and other elite colonized women, European ideas converged with Egyptian nationalism. Tutored at home as a child, Sha'arawi entered an arranged marriage at age thirteen. She lived apart from her husband for seven years, and they later had several children. Sha'arawi began to question whether Islam required female seclusion and the veil when she participated in a salon run by a French-born mentor. She helped found a charity for poor women, and after traveling to France she adopted the goals of educational and political rights for women. In the 1920s Huda Sha'arawi successfully campaigned for women's access to Egyptian universities. In 1923 she founded the Egyptian Feminist Union (EFU) and served as its president until 1947. The EFU published *The Egyptian Woman*, first in the French used by the elite classes and later in Arabic. The EFU's demands included access to higher education and the reform of marriage, divorce, and child custody laws. Like middle-class European women reformers, the members also worked to end prostitution and improve employment opportunities for women.

To help achieve Egyptian independence, Sha'arawi mobilized women politically. Over three hundred women handed a petition to the British governor from the "mothers, sisters, and wives of those who have been the victims of British greed and exploitation."[6] In 1919 hundreds of veiled women marched through the streets of Cairo to denounce British violence against the independence movement. "Down with oppressors and tyrants," their banners read. Many of these women considered feminist goals integral to the nationalist cause. Yet Sha'arawi also criticized Egyptian customs. When she returned from Europe in 1923 she rejected the traditional veil. Newspaper photographs of her unveiled face inspired other urban middle- and upper-class Arab women to remove their veils, not only in Egypt but also in Lebanon and Syria.

In the next decades the EFU continued to address women's work conditions and to oppose prostitution. In the meantime, other elite Egyptian feminists, such as the Sorbonne-educated Doria Shafik, also sustained the movement for women's rights. In 1948 Shafik formed the Daughters of the Nile Union, which appealed to middle-class urban women throughout Egypt. Shafik believed that national progress required female literacy and professional jobs for women. An outspoken feminist, she organized an invasion of the Egyptian parliament in 1951 and two years later created a women's political party. The Egyptian government quickly suppressed the organization.

To her conservative religious opponents Shafik pointed out that
Islamic law made women equal in marriage. She wanted to extend that
principle to politics. Since an Islamic woman could choose her husband,
she "should have the same right as men to select whomever she wants
to represent her concerning public matters."7 In 1954 Shafik staged a
hunger strike for woman suffrage, which Egyptian women gained in
1956. By then, however, a new government denied the right to any political opposition. The legacies of activists such as Sha'arawi and Shafik—
higher education, professional jobs, and an insistence that feminism is
compatible with Islam and nationalism—continue to influence Egyptian
feminists.

Alongside women's movements led by European-educated feminists, working-class women participated in national independence or
self-determination movements through their long-standing mutual support networks. In South Africa, for instance, traditional women's organizations, such as Manyano (the name is taken from the local term for a
prayer union), originated as savings clubs to help families in times of
need. Their members later opposed the system of racial control imposed
by the Afrikaner white minority rulers descended from Dutch and British colonial settlers. In 1913 grassroots African women's organizations
demonstrated against a law requiring black women to carry passes in order to move about. Many protesters who destroyed their passes served
harsh prison terms. Manyano became a model for the Women's League
that formed after World War II within the African National Congress
(ANC), the democratic movement to abolish the apartheid system of segregation and enfranchise the black majority. In the 1960s the Women's
League protested revived pass laws and its leader, Gertrude Shope, was
exiled. Alongside these political protests, Indian and African women's organizations continued to attend to the welfare of women and children.

During most of this era white South African women met in segregated groups that supported apartheid. The exceptional white women
who actively opposed the system, such as early ANC activist Ruth First,
were often members of the Communist Party. Eventually some white
women's organizations joined the antiapartheid fight through the Federation of South African Women. African members of this cross-race alliance appealed to women's common identities as mothers when they

pointed to apartheid and asked white women, "Can you as a woman, as a mother, tolerate this?"[8] In the 1950s the Federation of South African Women marched en masse to protest the effect of pass laws on women.

Women active within the South African antiapartheid movement always addressed broad social justice issues. The Women's League within the ANC combined concerns about child and family welfare with feminist demands for political rights. When they drafted the Women's Charter, the Women's League called not only for the right to vote but also for the redistribution of land, the reform of marriage laws, and an end to child labor. The middle-class white women's organization Black Sash, founded in 1955, protested racial injustice long before they turned to women's rights. In the final push for democratic rule, while African women's grassroots activism focused on the needs of children and families, a revived Federation of South African Women added individual women's rights to their agenda. After white minority rule finally ended in 1994, South Africa guaranteed women equality under the law.

Nationalism, Modernization, and Reaction

Anticolonial movements could extend the principle of self-determination to women, but nationalism did not always coincide with feminist politics. In Turkey and Iran, for example, heads of state who declared women's rights as part of a program of Westernization imposed their will without women's participation. Formerly the core of the Ottoman Empire, Turkey successfully fought off European rule at the end of World War I. Educated Ottoman women, some of them influenced by European feminism, participated in both the war effort and the nationalist movement. The new government of Kemal Ataturk, eager for Turkey to be seen as a "civilized" nation, adopted Western standards of secular government and popular literacy. Through education women would achieve their "highest duty," motherhood, and train patriotic citizens. By rejecting the Islamic family code and adopting European laws, Ataturk greatly affected women's lives. Turkey outlawed polygyny in 1926 and gradually adopted woman suffrage during the early 1930s, well before other nations such as France. Similarly, as part of his Westernization campaign in the 1930s, the shah of Iran declared a ban on women wearing the veil in public and extended university education to women.

[handwritten: suffrage — right to vote]

Top-down reforms, however, did not necessarily grant women political authority. For one, Ataturk crushed or co-opted Turkish feminist organizations, along with other social movements. In Iran, when women's movements formed during the 1950s as part of opposition to the government, the ruling shah ordered state control of women's organizations and placed his sister at their head. In addition, because the imposition of secular law fostered religious resentment, women's rights became a target of the conservatives who overthrew the shah in 1979. The religious state led by Ayatollah Khomeini quickly mandated Islamic dress for all women and curtailed women's higher education and access to the professions. When women protested the new laws, the state banned women's organizations.

Other anticolonial and nationalist movements overturned women's rights as Western imports. In Algeria, the association of women's emancipation with French colonialism created a political backlash. A history of forced, public unveiling of women by the French made reveiling a symbol of resistance. Although women participated widely in the war to overthrow the French, the independent Algerian government established in 1961 soon dismissed calls for women's emancipation along with most things European. Because the leaders of the women's movement, like other nationalists, were steeped in French culture, their feminism seemed to conflict with independence. Women could vote and the new constitution professed equality, but the law was not necessarily enforced. Equally important, in a compromise with those calling for Islamic law, the new Algerian government adopted a strict family code that limited women's access to divorce and contraception. As Algerian feminist Marie-Aimée Hélie-Lucas explains, women hesitated for years to speak out against unjust laws because they felt "silenced by fears of accusations of betrayal and by the nationalist myth."9

nationalism — patriotic feeling or efforts
— desire + plans for national independence
— desire of a people to preserve on
lang-relig + traditions

THE ORIGINS OF INTERNATIONAL FEMINISM

Because such diverse local contexts forged women's politics, early efforts to create an international movement faced formidable challenges. European and U.S. feminists had corresponded and met since the 1840s. Beginning in the 1880s they built organizations to promote goals ranging from temperance and pacifism to socialism and suffrage. Until World War I, the movement was international in name only. Western European and American women initiated the groups and then encouraged local chapters to form in other parts of the world. As European world domination declined after the war, however, women in Latin America, Asia, and Africa increasingly took part in the International Woman Suffrage Alliance, the International Council of Women, and the Women's International League for Peace and Freedom. The leadership remained dominated by elite, white, Christian women from northern and western Europe. Anti-Semitism placed limits on the roles of European Jewish women, while Huda Sha'arawi from Egypt was the only Muslim among leaders of the suffrage alliance. Significantly, although Sha'arawi aligned with Western feminists on suffrage, she chastised these allies when they supported colonialism. Aware of the limitations of European women's "universalism," she also fostered pan-Arab women's movements, including the establishment of the regional Arab Feminist Union in 1945.

The earliest efforts to create an international women's movement often reproduced colonial relations. When European women spoke of aiding "primitives," for example, they relied on the same stereotypes of passive, helpless others that characterized missionary and colonialist rhetoric. Just as women of color within the United States challenged white feminists to recognize their racial biases, so too women from Asia, Africa, and the Middle East took issue with what scholars later termed "feminist orientalism," the tendency to view all women outside the West as exotic, sexually oppressed others.[10] In 1920 black women from the United States and Africa responded to comments demeaning to them by forming the International Council of Women of the Darker Races. At an international conference in 1935 Shareefeh Hamid Ali of India spoke for women "of the East" when she explained to "you of the west" that "any arrogant assumption of superiority or of patronage on the part of Europe or America" would alienate "the womanhood of Asia and Africa."[11] These women expected support from Western feminists in their dual struggle for personal and national independence.

Some Western feminists understood that they could learn a great deal from other women, many of whom already enjoyed privileges not available in Europe and North America. In the early 1900s the *Jus Suffragii*, the international suffrage journal, reported on the economic and political rights that women enjoyed as traders in Africa or as municipal voters in Burma. The U.S. suffrage leader Carrie Chapman Catt could be patronizing about the need to "uplift" women outside the West, but she also recognized that millions of these women "have always enjoyed more personal freedom than was accorded to most European women a century ago, and more than is now permitted to thousands of women under our boasted Western civilization."[12] Articles in the suffrage journal also pointed out how European efforts had eroded women's customary authority, and they acknowledged that Islam was not necessarily oppressive to women. Eventually the international women's movement recognized that women outside the West were perfectly capable of establishing their own women's movements, which could meet on equal terms with European and American organizations.

Most of the European women involved in international feminist organizing espoused liberal goals of educational, property, and voting rights; many shared maternalist sympathies for improving women's family lives through temperance and antiprostitution movements. In addition, socialist women influenced international movements, largely in those countries with strong Marxist politics. The Socialist Women's International organized by Clara Zetkin in 1907 favored woman suffrage for all classes along with social justice. After World War II a Communist Party women's international backed by Moscow raised women's issues but avoided the word *feminist*.

The United Nations and International Feminism

World War II represented a turning point for women's organizing, as it did for international relations generally. Aside from women's cooperative relief efforts, the war gave rise to political institutions, such as the United Nations, that fostered international feminism. In the decades after the war, the rhetoric of democratic rights first articulated two centuries earlier during the European Enlightenment extended far beyond its original geographic boundaries. The remaining colonial empires soon gave way to independent states. This expansion of the ideals of human rights had important implications for both the former colonies and women's movements.

Despite the extension of national self-determination beyond the West, the postcolonial world faced huge economic disparities. Former colonies, termed the "Third World," "developing nations," or the "South," remained dependent on the advanced industrial nations for financial and technological investments. They also became a battleground in the Cold War struggle for alliance with either the "First World" of the West or the "Second World" of the Communist bloc. True independence—for countries or for individuals—required not only national sovereignty but also economic stability and international security.

The United Nations provided a potential global forum for discussing human rights, economic justice, and international security. The 1945 UN charter incorporated both Enlightenment ideals and the language of liberal feminism when it reaffirmed "faith in fundamental human rights, in the dignity and worth of the human person, in the equal rights of men and women." The document repeatedly called for rights, freedoms, and respect for all "without distinctions to race, sex, language, or religion."

In 1947, as part of its mechanisms to foster economic and social progress, the UN established the Commission on the Status of Women. Two years later the General Assembly agreed upon the Declaration of Human Rights, which applied the principle of equal rights to thought, opinions, privacy, education, work, leisure, and peace. Significantly, it also incorporated the domestic concerns of maternalist reformers such as

Eleanor Roosevelt, who provided the driving force behind its adoption. Along with adult men and women sharing "equal rights as to marriage, during marriage and at its dissolution," the declaration proclaimed that "motherhood and childhood are entitled to special care and assistance," whether a child was born "in or out of wedlock."[13] However idealistic these pronouncements, the UN has had a wide-reaching practical impact on the kinds of health and welfare issues long championed by maternalist reformers. Nongovernmental organizations (NGOs) such as the World Health Organization (WHO) and the United Nations International Children's Emergency Fund (UNICEF) have both channeled aid and nurtured cross-cultural communication among those concerned about the status of women.

The Decade for Women

These networks expanded after the UN declared 1975 to be International Women's Year, launching the Decade for Women. Three international conferences on women's issues punctuated the decade. Delegates from 133 nations gathered in Mexico City in 1975; in 1980, 145 nations were represented in Copenhagen; and in 1985 representatives from 157 countries met in Nairobi. These conferences provided a critical intersection where Western feminists encountered the political and material realities of women's lives outside the West.

Although a majority of the participants were women, men dominated the speeches and leadership at Mexico City in 1975. The official delegates often represented the interests of their governments, not necessarily those of women's organizations. At Copenhagen, for example, a male delegate from the USSR declared that there was no discrimination against women in the Soviet Union because the law forbade such discrimination, and there was no such thing as sexism in his country because there was no such word in the Russian language. As women at the UN pressed for equality, however, the conferences included more female leadership and the discussions turned to the gaps between male and female opportunities.

Equally important, women from around the world who were not official delegates gathered at parallel meetings held during each of the UN conferences. A tribune outside the Mexico City meeting attracted six

thousand activists; the forums at Copenhagen and Nairobi grew from
ten thousand in 1980 to fifteen thousand in 1985. Though Western-
dominated at first, 65 percent of the participants at Nairobi came from
developing countries, and women of color from the West now played
leading roles. With no formal governmental agendas, these forums provided opportunities for intense communications, at times quite heated.
Representatives of NGOs ran workshops and panels to share their efforts to combat poverty, violence against women, female genital cutting,
and illiteracy. Each topic provoked conflict over political strategies. In
Copenhagen women spontaneously organized sessions every day, such as
one sponsored by Norwegian women called "Sisterhood—A Myth?" A
daily free newspaper announced workshops and criticized the politics of
the official conference, whose delegates could not avoid the radical ferment around them.

The political tensions that reverberated through each meeting reflected the imbalance of power between advanced industrial and developing nations. When U.S. feminists arrived in Mexico City to talk about
equal rights, for example, they immediately encountered criticism from
delegates who did not want to discuss gender outside the context of movements for national self-determination. The U.S. government did not want
the politics of apartheid in South Africa or the Israeli-Palestinian conflict
on the agenda. Greek delegate Margaret Papandreou called this U.S. position "antifeminist" for trying to separate politics from women's issues.[14]

At the NGO forums women did debate international politics as well
as economic development policies. Western feminists arrived with a focus on equal rights to education, property, and political authority. For
women from Asia, Africa, and Latin America, however, rural and urban
poverty represented the most pressing challenges to human rights. "To
talk feminism to a woman who has no water, no food and no home is to
talk nonsense," the *NGO Forum* newspaper at Copenhagen explained.[15]
Responding to this sentiment, the 1985 NGO Forum in Nairobi convened workshops to discuss the variety of regional contexts that feminism must address.

The exchanges at the official UN conference and the unofficial NGO
meetings proved highly educational for Western feminists. Delegates
learned about the daily problems that confronted women globally: living

under apartheid in South Africa; struggling for self-determination in Palestine; bringing water, sewers, and electricity to poor Brazilian women; trying to feed families throughout the world. The NGO gatherings especially convinced many Western women that world poverty and national liberation were feminist issues because they affected women's lives around the globe. After attending the Copenhagen conference, Charlotte Bunch, a radical lesbian feminist in the United States during the 1970s, began to address international women's issues. In preparing for the 1985 NGO forum in Nairobi, she came to the conclusion that "the beginning point at both conferences must be that *everything* is a woman's issue. That means racism is a woman's issue, just as is anti-Semitism, Palestinian homelessness, rural development, ecology, the persecution of lesbians, and the exploitative practices of global corporations."[16]

Women from developing nations also felt the profound effects of these conferences. Valsa Verghese, who came from India to attend the Copenhagen conference, initially felt "frustration and confusion" at the multitude of choices at the NGO Forum. By the end she found it "heartening to realize that in spite of cultural differences there was so much in common to unite us, to feel the bond of sisterhood, to break the isolation of women and to feel the growing power within us."[17] The meetings also exposed women to the potential of feminism for their own local politics. A Latin American woman who was "not at all interested in feminism" before attending the Copenhagen conference wrote that "after seeing how governments and the UN treat women and what has and has not happened in the Forum, I am now considering the potential of feminism seriously."[18]

The Ripple Effect

The UN conferences set in motion waves of organizing among women throughout the world. In Brazil the International Women's Year in 1975 helped revive the feminist movement during a conservative period of military rule. A women's conference in Rio de Janeiro that year led to the formation of dozens of new groups, including the Brazilian Women's Center, several feminist newspapers, and organizations of students, professional women, and lesbian feminists. The effect continued for decades, with more than eight hundred Brazilian groups involved in planning for the Beijing conference in 1995. In Manila a Sisterhood Is Global Dialogue in 1988 and two international women's health conferences in the early 1990s inspired Filipina lesbians to create their first regional organization.

Just as women of color in the United States built their own feminist support structure, Latin American, African, and Asian women met to define their feminist agendas. At the Copenhagen conference feminists from Colombia decided to hold a regional meeting the next year. Since then grassroots activists and women professionals from Latin America and the Caribbean have held Feminist Encuentros. From two hundred participants in Bogotá, Colombia, in 1981 the meetings grew to over twenty-five hundred women in San Bernardo, Argentina, in 1990. One theme of the Feminist Encuentros was the way class and race influenced the lives of women; another was how participants could bring women's diverse concerns to national institutions such as labor unions and political parties. In local and regional meetings, historian Cheryl Johnson-Odim explains, women treated "feminism as a fundamentally political movement connected as much to the struggle of their communities for liberation and autonomy as to the work against gender discrimination."[19]

The international women's meetings reverberated in national politics as well. When UN member nations sent delegates to the Decade for Women conferences, they had to take stock of their own laws and social practices concerning women. Each official UN conference issued statements for approval by member nations, such as the Plan of Action, and these prompted further political activism back home. In 1975, for instance, Japan responded to the Mexico City Plan of Action by establishing the Headquarters for the Planning and Promotion of Policies Relating to Women as well as an Advisory Council on Women. Each prefectural government also set up a network for implementing the plan. In addition, the Mexico City delegations drafted the Convention on the Elimination of All Forms of Discrimination Against Women (CEDAW), which the UN General Assembly passed in 1979. CEDAW reiterated earlier UN commitments to both women's rights and the importance of families; it also incorporated the effects of poverty on women, the need to abolish apartheid and all forms of racism and colonialism, and the importance of national self-determination for "the attainment of full equality between men and women."[20] When feminist lobbyists convinced the Japanese government to sign CEDAW, they won official commitment to reforming discriminatory national laws.

The UN Decade for Women and its regional offshoots also inspired opposition to feminism. In Brazil and Chile conservative women's organizations formed to uphold not only traditional gender roles but also military dictators and Catholic religious authority. In the United States, Phyllis Schlafly's right-wing Eagle Forum opposed ratification of CEDAW. She cited in particular the article that required textbooks to eliminate stereotyping of women and men. "Unable to persuade Americans voluntarily to go along with their censorship attempts," Schlafly explained, "the feminists are trying to get the UN to do this job for them."[21] With support from conservative national legislators such as Senator Jesse Helms, the opposition to CEDAW prevented the United States from joining the more than 165 nations (two-thirds of UN members) that had ratified the treaty by 2001. The Roman Catholic leadership at the Vatican also continues to oppose CEDAW because it promotes women's control of reproduction, which, they fear, will foster abortion.

RETHINKING FEMINISM IN THE POSTCOLONIAL WORLD

Creating a transnational women's movement requires that feminists overcome the legacies of colonialism. That challenging task means reaching across cultures without imposing Western notions of superiority and acknowledging the multiple forms that both injustice and emancipation may take. Two international issues embody the tensions inherent in women's global encounters. The first, international development programs, highlights the dilemmas of liberal feminist politics, which founder over the role of gender difference in efforts to achieve gender equality. The second, the notion of "global feminism," highlights the weaknesses of both liberalism and a radical feminism that overlooks class and race distinctions among women. Both serve as reminders that economic and political strategies must take into account the particular strengths of women's local heritage.

International Development and Women's Labor

During the 1970s and 1980s the United Nations and other international organizations began to rethink the role of women in economic development programs. The international efforts to stimulate economic growth in the developing regions begun after World War II had failed to undermine the extensive poverty in these countries. Along with the earlier goal of expanding national productivity, UN agencies turned their attention to the growing inequalities of wealth. The impoverishment of women represented a major obstacle to economic justice, and the UN Decade for Women provided a forum for reviewing development policy through the lens of gender.

In *Woman's Role in Economic Development* (1970) Ester Boserup argued that most development programs had failed to take into account women's productive roles. In the rush to increase productivity in developing nations, planners and lenders such as the World Bank and the International Monetary Fund concentrated on male workers. Foreign aid provided men with land, credit, and tools and expected wives to provide domestic labor. As a result, the gender gap in technology, wealth, and status widened. Describing West Africa in the mid-twentieth century, Boserup observed that "men ride the bicycle and drive the lorry, while women carry head loads, as did their grandmothers. In short, men represent modern farming in the village, women represent the old drudgery."[22] When development programs considered women at all it was usually in their capacity as mothers targeted by family planning efforts to reduce population growth.

In the past, African women had contributed to the economy, especially as producers of food. Boserup and other scholars wanted to integrate rural women into new forms of production though education and training. A school of thought termed Women in Development (WID) made the case that full economic development required a recognition of women's contributions to the economy and their integration into production. Rather than viewing women as dependents in families, WID argued, they should be encouraged to generate income, either as small entrepreneurs or as factory laborers.

WID advocates helped extend modernization policies to women in the developing regions by drawing women into the market economy. As several scholars have noted, WID represented "liberal feminism writ global," for it rested upon liberal values of individualism, self-interest, and private property.[23] To an extent, this approach succeeded in adding gender to the policy debates on international development. In practical terms, WID also laid the groundwork for the influx of young Latin American and Asian women into manufacturing jobs in the free-trade zones where multinational corporations established factories. It also lent support for efforts to educate girls.

Even as international development programs began to integrate women into national productivity goals, criticisms of WID emerged. The South Asian feminist scholar Naila Kabeer summarized the problem: WID recognized women's productive potential at the expense of appreciating their unpaid work in the household. Ignoring reproductive and household labor placed women in a double bind. Women workers could not earn enough money to purchase the household and child care services they needed in order to be able to leave their homes to work for pay. By assuming a similarity between female and male workers, WID overlooked important differences, particularly the realities of motherhood. Without taking into account both women's biological capacity for childbearing and the structural inequalities of race and class, WID could not contribute to solving the problems of women's, and world, poverty.

Moreover, simply mobilizing women as workers did not necessarily empower them, a lesson that women of color in the West long realized. In her study of Malaysian factory workers, anthropologist Aihwa Ong concluded that these women may have exchanged patriarchal control within their families for industrial surveillance and discipline in the factory. As one worker complained of her foremen, "They give this job, that job, and even before my task is done they say do that, do this, and before that is ready, they say do some other work." In the words of another Malaysian factory worker, "It would be nice working here if the foremen, managers, all the staff members and clerks understand that the workers are not under their control."[24]

The flaws of merely drawing women into the labor force became apparent by the end of the UN Decade for Women. During the period when WID policies dominated, women's economic resources had declined, not improved. In response to the shortcomings of WID, feminists recommended a new approach known as Gender and Development, or GAD. Since the 1980s GAD advocates have attempted to take into account women's customary economic and family responsibilities when they implement development policies. GAD addresses issues such as the relationships of men and women to natural resources and the impact of male migration on women's work and responsibilities. Rather than exclude women from, or integrate them into, a male model, the GAD approach builds upon rural women's practices, such as their traditional knowledge about agriculture. In projects that recognize female expertise in native plant diversity, development agencies turn to local women as authorities for seed selection. As Mona Khalaf, of the Institute for Women's Studies in the Arab World in Beirut, Lebanon, explains, GAD has broadened development analysis to discuss "sustainable human development, a development achieved by people and not for them."[25] The UN has adopted the goal of "stimulating growth with equity" by providing resources to both women and men in sustainable development projects.

The Challenge of Local Feminisms

A second feminist dilemma concerns the controversial notion of a "universal sisterhood" that presumes the relevance of Western politics to the rest of the world, regardless of local conditions. In Amrita Basu's terms, the "challenge of local feminisms" complicates sisterhood.[26] Although patriarchy may subordinate women all over the world, as a group of African women scholars explains, "women are also members of classes and countries that dominate others. . . . Contrary to the best intentions of 'sisterhood,' not all women share identical interests."[27] Just as women of color in the West testified about their racially specific identities, women outside the West have explained why gender cannot be the sole determinant of their politics. Peasant and working-class women in Africa, Asia, and Latin America have been adamant that for them, economic justice, along with cultural and national sovereignty, must become a priority of feminism. In contrast to European and North American drives for individual rights, these local activists often stress women's domestic identities and the needs of family and community. At times they turn to innovative cooperative structures rather than purely individualistic ones, building upon women's mutual support networks.

The life of Domitila Barrios de Chungara suggests how these complex politics of location operate. The wife of a Bolivian miner and mother of seven children, Barrios de Chungara first became involved in politics in 1961 as a housewife when local women protested the arrests of their husbands during a strike. After the women staged a nine-day hunger strike outside the prison, the miners were released. Back home the women formed a union of their own, the Housewives Committee of Siglo XX. When her husband opposed her joining the committee, Barrios de Chungara staged her own work stoppage in the house; he soon realized the value of her labor and accepted her decision. The women of the Housewives Committee monitored the prices of consumer goods in the community, demanded adequate medical supplies at the local hospital, and forced government officials to bargain with them by blockading the roads.

From her experience organizing the wives of miners, Barrios de Chungara became active in leftist politics and ran unsuccessfully for national office. She also worked to educate peasant women about their rights, calling on her *compañeras* to resist intimidation from their husbands or from the state. "Where would the world be without women?" she wrote in 1980 in a pamphlet well illustrated with drawings to reach those with limited literacy. Citing the United Nations charter, she assured women that they had the right to education, equal wages, and political participation. For the future of their children, she argued, women had to learn new skills, which meant overcoming the socialization that had taught them to defer to men. To do so she urged women to educate each other. "You must find ways, places where you can talk. . . . You must talk about your problems."[28]

Domitila Barrios de Chungara sounded a theme that recurs around the world: the need to empower women as full participants in larger movements for economic and social justice. Yet she consciously rejected the equal-rights strategy of liberal feminists. As she told the UN conference in Mexico City in 1975, she identified two kinds of liberation: "One type involves those who think women will only be free when they equal men in all their vices. This is called feminism. . . . But *compañeras*, do we really want to smoke cigarettes?" The other type consisted of "women being respected as human beings, who can solve problems and participate in everything—culture, art, literature, politics, trade unionism—a liberation that means our opinion is respected at home and outside the home." Echoing maternalist beliefs in women's moral superiority, she insisted that women were "more thoughtful, more firm in their positions, more honest" and were therefore critical to the success of working-class movements. Her politics foreshadowed a critical shift in emerging transnational feminisms: from a focus on rights and entitlements to a struggle for empowering women as agents of change.

Western feminist politics achieved its earliest victories by calling for the extension to women of men's growing political and economic rights. Transnational women's movements recognize as well the political importance of alternative strategies that draw on women's heritage of raising their families, maintaining their cultures, and empowering themselves. Women throughout the world developed these survival skills under patriarchy; before a politics of rights, they often relied on reciprocal family and social obligations to maintain a balance of power between men and women. By insisting on adequate care for women's families, these strategies complement equal rights arguments and broaden the reach of women's movements.

REDEFINING FEMINISM

By the end of the UN Decade for Women, women in the developing world had redefined feminism, rejecting the myth of global sisterhood in favor of a more heterogeneous and flexible framework. As participants at the Nairobi conference explained in 1985, feminism "constitutes the political expression of the concerns and interests of women from different regions, classes, nationalities, and ethnic backgrounds. . . . There is and must be a diversity of feminisms, responsive to the different needs and concerns of different women, and defined by them for themselves."[29] For

Western women, the myth of global sisterhood had to give way to the politics of location. The result has been a more realistic notion of transnational feminism. In this model, an understanding of historical and cultural differences among women provides the base for alliances across those differences.

This transnational approach has enabled more activists from a range of cultures to embrace feminism as a political identity. From *La Red Feminista Campesina* (The Feminist Peasant Network) in Mexico to the Feminist Network (*Feminsta Hálózat*) in Hungary, women's organizations have accepted the term as well. The Filipina group Kalayaan, founded in 1983, defines itself explicitly as "a feminist membership organization." In response to the claim that feminism, as a Western idea, had no place in the developing world, a member of Women in Nigeria explained that "African men see nothing wrong in their relationship with Western governments and institutions, but object to African women having relationships with these same institutions. Why? Because they feel threatened by the prospects of feminism."[30] When the Women's League of the African National Congress returned from exile in 1990, they proclaimed that "feminism has been misinterpreted in most third world countries . . . there is nothing wrong with feminism. It is as progressive or reactionary as nationalism." With the establishment of a democratic government, they dropped their call for "liberation before feminism" and began to negotiate for equal representation of women in the ANC.[31]

In the West, liberal feminism called for the extension of men's individual rights to women, socialism concentrated on organizing women as wage laborers, and radical feminism emphasized the power relations between men and women in familial and personal relationships. The expansion of feminism internationally makes even clearer why all of these political streams must converge. Seventy percent of the world's women live in developing regions, where economic survival depends on their work both in families and for pay. While class-based liberation movements address wage labor, and feminism insists on political rights, the particular economic needs of poor women require new forms of activism. Their concerns include the protection of women's customary land rights, the creation of women's economic cooperatives, and the drive for female literacy. To support women's rights, feminists must also recognize the family as a central social institution in the lives of most women in the world. At the same time, movements for economic, political, and environmental justice must consider their impact on women's lives and ensure women a role in decision making.

Acknowledging the interconnections of women's rights, economic justice, and world politics, United Nations Secretary-General Boutros Boutros-Ghali opened the 1995 UN-sponsored Fourth World Conference on Women in Beijing by declaring that the "great political project of the twentieth century" was to secure equality for women and men, in fact as well as in law. The Declaration and Platform of Action adopted at that gathering insisted that women's rights were human rights. Equally important, the expanding political agenda of feminism confronted over twenty thousand delegates at the NGO gathering outside Beijing, where demonstrations took place each day, led by disability rights organizers, lesbian activists, women of color, indigenous women's rights groups, and pacifist groups such as Women in Bosnia/Rwanda/Somalia/Palestine-Israel for Peace. Cambodian women testified to the devastating effect of land mines on their daily lives, AIDS educators from Thailand shared ideas, and rural African women insisted that they were "no longer invisible and voiceless."[32] The global stage had expanded to include the voices of women whose politics of location, both geographic and personal, strengthened the feminist movement.

PART III

THE POLITICS OF WORK AND FAMILY

SIX

NEVER DONE: WOMEN'S DOMESTIC LABOR

A mother with a family is an economist, a nurse, a painter,
a diplomat and more. And yet we take back seats. . . .
We put ourselves there. How often do you hear a colleague say,
"I am only a housewife"?
—BUCHI EMECHETA, NIGERIA/ENGLAND, 1985

The growing appeal of feminist politics rests in large part upon historical changes in the meaning of women's work. Always critical to human survival, the labor of women has not always been rewarded equally with men's. Take for example the case of Ellen Skaar, a midwestern U.S. farm wife. For twenty years Mrs. Skaar worked alongside her husband to keep their Wisconsin farm profitable. During a typical twelve-hour day she milked the cows in the morning and evening, cared for the chickens, and helped plant, harvest, and strip the tobacco crop. She regularly baled hay and drove a tractor as well. The Skaars agreed to share their farm revenues. When they divorced in the 1970s, however, a court ruled that all profits from the farm belonged to Mr. Skaar. In marriage, he was legally "entitled to his wife's services."[1] Ellen Skaar's work was never done. As a farm wife, however, she could not reap the profits of her labor.

The invisibility of women's labor lies at the heart of feminist critiques of work and family. We often link feminism to the entry of women into the workforce, but as Ellen Skaar's life illustrates, that phrase is misleading. Women have always worked. Well before a wage labor system came to dominate in industrial economies, women raised food, children, and animals; made clothes and meals; healed bodies and spirits. Folk and popular cultures recognize that women toil longer than men. "Man must toil from sun to sun," an aphorism goes, "but a woman's work is never done." The folktale of a farmer who tried to switch places with his wife ends with his realization that "she could do more work in a day than he could do in seven." Yet a powerful contemporary myth holds that women in the home do not work, or when they do, their jobs are "natural," merely the biological functions of mothering, nurturing, reproducing daily life. Performed for love, not money, domestic work does not count in the same way that men's labor does.

How did women's labor in the home become invisible? As capitalism and industrialization drew workers out of the home and measured labor's worth through wages, the gap in the value of men's and women's work widened. Unpaid domestic duties limited most women's options when men first joined the wage labor force. When women did work for pay, they faced a "double day" of performing both household and wage labor. Having to juggle competing identities as mothers and workers further disadvantaged women in the labor market.

This economic process has occurred unevenly across the world. The historical shift from agriculture to industry began in England and northwestern Europe around 1800, spread across the United States and most European nations by 1900, and affected the global economy by 2000. In each locale, in each era, the meaning of work changed for everyone, but in different ways. As men entered labor markets they came to be judged by a "breadwinner" standard. A Western ideal of natural female domesticity masked both women's economic contributions in the home and men's familial labors. The model of male breadwinner and female caregiver required an income rarely available to working-class men or women. For family or personal survival, working-class women often marketed their domestic labor. They worked as servants, sold food or household products, or provided sexual services. Women received neither a full living wage nor social rewards for these forms of labor. At the same time their dual labors, in the home and for wages, put them at a disadvantage compared to men.

Many of the economic problems faced in the world today, from

hunger and poverty to crises in welfare systems, have roots in this disparity between the values placed on women's and men's labor. By valuing
men's labor more than women's, industrial economies have exacerbated
earlier gender asymmetries. Indeed, defining work in a way that overlooks women's unpaid labor creates a false distinction between selfless,
unpaid caregiving by women and competitive wage earning by men. In
fact, women's domestic labor has been essential to the growth of capitalist economies. Feminists recognize this value and criticize the domestic/
breadwinner gender divide for relegating women to a dependent status.

THE FAMILY ECONOMY AND HOUSEHOLD LABOR

Whether in the past or in rural regions of the world today, subsistence
and agrarian cultures rely on the labor of both men and women. In preindustrial agricultural societies family members raised the food they ate,
made the clothes they wore, and crafted the tools they needed. Each person contributed a share to what has been called the "family economy."
When husbands worked in the fields and tended livestock, wives worked
closer to the home, raising not only children but also some crops and
barnyard animals. In much of the world farm wives provided family
health care, prepared and cleaned up after several daily meals, and produced cloth for family garments and other household items. Even when a
male head of household had legal authority over his wife and children,
economically husband and wife relied on each other's labor.

Farm women knew that they performed important tasks, and they
let others know that their labor was, indeed, never done. Mrs. Sara Price,
a midwestern U.S. housewife and mother of six, lamented in a verse written in her diary in the 1800s: "It's sweeping at six and it's dusting at
seven, it's victuals at eight and it's dishes at nine / It's potting and pan-
ning from ten to eleven; we scarce break our fast 'til we plan how to
dine." A British agricultural laborer, Mary Collier, complained in her
poem "The Woman's Labour" that when she turned homeward in the
evening after working the fields all day, her "domestick Toils incessant
play." These toils included cooking dinner, making beds, feeding swine,

and setting the table. In the morning, after she dressed and fed the children and mended their clothes, she had to leave again for the fields, "Soon as the rising Sun has dry'd the dew."[2] Like Collier, African American women worked both in the fields and in their own homes, even after the end of slavery. As Frances Harper observed in the 1870s, rural southern black women "do double duty, a man's share in the field, and a woman's part at home."[3]

Family farming and farm labor have declined in much of the Western world, but at the start of the twenty-first century three-quarters of the world's women lived in developing countries, where they produced over half of the food raised. In other words, the challenge of feeding the world falls heavily upon women, who often have the fewest resources for the task. In Africa, with its long tradition of female farming, 80 percent of the food is still raised by women. Many of them continue to sell their produce in local markets. In Asia women constitute one-half of the agricultural labor force.

In all regions farmwork remains physically demanding. In rural sections of Africa and Asia women draw and carry water for up to five hours each week; in the dry season in Mozambique women may spend fifteen to seventeen hours a week procuring water for their families. In Latin America indigenous peasant women participate in the harvest. In South and Southeast Asia women labor on individual family plots; in China they harvest rice or wheat and raise animals. Almost everywhere rural women continue to have primary responsibility for the maintenance of family members and the household, even as they produce goods for consumption or sale.

The story of Om Naeema, who grew up in Egypt during the 1970s, illustrates the persistence of the family economy in developing countries and the varied labors of rural women, who still constitute over half of Egypt's female population. Om Naeema's father would wake and feed the children before they all walked to the fields, where the children guarded the farm animals while their father plowed. In the house her mother ground wheat and corn for bread, cooked, cleaned, and washed clothing; after her husband died, she worked in the fields while the children planted crops and tended animals. Om Naeema began training for women's work as an adolescent. She learned to rise before dawn, milk the buffalo and feed the animals, collect dung for fuel, haul water from the river, clean house, wash clothes, bake bread, and then, "if they needed my help in the fields, I would go with them." At age fifteen she married and took her skills to her new household.[4]

Despite their hard labors, most farm women have not had the same ownership rights as men to the land they work. In Europe and America males customarily inherited family holdings. West African women have maintained some of their customary land use rights, but women rarely inherit land in Asia and Latin America. Women's farm labor, in other words, has contributed to a family economy that is legally "owned" by husbands. The case of the hardworking Wisconsin farm wife, Ellen Skaar, reflected this principle. Although not all farm families consider women merely laborers rather than owners, deeply held beliefs that women work for their families and not for themselves continue to influence the meaning of female labor.

INDUSTRIALIZATION AND THE FAMILY ECONOMY

Over the past two centuries industrial production and wage labor have supplanted self-sufficient household economies. Mechanization allowed specialized mass production of many goods once handcrafted in households, such as clothing, furniture, and foods. Capitalist economic organization stimulated industrial growth. When factory owners hired wage workers to run machines they reaped profits by selling the manufactured products to workers' families. This system of production for consumer purchase gradually reshaped national and then world economic systems.

The industrial revolution affected the family economy in the West in complex ways. Some writers have described this impact as the "separation of work and home" because workers now left the household to earn wages. Since women continued to work within the home, a more accurate statement is that wage labor drew certain workers out of the family, creating a distinction between work performed for wages in the labor market and work performed for families in the home.

Any family member might enter the wage labor force. Indeed, the earliest textile mills in the 1780s employed whole families, including women and children. Farm daughters in the United States and England flocked to mill jobs in the 1820s and 1830s. But married women remained more tied to the household, where they cared for their children. In the early stages of industrialization fathers, sons, and unmarried daughters were more likely to work for wages. If poor families could not survive, however, married women joined the wage labor force from necessity. In the United States, African American and Irish American families included more wage-earning married women. By the late twentieth century most married women worked for wages in the United States, but initially the new work patterns affected men. (See Appendices B and C.) Once they had worked long hours in or near the household; now men left home for up to twelve hours of wage labor, six days a week. Early critics of industrial capitalism used the term "wage slavery" to describe their lives.

Middle-class families could afford to keep wives out of the labor force, a practice that exaggerated earlier gender distinctions between public and private spheres. The elevation of domesticity as the ideal vocation for married middle-class women contrasted with a male ideal of sole breadwinner. As Isabella Beeton advised British women in 1861, "Of all those acquirements, which more particularly belong to the feminine character, there are none which take a higher rank, in our estimation, than such as enter into a knowledge of household duties; for on these are perpetually dependent the happiness, comfort, and well-being of a family."[5] According to the abundant Anglo-American domestic literature, mothers were supposed to provide a comfortable, pious, loving home not only for their children but also for their husbands. Urged to be ambitious, competitive, and profit-seeking, these men served as the clerks, merchants, managers, and professionals in the industrial economy. No longer an enterprise headed by a patriarchal father, the private home became a zone of affection, morality, and cleanliness under maternal rule. In contrast to the individualism of the capitalist marketplace, the female-dominated home incorporated an ethic of caring, which was designated as women's labor.

In fact, the reproductive labor of motherhood diminished for these white middle-class women. When commerce and industry supplanted agricultural life, large families were no longer needed for farm work, so women had fewer children. In the United States, for example, married women bore on average over eight children in 1800 but under five children in 1900. The shift occurred first for white women, later for predominantly rural groups such as African Americans and Mexican Americans. Despite these lower birth rates, American society celebrated motherhood as woman's primary vocation. Other industrializing cultures also created a specialized female identity: the mother who worked in the home for love, not money. This ideal influenced even those women who could not afford the luxury of remaining at home.

Although housewives did not receive pay, their work had enormous value for industrializing economies. Women's unpaid labor in the home made it possible for families to survive on working men's modest wages. Both working and middle-class housewives saved, sewed, and managed finances; they continued to produce for home use well into the twentieth century. Eventually housewives would spend more of their time as consumers, selecting goods from the market, and sometimes doubling as wage laborers to help families afford the expanding range of consumer products. As mothers, they prepared children for the tasks they would have in the industrial and consumer economies.

So diverse are housewives' contributions that it is difficult to place a monetary value on their labor. Some economists have attempted to do so by calculating the annual cost of purchasing women's services. In 1993 a family in the United States would have had to pay as much as $50,000 a year to buy all that a housewife contributed. In 1995 the United Nations Development Programme estimated that the worldwide annual worth of women's unpaid or underpaid work was $11 trillion.

Despite the value of their labor, most housewives have been economically vulnerable. Historically, widows could earn very little by selling their skills as laundresses or seamstresses. If they had children to support, they could rarely survive without familial, charitable, or state assistance. When states established welfare systems in the early twentieth century, benefits for widows were inadequate and discriminatory. In the United States the "spouse benefit" for a surviving homemaker was half of what a husband received from the social security system. In other cultures as well,

housewives are underpaid and undervalued for their economic contributions to both family and society.

Many women, including feminists, have internalized this devaluation of housework and motherhood. Reacting against the revival of
domesticity after World War II, Betty Friedan portrayed housework as a
trap in *The Feminine Mystique* (1963). Her solution—for the middle-class
woman to hire a maid—shifted the burden to working-class women but
left the demeaning attitude in place. Surveying women's lives in the
United States during the 1980s, Nigerian-born writer Buchi Emecheta
was surprised by the distaste for the work of homemaking, including
mothering. Women wash, cook, and teach their children "to love and to
hate. What greater work is there than that?" she asked. From her West
African perspective, Emecheta questioned the devaluation of women's
work: "I do not think it low. A mother with a family is an economist, a
nurse, a painter, a diplomat and more. And yet we take back seats. . . .
We put ourselves there. How often do you hear a colleague say, 'I am only
a housewife'?"[6]

Domestic Identities

Reclaiming the joys of homemaking would be less problematic if the
ideal that women "naturally" worked in the home for love, not money,
did not have such profound implications for their identities. Historically,
homemaking has been set in contrast to full citizenship. Under the British and American principle of coverture, wives legally owed domestic
and reproductive service to their husbands. The Wisconsin court followed this precedent when it ruled that the labor of farm wife Ellen
Skaar belonged to her husband. A wife's economic standing depended on
that of her husband. As Alva Myrdal wrote in 1945 of married Swedish
women, "Their incomes are never directly related to their toil but only to
the level of the husbands' incomes."[7]

Coverture had important implications for women's identities as citizens. The expectation that family responsibilities come first has justified
women's exclusion or exemption from military service and jury duty. In
1961 a state assistant attorney general in the United States ruled in favor
of women's exemption from jury duty by invoking the more pressing
"burden of providing palatable food for the members of the family." The

Supreme Court agreed that "woman is still regarded as the center of home and family life." Not until 1975 did feminist lawyers succeed in overturning this reasoning to establish women's right and responsibility as U.S. citizens to serve on juries.[8]

Women's domestic identities have proven to be quite tenacious, even after commercial markets transform their lives. Wage earning by women does not necessarily exempt them from performing domestic tasks, even though breadwinning exempts men from most familial labors. During the "putting out" stage of industrialization, when women often performed piecework in their homes, they continued their domestic duties as well. Immigrant mothers who sewed garments in London or on New York's Lower East Side in 1900 also cooked, cleaned, and tended children, many of whom labored as well. The pattern recurred when this system moved to developing regions in the twentieth century. A study of lace makers in an Indian village in the 1970s found that even though these women earned cash that was critical for family survival, the sexual division of labor in the family remained undisturbed. Since women crocheted lace in the home, they were expected to perform all of the housework and child care. As one lace maker complained: "No man helps a woman. Even when the wife is busy making lace, when her husband comes home she has to get up quickly and make tea for him. It is not correct on the part of the men."[9]

When men and women both leave the home to earn wages, women continue to perform more of the unpaid domestic work. In southern Asia, for example, working women generally spend three to five hours more per week in unpaid subsistence work than men do, as well as twenty to thirty hours more per week in unpaid housework. The disparity has implications for perpetuating gender inequality in children's lives as well. In rural India girls spend twice as much time per day doing chores as boys; boys spend more than six times as long as girls reading.[10]

Nor is this imbalance in domestic work unique to the developing world. A 1995 UN study found that in most developed countries women contributed over thirty hours of housework per week, men only ten to fifteen hours. The disparity was even higher in Japan and Korea, where women do nine times as much unpaid labor as men. A study of the United States found that husbands contributed less than 25 percent of the total time spent on the four most time-consuming tasks—cooking, cleaning, dishwashing, and laundry. As Pat Mainardi once caricatured men's attitudes, "Unfortunately, I'm no good at things like washing dishes or cooking. What I do best is a little light carpentry, changing light bulbs, moving furniture (*how often do you move furniture?*)."[11]

Even when wives earn wages, and even when men and women profess equality, the disparity holds. A 1986 California poll asked who should be responsible for housework when both partners worked full-time outside the home. Men and women agreed overwhelmingly (89–90 percent) that both should share equally, but when asked who actually performed most of the housework, less than half of the men (44 percent) reported sharing it equally (and according to their wives, only 30 percent of them actually did so). At the end of the century, comparative data for Norway, Canada, Australia, Sweden, and the United States reveals, husbands in dual-earner couples perform between 18 and 27 percent of household labor (depending on whether the husband or wife is reporting). In Sweden men contribute the most and the reports of husbands and wives are more likely to agree.

Modern household technology has not necessarily lightened the burdens of housework in the West. Historical studies of time spent in housework show that rural women who lacked electricity, with its "laborsaving" appliances, spent the same or less time per week on housework as urban women who had access to laborsaving devices. Housework can actually expand with new appliances. Although washing machines eased the physical labor of doing laundry, standards of cleanliness rose along with technology. Women who washed clothes by hand did so only weekly, while those who had machines used them several times a week. Rugs previously hand-beaten twice a year could now be vacuumed weekly. Refrigerators and stoves made cooking less time-consuming, but now women spent more time shopping. The automobile, which encouraged urban sprawl and suburbanization, meant that mothers increasingly provided transportation for family members. Women's greater time spent in family maintenance means less time for either paid labor or leisure, confirming the old adage "never done" and disadvantaging women in the world of paid work.

Men have increased their overall share of housework in industrial societies where women work for wages and feminists have questioned their double day. From the 1970s to the 1990s husbands in U.S. dual-income couples gradually added an hour of household chores to each day, while their wives reduced housework by about a half hour each day. Changing attitudes about gender affect these patterns. In western Europe, men with more egalitarian attitudes perform more housework than do other men. The gains are limited, however. In the 1960s women in the United States worked six times as long as men at domestic tasks; by the 1990s they still worked twice as much. And when paid jobs demand more hours from workers, men reduce their housework more than women do.

Women's greater responsibility for child care helps to account for this persistent imbalance in household labor. Historically, more men have helped raise children, whether training their sons as helpers or supervising religious instruction at home. In the past few centuries men's absence from the home for wage labor, along with the cultural elevation of motherhood as woman's primary vocation, has deepened the parental divide. Socialized as girls to care for others, many women flourish as mothers and pass on their caretaking skills to the next generation. They clearly remain the primary parent around the world. In Australia and New Zealand, for example, when a couple has children, the wife's unpaid work increases by 25 to 30 percent, the husband's not at all (although his hours earning wages do increase). In the United States, when both parents hold jobs, a mother is about four times more likely than a father to take time off from work to care for a sick child. Fathers who live with their children in the United States now spend more time on caretaking than in the past, but given fathers' absence after divorce and separation, the overall tasks of parenting still fall primarily to mothers.

Extended Mothering

Despite the annual outpouring of sentimental tributes to motherhood, most cultures assume that women require neither compensation nor recognition for their daily personal labors. Yet the job is a critical one. It is impossible to calculate its value to children. Joy Kogawa captures well the physical and emotional power of mothering in her 1981 novel *Obasan*, about a Japanese Canadian family. Describing the "alert and accurate knowing" of a mother and grandmother, a child explains: "When I am hungry, and before I can ask, there is food. If I am weary, every place is a bed. . . . A sweater covers me before there is any chill and if there is pain there is care simultaneously."[12] Such daily mothering can also be performed by siblings, aunts, and "other mothers," including males, but women still dominate in this valuable yet undervalued work.

Women not only respond to the daily needs of children more than men do; they also spend more time maintaining family and community ties. Holiday preparations have become largely women's work. In the United States Thanksgiving, Passover, Kwanzaa, and other feasts where relatives assemble and affirm their common cultural background require days of preparation and hours of serving and cleaning, as well as invaluable crisis management skills necessitated by many a family gathering. Typically women send the family Christmas cards, the thank-you notes, and the modern computer-generated family annual reports. In the United States they do most of the planning for life-cycle celebrations such as weddings, the Jewish bar or bat mitzvah, and the Mexican American *quinceañera*.

The service dimensions of housework extend well beyond the private or extended family. Women's caregiving work has softened the impact of the competitive marketplace. A veritable army of female volunteers has cushioned the effects of industrialization on urban poverty and social anomie. In the 1800s both married and single women became "civic mothers" in North American, British, and Latin American cities. They collected food and clothing for the poor, established settlement houses to assist immigrants, and held bake sales to build hospitals and clinics. In churches and in synagogues, unsalaried women created the precursors of social service agencies, often aiding members of their own religious, ethnic, or racial communities. Parent-teacher associations long depended on women who did not earn wages. In the twentieth-century United States the statistically typical volunteer was a married, middle-aged, college-educated woman in a midwestern urban household who was not employed for wages.

Along with a service ideal, the Western ideology of domesticity also required women to play a spiritual role, creating households that would serve as "havens in a heartless world." In the industrial era, greeting-card paeans to motherhood began to invoke an ideal of selfless, even sacrificial, behavior, expectations that persist into the present. In many cultures, for example, women provide more care for aging parents than men do. In Puerto Rican families daughters have primary responsibility for older parents as well as for the mental health of their children and husbands. In Japan almost 90 percent of the care of elders falls to wives, daughters, and daughters-in-law.

Emotional mothering—whether of children, parents, or members of extended kin networks—takes a particularly high toll on women whose families have the fewest resources, including the growing number of single mothers in industrial societies. Poor, immigrant, and ethnic or racial minority families in every culture can face a particularly heartless world, necessitating greater healing work in the home. In communities with higher male unemployment or alcoholism, or a higher incidence of racism, women often serve as the shock absorbers for their families.

A powerful image of this phenomenon appears in a poem by the African American writer June Jordan, set to music by Bernice Johnson Reagon. The song, "Oughta Be a Woman," which honors Reagon's own mother, describes a woman who provides paid domestic labor by day for white families. After a day of "Washing the floors to send you to college," she returns home to her children, where "She listens to your hurt and your rage." Not only her family members but also "everybody white turns to her." She listens to all of them, but there is no one for her to turn to, for she is "Alone in the everyday light." Carrying this overload without relief, Reagon sings, is "too much to ask" of any woman:

> There oughta be a woman can break
> Down, sit down, break down, sit down
> Like everybody else call it quits on Mondays
> Blues on Tuesdays, sleep until Sunday
> Down, sit down, break down, sit down.[13]

Jordan and Reagon value this emotional labor, but they also lament the price extracted by a mother's sacrifice for her children.

PAID DOMESTIC WORK

The domestic worker of "Oughta Be a Woman" represents an important historical figure, for domestic service has been the main entry point for women making the transition from unpaid to wage labor. That transition occurs at different historical moments across the world, and its impact depends on a woman's social position. Certain groups of women, often members of ethnic or racial minorities, take service jobs that relieve other women of household work.

Domestic service is not unique to modern societies. Historically, both men and women have performed domestic tasks for wealthy families. Under slavery, house servants assisted with cooking, cleaning, and child care. Farming families sometimes apprenticed older daughters to neighbors to continue the lessons in homemaking they first learned by assisting their own mothers. In commercial and industrializing societies the demand for domestic servants expanded. Urban middle-class families could afford household help, and their higher standards of cleanliness required it. Lower birth rates meant fewer daughters who could assist with this housework. During the 1800s the middle class in industrializing cities around the world came to rely on hired maids and nannies. The practice continues today, especially when mothers have jobs outside the home.

Migrants from the countryside to cities provide a pool of domestic workers whenever subsistence agriculture gives way to an industrial economy. In the United States unskilled white male migrants and immigrants found jobs in factories and mines in the 1800s. Although textile mills hired young women, the expansion of heavy industry, such as steel production, created jobs reserved primarily for men. Working-class women earned money providing personal services such as cleaning, either full- or part-time. "I choose housework," a servant explained, ". . . for the simple reason that young women look forward to the time when they will have housework of their own to do." Aside from preparation as a future housewife, live-in service provided food, lodging, and an introduction to urban life for impoverished migrants. "I came to a strange city and chose housework," another domestic recalled, "because it afforded me a home."[14] For all of these reasons, domestic service for women expanded along with migration, urban growth, and industrialization.

The rise of female service occurred internationally, though at different times. At the end of the 1700s up to half of all European women employed outside their homes worked as servants. Over the next century young unmarried women who moved to Victorian London from the countryside swelled the ranks of female servants, which doubled in the last half of the nineteenth century. Ethnicity and race strongly affected the composition of the female domestic labor force. In the United States, middle-class families in the 1800s hired Irish and Scandinavian immigrant women in the North, Mexican migrant women in the Southwest. When African Americans left the rural South after 1900, black women dominated domestic service in northern cities. When Latin American and Caribbean women immigrated to the United States after 1960, many found work as household maids. After 1950, women from the Latin American countryside entered urban economies with few options except domestic service in middle-class homes. In Mexico City, for example, they remained in domestic service for around seven years, and when they left, new rural migrants filled the vacated jobs. In the late twentieth century domestic service provided a major source of income for black women in South Africa; it was the second largest occupation after agriculture.

High turnover rates for domestic workers in each period of urbanization reflected migrants' views of service as a temporary vocation, to be practiced only until marriage or advancement to a better job. Few women wanted to remain in service because the job was both demanding and often demeaning. Live-in maids could be on call twenty-four hours a day. "You are mistress of no time of your own," one worker complained.[15] Even day workers faced long hours and low pay rates. An African American woman wrote in 1912 that she worked fourteen- to sixteen-hour days.

Moreover, the domestic work environment depended entirely on the personality of the housewife, which could range from authoritarian to maternalistic. With no job security, servants could be fired at the whim of their employer. The job was notoriously dangerous for young women. Well into the 1900s male household members impregnated servant girls with impunity, for the servant was usually blamed for her plight and dismissed. When twentieth-century labor unions and labor laws began to protect Western industrial workers, domestic servants enjoyed neither a minimum wage, sick leave, vacation with pay, nor bargaining power. For these reasons, most women considered working in another home the least desirable kind of employment. As one British servant recalled, "The system was a continuation of slavery, except that you were able to hand in your notice and leave instead of having to stay for life."[16]

Where racial barriers prevented other forms of employment, however, domestic service remained women's primary occupation. Because so many other jobs were closed to them until the 1960s, African American women in the United States worked as maids long after white women left these jobs. They continued to work after marriage to help support their families, since black men earned so little in the menial jobs available to them. For Japanese immigrants to the United States from 1910 to 1940, both language difficulty and a racially segregated labor market drew women to domestic service. For both groups even well-educated women could not find work in any other sector. Yet employers treated all maids as if they lacked intelligence and ambition. "They say do this, do this, how to do," a Japanese American domestic recalled. "I know already everything, but still people try to tell you different ways."[17] As Judith Rollins points out in her study of contemporary domestic workers, African American women often concealed the fact that they had children in college because it might threaten the status of their employers.

Ethnicity and race still structure the domestic workforce. Immigrant women enter labor markets through service jobs, although by the late twentieth century they worked not only in private homes but increasingly cleaning hotels, office buildings, or hospitals. In several U.S. cities, Hispanic, and Asian/Pacific Islander women filled between 75 and 90 percent of the jobs cleaning office buildings. In addition, a growing number of immigrant women nannies from developing countries care for the children of middle- and upper-class families in Europe, North America, and urban centers in other regions. In 1993, for example, public attention focused on the practice of professional women hiring immigrant nannies when lawyer Zoë Baird withdrew from consideration for the post of U.S. attorney general because she had employed a Latin American baby-sitter who was an illegal immigrant.

Especially if they are not legal immigrants, cannot speak the language, or cannot become citizens, foreign domestic workers can be highly vulnerable to exploitation and abuse. "They dictated to me everything that I should do," Rosalie Vista complained of her job caring for a family of eleven. "I could not stand the way they treated me. . . . They just shouted and insulted me."[18] For young and impoverished women from the Philippines, Sri Lanka, and other Asian countries who have been recruited as maids by employment agencies in Kuwait and Saudi Arabia, working conditions can be intolerable. Confined to their employers' homes, forced to work up to eighteen-hour days, and beaten by female as well as male employers if they resist, many of these women try to escape. Some find refuge in their national embassies, where new employers seek them out. Few can afford the passage home. One Filipina woman working in Saudi Arabia in the 1990s who could no longer tolerate her mistreatment turned to a man who offered to help her leave the country. When she refused to provide sex in return, he drugged and raped her.

Domestic service still provides an important foothold into the labor market for urban migrants, but as soon as sales and service jobs open, women flock to them. This shift to a consumer-based economy occurred gradually over the 1900s in Europe and the Americas. In Brazil, for example, one-half of working women were servants in 1900 but only one-fourth were in 1985. In the United States the proportion of wage-earning women engaged in domestic service declined from 20 percent in 1920 to under 3 percent in the 1990s.[19] In contrast, the proportion of women in domestic service remains high where economies offer few other options.

Along with its shrinking share of the female labor force in consumer-based economies, domestic service has changed considerably since the early period of industrialization. Employment agencies have begun to shift the nature of service, eliminating the personal interaction with homemakers and providing benefits for workers. A few cooperative cleaning services have been able to achieve greater control over work conditions. Domestic workers themselves have attempted to transform the role of servant into that of expert. In her study of Mexican American domestic

workers in the United States, Mary Romero observed myriad forms of ne-
gotiation to improve the job, ranging from clarification to confrontation
to quitting. "I'm not your maid," Angela Fernandez told the children of
her employer, "I'm your housekeeper." Mrs. Montoya echoed the theme:
"I figure I'm not there to be their personal maid. I'm there to do their
housecleaning—the upkeep of their house."[20]

WOMEN ON THE STREETS

Not all women who needed to earn cash became domestic servants.
From the early years of urban industrial life, mothers with small children
who could not leave home took in sewing or laundry. Some worked regularly, others only in times of dire economic need. Housewives could also
increase family income by providing food and lodging for boarders, many
of whom were new migrants to the city. Some mothers provided paid
child care for other working mothers.

Outside their homes, women marketed goods or services on city
streets. In industrializing New York City in the 1840s, poor women and
children could be found scavenging for discarded goods that they could
use or resell. In the 1990s women migrants to Latin American cities sold
fruit or other food in street stalls. From Mexico to South Africa, women
continue to peddle food, matches, and tourist goods to earn enough to
survive. This informal sector of the economy, characterized by part-time
and seasonal activity, provides very meager income and evades government regulation. Because economists rarely recognize this labor as part of
national productivity, they often underestimate the number of women
who are in fact working for pay.

While both men and women participate in this kind of street peddling, one occupation within the informal economy is highly skewed by
gender: prostitution. Some men do engage in the sale of sex to other
men, and impoverished boys have been particularly vulnerable to sexual
commerce. Historically and today, however, women have dominated the
ranks of sex workers. Just as women migrants sold goods and domestic
services in the informal sector of the economy, so too they marketed
sexual services. The expansion of prostitution and the conditions under

which prostitutes work have fueled feminist critiques of both sexual and economic exploitation.

The History of Prostitution

Sometimes called the "oldest profession," prostitution has rarely been accorded the status of a true profession, which is marked by educational and licensing requirements. In some settings, though, prostitutes have enjoyed social respectability. Ancient Babylonian and Greek cultures accorded status to temple prostitutes who served the gods and goddesses in a religious, rather than commercial, role. In Asia some courtesans enjoyed the respect of colleagues for the social and sexual skills provided for their patrons. More frequently, however, prostitution has been a disreputable and demeaned occupation. Forced on women who were either captured by conquering armies or sold into service by desperately poor families, it is widely condemned in law and religion. Nonetheless, in many premodern societies prostitution was not necessarily a lifelong status. In fifteenth-century France, for example, a prostitute could repent her past, enter a Magdalene home, and later marry respectably. Because daughters sold into sexual service by impoverished Chinese or Japanese families fulfilled an obligation to filial piety and sacrificed for their families, they too might eventually leave the trade and marry.

In the 1800s, however, the prostitute in European and American cities acquired a permanent identity as a "fallen woman," the antithesis of the pure, middle-class mother in the home. Viewed as a sexually depraved creature, to be shunned by all respectable women, the prostitute in fact protected the virtue of pure women. According to the concept of "necessary evil," society had to tolerate the existence of prostitutes because they siphoned off male lust. Brothels, an editorial explained in 1892, "are necessary in ministering to the passions of men who otherwise would be tempted to seduce young ladies of their acquaintance."[21] Because the boundary between pure and fallen woman mirrored racial and ethnic lines, it reinforced social hierarchy by ranking sexual purity by race.

The rapid expansion of commercial prostitution in industrializing societies exacerbated the stricter divide between pure and impure women. So great was the increase of prostitution during the 1800s that the spread of venereal disease created a public health crisis in the major Western metropolitan centers of London, Paris, and New York City. Reformers and government officials associated prostitutes with infection. According to a vice commission report, prostitutes carried "a disease to be feared with as great a horror as a leprous plague."[22] Nonetheless, sexual commerce grew wherever wage-earning male migrants lived apart from families and women sought income. Commercial prostitution seems to peak during the first stage of industrial growth, when men have greater choices for wage labor, and then decline when more service jobs open to women. Indeed, prostitutes seemed omnipresent wherever men congregated in early industrial England and America, in cities, on frontiers, or near military bases.

Women became prostitutes for a variety of reasons. Some enterprising women entrepreneurs established their own brothels and employed other women as residents. More typically, poor and working-class women who could not otherwise support themselves entered prostitution. "It was absolute want that drove me to it," a seventeen-year-old reported in 1856.[23] Some preferred the work to domestic service. Others had no choice, especially those "fallen women" who bore children outside marriage. As a group of American prostitutes asked in 1914, "How many citizens will give employment to women of our class?"[24] Neither housewives nor factory owners wanted to hire these women, and other workers often shunned them as well. Child prostitution has always drawn in the poorest and most vulnerable workers, whether in Victorian-era London or contemporary Bangkok. Thousands of young girls continue to perform sexual labor, some of them kidnapped, others sold by families into labor contracts.

Colonialism also affected the spread of prostitution. In the early 1900s prostitution flourished in Africa when colonialism removed men from their villages to work compounds. Officials tolerated an influx of prostitutes because they helped to stabilize the male workforce. In Kenya rural men who migrated to Nairobi for jobs could not bring their wives, who continued to farm at home. In the city prostitutes charged men for a range of domestic comforts once offered in their homes, including food, water, and a bed in which to sleep.

In multiracial societies the harshest conditions have been experienced by racial minority women. In the 1860s and 1870s Chinese women sold into prostitution in America worked between four to six years in the small "cribs," or rooms, that lined Chinatown alleys, servicing white men for a small fee per customer. Disease, despair, and early death took a large toll on these assembly line sex workers. After 1900 cities cracked down on tolerated vice districts, making street prostitutes more vulnerable to arrest. Although women of color represented less than half of all streetwalkers in the United States, they constituted 85 percent of those imprisoned for prostitution.

The Contemporary Business of Prostitution

Prostitutes continue to play an important role in modernizing economies. They provide sex for male workers, soldiers, and sailors and fuel a huge international sex industry. In the contemporary United States an estimated quarter million prostitutes service a million and a half customers each week. The gross annual revenue from prostitution ranges from $7 billion to $9 billion, not including the sale of pornographic depictions of sexual acts. In Indonesia estimates of annual profits from prostitution range from $1 billion to $3.5 billion. Australian police estimate that prostitution grosses $30 million a year there, while the sex industry accounts for 1 percent of Japan's gross national product (equal to its defense budget).

As capitalism expanded globally, so has sexual labor and its racial hierarchy. The contemporary rise of international entertainment zones has precedents in earlier colonial outposts, such as Havana before the Cuban revolution of 1959. A playland for wealthy Europeans and Americans, the city offered heterosexual and homosexual prostitution, along with alcohol, gambling, and drugs. In another former American colony, the Philippines, poor rural women flocked to U.S. military bases to earn low wages as bar girls and prostitutes. The Marcos dictatorship encouraged the so-called hospitality industry as a source of foreign income, and by the time these bases closed in the 1990s an estimated one hundred thousand Philippine women, including five thousand children, served as prostitutes. In the Philippines, Thailand, and South Korea a form of sexual tourism has now developed to serve some Asian but mostly European men seeking allegedly "docile" Asian women, either as mail-order brides or short-term prostitutes. As the brochure for one Dutch sex tourism company explains, men can find "little slaves who give real Thai warmth."[25]

Today, wherever poor women seek income, prostitution persists. In Calcutta Pushpa Das once worked as a domestic servant, but the $10 a month she earned could not support her unemployed husband, daughter, and other dependent relatives. When Das turned to prostitution, she could earn $50 a month. Women seeking income have produced new forms of regional labor migration. In the 1990s Egyptian prostitutes faced competition from Russian women who had lost their jobs with the economic restructuring from communism to capitalism. Migrating to the Middle East, blond Russian women represented an exotic racial other in the sexual marketplace. In Japan local prostitutes now face competition from Chinese immigrants, who can earn more selling sex to businessmen than they could in other jobs at home. In the words of one young woman, trained as a doctor in China but working as a prostitute in Tokyo, "Here, if you work hard, you can make money and get ahead. . . . You just have to be willing to work hard and take the tough jobs."[26]

During the transition to industrial life, the association of women and domesticity profoundly affected women's economic status. It still shapes which jobs women hold, the wages they can earn, and the double day of caretaking at home after paid labor. The legacy of unpaid work within families meant that domestic work performed for others tended to be devalued. Even nondomestic employers would justify lower female wages by assuming that all women depended on male breadwinners who earned a "family wage." When women worked, they reasoned, it was to earn "pin money" to purchase luxuries. Since not all men could support families, however, women's earnings often went directly to household expenses, but they were never enough to provide for self-support. In short, during the industrial era domesticity contributed to women's economic dependence. Ultimately, feminism would respond by mobilizing women workers and envisioning social policies to bridge unpaid and paid labor. But that political response awaited the massive entry of women into wage labor.

SEVEN

INDUSTRIALIZATION, WAGE LABOR, AND THE ECONOMIC GENDER GAP

Women's work is looked down upon. It's not really considered important, and you're not going to be paid wages for something that's considered trivial.
— OFFICE WORKER, UNITED STATES, 1979

Work strengthens a woman's position.
—FACTORY WORKER, EGYPT, 1985

In the 1970s a New England telephone operator named Chris recalled her work history. Her mother, the daughter of immigrants, had to quit school at age twelve to work in a textile mill. Determined that no daughter of hers would work in a factory, she insisted that Chris finish high school. Like many young women in the United States and Europe, Chris completed a commercial course so that she could get a better-paying job in an office. After graduation she found a clerical job at an insurance company, but "it was just like a factory. They had piecework and everything." The phone company was not much better, with constant surveillance and pressure to speed up the calls. Rather than protest, Chris noticed, workers took their frustrations out on each other. "Where can they go?" she asked rhetorically. "It's either a factory or an office. There are not that many things that a woman can get into. Most women have been trained to feel that this is all you should expect."[1] But in the 1970s women like Chris began to expect more. Then a working mother in her thirties, she enrolled in a community college with hopes of becoming a social worker, one of the few professions dominated by women.

Chris' story reflects two equally important historical trends in the past century: expanding opportunities for women to earn wages and persistent limits on their careers. Working women, and especially working mothers, have reshaped family life, the workplace, and social policy. By the year 2000 women accounted for over a third of the world's paid workers and up to half of the workforce in the United States, western Europe, Russia, and Australia. Wherever married women entered the paid labor force, they challenged the artificial divide between home and work. Wage earning potentially weakened the patriarchal family by providing women a measure of economic independence or at least greater leverage within their families. Despite their long hours in paid work outside the home, however, working women can only rarely support themselves. Their jobs cluster in "female" sectors of the economy: light manufacturing, clerical and sales, or providing services once offered in their homes, such as serving food or caring for children. In the professions as well, they have not had the same opportunities for advancement that men enjoy. And women's wages have never been equal to those of men, even in the same job categories.

Equally important, when women participate in paid labor, they continue to care for others in their homes, particularly husbands and children. The legacy of unpaid work in the home perpetuates economic inequality in several ways. It masks women's full economic contributions, it creates the double day for women workers, and it leads to perceptions that women are not dedicated to their jobs. The continual devaluation of caring labor in the home also ignores the truly interdependent relationships within families. Underlying the contradictions of contemporary women's wage labor is a history in which women have been viewed first as women, then as workers.

FROM FACTORY GIRLS TO
WORKING MOTHERS

Women have entered the formal labor market for two main reasons: employers' expanding demand for cheap workers and the greater availability of women seeking income. Commercial and industrial growth required a larger workforce. Since most men had job choices, they could demand higher wages. Employers could cut costs by filling new jobs with cheaper female workers. At the same time, more women became available for wage labor because they were having fewer children than in the past. As children ceased to be an economic asset to families in industrializing economies, birth rates declined. With fewer children to tend at home, first older daughters and later their mothers sought wage labor. The expanding demand for cheap labor, along with the increasing availability of female workers, drew women first into textile mills and later into clerical, sales, and other service jobs. This process continues today in developing nations, so that women's participation in wage labor now affects families throughout the world.

Labor Needs and Women Workers

The initial stage in this movement from housework to wage work took place in western Europe and the United States after 1800. Industrial production began to make finished goods from raw products, such as cloth and clothing from the cotton harvested by southern slaves. Textile production was critical to the growth of world capitalism, and women's labor played a central role in this phase of industrialization. British women had traditionally performed much of the spinning, weaving, and sewing within their families. After 1800 many of them followed these crafts into the new textile mills, working long hours at pay rates significantly lower than men's. Single women who lived at home, as well as some married women, swelled the ranks of factory hands. By the 1850s, almost 60 percent of the workers in the British textile industry were female. Similarly, the first textile mills in the United States welcomed young rural women who tended the looms, while men earned higher wages as mechanics or overseers. In the 1820s these "factory girls" lived in supervised dormitories for a few years, saving their wages for the time they would leave the mills. "Now soon you'll see me married, to a handsome little man," went the words to one of the factory girls' songs. "Then I'll say to you factory girls, come see me when you can!"[2]

The surge in women's participation as factory workers in England and America declined around the middle of the nineteenth century. After the passage of the British Factory Act of 1833 and subsequent laws limiting work hours and child labor, fewer women entered the factories. In addition, with the rise of trade unions, male workers insisted that they should earn a "family wage" that would enable them to support their wives at home. Yet women continued to produce textiles as pieceworkers in their homes or in tenement sweatshops. In New York, London, Paris, and Berlin, women sewed garment parts or made hats and gloves for a few cents each. Though suitable for married women caring for young children, piecework in the home was a notoriously harsh trade, with low pay that required ten- to twelve-hour days to earn enough for survival.

Over time and place, textile production drew rural women into manufacturing jobs. In the United States cotton mills moved to the southern states after 1900, employing members of poor white families, including women and children. Now southern factory workers sang their own lament: "Hard times, cotton mill girls, hard times everywhere." At the same time, when Mexico, Brazil, and Argentina began to industrialize, their first textile factories hired female workers from the countryside. During World War I, for example, Luiza Ferreira de Medeiros began working in a textile factory in Brazil. Her workday lasted from 6 A.M. to 5 P.M. daily. In the 1920s Indian women toiled in textile factories, and young Chinese women worked twelve-hour days in the Shanghai cotton mills. Like the earliest textile workers, they earned wages for several years before returning to their villages to marry.

Even after textile factories created paid jobs for women, piecework at home continued to provide an important source of family income. A Greek garment worker explained the pressures of home work in the 1980s. After paying for thread, electricity, rent, and maintenance of her sewing machine, she could earn as much as a factory laborer only by working fast and for long hours. "When you spend sixteen hours working at home at least nine have to be pure work if you really want to break even." Though taxing, working at home did avoid the supervision of factory work, where "you have so many people above you controlling you and treating you like a 'thing.' "[3]

Textile factories continue to employ women throughout the world, but the next stage of economic growth created yet another demand for low-paid workers, this time in clerical and sales jobs. Although heavy industry such as steel manufacturing employed only male workers, new technologies were transforming the nature of business. By the late 1800s the railroad, telegraph, and telephone fostered the amalgamation of local businesses into national corporations in both the United States and western Europe. This process of consolidation created huge bureaucracies that required an army of clerks. Literate white women filled the new jobs in business firms. In Europe the expansion of government services created jobs for women as postal clerks and telephone operators. Almost a third of European working women held service sector jobs by the 1930s. At the same time, the growth of mass marketing created a demand for a retail sales force. Women swelled the ranks of salesclerks in the newly established department stores of Western nations.

Professional jobs were also opening to educated women for the first time. A bureaucratic society required literate workers, so public schools and public libraries became essential institutions. Once middle-class women in the United States and western Europe could attend college, they sought professional jobs as teachers and librarians. Although men once performed these tasks, women cost less and seemed well suited to working with children. By 1900 women teachers outnumbered men by a ratio of two to one. Outside the West as well, educated women gained access to the professions in sex-segregated jobs, such as teaching and social work. In South Asia, for example, educated women became public health officials, largely serving women and children.

As the case of teachers suggests, when women entered the paid labor force, they continued to be viewed as women first, workers second. This identity has shaped the meaning and the value placed on women's labor. Many of the jobs created in the past century could be viewed as an extension of women's familial work. Along with white-collar jobs in offices, classrooms, and department stores, a pink-collar sector employs women as health care aides, beauticians, and waitresses. In all of these jobs wages remain low in part because the work is typed as female, in part because employers consider women secondary earners in families headed by male workers.

Which Women Work for Wages?

The economic processes that draw women into paid labor occur unevenly across the regions of the world. More women earn wages where industrialization first emerged, where service sectors have expanded, where states have explicitly recruited female workers, and where employers or states provide social services such as child care. Even in countries with similar economies, however, cultural attitudes affect women's labor force participation. While rates vary across the globe, the overall trend is toward women's participation in paid labor through much of the adult life cycle. (See Appendix D.)

The U.S. labor force illustrates women's increasing participation in wage labor. In 1800 the U.S. census listed under 5 percent of all women as gainfully employed. By 1900 that figure had climbed to 21 percent, and by 2000 it reached 60 percent, or around 40 percent of all paid workers. Figures for other industrial economies are also striking. By the 1920s women constituted over half of the paid workers in Japan. The Soviet Union could not have industrialized in the twentieth century without women's workforce participation. By the 1960s, 80 percent of working-age women in the USSR were employed, and by 1990 women represented half of the labor force in the former Soviet Union. In Europe during the 1990s the proportion of women in the paid labor force ranged from over half in Great Britain and Scandinavia to around a third in southern Europe. Since men's wage labor has declined slightly, the work experience of men and women is becoming more similar.[4]

In contrast, where agriculture dominates the economy, fewer women earn wages. Only one-fifth of Latin American wage laborers were women in 1970, although that figure increased to one-third by 2000. In much of the Middle East women's share of the labor force remains low, under 30 percent in 2000. Keep in mind that all of these figures underestimate women's paid labor force participation, since so many women continue to work in the informal sector of the economy. The UN also measures "total economic activity," which includes more of this production but still excludes unpaid domestic or volunteer labor. (See Appendix D.)

The national figures do not tell the whole story about which women work for wages and when. The impact of racial discrimination on family income creates unique work patterns. In the United States, African American women long exceeded all other groups of female wage laborers, with twice the overall rate for women in 1900. Because African American men earned so little in the few jobs open to them, and because they were more likely to experience seasonal or chronic unemployment, black women had to help support their families. Until the 1940s race remained more important than gender in determining whether a woman worked in the United States. After World War II, however, the race gap narrowed. White married middle-class women sought paying jobs to help their families afford homes and consumer products, or to save to send their children to college. More white women supported themselves as single or divorced mothers. By 1980 the black-white race gap among women workers had almost disappeared, with about half of each group working for wages. By 1999, 64 percent of black women were in the workforce, compared to 60 percent of white women. Other cultural gaps persist, in part because ethnic groups differ in their views of women's wage earning or in their birth rates. In the United States, for example, a higher proportion of Asian American than Puerto Rican women worked for wages in the 1990s. (See Appendix B.)

Along with the young, single workers first drawn into the labor force, older and married women now earn wages, and so do mothers of young children. In 1890 under 5 percent of married women in the United States worked for wages; in 1980 half of them did, as did half the married women in Great Britain. In 1995 the U.S. paid labor force included 61 percent of all married women (compared to 77 percent of all men). The U.S. labor force participation rate of mothers has increased every decade since 1950. While African American mothers had been laborers for decades, by the 1980s white women with both school-age and preschool children had joined them. By 1995 two-thirds of all mothers, and over half of the mothers with children under age two, earned wages.[5] (See Appendix C.)

Another way to think about this important historical shift is through the life cycles of generations of women. In 1800 a married woman in the United States could expect to live to around age forty and bear more than seven children. In 1900 her great-granddaughter lived into her fifties and had only four children. By 2000 that woman's great-granddaughter could expect to live to age eighty but would bear only two children. Over each century, women's reproductive labors dropped by half while their life span expanded. As a result, married women now have many more years without child-care duties. Although the dates differ for other industrial countries, the direction of change is the same. Since 1900 birth rates have fallen while life expectancy and women's wage labor have increased throughout the industrial world. (See Appendices D and E.) In the United States and Japan, for example, over half of all married women now work for pay. In Sweden over 80 percent of married women earned wages in the 1980s, compared with just under half in the 1960s.

Even during their child-rearing years, however, mothers increasingly enter the paid workforce. For some, divorce and single parenthood make jobs an economic necessity. Births to unmarried women have tripled in many industrial countries since 1970.[6] In the United States about two-thirds of single mothers and three-fourths of divorced women earned wages in the 1990s. Even in two-parent families, higher costs of living, desires for a higher standard of living, and hopes for their children's futures make two wage earners a necessity. "The reason I turned out to work," a Mrs. Turnbull of England explained in the 1960s, "was that my husband was only on £8 a week and there were five of us to keep."[7]

Women's wages have become critical to family support throughout the world. In Ghana women maintain a third of the households with children. In the Philippines women provide a third of the cash income for their families while continuing to contribute unpaid household labor that brings their full contribution to over half of household support. As in industrial societies, women work both to help support their families and to improve the lives of their children. According to the U.N. Population Fund, "Parents increasingly recognize the need for education to improve their children's chances in life."[8] Mothers take jobs to pay for school fees and uniforms, especially in poorer countries that have had to cut their educational budgets.

As families increasingly depend on the wages of women as well as men, attitudes toward women's paid labor slowly change. As a British husband who once felt that his wife's "place was in the home" recalled, "I modified my views in the 1960s. I accepted the fact that she really needed some other interest outside the home."9 Opinion polls reflect the shift. In Great Britain beliefs that husbands should be breadwinners and wives should care for their families declined by about half from the 1980s to the 1990s. Similarly, U.S. polls show that disapproval of women's work outside the home dropped significantly.10

Yet ambivalence toward working mothers persists as well. Among South Asian women interviewed in East London in the 1990s, over a third felt that women should remain in the home to care for their families. Echoing broader opinion around the world, one of these women explained that "she's the one who has the children and she's the one who has to breast-feed them, and so she should stay at home and be the housewife."11 In the United States a large majority of women and men agree that a woman can be both a good mother and successful in a high-paying career. Yet most also feel it would be better for a mother to stay home and take care of the children, even when her income is needed.12

Cultural attitudes have not kept up with economic realities. Despite desires for mothers to remain at home, women are unlikely to leave the paid labor force. While some women initially took paid jobs because of economic need, a recent survey of American workers found that only 31 percent of female workers (and 21 percent of male workers) would remain at home if they could afford to. In her study of workers at a "family-friendly" corporation, sociologist Arlie Hochschild found that some women in the U.S. found the workplace more appealing and less stressful than their homes. "I usually come to work early just to get away from the house," one mother of two explained. Since she had to perform most of the housework at home, she found that "the more I get out of the house, the better I am. It's a terrible thing to say, but that's the way I feel."13 Although the notion that women are temporary workers continues to influence wages, promotions, and social policy, it no longer accurately describes the lives of most women in most industrialized nations.

THE GLOBAL ASSEMBLY LINE

In the 1990s nineteen-year-old Adelia Ramírez Hernández took a job in an American-owned electronics factory in Reynosa, Mexico, earning $30 for her forty-five-hour week. She was one of a million and a half women who worked in export manufacturing plants in developing countries, almost half of them for multinational corporations, usually based in the United States. These plants contribute to the economic development of largely rural nations in Southeast Asia, Africa, and Latin America.

With the end of colonialism after World War II, many newly independent nations remained economically dependent on the West. To bring much-needed capital into these areas, governments in Hong Kong, Taiwan, and Mexico encouraged local companies to manufacture goods for export abroad, rather than consumption at home. Since the 1950s these governments have offered tax and tariff incentives for foreign factories to locate within designated areas called free-trade zones. They also allowed foreign ownership of these companies, encouraging Western-based multinational corporations to move their production offshore to save costs. In the 1960s, with the help of loans from the World Bank and the International Monetary Fund, production of computer parts and garments increasingly moved to countries such as Sri Lanka. By the late 1970s, American and Japanese factory owners were relocating their plants to Mexico or Southeast Asia.

Sometimes called "runaway shops," these factories escaped minimum wage and other labor laws as well as environmental regulations. As a result, they paid low wages, had lower production costs, and reaped higher profits. At a time when American workers earned $3 to $5 an hour, Mexican workers in the *maquiladoras* (subcontracting shops) on the border earned only $3 to $5 each *day*. Young single women such as Adelia Ramírez Hernández continue to fill the demand for cheap labor in Mexico, as they do in Southeast Asia. About 80 percent of the global assembly line workers in electronics and clothing factories are young women between the ages of thirteen and twenty-five. In Asia, where the majority of them work, most are unmarried, though Latin American and Caribbean women factory workers, who are slightly older, are more likely to be married or divorced than those in Asia. Some of these Latin American women have migrated to factory jobs from rural areas, and some attended high school. Most of them are not from the poorest families, for those women still work in domestic service and prostitution.

These women factory workers earn much less than men—sometimes only half of male wages. Their jobs, however, provide better wages and more security than they can find in agriculture or the informal economy. Women's factory wages often help support families. A study of Hong Kong in the 1970s showed that 88 percent of women workers gave over half of their earnings to their parents. Families might use this money to enable sons to go to school, thus perpetuating gender inequality. But wage earning allowed daughters more leverage in their households: They became exempt from domestic labor, and they gained greater control over their futures by choosing their own spouses. A married Egyptian worker emphasized this link between her factory earnings and authority at home: "Work strengthens a woman's position. The woman who works doesn't have to beg her husband for every piaster she needs. She can command respect in her home and can raise her voice in any decision."[14]

Wage earning may challenge gender subordination, but the global assembly line leaves many forms of hierarchy undisturbed. Some women workers themselves strive to retain customary gender relations. In Bangladesh, for example, women who observe the gender seclusion of *purdah* cannot wear the tentlike *burkah* when they go to work, yet some affirm rather than abandon the system. "The best *purdah* is the *burkah* within oneself, the *burkah* of the mind," one factory worker explained.[15] Many employers base their hiring practices on ideas about innate qualities of gender and race. As one Malaysian government official explained, "The manual dexterity of the Oriental female is famous the world over. Her hands are small and she works fast with extreme care. . . . Who, therefore, could be better qualified by nature and inheritance, to contribute to the efficiency of the bench assembly production line than the Oriental girl?"[16] Employers also invoke gender stereotypes when they hold beauty contests for women workers. At one Mexican *maquiladora* the management announced a bikini contest as a "benefit for the workers," some of whom felt insulted enough to file complaints.[17] Many employers assume that because women in certain developing countries have been socialized to be subordinate they will make docile workers, unlikely to complain or unionize.

This concern about employee protest is well founded. Assembly line work is extremely taxing, requiring intense visual concentration and physical stamina. Companies set quotas for production, and rush orders can mean forced overtime with long, stressful hours spent assembling computer parts or garments. One South Korean study showed that most of the electronics workers had severe eye problems within one year on the job. High-tech data entry workers also complain. "Everything you do has to go on a time sheet. I personally call it slavery," one Caribbean woman worker concluded.[18] Women working in factories with few safety regulations risk accidents and exposure to toxic substances. As a sewing machine operator wrote, "When [apprentices] shake the waste threads from the clothes, the whole room fills with dust, and it is hard to breathe. Since we've been working in such dusty air, there have been increasing numbers of people getting tuberculosis, bronchitis, and eye diseases. Since we are women, it makes us so sad when we have pale, unhealthy, wrinkled faces like dried-up spinach."[19]

The global economy affects women workers not only in developing countries but also in the industrialized West. Runaway shops can mean lower wages for all workers, while the threat to move production offshore can undermine efforts to unionize. When women immigrate to the West they may find work in electronics factories in Silicon Valley that resemble the global assembly line. At the same time, many immigrant women continue to find employment as did earlier generations, sewing garments in unregulated sweatshops, where they earn less than the minimum wage, and returning at night to care for their homes and children. In the words of one Asian woman immigrant, who could have been speaking for the women of the world, "After sewing, laundry, cleaning and cooking, I have no breath left to sing."[20]

FEMINIZATION AND
PROFESSIONAL WORK

Even when women enter male-dominated professions, gender ideology creates a significant divide in the meaning of labor. The history of the professions in the West illustrates that when significant numbers of women gain access, a profession is likely to become "feminized." Teaching, nursing, and librarianship were feminized by the late 1800s, as were clerical, sales, and bank teller positions in the 1900s. Feminization creates positions for more women but with lower pay and status than that of the men who once worked in each of these jobs. Once women outnumber men, a profession loses prestige and pay rates deteriorate. At the same time, gender hierarchy persists, for the men who remain hold the best-paid and most prestigious positions as supervisors and managers.

Teaching provides a good example of an occupation that tipped from male to female as the need for cheap workers expanded. After 1800 commercial growth in the United States required literate workers. Local governments established schools to support universal primary and later secondary education; compulsory school laws enforced attendance. To control growing expenses, school boards began to hire women, and by the 1880s the male schoolmaster had given way to the female schoolteacher. The feminization of teaching rested upon gender ideology: Women were considered well suited to work with children in low-paid teaching positions, while men monopolized the offices of principals and school superintendents. Furthermore, schoolteachers in the United States once had to resign after marriage, reinforcing the idea that woman's primary work remained in the home.

The process of drawing women into the lower ranks of education recurred in other countries undergoing the transition to commercial and industrial economies. In the Soviet Union from the 1940s through the 1970s women held 80 percent of primary-school teaching and administrative jobs but only 30 percent of secondary-school administrative positions. At the end of the twentieth century women in Denmark held

60 percent of the staff positions in schools but only 16 percent of senior posts.

Some professions proved more resistant to women's encroachments, including medicine and law. Women once served as healers in many cultures, and midwives continue to attend births. By the 1860s, however, the professionalization of Western medicine created an exclusively white male domain. In England and France, male students physically barred and taunted women who tried to study medicine. Only the Russian government encouraged women to become doctors because the need there was so great. In the United States most medical schools and professional organizations refused to admit women and African Americans. The American Medical Association did not admit female physicians until 1915.

In response to exclusionary admission practices in the United States, both women and African Americans founded their own medical schools. The New England Female Medical College graduated 364 women physicians before 1900, including Rebecca Lee, the first black woman doctor in the United States. The women doctors in turn established clinics and hospitals that served primarily female patients. Because of this separatist strategy, 6 percent of the doctors in the United States were women at the beginning of the twentieth century (compared with 10 percent in Russia). After 1900, when male medical schools began to admit a small number of women, the women's colleges declined. Although medical school applications from women soared, strict quotas at formerly all-male schools restricted women's enrollment to 5 percent of the student body. Thus the integration of medical education in the United States actually halted the increase in female physicians. Only after feminist pressure forced the end of quotas in the 1960s did women in the United States achieve full access to medical education.

American women also tried to enter the legal profession in the 1800s, but they met strong resistance from law schools, employers, and the courts. One brave woman from Illinois, Myra Bradwell, took her case to the Supreme Court, which ruled against her in 1873. "The constitution of the family organization," the Court explained, ". . . indicates the domestic sphere as that which properly belongs to the domain and functions of womanhood . . . [and] is repugnant to the idea of a woman adopting a distinct and independent career from that of her husband."[21]

After women gained entry to law schools in the twentieth century, quotas kept their numbers small, and employers discriminated against even the most highly qualified women graduates. In the 1950s, for example, no law firm would hire a distinguished Stanford Law School graduate named Sandra Day O'Connor. Ultimately she went on to become the first female associate justice on the U.S. Supreme Court.

In the 1960s and 1970s, encouraged by the revival of feminism, women in the United States and Europe applied to professional schools in record numbers and quotas began to fall. Between 1970 and 1990 the proportion of female lawyers and judges in the United States increased from 5 percent to 24 percent. In Great Britain over half of the new solicitors during the 1990s were women. Occupational segregation persisted, however, in the kinds of legal work open to women. Female lawyers remain in the lower ranks of the profession because they cluster in low-prestige, lower-paying jobs as public defenders or family law attorneys. Holding age and qualifications constant, men still fared far better than women. In one U.S. study eligible men were twice as likely to become partners in their firms than eligible women. Women solicitors hold only one-fourth of the partnerships in British law firms. The divergence affects income. Although entry-level lawyers earn similar salaries, over the course of their careers a gender gap emerges, in part because men are more likely to be promoted. In the United States, even as women increased their share of law degrees, their earnings ratio declined.

In medicine as well, the surge of women doctors did not preclude occupational segregation. With the elimination of gender quotas, women in the United States entered medical school in record numbers. By 1976 almost 25 percent of all medical students were female, and by the 1990s women made up half of the entering class at many medical schools. Similarly, in Great Britain the proportion of women medical students increased from under a fourth in 1968 to over half in 1991. In both countries, however, women are often encouraged to choose family practice and pediatrics, while men continue to dominate higher-paying specialties such as surgery. Much of the income differential between male and female physicians arises from their different specializations.

Occupational segregation persists in a variety of professions. As women enter professional jobs men continue to hold the higher-prestige, higher-paying positions; most women gain access only to the more routinized jobs—the part-time instructors, the legal clinic workers. Through a process known as deskilling, a job that once carried prestige drops to a lower status within a gender hierarchy. Women often perform the routinized, deskilled tasks for less pay. The earliest computer programmers, who were male, belonged to the category of technical workers; as women entered the field, the work they performed became reclassified as clerical. As women became pharmacists they found lower-paid jobs in retail stores, while male pharmacists tended to work in research or management.

Academia also illustrates the persistence of a gender hierarchy within the professions. Although women's share of faculty positions doubled in the United States between 1960 and 1990 (to 40 percent), women are overrepresented in less prestigious schools and among part-time workers in non-tenure-track jobs. In 1997 white males held 70 percent of the full-time tenured faculty positions in the United States, and at elite universities such as Stanford and Harvard, only 15 percent of tenured professors are women. The tenured staff at medical schools are still predominantly white and male. Reviewing the U.S. data on women in academia in 1998, Virginia Valian concluded that "since 1976 there has been zero progress in closing the tenure gap between men and women."[22]

In some countries that academic gap is even wider. During the era of the Soviet Union, despite state encouragement for women's entry into scientific research, a clear gender hierarchy emerged in research and teaching institutes: Women held one-fourth of the junior appointments, 10 percent of the senior appointments, and only 2 percent of academic professorships in science. In the post-Soviet era women constitute slightly over half of the college faculty in Ukraine, but they remain at the lowest levels of lecturers and assistants. In the 1990s only 4 percent of professors in Germany and under 10 percent in Japan and Korea were female. Whether drawn into the learned professions under communism or capitalism, women occupy an inferior economic position.

If women's job categories merely differed from men's, the feminization of the professions would not necessarily contribute to economic inequality. If teaching had carried the same recompense as medicine in

1900, the fact that more women taught and more men practiced medicine would not have been problematic. The process of feminization, however, has involved a devaluing of tasks simply because they are performed by women. Like the New Guinea culture in which women cultivate sweet potatoes and men raise the higher-prestige yams, modern societies attach greater value to male activities. Gender ideology divides the professions, as it divides the workforce in general, creating inequality not only in status but also in wages.

LABOR FORCE SEGREGATION AND THE WAGE GAP

As women pour into the paid labor force in expanding economies, they do not necessarily compete for men's jobs. Rather, workers typically enter specialized labor markets that are segregated largely by sex and race. In 1960, for example, only 3 percent of skilled (blue-collar) workers in the United States were female, and only 2 percent of service (pink-collar) workers were male. In 1990, out of 260 occupational categories in the United States, only 12 percent were sexually integrated. The majority of jobs were either male- or female-dominated.

Female jobs vary by regional economies, but in every region most jobs are sex typed. In developed market economies almost 80 percent of women workers can be found in service sector jobs, such as teachers, health care workers, or waitresses, with about 15 percent in industry and the remainder in agriculture. Throughout the world, women wage earners dominate as child care workers, nurses, and primary-school teachers. Jobs sometimes typed as female in one culture may be considered male in another. In the Soviet Union most doctors were women, but the profession carried low status and low pay. In North America women dominate in the garment industry and as bank tellers. In China they harvest cotton and rice. In Southeast Asia they work in textile or electronics plants.

Race and ethnicity further divide the workforce, creating internal job ghettos. Women from minority groups cluster in domestic service or factory jobs, while women from dominant groups have greater options as professionals and managers. In South Africa, for example, black women predominate in agricultural and domestic service, while white women represent two-thirds of all teachers and 85 percent of all social workers. In the United States, immigrant, Native American, and African American women work as nurse's aides and Chinese American women work as textile operatives, while women of European backgrounds are secretaries, teachers, and nurses.

This sexually and racially segregated labor force creates many of the economic inequalities that feminists challenge. Changing these patterns is a daunting task, given their deep historical roots. Employers first hired women in large part because they could pay them less than men. They assumed that women workers earned supplemental wages but did not have to support themselves or their families. Since employers expected women to leave the labor market when they married or had children, they saw little reason to advance them. In short, women workers constituted a secondary labor force, viewed differently from male wage earners who were, or would become, heads of households. Women's very economic advantage in the labor market—that they worked for less pay and did not seek advancement—created their disadvantage. In practice, of course, individual women do need to support themselves and their children, and women often aspire to better jobs. But the view of women as secondary workers affects all women in the labor force.

Occupational segregation contributes to the persistent gender gap in wages. Although this gap has narrowed over time, it continues to reflect unequal labor practices. In 1900 women in the United States earned on average around 50 cents for every dollar earned by a man; by 1950 the ratio had increased to 60 cents, and by 2000 American women earned approximately 75 cents for every male-earned dollar. The wage gap is narrower in other industrial nations in which public policies support women workers. During the 1980s and 1990s women's share of male income was 90 percent in Sweden and Australia and around 80 percent in France and the United Kingdom. Although women in the USSR once averaged 70 percent of men's earnings, in postcommunist Russia their earnings fell to 40 percent of men's. Yet socialist governments do not necessarily ensure higher earnings. In the 1990s women in China earned 59 percent of men's wages. Women in the European Union (EU) nations as a whole fared much better, earning three-fourths of male income. Much of the EU gap can be explained because men held better-paying manual jobs and women dominated lower-paid clerical jobs.

Even without occupational segregation, however, the wage gap persists. In 1990 Japanese women in manufacturing jobs earned less than half of what their male coworkers made. In the United States saleswomen earn 52 cents for every dollar a salesman takes home. Whenever women enter male-dominated jobs, the earnings gap is wide, but when men enter female-dominated fields as nurses or secretaries, they actually earn more than women.[23] Professional workers face a wage gap as well. Women who graduate from business school earn 12 percent less than their male classmates. Women physicians in the United States take in 82 percent of male doctors' earnings. One study of Stanford University graduates found that within similar jobs, and holding constant the number of hours worked each week, women still earned only 75 percent of male earnings. Although younger women workers often receive wages similar to men's, over the life cycle the gap increases.

The wage gap, like the segregated labor force, has historically reflected race as well as gender hierarchies, but gender has become more important over time. In 1940 white women earned 61 cents, black men 45 cents, and black women 23 cents to the white male dollar. In 1976 black men earned 75 cents, but white women 59 cents, and black women 56 cents to the white male dollar. Holding education constant, gender still influenced income more than race. For example, college-educated Hispanic women earned 62 percent and college-educated Hispanic men 75 percent of white male earnings. These figures can be confusing, but the overall picture at the close of the twentieth century showed that white males in the United States enjoyed almost twice the income of Hispanic women, a third more than white and African American women, and almost a quarter more than minority men. While racial differences persist, gender has become a more salient factor in the U.S. wage gap.

EXPLAINING THE WAGE GAP

How feminists and public officials respond to the wage gap depends in large part on how they understand its causes. Do women choose to remain in lower-paying jobs, or do employers discriminate to keep them from advancement? Is discrimination conscious and malicious, or do cultural ideas about gender inadvertently perpetuate job segregation and the wage gap? Is the economic gender gap a permanent, structural force, or are attitudes and workplace practices malleable?

To some economists the sexually segregated labor force makes good sense for both employers and women workers. From the perspective of employers, women may be temporary or inefficient workers, given their household and maternal work. As less valuable workers, they receive lower wages. From the perspective of women who may choose to leave the workforce and raise children, entering lower-paying jobs makes sense because these jobs require less training. Why invest in a career that will be interrupted by childbearing? Assumptions about employee choice recur in many cultures. For example, many Japanese companies have distinct career tracks: All men enter the managerial track, which requires overtime that cuts into family life. Until 1985 all women had to enter the second track, which involved routinized work without promotion but more time for family. Even women university graduates had no promotion possibilities. Although equal-rights laws now allow women to choose the "male" track, they know they are giving up expectations of family life if they want economic advancement.

The theory that women employees choose less demanding jobs has been influential in the United States. It provided a successful legal defense when the U.S. Equal Employment Opportunity Commission filed a suit against the large retailer Sears, Roebuck and Company. Saleswomen at Sears earned lower commissions than did salesmen. The company argued that women rationally chose sales jobs involving products with lower commissions because selling high-ticket items required long evening hours apart from their families. Rather than a result of employer discrimination, the company claimed, the gender disparity in commissions was a product of the free choice of workers. In 1986 a district court ruled in favor of Sears.

The arguments that women workers either deserve or choose lower-paying jobs are deeply flawed, however. For one, the view of women as less efficient workers rests on erroneous assumptions. Women may temporarily stop working to bear children, but that does not mean that they are less productive than women or men who remain in the labor force. Reentry workers, it turns out, are more productive than entry-level workers. It would be more rational for an employer to hire a mother who is returning to work than a young unskilled worker. Second, simply having family responsibilities does not affect incomes across the board. When middle-class men increase their share of housework, their earnings do not decline. Working-class women also maintain their wage levels even as they maintain their homes, and African American women with children tend to earn more money than those without children. Something other than choosing to perform domestic tasks must be affecting white women's salaries. Moreover, holding constant the factors of age, educational experience, hours worked for pay or spent in child care, and length of time in the workforce, the wage gap does not go away. Women in the same jobs, with the same backgrounds, working the same hours, and with the same domestic and parental duties as men earn 75 to 90 percent of men's wages.

More plausible is the finding of a 1981 National Academy of Sciences study that employer discrimination explains up to 50 percent of the wage gap in the United States. Employers perpetuate the segregated labor force when they base their expectations of workers not on individual performance but on group stereotypes. Once hired, members of certain groups (such as white males) are given internal promotions because they are assumed to be high producers. Members of other groups, such as women and minorities, are believed to be less productive; they are relegated to the most strongly sex- and race-stereotyped jobs. In the phenomenon known as "crowding," women who enter the labor force are not necessarily competing openly for jobs; rather, women and minority men often compete with each other at the lower end of the job scale. The existence of this artificially enlarged pool of workers who are excluded from the best jobs helps keep their wages low.

Even slight employer bias can set off a vicious cycle that perpetuates inequality. Imagine that an economically irrational distaste for women as primary workers leads an employer to hire more-expensive male workers. To make up for paying more to these men, the employer has to pay less to the women who are hired. Once women enter these lower-paid, dead-end jobs, they are more likely to choose to leave their unrewarding and unrewarded positions, creating a self-fulfilling prophecy. Paid less in dead-end jobs, women learn to act like dead-end workers, while men get better, higher-paying jobs. Such was the case historically for secretaries, who once had no chance of promotion and dreamed about escape from their jobs through marriage.

According to feminist economists such as Heidi Hartmann and Myra Strober, the structures of capitalism and patriarchy combine to perpetuate discrimination against women workers. For one, women's cheap labor is critical to increasing profits, since women represent a "reserve army" of workers who compete with each other rather than with men. But these structures also contribute to maintaining male power over women, both in the family and in the workplace. For example, capitalism supports patriarchy in the family in another vicious cycle: Because women get low-paid jobs, they are economically dependent on men in their families. As lower-paid workers with less leverage at home, women must take on more responsibility for housework and child care. Given their double day, women often get low-paid, secondary-sector jobs that make them more dependent on the men in their families.

The patriarchal family serves capitalism as well. Women's domestic labor plays a large part in allowing men to be productive workers earning high wages. Women literally reproduce the labor supply—through unpaid childbearing and household labors. Many men who succeed at work do so with the support of wives who perform most of their domestic work. Nine out of ten corporate executives in the United States have nonworking spouses, while women executives only rarely have a nonworking spouse running the household and taking care of their children. In a sense, women workers are at a disadvantage because they do not have wives. The patriarchal family also serves capitalism when it siphons off protest from male breadwinners who may feel powerless on the job but know they have power over women in the home. As sociologist Barbara

Reskin points out, men maintain their gender power when they exclude women from the best jobs. Finally, structural discrimination that keeps women and minority men in competition for a limited group of jobs undermines worker solidarity, weakening the chance that unions can challenge employers over wages, benefits, and work conditions.

Gender Ideology in the Workplace

Structural discrimination operates through the everyday practices of individuals. A good example are the social practices that can create informal barriers to hiring or promoting women and minorities. The men's-club atmosphere in certain jobs, ranging from blue-collar trades to surgery to executive boards, makes it hard for women to be taken as seriously as men. One successful female investment banker could not make the social contacts necessary for promotion in part because she found herself excluded from the male-only excursions to golf courses and strip clubs. Women who work in blue-collar trades go through uncomfortable hazing for encroaching on traditionally male territory. Coworkers put enormous obstacles in their way. "For a long time I wasn't allowed to do certain jobs," a pipe fitter recalled. Not surprisingly, in the early 1990s only 2 percent of the construction workers in the United States were female. For those who persisted, however, the jobs could be enormously satisfying. "I loved carpentry immediately and still love it," explained Pat Cull. "It doesn't matter if it's digging ditches or doing a fine piece of cabinetry—it's honest work that I can be proud of. The problems I've had have always come from the attitudes of the men I work with and for."[24]

In addition to obstacles and hazing, up to 50 percent of all women workers in the United States and Europe report that they have experienced some kind of unwanted sexual advances. Subtle sexual harassment can serve to exclude women from higher-paying male jobs. In the late 1970s, for example, a female medical student preparing for surgery received an unwanted neck massage from the supervising male surgeon. When he whispered in her ear, "Wish I could be doing this with you somewhere else," he sent a clear message that he thought she belonged in the bedroom rather than the operating room.[25] When women protest about harassment, they risk accusations that they are prudish, humorless, or imagining harm. As the Czech sociologist Lenka Simerska put it, sexual harassment is "omnipresent, but it's not considered a serious problem. You're supposed to laugh about it and say that it's a stupid invention of hysterical American feminists, and that, actually, it does not exist here at all."[26]

Many of these discriminatory practices originate in our attitudes about gender. Every culture views men and women through what psychologist Sandra Bem calls "the lenses of gender." These lenses may vary from a belief that male domination is "natural" to an emphasis on the complementarity of male and female spheres. The egalitarian values professed by most contemporary industrialized societies coexist with underlying beliefs about natural sex roles. Individuals internalize these cultural lenses and apply them unconsciously in the world of work. Even small, unconscious biases can accumulate over time to create major inequalities.

Social science experiments and the attitudes of employees attest to these gendered expectations. Take the response to a test or essay, sign a male name to it, and evaluators score it more highly than if the exact same response is signed with a female name. Expectations that men perform better than women become self-fulfilling prophecies. Both male and female workers bring their deeply internalized understandings of proper gender roles to the job. In China some women insist that they cannot handle highly technical work in a factory; some North American and European men refuse to take "women's" jobs. An office worker in Baltimore blamed the lack of respect for women's work for its low pay: "If people would respect women's work, naturally your wages are going to go up. . . . Women's work is looked down upon. It's not really considered important, and you're not going to be paid wages for something that's considered trivial."[27] Sociologist Cynthia Fuchs Epstein points out that this pattern mirrors family relations in which sons have been raised to have higher self-esteem and expectations for success than daughters.

Employers can manipulate expectations about female behavior to discourage workers from seeking advancement or voicing discontent. In many Japanese companies, women, no matter how well educated or competent, are not considered for advancement because they are seen primarily as *shokuba no hana* "flowers in the workplace," whose fashionable clothing provides a decorative atmosphere. In a Silicon Valley electronics factory, employers played upon gender assumptions to control their low-paid workers. Supervisors felt free to flirt with female employees, claiming that they did so to make women feel feminine, as if this act compensated for their lower wages. At least one Chinese immigrant worker explained that she did not file a claim about unsafe conditions because she feared losing the flirtations of her white male supervisor; she also would not consider joining a union because union women, she believed, were "a bunch of tough, big-mouth dykes."[28] In this case, homophobia and gender ideology jointly controlled workers.

But these same electronics workers could turn gender ideology to their advantage. A Salvadorian immigrant, fed up with her boss for admonishing Hispanic women to "work faster if you want your children to eat," brought her own children, as well as her nieces and nephews, to the factory. She lined them up in front of the boss, and one child explained that his mother was so tired after work that she never had time to play with her children. From then on the supervisor eased the pace of work and began to take her more seriously. She had successfully used her identity as a mother to protest and improve work conditions. Similarly, a woman who tested chips in the factory manipulated her male supervisor's misconceptions about women: "He thinks females are flighty and irresponsible because of our hormones—so we make sure to have as many hormone problems as we can. I'd say we each take hormone breaks several times a day. My next plan is to convince him that menstrual blood will turn the solvents bad, so on those days we have to stay in the lunchroom!"[29] While this strategy brought short-term relief, it left intact the gender stereotypes that largely disadvantaged women workers.

Subverting gender meanings is not the only tool available to working women. The double day, women's lower pay, and gender and race biases in hiring and promotion create fertile environments for feminist politics. As the global economy continually expands the ranks of female paid laborers, women's movements seek to alleviate the economic burdens of these practices. Wherever a sexually segregated, lower-paid female labor force combines with women's primary responsibility for family care, feminists have introduced social policies to challenge both workplace inequities and the double day.

-EIGHT-

WORKERS AND MOTHERS: FEMINIST SOCIAL POLICIES

It is not only a matter of women entering the social world more boldly. . . . It is also a matter of men sharing life in the family's intimate world more fully.
— ALVA MYRDAL, SWEDEN, 1944

We are women, illiterate women,
Coming together to make a union. . . .
We challenge everyone with our strength.
— SELF-EMPLOYED WOMEN'S ASSOCIATION, INDIA, 1990S

Working women have used every means available to force employers and governments to adapt to their needs. In the 1970s, for example, Sonia Oliva, the daughter of a Guatemalan peasant, took a job in a chemical laboratory in Guatemala City. She became an activist in her labor union, which negotiated a contract providing day care for the children of workers. When the company failed to fulfill its obligation, Oliva brought her son Pavel to work, along with his diapers and bottles. The lab manager told her, "You have to work, you can't have a child here with these chemicals." Oliva reminded him that "there was supposed to be a day care center, and if they wanted to, they could give me a paid holiday until they built one, but until that time I would come with Pavel. They said they'd call a labor inspector. I said, 'Great!' "[1]

For workers such as Sonia Oliva, neither union contracts nor government regulations can ensure the support needed to raise a family while earning wages. But Oliva's knowledge that the law recognizes both her needs and her rights is the result of decades of activism. As women increasingly work for pay, feminists advocate a range of policies that can help resolve the dilemmas of wage labor and motherhood. On one hand, these policies secure equal opportunity, pay, and promotion so that women workers can aspire to incomes sufficient for self-support. On the other hand, they recognize women's reproductive aspirations and try to protect their caregiving labor in the family.

Over time feminists have tried to reconcile these dual strategies by rejecting policies that reinforce the public/private divide. The model of male breadwinner and female caregiver has never fit well with the experiences of working-class and minority families in the West, nor does it describe most families in developing regions. Increasingly, feminist social policies try to reshape the workplace to accommodate the realities of parenting; this includes drawing men into caretaking tasks at home as much as opening paid jobs to women. By the close of the twentieth century Western feminists were supporting the ideas first articulated by Alva Myrdal in Sweden during the 1930s and 1940s, when she insisted on sharing both work and family tasks between men and women. Because the admittedly artificial worker/woman divide has been so influential, it provides a critical framework for understanding contemporary social policy debates.

WOMEN AS WORKERS: LABOR POLICIES

Wherever women took paid jobs in industrializing economies, they participated in movements to improve wages and work conditions. In the 1840s both the Lowell "mill girls" in the United States and the young lace makers in Great Britain "turned out" by stopping their work in protest. In the 1920s militant women protested conditions in textile mills in India and female cotton mill workers in Shanghai went on strike. When trade unions earned the right to bargain for wages and hours, women workers benefited. In countries such as Germany, France, and Russia, organizing women workers through the trade union movement took priority over woman suffrage.

Throughout the world, however, women workers have been under-represented in unions. For many years the labor movement's focus on organizing male-dominated, heavy industries ignored much of women's work. Gender ideology also hindered full inclusion. In the United States and Europe, trade unionists long expected men, but not women, to earn a "family wage." In addition, women workers themselves posed obstacles to unionization. The double demands of wage labor and family care left little time for meetings. "If the woman has to do everything at home there is no chance of her going to meetings," a South African union organizer explained.[2] As with men, ethnic differences among workers constrained organizing efforts, whether in New York's garment trades or Shanghai's cotton mills.

The most successful women's labor organizing has emphasized gender as much as class. The long history of gender solidarity continues to influence feminist strategies. In China, for example, Shanghai cotton mill workers pledged sisterhood in mutual aid organizations as a means of supporting each other. Like rural women who migrated to cities in the United States, urban Chinese migrants often turned to the Young Women's Christian Association for lodging. In England and the United States chapters of the Women's Trade Union League (WTUL) forged alliances between middle- and working-class women. In 1909, for example, middle-class allies contributed to strike funds and stood on picket lines with women garment workers during the "Uprising of the 20,000" in New York City.

Women's movements also mobilized housewives to support workers through consumer boycotts. If companies paid low wages to women or permitted unhealthy work places, consumers would not buy their products. In the early 1900s the Consumers Union sponsored a "white list" of manufacturers who treated women workers fairly, to encourage the purchase of their products. In India as well, mass movements relied on the power of organized housewives. When a United Women's Anti-Price-Rise Front formed in 1973 "to mobilize women of the city against inflation," thousands of Indian housewives demonstrated by banging plates and rolling pins.[3] Consumer activism revived in the United States in the 1990s with boycotts of apparel manufacturers who relied on sweatshop labor or condoned factories that do not meet safety and wage standards.

Meantime, the huge growth in service jobs filled by women in the decades after World War II set the stage for a renewed burst of labor organizing, this time in traditionally female occupations. In the 1970s French nurses went out on strike to insist on greater respect for their skills as professionals. In the United States a group of office workers in Boston formed a new union called 9 to 5. They joined the Service Employees International Union and demanded "raises, not roses" as appreciation for their labors. The group won significant victories when they went on strike against employers such as Harvard University. Hotel workers also joined unions. When flight attendants (formerly called stewardesses) organized, they won not only better wages but also the elimination of the arbitrary weight and height requirements that emphasized youth and beauty over work skills. (One flight attendant, Patricia Ireland, became an activist when she found out her family medical benefits did not equal men's. She later became the president of the National Organization for Women.) Major strikes, such as the 1974 walkout of Asian women workers at a Leicester, England, typewriter company, signaled the new militance of working women of color. By the 1980s women represented on average one-third of the union members in Europe, a figure only slightly lower than their overall labor force participation rate. The advantages of unionization could be dramatic. Union women in the United States earn almost 40 percent more than nonunion women workers. As a result, the pay gap has narrowed for all union workers.

Labor feminists sought leverage within unions as well as with employers. In England and France women pressured unions to drop their historical support for the male family wage in favor of equal hiring opportunities for women. One North American group, the Coalition of Labor Union Women (CLUW), trained women for union leadership and created a network of activists. By participating in the National Organization for Women, CLUW members kept labor issues on the liberal feminist agenda. By the 1980s about half of the members in CLUW's seventy-five chapters were women of color. In Brazil women forced their trade unions to address both sex discrimination at work and the double burden of family care. In the 1990s one of Brazil's largest unions, the Workers Union Central, reserved 30 percent of its leadership positions for women workers.

In a distinctive new form of organizing, women in the informal sector of the economy also sought collective power. Domestic workers organized in parts of Africa; in India domestics went on strike in 1982. Household workers in Latin America first formed unions as early as the 1920s, but their organizing expanded regionally. In 1988 domestic workers from a dozen countries formed the *Confederación Latinoamericana y del Caribe de Trabajadoras del Hogar* (CONLACTRAHO), a domestic workers federation that has called for a minimum wage, sick leave, and protection from sexual harassment. Even prostitutes began to mobilize. In the 1970s they demanded the decriminalization of their trade as a means to improve work conditions. In Lyons, France, prostitutes staged a work stoppage to protest exploitation. One U.S. group, COYOTE (Call Off Your Old Tired Ethics), recommended not only a prostitutes' union but also worker-owned collectives that would eliminate madams and pimps. In South Asia the Women's Collaborative Committee, formed by prostitutes in 1995, soon had over thirty thousand members. Along with insisting that customers use condoms to prevent the spread of HIV, they demanded police protection from assault and exploitation.

Labor organizing in the informal sector can have a powerful impact on women's lives. In India, the Self-Employed Women's Association (SEWA), founded in 1972 by Gandhian socialist women, offers job training, economic aid, and bargaining skills to street vendors and pieceworkers. These women produce weaving and embroidery, sell vegetables and junk, and collect firewood. Anticipating the microcredit movement of the 1980s, SEWA established the Mahila (Women's) Bank, one of the first cooperative banks to provide loans for the poorest, illiterate women. By the 1990s two hundred thousand self-employed women belonged to SEWA. As bank director Lalita Krishnaswami explained, when women join SEWA they gradually "start feeling confident. They get a little respect from their family. The children begin to view their mothers differently. Domestic violence can be reduced. . . . Each change creates new possibilities for change." The SEWA organizing song captures the spirit of this movement to organize the least privileged workers. "We are poor women in a hostile land," it proclaims.

We have neither land nor work.
Our houses are as small as our hands
And our needs are many. . . .
We are women, illiterate women,
Coming together to make a union. . . .
We are illiterate, but what of that?
We challenge everyone with our strength.[4]

Legal Strategies: Protection or Opportunity?

The plight of women workers during early industrialization inspired demands for laws regulating women's labor. This legislative legacy still influences feminist policy debates. Like the anti-child-labor laws first passed in England in the 1840s, the protective legislation enacted in many European countries by 1900 limited women's access to night work and certain kinds of physically demanding work such as mining. Socialist politicians generally accepted protective legislation, calling for an eight-hour day for women workers before extending that demand to include all workers.

The history of protective legislation in the United States reveals how strongly gender ideology has influenced working women. American courts considered maximum-hours and minimum-wage laws unconstitutional because they infringed on the contractual rights of employers and workers to bargain. Ideas about gender, however, provided a significant legal loophole that could justify protective labor laws for women. In 1908 a coalition of women's and labor activists successfully argued before the U.S. Supreme Court that the state had a compelling interest in protecting the health of future mothers. In *Muller v. Oregon* the Supreme Court accepted this reasoning and ruled that states could pass laws to limit hours and work conditions for women only. The language of the decision reflected reformers' views that women required special treatment: "That woman's physical structure and the performance of maternal functions place her at a disadvantage in the struggle for subsistence is obvious," the justices concluded. "The physical well-being of woman becomes an object of public interest and care in order to preserve the strength and vigor of the race."[5]

The protective labor regulations permitted by the *Muller* decision proved to be a double-edged sword. Laws could limit women's total work hours, thus protecting maternal health, but at the same time they could prohibit women from working overtime or at night, thus limiting their ability to earn higher wages. In some states women could not work as bartenders, or waitresses could not serve cocktails after a certain hour. Employers could refuse to hire women who had school-age children, since paid work interfered with maternal tasks. At the time, most American reformers considered the *Muller* decision a huge victory, given their commitment to empowering women as mothers. In the 1920s, however, the younger women who introduced the Equal Rights Amendment rejected this strategy of protective legislation because they wanted women to compete as equals with men in the workplace. The bitter split between equal-rights feminists and those who favored protective legislation echoed among international feminists and lasted until the 1960s.

Equal-Rights Law

The resurgence of feminism in the 1960s, spurred by the widespread participation of women in the paid labor force, revived questions about protective legislation. By then even the U.S. government had gradually extended labor standards to male workers, so that women no longer had to rely on maternal identities as a basis for demanding minimum-wage and maximum-hours laws. Because of occupational segregation in the labor force, the economic gender gap persisted. To close it, feminists in both the United States and western Europe recommended legislation prohibiting discrimination in hiring, pay, and training.

The first such policy initiative, equal-pay laws, had strong support from trade unions. Allowing employers to pay women workers less for the same tasks threatened to lower the wage scales for male workers. As much a labor cause as a feminist one, equal-pay guarantees enjoyed widespread support after World War II. France, Germany, Italy, Belgium, and the Netherlands included a guarantee of equal pay in the 1957 Treaty of Rome, the precursor to the European Union. The Scandinavian countries began to pass such laws in the 1960s. The U.S. Congress passed an Equal Pay Act in 1963, outlawing separate pay scales for men and women in the same jobs, and Great Britain implemented equal pay in 1975. Governments created a variety of enforcement mechanisms, including the Equal Opportunity Commission in Great Britain and a secretary of state for women's rights in the French labor ministry. The measures had an important impact. After an equal-pay law took effect in Portugal in 1973, for instance, women's earnings increased from 52 to 71 percent of men's.

In the context of a sexually segregated labor force, however, equal pay for equal work could not eliminate the wage gap, since men and women rarely held the same jobs. Only a ban on discrimination in hiring, salary, and promotion would open male-dominated jobs to women. In response to the movement for racial justice, the U.S. Congress enacted such a ban. Once Title VII of the 1964 Civil Rights Act prohibited employers from discriminating on the grounds of sex as well as race, women workers flooded the enforcement agency with complaints. By 1969 the Equal Employment Opportunity Commission (EEOC) had received over fifty thousand accusations of workplace sex discrimination.

Second-wave feminists set off a worldwide demand for both equal-pay and antidiscrimination laws. In 1975 a British law banned sex discrimination in employment, and Ireland and Italy passed equal employment laws in 1977. France enacted legislation in 1983 prohibiting employment discrimination by sex (though allowing special leave for pregnancy and maternity). Japan enacted its Equal Employment Opportunity Law in 1985, which opened the previously male-only career track to women. In the 1990s, after export manufacturing zones had increased women's factory labor, feminists in both Mexico and the Philippines abandoned the protective-law approach in favor of equal-treatment legislation that would lift restrictions on women's work.

Civil rights legislation affected hiring practices in male-dominated fields. Employers could no longer rely exclusively on word-of-mouth referrals to recruit workers, for such "old-boy network" hiring perpetuated the gender and racial inequalities of the workforce. Now they had to advertise jobs openly to fill vacancies. Nor could employers or agencies screen applicants in discriminatory ways. Help-wanted ads, once segregated into male and female job listings, could no longer state preferences for one sex without good reason. Jobs once gender-coded as "policeman" or "mailman" acquired the neutral labels of "police officer" and "mail carrier." Antidiscrimination law also made it illegal for employers to ask job applicants about their marital status, nor could they screen out pregnant women or mothers.

In a series of landmark cases, Western feminists used equal-rights laws to gain access to jobs, back pay, and guarantees of fairer treatment in the future. In the city of San Francisco a court order mandated the hiring of women and minorities for police and fire department jobs. Women employees won an out-of-court settlement with Smith Barney, a U.S. brokerage firm, that included programs to achieve fair treatment of both women and minority workers. By desegregating occupations, equal-rights laws helped alleviate some of the wage gap. The stricter the enforcement, the greater the inroads for women in construction, mining, banking, and telecommunications.

Equal-rights laws helped challenge the biases that have restricted women's workplace advancement, including invidious gender stereotypes. One plaintiff in a sex discrimination case, Ann Hopkins, confronted these biases when she worked as a senior manager for the global accounting firm of Price Waterhouse. Hopkins earned outstanding performance evaluations and brought in most of the business for her home office. Yet the proposal to make her a partner failed on the grounds that she lacked charm and femininity. Her work review described her as "macho" and advised her to take a course in "charm school," counseling that she would advance at work if she would "walk more femininely, talk more femininely, dress more femininely, wear makeup, have her hair styled, and wear jewelry."[6] In 1989 the U.S. Supreme Court ruled that the evaluation of her work contained discriminatory sex stereotyping. After eight years Ann Hopkins finally got her partnership, with back pay and promises of no retaliation.

Beyond Liberal Rights: Alternative Legal Strategies

Equal-rights laws, however, could not entirely eliminate men's advantage in the labor market. For one thing, the law is hard to enforce. Working women who sensed unfair treatment had to invest much time and energy in filing suits; behind each of the practices outlawed lies a long and often torturous trail of legal cases, appeals, and hard-won verdicts. In the United States the number of complaints far exceeded the resources allotted to the EEOC, so some cases were never investigated. Even when the government pursued employers, it did not always prevail in court. Recall how Sears successfully defended its record of unequal earnings by arguing that women chose less competitive sales positions because they preferred to spend time with their families. Some kinds of discrimination proved hard to eliminate. Veterans' benefits, which gave those who had served in the military priority for civil service jobs, did not intend to discriminate against women, but men had a de facto advantage since historically the military had accepted so few women.

Although the legal cases chipped away at sexual segregation and the wage gap, women's secondary status as workers remained deeply entrenched. New strategies emerged to supplement equal-rights laws, including affirmative action and comparable worth. These approaches attempt to acknowledge women's difference as workers and to reevaluate the kinds of jobs they have historically held.

Affirmative Action

During the U.S. civil rights movement of the 1960s, a new government policy known as "affirmative action" attempted to remedy the past systematic exclusion of racial minorities from the best-paying and most secure jobs. In 1967 an executive order expanded the policy to include women. The term "affirmative action" referred to employers taking proactive steps to recruit and train members of underrepresented groups. Its formula—that, all other things being equal, employers could and should choose a woman or minority candidate—provided one means of reversing historical patterns of discrimination.

The original U.S. affirmative-action policy had support from women's caucuses in the trades and professions, the Coalition of Labor Union Women, and welfare reformers. It called for government contractors to set goals of hiring women in 20 to 25 percent of the places within their apprentice programs. The policy expanded to private employers who established affirmative-action programs as part of legal settlements when found guilty of sex discrimination. For example, in 1974 the women's caucus at the *New York Times*, with support from the black workers' caucus, brought a class action suit against their employer. They realized that women at all levels of employment were earning less than men and that women simply could not advance into certain jobs. The out-of-court settlement in 1978 included an affirmative-action program to remedy past discrimination at the newspaper. In addition to employers, colleges and universities that accepted government funds also created affirmative action programs to recruit students and hire faculty from underrepresented groups. In an important challenge to affirmative-action policies, the U.S. Supreme Court ruled in the 1978 *Bakke* case that employers or schools could not set strict numerical quotas but could set more general goals for hiring women and minorities.

In many cases, affirmative-action settlements expanded opportunities for women. In California, for example, a court found a utility company guilty of race and sex discrimination in hiring. The company had defended itself by claiming that only white males ever applied for their jobs as "linemen." Under a federal order to change, the company became more creative, advertising the position in women's gyms. Soon strong, qualified women applicants eager to earn good wages started to apply for these jobs. The simple act of reaching out where women might learn of opportunities had expanded the qualified labor pool. In another case, advertising blue-collar jobs changed a woman's life. As she explained, "I didn't think about nontraditional work until I heard the carpenters were looking for women. . . . But as soon as the possibility was mentioned, my imagination went with it."[7] Job training programs provided another mechanism for recruitment under affirmative action. In New York the United Tradeswomen brought black and Latina women into skilled jobs. In San Antonio the Chicana Rights Project and the National Organization for Women trained Mexican American women for skilled work. Initially a race-based program, affirmative action expanded to benefit women of all races as well.

Other countries have also adopted forms of affirmative action to redress past gender, racial, or religious discrimination. In southern African nations, affirmative action has helped incorporate black Africans into jobs once monopolized by whites. Northern Ireland has tried to assist Catholic workers who had been discriminated against in the past. In Asia both Sri Lanka and Malaysia have implemented affirmative-action policies for women workers. During the 1980s the governments of Sweden, Finland, and Norway offered strong incentives to government employers and unions who met quotas for hiring women. The French *Loi Roudy*

(1983) required companies to report annually on recruiting, training, and promoting workers, while Italy's Measures for Positive Discrimination (1991) encouraged employers to set targets to achieve gender parity.

In 1995 the European Union high court upheld hiring preferences, but not quotas, for women in public sector jobs, although member countries do not have to implement them. More typically, European countries incorporate the principle of "positive action," or voluntary efforts to accommodate the workplace to meet women's needs by adjusting work schedules and providing child care and job training. In Belgium, for example, efforts to redress past discrimination include assertiveness training, career planning, and day care for women seeking jobs.

Even as affirmative action has spread internationally, it has become increasingly controversial in the United States. Critics have challenged affirmative action in part because its emphasis on group membership goes against the liberal principle of individual merit. Opponents also accuse affirmative action of "reverse discrimination" for turning the tables on some white male job applicants. Affirmative-action policies, they argue, create gender and race preferences that disadvantage white men and do not necessarily help women and minority group members, who will be stigmatized as less qualified. In public opinion polls, white women oppose affirmative action as strongly as white men, even though they benefit from its policies. Building on this discontent, during the 1990s successful political campaigns overturned the policy in higher education in several U.S. states.

In response to charges that affirmative action advocates hiring by group membership rather than individual merit, supporters point out that women and racial minorities are already being treated as group members. Barbara Babcock, who was the first woman to serve as an assistant attorney general in the U.S. Department of Justice, made this point when asked how she felt about getting the job because she was a woman: "It feels better than being rejected for the position because you're a woman."[8]

Furthermore, because evaluations of individual merit are highly subjective, they are vulnerable to deeply rooted, subtle biases that arise from gender schemas. Such unconscious discrimination can affect hiring and promotion. All other things being equal, white males used to get the judgment call in their favor, just as children of alumni have historically been favored in college admissions. Affirmative action attempts to tip the balance toward women and minorities, not in order to achieve reverse discrimination but rather to ensure equal opportunity. As legal scholar Ronald Dworkin explains, when inequality has been long-standing, merely equal treatment can be insufficient to secure treatment as an equal.

Equal Pay for Work of Equal Value

In one sense, affirmative action falls under equal-rights law. But it also argues that women and minorities should be valued not only because they are qualified (equality) but also because they bring fresh perspectives (difference). Affirmative action is not the only feminist legal strategy that questions whether integration is sufficient to achieve equality. Many feminists have argued that the law must also take into account the unique value of what women bring with them, whether as coworkers in jobs or as role models in the classroom.

Pay equity, or comparable worth, also addresses the importance of valuing women's contributions. Pay equity responds to the reality that equal pay for the same work leaves the sexually segregated labor force intact. Even though a few women earn male wages because of affirmative action programs, most women earn less in their job ghettos. Desegregating those low-paid ghettos is a challenging task. Jobs such as carpenter, sailor, or painter command higher wages by virtue of their association with men. Jobs traditionally performed by women, such as maid, secretary, or nurse, offer lower wages. The legacy of domestic identities plays a key role in sustaining this hierarchy. What else can account for disparities in which some schoolteachers earn less than liquor store clerks, while librarians may earn less than tree trimmers or water meter readers?

The strategy of pay equity originated as early as the 1960s, when the Scandinavian 'equality ombudsperson' began to enforce equal pay for work of equal value. Only a few European states have incorporated a similar law, however. Canada adopted the principle in its Human Rights Act of 1985 by outlawing discrimination in wages for men and women "performing work of equal value."9 In the United States states such as Michigan and Pennsylvania, along with cities such as Los Angeles and San Jose, reclassified jobs according to comparable worth. In 1999 the

American Federation of Labor—Congress of Industrial Organizations, long an advocate of equal pay for equal work, called for legislation to require employers to pay men and women equally for comparable jobs.

To enact pay equity, an employer reevaluates the skill and pay levels of all jobs according to a gender-neutral schema. One pay equity evaluation found that despite similar duties, predominantly female social workers had been earning a third less than the predominantly male probation officers. New job categories would eliminate this disparity. Similarly, a comparable-worth evaluation might set similar wages for labor performed by a "maid" and a "janitor" and possibly rename their job with a gender-neutral term such as "maintenance worker." Divested of the historical devaluation of women's work, the new categories and fairer wages could help close the gender gap in salaries by enticing men into historically female occupations and by paying women more for their worthwhile labors.

Comparable-worth policies have benefited all women and minority men. In the United States a 1992 study found that "comparable worth raised the pay of workers in jobs performed primarily by white women and by women and men of color."[10] In Australia, which gradually instituted comparable worth between 1969 and 1975, the female wage ratio increased from 65 to 86 percent of men's wages. Fourteen of the twenty U.S. states that enacted pay equity for state workers by 1989 brought women's earnings ratio up from 74 to 88 percent of men's wages (compared to a national average of 71 percent). Opponents criticize the policy for interfering with the operation of the free market and warn that realigning wage scales could increase public costs. Thus far in the United States the practice has not created new tax burdens, although it can slow employment growth slightly. Pay equity alone cannot close the wage gap, but it introduces an important element of valuing women's labor to supplement equal opportunity law.

Giving Women Credit

Affirmative action and pay equity both aim to give women a boost up in the workplace, where they have historically encountered sex discrimination. Employment law affects only part of the economic gender gap, however, for women also need equal access to credit, whether as self-employed workers or as consumers. Since the 1830s the women's rights movement in the West has campaigned for property rights to allow married women to control their own wages and property. Second-wave feminists have also insisted that all women should have independent access to credit, so that married women do not have to rely on their husbands to get bank loans. In the United States the 1974 Credit Opportunity Act prohibited banks from refusing to grant women loans in their own name. This right to credit enables women to form businesses on their own, and more and more women have done so.

Outside the West the issue of credit has been especially important. Equal-rights law and pay equity may help workers in advanced industrial economies, but poor women in developing nations will not benefit from labor laws until they find some kind of income-generating labor. Most of these women work either on the land or in the informal sector of the economy. For them, the most pressing economic issues have been women's right to land ownership and access to credit. In the Philippines and in Mexico, for example, women participants in peasant movements have demanded independent ownership of farmland. In parts of Africa, South Asia, and Central America poor women seek bank loans to start income-generating enterprises near their homes so that they can continue to care for families.

Providing loans to poor women is now a priority of women's movements in the developing world. The impact is well illustrated by an Indian textile hauler named Gafoorbhai. A small loan of $50 from SEWA's women-owned bank allowed this hardworking grandmother to purchase a handcart. Because she could haul twice as much cloth than she had been able to balance on her head, her profits more than doubled.[11] In Bangladesh the Grameen (Village) Bank, established in 1983, instituted a unique credit system that has become a model for world lenders. A group of five women may apply for small loans (on average about $150) to help them establish income-generating enterprises. Every member of the group is responsible for all five of the loans.

By creating a support network and peer pressure, microlending has been enormously successful. An unprecedented 90 percent of the borrowers repay their loans, while women in poor families are able to find an economic foothold by selling goods or farming land. Similarly, the Chinese organization Rural Women Knowing All, which follows up loans with literacy and skill training programs, has a 100 percent return rate. Microcredit has become a world movement, spreading from South Asia to fifty countries. In Guatemala a $50 loan enabled one group of women to buy a used washing machine that they rolled around their village to take in laundry. A Brooklyn, New York, credit union formed a Sisters in Lending Circle to help women on welfare gain economic independence.

Microlending has improved the lives of poor women and their families. Women borrowers tend to reinvest their income in food, shelter, and schooling for their children. The positive effect on communities can reduce opposition to women's newfound labor outside the home. In Bangladesh, for example, some Muslim husbands and clergy objected to women taking loans and starting businesses. "I explained to everyone what I was really doing," a village woman named Osima recalled, and her husband relented. Because of women's business, she reported, the village "has received sanitary latrines and violence against women has gone down."[12]

WOMEN AS MOTHERS: FAMILY POLICIES

The innovative policies advocated by feminists to expand working women's opportunities have achieved impressive gains in jobs, wages, and loans. However, most women continue to perform unpaid child care in their homes, which deeply affects their wage earning. Only by addressing the major biological difference between male and female workers— women's capacity to bear children—can feminist strategies transcend the sexual division of labor that disadvantages women workers.

Not all women choose to become mothers, but a large proportion of women laborers do bear children at some time. Eighty percent of wage-earning women in the United States are of childbearing age, and over 90 percent of them will become pregnant during their careers. Combining child care and other labors posed fewer problems in preindustrial families, when women and men worked in or near the home. When married women first entered the industrial labor force, they often left their paid jobs when they had children, either by choice or because employers refused to allow pregnant women or mothers to continue in their jobs. Since the 1950s, as expanding service jobs have attracted more Western women into paid labor, increasing numbers of mothers with small children have remained in the labor force. The dilemmas they face—the double day of paid and unpaid labor, the search for reliable and affordable child care, the conflicts that arise when children are ill—have inspired feminist political responses.

Although equal-rights laws enable more mothers to work, these women remain at an economic disadvantage when they bear children. One U.S. study found that a working woman's earnings declined by $3,000 in the first year after the birth of a child and even more in subsequent years. In Great Britain the lifetime "mother gap" in earnings for a woman with two children amounts to £140,000. Taking time off for childbirth accounts for only part of these losses. Reentry into the labor force often means finding a lower-paying job, and some mothers cannot find new jobs at all. Divorced mothers rarely receive alimony and often cannot enforce child support payments. Nor do divorce settlements usually compensate women for their years of unpaid family labor (although a 2001 German federal court ruling did increase alimony for former housewives). Mothers who are widowed, divorced, or deserted often rely on state welfare payments. In the United States and elsewhere, the majority of recipients of welfare are the children of low-paid or unemployed single mothers.

Motherhood, in short, contributes to the pay gap between women and men. But it also creates a double burden of parental labor that exhausts working mothers and deprives them of leisure time. Some professional women resolve these problems by hiring full-time nursemaids or nannies. Even those who can afford paid helpers often experience anxiety over the quality of child care. Given strong societal messages in many cultures, mothers may feel conflicted about not remaining at home with infants. For most wage-earning mothers, private child care is too expensive. Outside of socialist states or western European countries such as Sweden, Denmark, Belgium, France, and Italy, public day care can be hard to find. When women cannot afford to hire child-care providers and governments do not provide it, extended kin networks and neighborhood cooperative arrangements offer a patchwork of solutions.

Not surprisingly, grassroots feminist activists of the 1960s and 1970s often pointed to the need for quality, affordable child care. In New York City one group established the Liberation Nursery by turning a storefront into a day care cooperative; they then hired local mothers to run it. In Japan an early feminist commune provided child care for activists. By the end of the twentieth century, however, affordable, safe, and available child care for working mothers remained an unfulfilled goal for most Western feminists. In Great Britain two-thirds of wage-earning women relied on friends and family members to provide informal child care. To date, countries that have provided care for children and the elderly, along with minimum-wage laws, have done the most to close the economic gender gap.

Socialist Policies and Socialist Feminist Alternatives

The history of socialist governments and socialist feminists provides both positive and negative models for resolving the dilemmas of working mothers. Communist countries have provided child care to free mothers' time for "productive" labor. China, Cuba, and the USSR all established state-run nurseries and day care. In the 1970s Cuba spent a greater share of its resources on child care than almost any other country, and its Family Code of 1974 mandated an equal share in housework for both parents (a goal more easily articulated than achieved). China's working mothers have enjoyed paid leave for childbirth, nursing, and housework, and rural communes collectivized household labor. Yet most paid child-care workers have been women, not only in China and Cuba but also in other socialist experiments, such as the Israeli kibbutzim.

Some socialist states introduced incentives for working women to have children. During the 1970s the German Democratic Republic combined birth control (free contraception and easily available abortion) with state support for motherhood. New mothers enjoyed one year of paid leave after their first child and six months after the second child, with a guaranteed job when they returned to paid work. Women—but not men—could have one day off a month to do housework and up to six weeks a year to care for sick children. They could also count on public child-care facilities. These policies gave East German women a measure of economic independence from men, for state-supported child and health care allowed even single working mothers to survive. These so-called mommy politics, however, excluded fathers from any responsibility, and they bred resentment about women's special privileges. When feminist organizing became possible after 1989, women's groups called for the extension of parental benefits to men so that women would not be typed as the "natural" parent. By emphasizing maternal, rather than parental, benefits, the state had reinforced women's identity as mother first, worker second. With the reunification of Germany in 1990 and the end of socialist policies, these child-care incentives ended, and women faced both high unemployment rates and the problem of finding child care.

In their Wages for Housework campaign socialist feminists in North America and England proposed, but never achieved, an alternative approach to women's labor in the home. Like early-twentieth-century feminists Charlotte Perkins Gilman and Virginia Woolf, they suggested payment for the valuable work women perform for their families. In contrast to the conservative, pronatalist policies of militarist states, who offer payments and honors for mothers of large families, the Wages for Housework campaign did not want to limit women to maternal labor but it did insist on treating domestic tasks as worthy of salaries. Strongest in England and Canada, the movement revised Marxian views of women's labor by demanding that the state pay women for "keeping everyone functioning." "We want wages for every dirty toilet, every painful childbirth," they declared. "And if we don't get what we want, then we will simply refuse to work any longer."[13] Besides recognizing the economic value of women's household labor, direct payment from employers or the state would free women from control by husbands. In principle, placing an economic value on women's work in the home would also improve wages for teachers, nurses, and secretaries in the female-dominated service sector.

These ideas may have seemed radical in the 1970s, but the attempt to revalue the unpaid work of women appealed to many feminists and ultimately influenced social policies. In 1976 the U.S. Congress passed displaced-homemakers legislation that set up hundreds of programs to help prepare divorced, widowed, or deserted women for paid jobs. Conservative administrations cut much of the funding, but the 1990s witnessed renewed recognition of the worth of homemakers. Feminists who once emphasized wage earning as a precondition for women's equality, such as the National Organization for Women, endorsed the Unremunerated Work Act. This bill simply called for establishing a measure of the unpaid work performed by women and men. Although it did not pass, by 1999 even conservative legislators in the United States were supporting the idea of a tax credit for "stay-at-home parents."

From Maternal to Parental Policies

The reference to "parents" rather than "mothers" in this recent legislation reflects an important political shift. Early social welfare programs in industrial countries usually emphasized motherhood, not parenthood. When social democratic governments protected working mothers they relied upon maternalist arguments about women's difference from men. On this basis Germany, Sweden, and France all enacted paid maternity leave by 1930, as did Norway, Mexico, and Brazil in later decades. After 1950 newly independent African states such as Zimbabwe mandated paid maternity leave as part of their labor laws. While useful for working women, the emphasis on gender difference in these measures reinforced the division of labor in which women provide care in the home while men earn wages in the labor market. In contrast, paid parental leave, as adopted by Scandinavian countries, extended inducements for men to undertake caring work. Reflecting these trends, the Convention to End Discrimination Against All Women (CEDAW), passed by the UN in 1979, stated that "the upbringing of children requires a sharing of responsibility between men and women and society as a whole."

Very gradually Western nations began to extend parental benefits to fathers. Swedish women's organizations first pushed for a welfare state that led the transition from maternal to parental policies. In 1936 a group of twenty-five women's organizations issued "A Call to Sweden's Women," demanding the right to work, paid vacations for housewives, legalized contraception, support for single mothers, and greater political representation for women. The programs they achieved from the 1940s through the 1970s, however, were not limited to mothers. As one of the leading Swedish activists, Alva Myrdal, explained in 1945, "It is not only a matter of women entering the social world more boldly. . . . It is also a matter of men sharing life in the family's intimate world more fully"—a world, she continued, "where women have been relegated alone."[14] Swedish national health insurance provided paid parental leave at birth for fathers as well as mothers, plus a year's paid leave for either parent during the first four years of a child's life. As an incentive to involve them in child care, fathers could get an extra ten days of paid leave.

At first only one out of five Swedish fathers took advantage of this opportunity, though even this rate was higher than that of men using the paid parental leave later enacted in France, Germany, Greece, Italy, and Canada. In the 1990s several Scandinavian countries initiated a further incentive of one additional month of paid leave if fathers shared in parental leave. As a result of this policy, the proportion of Norwegian fathers taking advantage of parental leave jumped from around 3 percent to 70 percent.

Although many industrialized countries provide some paid parental leave, few cultures have been as committed as the Nordic ones to sharing child care. Until 1999 Great Britain offered only maternity leave. Since then a new law has more than doubled the leave time to thirteen weeks and extended it to either parent. Leading the battle to expand the benefits were British trade unions, represented by lawyer Cherie Booth. To widespread publicity, Booth made clear that she expected her own husband, Tony Blair, to take some time off from his job as prime minister to help care for their newborn child. As a precedent, she cited the prime minister of Finland, who had recently taken a week's leave after the birth of his daughter. Although Blair merely spent more time with his family when his son was born, two-thirds of the British men polled shortly afterward claimed that they were likely to make use of the new parental leave.

Balancing Difference and Equal Opportunity

The United States, with its highly individualist and antisocialist heritage, lags far behind other industrialized nations in state support for working mothers. Until the 1960s most advocates for U.S. working women relied on maternalist arguments about women's unique roles as caregivers to support protective legislation and welfare payments to mothers. As in Europe, most second-wave feminists embraced equal-rights law, but they could not ignore the complications posed for working women by pregnancy and motherhood. Ultimately feminists expanded the equality argument from one in which women emulated traditionally male careers to one that would allow men to emulate traditionally female careers.

The issue of pregnant workers highlights the tension between difference and equal-rights legal strategies. According to the strict equality principle invoked by some employers, companies should not have to provide pregnancy leave since only women can benefit from it. Thus when bank receptionist Lillian Garland became pregnant in the 1980s, her employer refused to give her old job back after she gave birth. Garland sued the bank under a recently enacted law, the Pregnancy Discrimination Act of 1978. The law held that employers and insurance plans could not exclude pregnancy from coverage and that women had the right to the same disability leave as men, even though men cannot become pregnant. The Supreme Court ruled on her case in 1987, finding that the Pregnancy Discrimination Act allowed employers to treat pregnancy differently even if men had no comparable medical condition. Lillian Garland won her old job back.

The Pregnancy Discrimination Act struck fear in the hearts of some feminists, who predicted that basing public policy on biological difference would once again disadvantage women in the labor market. It also agitated employers, who warned that expanding job security and health coverage to pregnant workers would make it prohibitively expensive to hire women. In the decade after its passage, however, the act did not slow the entry of women of childbearing age into the U.S. labor force. According to one study, this "simple change in employer policy" led to significant increases in women's wages.[15] Workers who would have had to start over in new jobs could return to their previous positions and take advantage of opportunities for advancement.

A second example from the United States further illustrates the shift from integrating women workers into men's career patterns to recognizing the value of parental labor for both men and women. When U.S.

Representative Patricia Schroeder introduced the Family and Medical Leave Act (FMLA) in 1986, she purposely drafted legislation that included both mothers and fathers. The act, which passed in 1993, allowed three months of unpaid leave within two years after the birth or adoption of a child for either a man or a woman. Though unpaid, the parent on leave retains a guaranteed job and health benefits. In this sense, equality law worked in the direction of making men's lives more like women's.

Opposition from employers watered down the FMLA so that it covered only companies with fifty or more employees, which accounted for just half of the U.S. workforce. Once granted parental benefits, however, some fathers began to take advantage of them. Of the twenty million workers who used the law between 1993 and 1999, 40 percent were men. Maryland state trooper Kevin Knussman successfully invoked the Family and Medical Leave Act when he sued the state for denying him leave to care for a newborn child. As a man, he was told, he could not be the primary caregiver. Women's rights lawyers championed his cause, and his 1999 court victory forced a revision of Maryland law. Although the case took five years to win, Knussman considered the time well spent in fighting "illegal discrimination against fathers."[16]

Unpaid leave for parents, enacted in both the United States and Japan during the 1990s, represents only a small step toward reconciling job and family life. Only those parents who can afford to forgo income for several months can take advantage of it. If fathers continue to earn higher wages, mothers are more likely to take leave for child care. Even the paid parental leave offered by most other industrialized nations has time limits. Once parents return to work they still require affordable child care. Several Scandinavian countries have led the way in providing state-sponsored child care. By the 1990s half of Danish children under three attended public day care, as did 80 percent of Swedish children between three and six. On-site day care can ease the burden for wage-earning parents; companies in Great Britain and elsewhere now provide these services or subsidies for working parents. Expanded day care centers in Korean public schools, for example, allow some teachers to bring their own young children to work.

Flexible scheduling, which involves job security and benefits for part-time laborers, also promises relief to working parents. A Dutch law, for example, extends labor protections and benefits to part-time workers, many of whom are mothers. But offering flexibility only to mothers would reinforce the divide between male breadwinner and female caregiver. Thus when an American writer suggested that companies should create a "mommy track" that allowed business and professional women to work part-time, many feminists preferred a "parent track" that provided flexibility for men or women. Another model that recognizes the importance of care work for both parents is the adoption of family-friendly policies by employers. A German company, for example, instituted options of reducing the workweek and taking a career break for either male or female employees who wanted to care for their families. In the Netherlands, a 1996 labor law explicitly aimed "to promote the combination of work and care tasks, as well as other responsibilities outside the workplace."[17]

As in Sweden, these policies have to be combined with incentives for men to break through long-standing pressures to place work above family. As Alva Myrdal recognized in the 1940s, "there will probably be a long transitional period" before the duties of parenting cease to be primarily women's. She knew that only with widespread retraining— through the media and in families, schools, and churches—would men be "mentally prepared for the new mode of family living."[18] Pressured to work longer and longer hours, by the end of the century some men were beginning to change. In the United States between 40 and 50 percent of all the men surveyed said they would be willing to take a pay cut or quit their jobs in order to spend more time with their children. That figure rose to 70 percent among young men in their twenties. To shift from willing to able will require new social policies that help equalize family care across the gender divide.

Women and Welfare

Public welfare systems have played an important role in reinforcing women's primary responsibility for child care. These systems emerged in response to the social dislocations of industrialization, including unemployment and injury on the job. Most Western governments attempted to buffer the impact of illness, death, and unemployment. They established workers' pensions, unemployment insurance, social security in old age, and compensation for workplace injuries. In addition, another set of laws addressed the needs of working-class mothers who could not support their families, particularly widows.

In the early twentieth century, states such as France and Sweden facilitated wage earning by single mothers by providing public child care. In other countries, such as Australia and the United States, social reformers emphasized the sanctity of motherhood, the importance of child rearing, and the right of male breadwinners to earn a family wage. They initially supported "mothers' pensions" from the states so that widows could stay at home raising children rather than work for pay. When the United States created a social security system in the 1930s, the Aid to Dependent Children program (ADC, later AFDC) expanded assistance to any single mother caring for children at home. In practice, most poor mothers needed to work for wages because their small state stipends were inadequate to support a family.

Welfare, or family subsidies, became a feminist issue because women both bear the brunt of caregiving in families and have fewer economic resources to do so. In the United States, for example, a full-time worker receiving the minimum wage and supporting one child would be living below the official poverty line. Most single parents are female, whether they bear children outside marriage or raise them alone after divorce or desertion. Only half of these single mothers receive child support from fathers, and their wages are lower than men's. In addition, older women are more likely to be poor than older men because they started working later, earned lower wages, and thus accumulated less for their retirement. In short, the economic gender gap has given rise to the phenomenon known as the "feminization of poverty." The majority of the poor are women and their children. Whether in sub-Saharan Africa, Indonesia, the United Kingdom, North America, or Australia, far more women than men live in poverty.

Gender, of course, is not the sole determinant of poverty, for age and race compound its effect. In the United States, for example, Hispanic women are two times as likely and African American women three times as likely to be poor than white women. Race has strongly influenced welfare policies. In the United States, government stipends that helped mothers remain at home with children initially targeted white mothers. In the early twentieth century, social service workers often assumed that African American mothers could and should work for even the lowest wages. White women and their children continue to constitute the majority of welfare recipients in the United States, yet African Americans have been overrepresented among U.S. welfare recipients, largely because of racial discrimination in wages, housing, and employment. Popular stereotypes often demonize "welfare mothers" as young black women who bear children in order to profit from government stipends. This myth of the "welfare queen" ignores the fact that the states providing the lowest welfare payments actually have the highest birth rates. It also reflects the belief that black mothers should be working, based on a long history of their slave and wage labor.

Dissatisfaction with the U.S. welfare system arose among recipients themselves. A key grassroots activist, Johnnie Tillmon (1930–1995), had held a variety of low-paid jobs, from picking cotton to working in a laundry, even after she married and was raising six children. In the 1960s, when she left her husband and became too ill to work, Tillmon accepted government welfare payments. She found that after paying for her rent, utilities, and food from her monthly allotment, she was left with only $5 per family member. In 1975 Tillmon reflected on her experience: "AFDC is like a supersexist marriage. You trade in *a* man for *the* man. But you can't divorce him if he treats you bad. He can divorce *you*."[19] To protest this treatment, Tillmon helped form the National Welfare Rights Organization (NWRO), which reached a peak of ten thousand members in 1968. Their program called for a minimum annual income for families in need and a proclamation that woman's work is "real work—pay it a living wage." Although the NWRO dissolved in the 1970s, their ideas represented an important recognition of the value of women's labor in the family.

Feminist scholars echo Johnnie Tillmon's insights when they question whether welfare systems compound, rather than alleviate, women's dependency. According to Myra Marx Feree, communist benefits for working mothers created a form of patriarchy in which the state replaced husbands. Critics of capitalist welfare states point to a double standard in social policy. As Nancy Fraser, Theda Skocpol, and others explain, government entitlements honor men's breadwinning as opposed to women's caregiving. Veterans' benefits, workers' compensation for injuries, and unemployment insurance are rights due primarily to men from the state. In contrast, single mothers have to prove their desperate need for aid. State agents often dole out welfare payments with restrictions through means testing, applying rules that distinguish between deserving and undeserving mothers. According to Gwendolyn Mink, income support for caregivers should be "an affirmative right of poor single mothers" and "a condition of women's equality."[20] European feminist scholars such as Janneke Plantenga also call for welfare states to ensure not only an adequate income but also "that people have the time to provide for their own and each others' care needs."[21]

The American welfare system has moved in the opposite direction in recent years by demanding that poor mothers enter the paid labor force. The shift began in the 1960s, but in the 1990s a new welfare reform law cut off benefits after two years and placed a five-year lifetime cap on assistance. Without adequate child care, critics argue, former welfare mothers who cannot earn enough to support their children will become more dependent on male wage earners. The full impact of these reforms will not be known for years, but the effort to employ mothers of young children signals a complete shift from the initial goals of the U.S. welfare system, which was to keep white women from undertaking wage labor.

Grassroots feminists such as the Welfare Warriors in Wisconsin have responded to this restructuring of the U.S. welfare system by calling for a guaranteed income for those who care for children. Similarly, when Massachusetts eliminated state funding for poor mothers in the 1990s, feminists protested by occupying the governor's office. Without government assistance, they argued, some mothers would have to remain with or return to abusive husbands. The Massachusetts Welfare Rights Union continues to fight for the safety net they say is promised by the UN's Universal Declaration of Human Rights. In England and the United States feminists point out that without adequate child care provisions, welfare reform offers false hope to poor mothers. As an alternative, U.S. feminists point to the Scandinavian model: adequate public health programs, job training, and child care. Instead of targeting single mothers as the problem, they seek parental responsibility.

Holding men accountable is part of this approach. Feminist journalist Katha Pollitt satirically recommended that the U.S. government make all men choose between paying a special tax to support "children whose paternity is unknown" and having a vasectomy.[22] But her serious purpose was to make us think about men's responsibility for the welfare of the children they produce. In Denmark fathers do pay the state, which then allocates child support funds so that mothers do not have to go to court to get them. Even many conservatives share the goal of paternal responsibility, as evidenced by the U.S. Child Support Enforcement Amendments of 1984 and 1988 and the increased use of the term "deadbeat dads" as a counterweight to "welfare mothers." The British government established the Child Support Agency (CSA) in 1991 to try to extract payments from absent fathers. According to historian Sheila Rowbotham, however, like the U.S. efforts, "it was guided by the same ideological conviction that families should bear all the cost and responsibility of children with no help from the rest of society."[23] And even if fathers in the United States paid up, three-quarters of the families living in poverty would remain poor unless mothers found good-paying jobs.

The analysis of welfare echoes themes in the broader social debates on women workers. Alongside laws that enforce equality in the workplace, governments must value the labor that women perform in the home without limiting women to the job of mothering or excluding men from parental benefits. As Gwendolyn Mink observes, "Rights that accommodate mothers' caregiving work need not ascribe motherwork to all women, nor *only* to women; men can mother, too."[24] Not only would these policies reduce the economic gender gap, but they would also help alleviate poverty.

THE CHALLENGES AHEAD

At the end of the twentieth century welfare reform and reductions in government services set back the economic progress of women in both Western democracies and former socialist states. Even in Sweden, which pioneered the social policies that support working mothers, the elimination of social sector jobs contributed to a widening wage gap. In the mid-1990s Swedish women earned only 72 percent of male salaries, in contrast to 80 percent a decade earlier. In eastern Europe high female unemployment rates after the collapse of communism exacerbated women's dependence on men, and the economic outlook remains grim for many women in postcommunist states. At the same time, women in developing countries have suffered from the structural adjustment programs required by the World Bank and the International Monetary Fund. In the 1980s and 1990s stringent economic requirements to qualify for loans from these agencies forced reductions in social services such as health care and education in developing countries. As women absorbed much of the labor once supported by these states, structural adjustment programs became another target of feminist protest.

Despite the political obstacles, and despite the persistent legacy of women's domestic identities, feminists have initiated an impressive array of social policies to achieve greater equality for women. New strategies continue to emerge throughout the world. In the United States raising the minimum wage for all workers has become a feminist priority because higher wages will allow single mothers who head families to escape poverty. In Italy feminists target the "casualization" of work, in which more labor is performed by self-employed, largely unregulated workers. Setting new labor standards would benefit both female and male casual workers. In developing countries feminists monitor the health and safety features of world trade agreements, which affect so many women who work on the global assembly line. In those parts of South Asia and the Middle East where women continue to labor within their homes, feminists seek reform of family laws to ensure rights to property, child custody, and divorce.

The history of feminist social policies teaches us that only recognizing the connection between unpaid domestic work and paid market labor can resolve the dilemmas of working women. On one hand, work in the family contributes to the economy and deserves support. On the other hand, if support for family labor applies only to women, it reinforces the very gender divide that gives rise to women's economic vulnerability. In early periods of industrialization, an imaginary and unrealistic contrast distinguished between male wage labor and women's caretaking in the home. The social problems of poverty as well as gender inequality rest in large part on this outmoded construct. In advanced or postindustrial societies we now witness a blurring of gender lines. Powerful feminist arguments suggest that we will achieve both greater gender equality and greater economic justice when social policies recognize the value of women's work in the family, reward women equally in the workplace, and support the parental work of men as well as of women.

PART IV

THE POLITICS
OF HEALTH AND
SEXUALITY

-NINE-

MEDICINE, MARKETS, AND THE FEMALE BODY

One is not born, but rather becomes, a woman.
—SIMONE DE BEAUVOIR, FRANCE, 1949

Everyone I know is trying to be thinner.
—LIU YUFANG, CHINA, 1999

Biology is destiny," critics of feminism proclaim, pointing to female reproductive capacity to explain why women must depend on men, the "stronger sex." Yet biology is also variable, both culturally and individually. Most women have a monthly cycle of egg release, fertility, and menstruation, but not the !Kung, who live in the Kalahari Desert of southwestern Africa. These women forage for food, walk long distances, and eat primarily vegetables. They nurse their infants for several years and at frequent intervals. As a result of diet, exercise, and nursing practices, the !Kung are rarely fertile and menstruate only a few times during adult life. Without using contraception, !Kung women have only four or five pregnancies. Culture, not merely biology, determines their life cycle.

Nor is the biology of sex constant. Most of us distinguish between male and female by some kind of physiological markers: XX or XY chromosomes, ovaries or testes, estrogen or testosterone, vagina or penis. Males are generally taller, heavier, with more body hair, deeper voices, and greater upper body strength; females usually have the capacity to gestate, give birth, and lactate. But biologically sexed individuals vary greatly in ways that are not always clearly visible. Developmental biologist Anne Fausto-Sterling points out that about 4 percent of human bodies are physiologically intersexed, either because they have both testes and ovaries or because their external genitalia differ from their internal sex organs. A continuum, rather than a dichotomy, might best describe the range of human sexes.

Relying on physiology also obscures how frequently nonsexual factors account for human difference. On average, males may be taller, stronger, or more spatially adept than females, but some women exceed men on all of these counts. Imagine two overlapping bell-shaped curves that plot any number of characteristics by gender. Although the median (average) may differ for males and females, a large percentage of cases overlap. Even for statistically average males and females, sex difference determines little more than reproductive function until culture comes into play. Gender, or the social meanings attached to male and female, builds layers of difference upon a narrow biological foundation, affecting physiology as well as personality. As biologist Ruth Hubbard points out, if a society "puts half its children in short skirts and warns them not to move in ways that reveal their panties, while putting the other half in jeans and overalls and encourages them to climb trees . . . [t]heir muscles will be different."[1] Or, in Simone de Beauvoir's words, "One is not born, but rather becomes, a woman."[2] The same is true for men.

De Beauvoir's point can be taken even further to argue that the body has no fixed meaning prior to language and customs. Cultures create male and female as central identities, but we could as easily categorize humans based on behaviors or personality traits (loud or quiet, sweet or sour) that cut across reproductive biology. Deconstructing the male/female dualism would mean recognizing a range of possible identities that we miss when we focus on only two biological options. Admittedly, it is not that easy to deconstruct long-standing binary systems, for our histories have been deeply shaped by them.

If difference had no social consequences, if it did not disadvantage one sex economically and politically, feminists might not question the powerful hold of our biological definitions of male and female. Cultural elaborations of sex difference, however, move far beyond the bare facts of physiology to create inequalities. Beliefs about bodily strength, health, and beauty, as well as ideas about racial difference, help structure women's economic opportunities. Two historical forces, medicine and marketing, have exacerbated these inequalities by granting more bodily authority to men. Feminists have responded to modern science and market capitalism by raising questions about who defines, and who controls, the female body. Building upon the Western ideal of self-determination, feminist body politics seek both strength and pleasure for women.

THE MEDICALIZATION
OF THE FEMALE BODY

In articulating a "sexual politics," feminists have had to confront deeply conflicted associations of women with the body. The earliest civilizations both venerated and feared women's generative power. According to historian Gerda Lerner, worship of the great goddesses in the early Middle East "celebrated the sacredness of female sexuality and its mysterious life-giving force."[3] Both men and women prayed to images of the female body. Babylonians represented the goddess Ishtar with an image of the female vulva, while the Minoan snake-goddess exposed her breasts. Although we are not sure about the extent of ancient goddess worship, the association of woman with nature clearly granted power to women's bodies, and not only in the Middle East. In the Hindu religious traditions of South Asia, complex female goddesses included nurturing maternal fertility figures, such as Parvati and Sita, as well as more threatening icons of uncontrolled sexuality, such as Kali. The North American Anasazi pueblo dwellers honored Corn Mother as the source of life and celebrated both female sexuality and fertility.

Many of the rituals that associate women with nature have emphasized both power and danger. The onset of menstruation occasioned celebration among the West African Asante, who danced in honor of a girl's first menarche. But many cultures isolate menstruating girls and women for fear that their power could overwhelm men and undermine their ability to hunt. Pollution taboos often keep menstruating women secluded among themselves or, as in orthodox Judaism, physically off-limits to their husbands. In some parts of Africa fear that women's powerful sexuality would make them unfaithful wives contributed to the practice of female genital cutting, in which surgical removal of the clitoris is intended to suppress women's sexual desires. This practice, like the insistence on bridal virginity, also tried to ensure a husband's paternity by limiting the sexual activities of wives.

Although contemporary societies both venerate and fear woman's reproductive capacity, the worship of the female body as a powerful religious force has diminished over time. Lerner argues that kingships, early states, and horticulture demoted the mother goddess in favor of male deities. Christian cultures relied on a hierarchy in which males, as spiritual and rational beings, resided closer to God; while females, mired in the flesh, ranked closer to animals. As in Europe, Islamic cultures in the Middle East feared that women could drain men's energies and detract from their mental or spiritual pursuits. Over time the fear that women's sexual allure would debase men led to the public veiling of women and their seclusion in the home.

Remnants of the sanctified female body survive in some religious beliefs, including forms of Tibetan Buddhism. Elsewhere religions have provided, or women have seized, opportunities to transcend the flesh. Christian nuns, like monks, renounced the body for a life of spiritual contemplation. In the Middle Ages, lay Christian women attempted to conquer their bodies by seeking spiritual ecstasy through holy fasting (*anorexia mirabilis*) to prove that they could survive on spiritual sustenance alone. Jewish women ritually sanctified their bodies in the *mikvah*, a women's bath, after menstruating. Bodily purity provided a source of empowerment in these religious practices.

Modern Medicine

In Western cultures, the scientific revolution that began in the 1600s gradually shifted authority over the body from religious to secular and medical experts. New technologies such as machines driven by water and steam power seemed to promise human mastery over nature and did indeed transform economic life. The medical discoveries of the scientific revolution would have enormous effects on both men and women, extending the life span of both and ultimately reducing infant and maternal mortality. Yet scientific medicine could also enhance male control over the female body.

For centuries women had employed plant remedies and folk medicine when they attended the sick within their families as part of their domestic duties. Those who served as midwives had particular knowledge of reproductive functions and held a quasi-professional standing in their communities. Gradually, however, male practitioners began to replace women healers. Men had access to the new scientific knowledge spread through the universities, which excluded women. In the 1700s first male midwives and later male gynecologists monopolized the new technology of the forceps. When medical schools and state licensing requirements created a professional elite, they excluded women. Furthermore, in the late 1800s the germ theory of disease and the application of antisepsis boosted the claims to expertise and the status of professional medicine. Male physicians now held out greater promise of cures.

Along with expertise came professional authority, often exercised over women by male doctors who viewed their patients primarily as reproductive bodies. According to one nineteenth-century American physician, even when women had digestive, heart, or lung disorders, "these diseases will be found on due investigation, to be, in reality, no diseases at all, but merely the sympathetic reactions or the symptoms of one disease, namely, a disease of the womb."[1] The diagnosis of hysteria— from the Greek word for womb—applied particularly to women. Some physicians applied genital massage to invoke orgasm as a cure; in the late nineteenth century they began to use mechanical vibrators to achieve this end, implying that only men could induce sexual release in women. A prominent American physician, J. Marion Sims, developed more extreme treatments for female diseases. He pioneered the removal of ovaries or the clitoris by experimenting first on female slaves in the U.S. South and then on poor Irish women in the wards of a New York City women's hospital.

Less extreme but equally problematic treatments for those nervous disorders, labeled "neurasthenia," included the rest cure, invented by leading Philadelphia doctor S. Weir Mitchell. This approach ignored the mind entirely in favor of feeding and resting the female body. When

Charlotte Perkins Gilman suffered from a nervous condition after the birth of her daughter, she endured this cure of extended bed rest with no sensory stimulation. "I went home and obeyed those directions for some three months," she recalled, "and came so near the borderline of utter mental ruin that I could see over."⁵ In her 1892 short story "The Yellow Wallpaper" Gilman portrayed doctors as paternalistic authoritarians who infantalized women patients. The yellow wallpaper of her title filled the sickroom and surrounded its female patient like a domestic prison from which she had to escape.

Many middle-class women in Europe and North America internalized the belief that the body was the source of their discontent. In the nineteenth and twentieth centuries girls and women in the United States embarked on what historian Joan Brumberg has called "the body project," measuring their self-worth by the shape of their bodies. Previously interested in cultivating their characters and spiritual lives, Brumberg argues, young women increasingly concentrated on their physical appearance and especially their size. It is within this context that the medical profession "discovered" young women's eating disorders in the mid-1800s and termed them "anorexia nervosa." In previous eras, *anorexia mirabilis* was not considered a disease; some women even achieved sainthood through this practice. But the medical profession viewed fasting girls as physically sick. At first doctors attributed the condition to hormonal or endocrinological problems; later Freudians stressed eating as a symbol of sexual drive, fasting as symbolic of its suppression. Feminist interpretations of eating disorders would eventually challenge this medicalization, echoing Gilman's critiques of the economic and political restraints that forced women to overemphasize their physical condition.

Medicalization occurred largely in Western industrialized nations where scientific discoveries enhanced the professional status of medicine. It did not, however, entirely displace women's traditional roles as healers. In many rural areas midwives continued to attend births. In subsistence economies outside the West, women and male healers often coexisted, their authority resting on spiritual, rather than scientific, authority. Colonial governments often distrusted these customs. In the Philippines, for example, older women shamans specialized in rituals of birth and death, performing in song, story, and dance. When Spanish missionaries arrived, they labeled these women witches and urged converts to turn to Christian rituals and hospitals instead. Despite official opposition, women continued to practice a variety of healing arts. Unable to suppress them, by the 1870s the Spanish colonial administration in the Philippines established training schools for midwives.

THE BODY BEAUTIFUL IN CONSUMER CULTURE

Along with medicalization, commercialization has exerted an increasingly powerful influence on the cultural meanings of the female body. By the 1900s economies driven by marketing linked images of women with products that seemingly had little to do with sex—from cars to mouthwash to cigarettes. Playing on the female body as a desired sexual object, advertising and popular culture saturated the Western media with image and innuendo. In her 1963 treatise *The Feminine Mystique*, Betty Friedan dated this "sexual sell" in the United States to the years after World War II, but the practice had originated by the 1920s. An early cigarette ad, for example, showed alluring women who begged men to "blow a little smoke my way." In popular culture, songs about "hot lips" and "baby face" reached wide markets through radios and phonographs, displacing earlier religious music or secular anthems to motherhood and chaste sweethearts. Whether through ads or in the World War II photos of pinup girls, the postwar boom in pornographic magazines, or the lyrics to rock and rap songs, eroticized images of women sold products.

The sexualization of women in popular culture had particular racial connotations. A long-standing Western association of Africans with primitive sexuality created receptive audiences for African American entertainers. In the 1920s French audiences cheered Josephine Baker's erotic dance performances, while in the United States Ida Cox sang about her sexual prowess in "One Hour Mama" ("no one minute papa ain't the kind of man for me").[6] Along with exuding sexual power, however, these performers could reinforce the image of black women's sexual availability. Over time, most popular music about women of color perpetuated sexual and racial dominance. In their 1971 hit song

"Brown Sugar," the Rolling Stones exulted male mastery over a young female slave, including a chorus that invoked the sounds of his nightly whipping of a sexually appealing young girl.[7] More recent rap lyrics castigate women as bitches and whores. Like advertising, the Western pop music now so readily available around the world sends a message that women of color are both sexually desirable and subject to conquest.

By the end of the twentieth century the sexual sell had infiltrated vast regions of the world, wherever markets for Western popular culture expanded. A 1987 study of Japanese soft-drink ads found that over one-fourth displayed women in bikinis. Soon after communist China allowed private markets, sexualized female images proliferated there as well. An ad for a Chinese tire factory, for example, showed a seductive young woman wearing a miniskirt and high-heeled shoes. While some cultures resist the trend, tight pants, bare bellies, and female cleavage have become international marketing tools that highlight the female body as a commodity.

The Diminishing Female Ideal

Images of women's bodies have proliferated widely, but the female ideal in popular culture has quite literally narrowed over time. In the 1870s British music hall performer Lydia Thompson and her "British Blonds" exemplified the voluptuous, full-bodied ideal of female beauty. By the 1920s a smaller, boyish figure appeared in Europe and North America. When *Playboy* magazine introduced the full-bosomed centerfold model in the 1950s, the women who posed were about 9 percent under the normal female weight. By 1978 these models were 16 percent under normal female weight.

While advertising and pornography glorified a thin female image, mass production also contributed to a more homogenized female body. For centuries women had made their clothing at home to fit their own contours. With the shift to ready-made clothing, mass-marketed through chains of department stores, women's fashions became more standardized. Those whose size or shape did not fit the norm measured themselves against an impossible ideal. Philosopher Susan Bordo argues that the homogenizing effect of consumer capitalism created "boundaries on difference," narrowing the range of acceptable physical shapes and inducing women to discipline their bodies in an effort to conform.

Commercial products from cosmetics to hair dyes to diet foods perpetuate this quest for a perfect body. So do services such as exercise classes and cosmetic surgery. Weight Watchers, a hugely successful corporation that pioneered the profitability of fear of fat, has a clientele that is 95 percent female. Diet books sell hundreds of millions of copies, even though medical studies have shown that dieting does not produce long-term weight loss. "Fat farms" charge thousands of dollars a week to manage reduction routines. More extreme treatments such as jaw wiring, protein injections, and the potentially fatal gastric stapling are too costly for most women. Despite the health risks of some procedures, cosmetic surgery has boomed in commercial cultures. In Brazil the number of plastic surgery procedures jumped between 1996 and 1999 by 50 percent, to three hundred thousand, with the majority for purely aesthetic reasons. In the United States the number of women who had breast enlargement surgery increased from thirty thousand in 1992 to eighty-seven thousand in 1997. While the number of men getting tummy tucks and nose reductions also increased, women represent 86 percent of the total 7.4 million cosmetic surgeries performed in the United States.

Outside the West as well, women now go to great lengths to conform to a white, Western physical ideal. Young women in East Asia undergo cosmetic surgery to create creased eyelids, while in China dieting has become a fad for urban teenage girls. With rising standards of living and an expanding market for beauty products, the Chinese body ideal has changed from large to small. "When I was young, people admired and were even jealous of fat people since they thought they had a better life," the manager of a Chinese weight loss center recalled. She explained in 1999 that fat is now considered "awful."[8]

The extent to which women feel discontent with their physical appearance is evident by adolescence. In the contemporary United States over half of thirteen-year-old girls and three-quarters of eighteen-year-old girls express dissatisfaction with their bodies. A 1986 study found that 70 percent of fourth-grade girls reported concern about their weight and that about half of them dieted. By age eighteen 60 to 80 percent of American girls, but only 15 percent of boys, had been on diets.

According to British therapist Susie Orbach, up to 60 percent of six- to nine-year-old girls worry about their body shape and size. A study of both white and Asian girls in Great Britain revealed that a preoccupation with thinness among nine-year-old girls had a direct bearing on the development of eating disorders. Liu Yufang, a diminutive young woman in China, expressed the sentiments behind this widespread phenomenon: "I always want to lose weight. Everyone I know is trying to be thinner."[9]

Distorted body image—the result of comparison with unattainable ideals—motivates some of the preoccupation with dieting. Three-quarters of a large sample of American women considered themselves fat, even though one-quarter were not technically overweight and another 30 percent were actually underweight. Of those now diagnosed with anorexia and bulimia in the United States, 90 percent are female. Obsessed with the intake of food and control of their weight, these women can lose more than 25 percent of their body weight, either through dieting and exercise or through eating binges followed by purging. Long-term effects include loss of bone density and heart problems. Some, such as singer Karen Carpenter and gymnast Christy Henrich, have literally starved themselves to death.

Although the anorectic woman is usually portrayed as a white, middle-class American, other women are by no means immune from eating problems. In the United States, Becky W. Thompson argues, Latina and African American women may use food to anesthetize the traumas of racism and poverty. Between one-third and two-thirds of the American women of color she studied had been sexually abused, and Thompson found that these women were likely to dissociate from their bodies. As one of her subjects, Rosalee, put it, "dieting is one of those last-ditch efforts to make everything all right in your life when that is not the cause of the problems to begin with."[10] Dieting, Thompson suggested, provided a way to transform the abused body, while purging represented a rejection of the body held responsible for its own abuse.

The female quest for thinness rests upon both Western ideals of individual control of the body and the economic abundance that provides most people with enough to eat. Cultures in fear of starvation have historically favored larger body mass. In developing countries women continue to suffer more from the malnutrition of famine and poverty than from anorexia. In parts of West Africa, for example, "fattening rooms" prepare adolescent girls for marriage, fatness is associated with beauty, and obese women command a higher bride-price. In those areas of Africa and Asia where body weight can be an indicator of wealth, women shown drawings of female bodies ranked the images of heavy women more highly than those who were thin.

Contact with the West, however, can transform body image. African women who migrate to Britain soon come to share the Western aversion to body fat. In the South Pacific nation of Fiji, where full-bodied women have always been considered healthy, the introduction of Western television programs via satellite changed young women's body image. Girls who watched television frequently were more likely to consider themselves "too big or fat" and more likely to begin dieting. The rate of eating disorders increased among Fijian girls along with Western cultural influence.

The idealized female body creates not only health problems but also a social hierarchy of beauty that places women in competition with each other. This hierarchy privileges the white, thin, and able-bodied. For those who do not approximate the ideal, difference can extract a steep cost in self-esteem. The Asian American writer Nellie Wong captured this phenomenon in a poem: "[W]hen I was growing up," she explained, "my sisters with fair skin got praised / for their beauty . . . to become / a woman, a desirable woman, I began to wear / imaginary pale skin."[11] Historically, the use of skin-lightening cosmetics and hair straighteners among African American women in the United States reflected the internalization of a racial hierarchy.

The social hierarchy of the body has material effects as well, for it keeps those who are fat, dark-skinned, or disabled at the economic margins. Excluded from certain jobs in which women's conventional appearance is an asset, they earn considerably less money and are more likely to live in poverty than are the thin, white, and able-bodied. An extensive survey of Americans found that overweight women, but not overweight men, had lower household incomes and higher rates of poverty than those who were not overweight. Knowing that economic penalties await those who are different may well reinforce the quest for light-skinned, thin, "perfect" bodies among women.

FEMINISM AND BODY POLITICS

Western feminists initially responded to medicalization and commercialization by demanding women's control over their own bodies, a principle grounded in the political theory of individual rights. In democratic nations those admitted to the "body politic" of representative government—initially free white adult European males—enjoyed the right to physical liberty. Instead of the authoritarian control of bodies, democratic societies celebrated the virtues of personal self-discipline. Feminist politics have incorporated ideals of both individual physical freedom and internalized control of the body, but they have also changed over time to rethink the meaning of control.

Since its inception, feminism has tried to extend to women the physical rights enjoyed by men. Rather than being considered mere reproductive or sexual bodies, writers such as Mary Wollstonecraft insisted that women should be allowed a life of the mind. In the 1870s Elizabeth Cady Stanton reminded young women that "God has given you minds, dear girls, as well as bodies."[12] Conservatives of her era disagreed, fearing that higher education drained women's reproductive energies and reduced their fertility. (Smart female college graduates disproved this theory by showing statistically that education did not depress reproductive capacity.) Early feminists also sought freedom from bodily constraint. Dress reformers in England and the United States decried the tight-laced corset in vogue during the 1800s. Amelia Bloomer recommended the more comfortable pantaloons that later bore her name, although the fashion did not survive early ridicule. By the early 1900s both male and female reformers campaigned against female foot binding in China. "Deforming a natural foot . . . is just as abusive as that of binding the waist," wrote a Chinese American physician in 1909.[13]

When Western feminism revived in the 1960s, activists realized that they attracted their greatest media attention by publicizing women's bodily confinement. In 1968 U.S. radical feminists scored their first publicity coup by protesting the Miss America pageant to call attention to the sexual objectification of women. Outside the pageant young women created a symbolic funeral pyre in which they burned "instruments of female torture" such as "high heels, nylons, garter belts, girdles, hair curlers, false eyelashes, makeup, and *Playboy* and *Good Housekeeping* magazines."[14] Women around the world demonstrated against beauty contests, picketing the Miss World pageant in London. They also protested the medicalization of the female body. In the Netherlands a group of Dutch feminists bared their stomachs at a convention of gynecologists to reveal the slogan "Boss of Our Own Belly" written there.[15]

Reclaiming the Body: Women's Health

The Dutch slogan represents a central theme of contemporary feminist body politics: women's right to choose whether and when to have children. The reproductive rights movement encouraged efforts to restore medical authority once wrested from female midwives by male gynecologists. While women such as Elizabeth Blackwell had pioneered women's medical education in the 1800s, not until the 1960s did significant numbers of women around the world begin to integrate the medical profession. By the year 2000 over 40 percent of the medical students in the United States, Mexico, and Hong Kong, and about one-third in Egypt, were female.

Women doctors have affected the practice of medicine not only through specialized care directed at women but also by insisting that medical research and funding take women's health needs into account. Specialized women's health centers have expanded rapidly, from 19 percent of U.S. hospitals in 1990 to 33 percent in 1997. Reforms in health policy have improved treatment. U.S. legislation extended medical coverage for hospital stays after childbirth. Under pressure from the women's health movement, the U.S. Congress enacted a 1993 law requiring the inclusion of women in clinical trials of drugs. The act corrected the bias of previous research on disease that looked at male subjects and assumed that the results applied to women. In addition, women patients have pressed private health insurers, governments, and hospitals to cover their gender-specific needs.

Along with affecting mainstream medicine, feminists have also created a grassroots women's health movement with an emphasis on self-help. The consciousness-raising groups of the 1960s and 1970s inspired this focus. As women shared stories of bodily pleasures and pain, they admitted ignorance about sexuality and reproduction, learned self-examination methods, and claimed personal responsibility for health, reproduction, and sexuality. Soon these women took their concerns into the political arena. In 1969, for example, young feminists in Washington, D.C., disrupted U.S. Senate hearings on oral contraception because no women had been called to testify about the safety of the birth control pill. Others demonstrated outside the D.C. public hospital protesting, as activist Alice Wolfson recalled, "the disproportionate numbers of black women who were being maimed and were dying from botched illegal abortions."[16]

In Massachusetts one women's group that began meeting in 1969 decided to publish in accessible form the kind of medical information women sought. In order to reclaim a heritage in which women "have always exchanged experiences and wisdom with one another," in 1973 the Boston Women's Health Book Collective produced *Our Bodies, Ourselves*.[17] The book included chapters on formerly unmentionable topics such as lesbianism and sexual violence. It quickly sold 250,000 copies. Translated into nineteen languages (including Japanese, Spanish, French, Greek, Swedish, German, Hebrew, Dutch, Arabic, and Braille), it had sold over four million copies by the end of the century. The book exemplified the self-help theme of second-wave feminism by defining women's medical needs on women's own terms. Over the years collective members published specialized books on the health needs of older women and children. In 1999 a Latina version, *Nuestros Cuerpos, Nuestras Vidas,* tempered the language of individual bodily control with an emphasis on familial and community responsibility for life, translating "self-help" as "mutual help."

Since the 1960s local women's health groups have formed throughout Europe and the Americas. Some projects concentrated on reproductive rights and services, teaching breast and cervical self-examination and providing alternative birth centers. Feminists helped inspire a revival of midwifery and a reversal of the century-long medicalization of childbirth. Female kin and friends once again surround the birthing mother, but in contrast to earlier practice, more fathers now witness and take part in the delivery of their children. Acknowledging the stress of motherhood, the self-help movement has also established postpartum support groups.

Self-help fostered major advocacy projects to meet the specialized needs of women. Byllye Avery, who helped open a women's health center in Florida in 1974, insisted that southern black women faced particular medical problems, including teenage pregnancies, obesity, high blood pressure, and heart disease. After talking with many women about their health, she concluded that "the number one issue for most of our sisters is violence—battering, sexual abuse."[18] To combat violence and to educate women about health issues, Avery and others established the National Black Women's Health Project. By 1989 the organization had fostered ninety-six self-help groups in the United States, six in Africa, and two in the Caribbean. Similarly, Latinas in the United States formed the National Latina Health Organization in 1986 to promote "self-help methods and self-empowerment processes" as well as to ensure reproductive rights for Latinas. Their projects include a Girls Against Tobacco campaign as well as youth groups to promote Latina self-esteem.[19]

Advocacy and Activism

Feminists and health activists around the world have built upon the self-help model, but they have also lobbied governments to provide women's health services. In Brazil SOS Mulher, which provided health and contraceptive services during the 1970s, influenced the federal health ministry to create the Integrated Program for Women's Health in the 1980s. Brazilian feminists also created Committees in Defense of Women's Rights that targeted prevention of high-risk pregnancy. In 2000 the British government convened a Body Image Summit that developed health care initiatives to "understand the links between eating patterns and self-image, including eating disorders."[20] The women's health movement has also forced insurers to reimburse costs for mammograms and pelvic examinations. In Japan groups such as the Network for Women and Health protested the rapid government approval of the male impotency drug Viagra in light of the decades-long refusal to approve the female oral contraceptive. In June 1999 Japan finally rescinded its ban on the birth control pill. Similarly, U.S. women's groups pushed to require insurance companies to cover the costs of contraception in light of the enthusiastic embrace of Viagra.

A major insistence of the women's health movement has been more-extensive research, new treatments, and public education about diseases that specifically affect women. Activists have followed a path forged by the American environmentalist Rachel Carson, who first exposed the links between pesticides and cancer and herself died of cancer in 1964. Particular medical risks faced by women include DES and breast cancer. From the late 1940s through the 1960s pregnant women in the U.S. had received the drug DES (diethylstilbestrol) to prevent miscarriage; as their children came of age the incidence of cervical cancer among daughters revealed the tragic consequences of marketing drugs without thorough understanding of their long-term effects. Feminist watchdog groups, such as Breast Cancer Action, now closely monitor the drugs promoted by pharmaceutical companies. In addition, women's health activists of the 1970s challenged the routine use of immediate mastectomy whenever a biopsy revealed a cancerous tumor in the breast. Instead, they insisted on a period of time during which women could decide with their doctors on an individual treatment protocol.

The increasing rate of breast cancer has incited both grassroots and national activism in the United States. Dozens of organizations provide support services, raise funds for research, and educate the public about experimental treatments and the impact of environmental toxins. In the 1990s the National Breast Cancer Coalition in the United States successfully lobbied Congress to increase funding for research. Although death rates have fallen with earlier diagnosis and better treatment, breast cancer is still the leading cause of death for U.S. women age forty to fifty-five, and death rates remain higher for black women. Internationally, the incidence of breast cancer in all industrialized countries has increased from one in twenty just a generation ago to one in eight women in 2000. In response, women have formed outreach and prevention projects, such as the Organization Against Breast Cancer in Israel and *El Lugar* (The Place) in Tijuana, Mexico, which offers screening for breast and cervical cancer.

A broad range of health concerns now mobilize feminists. According to the U.S. Campaign for Women's Health, diseases that disproportionately affect women include osteoporosis, diabetes, lupus, gallbladder disease, and depression. In 1993 homicide was one of the top five causes of death for U.S. women age twenty-five to forty-four, and the rate for African American women was almost five times as great as that for all women. Although AIDS initially affected men, by the late 1980s the global pandemic was spreading most quickly among women. By the end of the century 46 percent of those infected worldwide were female, most of them living in sub-Saharan Africa. In the United States women initially contracted HIV from drug use but increasingly are infected by sexual partners; in Africa and Asia most of the women are infected through sexual contact with husbands or partners. In South Asia and Africa men who work away from home, such as long-distance truck drivers, have been accustomed to having sex with prostitutes at rest stops. Infected by prostitutes, they then infect their wives, greatly increasing the number of children born with AIDS. In 1997 half a million children in sub-Saharan Africa and almost fifty thousand in South and Southeast Asia were newly infected with HIV.

In response to the spread of HIV, women's health activists organized to promote safer sex practices and provide services for infected women. The Society for Women and AIDS in Africa, founded in 1988, quickly established branches in twenty-five African countries. Through grassroots education, support for infected women, and rehabilitation programs, it links the response to HIV with women's economic and human rights. In South Africa AIDS projects have drawn in traditional healers to help stem the spread of infection. In Zambia women volunteers have created social services to care for the tens of thousands of street children whose parents have died of AIDS. Women living with AIDS take an active role in many of these efforts. In the 1990s, for example, HIV-positive women in California founded WORLD—Women Organized to Respond to Life-Threatening Diseases. Through support groups and a bilingual newsletter, WORLD brings information to otherwise isolated women facing the disease.

AIDS is not the only international threat to women's health, for maternal and infant mortality remain pressing problems. At the end of the twentieth century the risk of maternal mortality ranged from one in twenty-three in Africa to one in four thousand in North America. (For African American and other minority women in the United States, however, the rate is four times as high as for white women.) While 98 percent of the women who live in developed nations receive prenatal care, only 59 percent of those living in developing countries do. Each day as many as fifteen hundred women die in childbirth, and half of all pregnant women worldwide suffer from anemia. Infant and child mortality disproportionately affects female children in parts of the world where food and health care are given preferentially to males.

Cognizant of these health challenges, the 1995 UN conference on women in Beijing proposed equal primary health care for women and urged countries to close the gender gap in infant and child mortality. The Beijing platform also recognized that world economic policies have a profound effect on women's health. Not only do poorer countries have high rates of communicable diseases and malnutrition, but in addition, when creditor nations force these countries to repay debts through economic austerity programs, health and human services funding dries up. As a result, disease and malnutrition spread, with mothers bearing the brunt of providing makeshift care and mourning lost children. Feminists from Beijing to Cairo to Moscow now argue that addressing women's specific health needs can vastly improve the quality of life and help reduce the economic inequalities among regions.

International Challenges

As in every transnational organizing effort, the legacy of colonialism affects the women's health movement. The controversy over female genital cutting (FGC), also known as female circumcision (FC), illustrates this legacy.[21] According to UNICEF, 130 million women have had some form of the procedure, which ranges from extreme infibulation, in which the genitals are sewn closed, to removal of the labia and clitoris, to a ritual bloodletting. Each year about two million girls undergo these sometimes crude surgical procedures. The majority reside in Egypt, Ethiopia, Kenya, Nigeria, Somalia, and Sudan. Although most sub-Saharan African countries have banned the practice, it persists in many areas. More widespread in the countryside, immigrants have imported the custom to cities in the

Middle East, Europe, and North America. Although they defy local law and practice, families practice FGC because they fear that their daughters will not be able to marry otherwise.

Egyptian writer Nawal El Saadawi called worldwide attention to female genital cutting in her 1977 book *The Hidden Face of Eve*, which was published in English in 1980. She described the pain of her own operation at age six and linked the surgically imposed limitation on female sexual pleasure with larger social constraints on women's political lives. Women in the Middle East and Africa, as well as in Western nations, increasingly condemned FGC. When delegates at the UN women's conference in Copenhagen in 1980 discussed the practice, Western feminists labeled it "female genital mutilation" (FGM), a term adopted by the UN's World Health Organization and in the Western press.

Women's groups in Africa, however, took issue with the tone and form of some Western interventions. In a statement issued in 1980 the Association of African Women for Research and Development (AAWORD) asserted that it "*firmly condemns* genital mutilation."[22] At the same time, however, AAWORD criticized the sensationalism and narrow focus of Western campaigns because they emphasized the impact of FGC on women's sexual pleasure. Western coverage also played into racial and religious stereotypes of Muslims, depicting them as a barbaric people. The custom in fact long predated Islam, is not supported by the Qur'an, and has been practiced by Christians as well as Muslims in Egypt. As Nawal El Saadawi explained, "female circumcision, like the veil, is a political issue rather than a religious one."[23]

AAWORD insisted that the defeat of female genital cutting required an appreciation of its underlying causes. These include widespread ignorance, exploitation, and poverty. Similarly, women's health activists in Egypt argued that FGC could not be viewed in isolation from a larger complex of gender inequality, including high rates of female illiteracy and unequal marriage and divorce laws. Because they recognized that taboos on discussing female sexuality made a public campaign unlikely to succeed, Egyptian activists concentrated on educating the nurses and midwives who historically performed the operation.

Many African women's groups have followed this broad strategy, beginning with female literacy, family law reform, and women's health education. This approach succeeded when a Senegalese women's organization, TOSTAN (Breakthrough), raised the issue in the context of literacy classes that discussed the health of girls and human rights. The village women participating in the workshops gradually began to question genital cutting. They enlisted their husbands and male religious leaders in the pledge not to cut daughters or have their sons marry women who had the procedure. After several villages pledged to stop, they brought their cause to the Senegalese parliament, which in 1999 banned FGC and established educational programs to ease the cultural transition.

African scholars emphasize that local efforts are more effective than top-down legislation, especially when they take into account the need for alternative coming of age rituals and compensation for the traditional female cutters. In some villages, symbolic cutting has replaced excision. A Nairobi-based NGO created a new ritual in which hundreds of Meru girls in a Kenyan village "graduated into womanhood" without FGC. In a ceremony in Guinea dozens of women renounced the custom by handing in the excision knives once used to cut female genitals. These local women's movements represent an important step in the process of extending to women the human right of physical self-determination while remaining sensitive to cultures that value communal responsibility.

THE POLITICS OF
REPRESENTATION—
RESISTING MARKETING

Along with reclaiming the body from medicalization, feminists have targeted commercial media representations that contribute to the sexual objectification of women. From Betty Friedan's exposé of the "sexual sell" in the 1960s to Naomi Wolf's critique of the "beauty myth" in the 1990s and academic analysis of the "male gaze" in popular culture, Western feminists have argued that images of women in advertising, films, art, and fashion can perpetuate gender inequality. "This ad is offensive to

women," activists scribbled across billboards that glorified male dominance or violence against women. At the same time, other feminists,
wary of portraying women as victims, call for new, more positive representations of female sexuality.

Responses to fashion illustrate the range of feminist strategies for
resisting the male gaze. Radical feminists of the 1960s and 1970s portrayed the media and the fashion industries as villains who perpetuate the
association of women as men's sexual objects. Miniskirts, for them, represented not liberation but sexualization. By the 1980s, however, feminists
disagreed over whether to condemn fashion or embrace it as a form of
self-expression. Lesbians elaborated a "femme" style of dress intended for
women's, not men's, pleasure. In the 1990s younger third-wave feminists
juxtaposed elements of traditionally feminine style, such as short skirts,
makeup, and bleached hair, with combat boots and quite unladylike demands for gender equality. One Asian American fan of the punk rock
"riot grrrl" band Bikini Kill wrote that when its founder, Kathleen
Hanna, "climbed on-stage in a mini-skirt, lipstick smeared, and sang/
screamed about incest or rape or girl-girl desire, she wanted you to know
that no matter what she wore, she wasn't asking for it."[24]

Tensions over feminism and fashion recur in Middle Eastern debates
over Western garb versus modest clothing. Whether worn only around
the face or from head to toe, the dark cloth covering of a woman's body
that signifies modest dress for Muslims has stood for the chains of slavery
in the eyes of the West. Historically, Muslim feminists such as Huda
Sha'arawi discarded their veils and adopted Western clothing styles as a
symbol of emancipation. When laws enforce the veil, they can in fact coincide with male control of women. Under the rule of the Taliban in
Afghanistan, women had to wear a head-to-foot body covering, supposedly to protect men from the temptations of the flesh. The clothing also
helped enforce a ban on women's wage labor by limiting their mobility.

Yet some Muslim women claim the veil as a woman's right. They
may choose it as a statement of personal modesty to protest the Western
objectification of women's bodies. Highly educated women professionals
have embraced the veil as a sign of their commitment to Islamic nationalism in the face of Western cultural imperialism. Why is the veil more

oppressive than a miniskirt? asks Nawal El Saadawi, who chooses not to veil.[25] In the view of one young Algerian woman, a commitment to personal choice can inform modest dress *(hijab)*: "I think it's scandalous how men dominate women in Algeria. Listen, if I am able to take on this *hijab* against the wishes of my father, another woman is also able to decide *not* to wear it, despite the wishes of her father. No woman should let herself be intimidated, a woman must stand up for her rights."[26] According to the Revolutionary Association of the Women of Afghanistan, who resisted the Taliban, "To wear, or not to wear, the Islamic veil is a completely personal issue and no one has the right to interfere with this decision or impose the veil upon us."

El Saadawi provides a unique perspective on the fashion debates because she is a critic of both the veil and Western women's fashions. When women wear makeup, she points out, "they hide their original features. This is a veil. This can be called a postmodern veil." Similarly, El Saadawi draws an analogy between female genital cutting and the cosmetic surgeries popular in the West, such as breast reduction or enhancement. "Cutting off part of the body, this is like female circumcision," she points out. "They think it is postmodern cosmetics, but really it is exactly like a clitoridectomy."[27]

Chinese women also struggle to find political meaning in women's changing fashions. Under communism and especially during the Maoist cultural revolution, Chinese clothing was uniformly dark, plain, and drab. Both male and female individuality was subsumed under a collective proletarian identity. With the opening of China to market economic forces and Western advertising, women's magazines encouraged a "new health and beauty craze," replete with makeup, high fashion, and a "Rapid Healthful Beauty Bust Enhancer." In reaction to decades of dictates that suppressed individual expression, many Chinese women justified the new fashions as a form of liberation. As historians Gail Hershatter and Emily Honig explain, however, "What looked like an increased scope for self-expression and individuality in women's attire may merely represent a new standard of conformity, one geared to pleasing men."[28]

WHERE MEDICINE AND
MARKETING MEET:
TRIM OR FIT?

Reclaiming the female body can be tricky. In cultures saturated with images of exuberant, slim, white female bodies, how can individuals resist the promise that control of their own bodies will make them happier, as well as healthier and wealthier? Two issues—dieting and sports—illustrate well the political tensions that feminists balance in seeking control over the body in a highly commercialized world.

Dieting is in part a response to women's historic economic dependence on men. As psychotherapist Carole Munter explains, "As long as our options are restricted, no woman will experience her body as her home, but rather as her meal ticket." Dieting also serves as a symbolic form of control for women in many cultures. While young men are encouraged to assert themselves, girls sometimes rebel by taking to an extreme the acceptable female concern with weight. For Munter, dieting provides a female fantasy that thinness will solve material and emotional problems. "We're taught to shape our bodies," she writes, "and not the world." Naomi Wolf has pointed out another political dynamic: When women do organize for social change, body image is turned against them. Backlash against feminism, Wolf explains, "uses images of female beauty as a political weapon against women's advancement."[29] Diatribes against feminism often invoke images of fat, hairy, ugly women, suggesting that to become a feminist, to claim an identity as a powerful woman, means losing all conventional physical appeal.

The line between strategic practices and internalized oppression is not always clear. The girl who refuses to eat may be trying to claim power within her family or in the society. But if this "hunger strike" is a protest of women's limited control in society, it is also, in Susan Bordo's view, a counterproductive act, "an illusory experience of power previously forbidden to her by virtue of her gender."[30] Some women argue that dieting or cosmetic surgery enhances self-image and even improves their work lives. Since losing weight can add to a woman's self-esteem in a culture that so often undermines women, no one should pass judgment on an individual decision to diet. Yet, as psychologist Esther Rothblum points out, since almost all dieters regain lost weight, any newfound esteem may later plummet.

Feminists tend to accept more enthusiastically the growth in women's participation in athletics. Women's sports strongly challenge earlier scientific beliefs in women's innate physical limitations. Once encouraged to exercise their bodies, women's athletic capacities have improved markedly. In 1964, for instance, the male-female time gap for running the twenty-six-mile marathon was almost an hour and a half; by 1984, the gap had closed to twenty-one minutes. Women's physiology had not changed; their access to athletic training did the trick.

Legal reform hastened the explosion of U.S. women's sports. In 1972 Congress prohibited discrimination on the basis of sex in schools that receive federal funds. Previously, school sports had been nearly monopolized by boys, in part because girls' teams had little if any funding. The gradual impact of Title IX of the 1972 Education Act vastly expanded girls' athletics. Only one in every twenty-seven high school girls participated in sports in 1971; by 1996 one in three did so. However, most U.S. schools are still not in full compliance, college scholarships for female athletes lag behind those for men, and only after women students file lawsuits do some colleges fund women's sports equally. Moreover, homophobia still haunts collegiate locker rooms. Nonetheless, by the time the young women raised with equal athletic opportunity since childhood reached college in the 1990s, the quality of their performance created greater public enthusiasm for women's sports. Under legal pressure, the National Collegiate Athletic Association organized national tournaments for women's teams, and when television began to broadcast them, the audience grew even wider.

In professional and Olympic sports as well, women athletes in a number of countries are reaping the gains long sought by feminists. At the 1970 Wimbledon professional tennis tournament, women players initiated a revolt against unequal pay. Feminists such as Billie Jean King challenged male prejudices against women athletes. Over the next generation, greater media coverage of players such as Martina Navratilova inspired younger women to take up the sport. By 2000 the women's game attracted international attention. Professional basketball expanded as well, first in Europe and later in the United States. In international amateur sports, women's participation increased from 15 percent of Olympic athletes in 1972 to 40 percent in 2000. Champion runners such as African American Florence Griffith Joyner and Aboriginal Australian Kathy Freeman, who lit the Olympic torch at the 2000 games, broadened the cultural repertoire of popular female images. The addition of women's Olympic team sports, such as basketball and soccer, along with greater media attention, further projected a vision of powerful female physicality.

Amateur sports also flourished as soccer, basketball, yachting, mountain climbing, and even hunting ceased to be single-sex activities. Women's participation in exercise, fitness, and bodybuilding soared in the developed nations. Even the Miss World and other beauty pageants that traditionally judged women's shapes in swimsuits began to incorporate fitness competition.

This health and fitness craze created new markets as well as new bodies. Clothing and footwear manufacturers such as Nike promote their goods by sponsoring female along with male athletes. Increasing sales reflect in part women's demand for athletic gear for each new sport and training activity. (A special Nike Web site announces the company's "responsibility to provide you with the shoes, apparel and equipment you need.")[31] Fitness has joined fashion in advertisements that proselytize a new female body ideal. In the United States magazines such as *Sports Illustrated for Women* and *Women's Sports & Fitness* feature covers with slim athletic female bodies, along with headlines like "Get a Body You Can Bare" and "Is Your Gym Making You Fat?"

As these titles suggest, traditional body ideals remain powerful. For example, a photo series on Olympic athletes that featured the heavyset U.S. weight lifter Cheryl Haworth obscured her size in a storm of fluffy white feathers.[32] Along with photos, much of the advertising in sports magazines perpetuates aspirations for a thin, white female physique. The quest for fitness can also overlap with extreme forms of bodily control, for many anorectic women exercise excessively to reduce weight, and the new emphasis on the fit body can reinforce physical hierarchies that relegate disabled women to economic marginality. As different as the new female athleticism seems from feminine fashion, it too can foster conformity unless women are able to choose freely how much they wish to adopt its values.

The finale of the women's World Cup soccer championship in July 1999 captured well the ambiguities involved in reclaiming the female body in cultures steeped in marketing. The long, tense final game between the United States and China came down to a single penalty shot that would determine the victory. When she saw that her kick had made the winning goal, the American player Brandi Chastain pulled off her soccer shirt, waving it with a victory cry while millions of spectators around the world witnessed her strong, fit body clad in shorts and a sports bra. For those who missed the televised game, newspapers carried front-page photos of the semibare champion.

As interesting as the photos were journalists' speculations about Chastain's act: Did she mean to claim equality with male soccer players who frequently stripped their shirts after making goals, or was she advertising her sponsor's sports bra in a clever form of marketing? The fact that Chastain had previously posed naked for a magazine raised further questions about whether she was also marketing sexual appeal. Like the third-wave feminists of her generation who reject dichotomies between fashion and feminism, between good girls and bad girls, Chastain may have found these questions inappropriate. Whatever her intention, though, her exuberant physical act captured the multiple meanings of the female body that had evolved by the end of the twentieth century—fit, fashionable, sexual, and strong.

TEN

REPRODUCTION: THE POLITICS OF CHOICE

If family planning had been available earlier, my life would have been different. That is my lifelong regret.
—MARRIED WOMAN, CHINA, 1990s

In her 1985 dystopian novel *The Handmaid's Tale*, Canadian author Margaret Atwood imagined a North American future in which totalitarian, antifeminist extremists seized control of government and the economy. Turning back the clock, these rulers ordained that women could no longer earn wages, spend money, speak out in public, or make choices about childbearing. Indeed, reproductive control of women was at the heart of this regime. In a world in which environmental toxins had produced widespread infertility, the few women who could still conceive had to serve as the "handmaids" whose sole purpose was to bear children who would be raised by barren, elite women. A revolutionary underground of women and men resisted these rulers, but Atwood kept their fate open to question, leaving to contemporary feminists the task of preserving women's reproductive rights.

Written at a time of growing conservative attacks on abortion in the United States, and a few years before the Canadian Supreme Court legalized abortion, Atwood's novel drove home the centrality of reproductive rights for North American feminism. By the 1980s reproduction had become politically charged and politically controversial because of the very historical changes that drew women into the wage labor force. In earlier eras women both welcomed motherhood and attempted to control reproduction. They prayed for fertility, turned to kin and neighbors to help rear children, and limited childbearing during times of famine or scarcity. Over the past two hundred years, however, the shift from self-sufficient agriculture to a commercial and then industrial economy encouraged smaller families. Women needed more reliable control over their fertility, especially when they entered the paid labor market. Economics, however, do not fully explain reproductive practices. Motherhood continues to have deep spiritual and cultural meanings, and both women and men are loath to undermine its power. Furthermore, recent medical technologies offer greater reproductive choices, but they also have the potential to exploit women's reproductive labor.

Given these historical complexities, feminists have proposed reproductive policies that balance an affirmation of women's capacity for childbearing with a recognition of the economic vulnerability that mothers still face. The principle of choice has become critical to feminists because it encompasses both of these positions. Choice allows women to claim rights to motherhood when they wish but to resist childbearing when they must. While the arguments for choice have shifted over time between individual rights and social welfare, the commitment to reproductive choice remains central to feminist politics.

REPRODUCTIVE STRATEGIES AND FERTILITY CONTROL

Almost all cultures have regulated births. When population threatened to overrun food supplies, earlier subsistence, nomadic, and agricultural societies found ways to limit growth. These methods included limiting or delaying marriage, punishing premarital sexual activity, and using herbal contraceptives or abortifacients. In many cultures, when food was scarce a child might be killed shortly after birth. Slave women sometimes committed infanticide to refuse forced reproduction. In most agricultural societies, however, children represent an economic asset. They work as farm laborers and eventually support their elders. In commercial and industrial economies children no longer provide labor for their families. Instead they require substantial investment of family resources and years of education to become productive workers. For this reason, wherever industrial economies expand, most families gradually adapt their reproductive strategies to invest more resources in raising fewer children.

The result of this shift in ideal family size is a decline in fertility rates (the average number of births to women of childbearing age). In the United States, for example, the marital fertility rate dropped by about half over the course of the nineteenth century, from slightly over 7 children per woman in 1800 to slightly under 4 children per woman in 1900. By 1950 the overall rate was under 3 births per married woman, and by 2000 it had fallen to 2.06. Rates differ by race and ethnicity, in part because African Americans and some immigrant groups worked the land longer than urban white middle-class populations. Yet family size declined over time for all groups. When other countries industrialized at different historical moments, their fertility rates declined as well. Before World War II Japanese women bore on average 5 children; by 2000 the figure was 1.41 children per woman. The rate for Russian women dropped to 1.25 by 2000. In Mexico, the average number of children per woman of childbearing age declined from around 7 in 1950 to 2.67 in 1999. (See Appendix E.)

Families reduced their fertility in any way they could. In the 1800s some couples in industrializing countries continued to use traditional herbal contraceptives or variations on the rhythm method, limiting intercourse to presumably safe periods of women's menstrual cycles. New contraceptive technologies, such as barrier methods, gained popularity in the nineteenth century. In the 1840s an early form of the diaphragm was patented in the United States under the name The Wife's Protector. Condoms made of animal membrane had been used earlier, especially among prostitutes, but with the vulcanization of rubber after 1880 a more reliable "sheath" became affordable for working-class couples in Europe and the United States. When these methods failed, women turned to abortifacients or folk remedies to end unwanted pregnancies. Well into the twentieth century some women tried to induce miscarriage by inserting knitting needles or other instruments into their own uterus, then turned to midwives when they hemorrhaged.

Both single and married women turned to abortionists. Before the nineteenth century religious and secular law in Europe did not condemn all abortions. Following English common law, American states allowed abortion if performed before "quickening"—when the mother felt the fetus move in her womb, usually around three to five months into the pregnancy. Legally, then, the mother could determine when life began. Early statutes did outlaw abortion if conducted against a woman's will. During the late 1800s industrializing societies such as the United States witnessed growing use of surgical abortion, particularly by married women attempting to limit family size. Movements to criminalize the procedure responded to this increase.

Early women's rights advocates had ambivalent attitudes toward contraception and abortion. They associated the condom with men's patronage of prostitutes and feared that contraception could lead to excessive sexual demands on wives. Without the excuse of avoiding pregnancy, they reasoned, wives might lose their ability to refuse marital sex. In contrast to what they considered "artificial" contraception, nineteenth-century U.S. feminists favored "voluntary motherhood," a phrase referring to a wife's right to refuse marital sex in order to avoid pregnancy. Some considered abortion a crime against women necessitated by the sexual demands of inconsiderate husbands.

But most married women desperately sought contraceptive information. They acquired it from women friends, druggists, or doctors, and through newspaper ads for abortionists or for elixirs that would bring on "delayed menses." Although private use of contraception was widespread, very few women spoke out publicly in its favor. The exceptions included the English feminist Annie Besant, who, like John Stuart Mill before her, tried to make contraceptive information available to poor women. Besant's arrest and trial in the 1870s brought the issue of contraceptive availability to public attention. Other women also defied the law to assist fertility control. In 1882 the first female doctor in the Netherlands, Aletta Jacobs, opened an illegal clinic where she provided diaphragms for women.

Even without easy access, married women's efforts to control their fertility were so successful that doctors and politicians worried about population decline. From 1860 to the 1930s, a movement to criminalize contraception and abortion contributed to the medicalization of women's health. Germany outlawed abortion in 1871, and in the United States the Comstock Act of 1873 prohibited the circulation of "obscene materials" through the postal service, including any contraceptive information or devices. At the same time American physicians led state campaigns to criminalize abortion. They portrayed married women who sought abortions as selfish pleasure seekers who shirked their maternal duties and cared only about "personal indulgence." New state laws banning abortion forced the practice underground from the 1870s to the 1970s. Wealthier women could either find private practitioners who would help them or hospital boards that would exempt them from the law, but most women resorted to back-alley abortionists at great risk to their health.

Legal restrictions on reproductive choice took another form in the early 1900s, when fears about population decline coincided with the rise of eugenics, the science of selective breeding. In the United States racial prejudice incited fears that white Anglo-Saxon Protestant women were committing "race suicide," given higher birth rates among Catholic and Jewish immigrants to the United States as well as African Americans. Elite classes worried that the country would come to be dominated by voters from the masses, whom they considered of inferior genetic stock. Similar fears of race degeneration in England prompted efforts to remove middle- and upper-class women from education and jobs by invoking their imperial duty to bear children. Faced by a population decline, the French government initiated campaigns to encourage motherhood and outlawed contraception after World War I.

Following the Malthusian tradition of population control for the poor, eugenicists also supported state sterilization of certain groups, including not only the poor but also immigrants, the "feebleminded," or the disabled. Sterilization involved surgery to tie the Fallopian tubes so that a woman could not become pregnant or vasectomy for males. Many women chose sterilization to avoid repeated pregnancies, especially if they already had several children. For other women, however, sterilization was involuntary. In Sweden, for example, over sixty thousand people were forcibly sterilized between 1936 and 1976, most of them women considered to be racially or socially inferior. In the United States compulsory sterilization laws initially targeted "mentally defective" women in state institutions to prevent them from bearing "defective" children. The laws applied to men or women of any background, but they disproportionately affected immigrants, African Americans, Native Americans, Puerto Ricans, the poor, and disabled women. Twice as many American women as men underwent compulsory sterilization.

Toward Birth Control

The feminist movements of the twentieth century increasingly embraced contraception and abortion as necessary for reproductive choice. As greater numbers of women, and especially married women, entered the paid labor market, control over fertility became more critical. Sexual mores were changing as well, with greater acknowledgment of premarital sexual activity among the young. Feminists moved away from an insistence on voluntary motherhood and began to call for contraceptive access for both working- and middle-class women.

Margaret Sanger, a nurse from a working-class background, first used the term "birth control." In 1916 Sanger opened the first U.S. clinic that distributed information on contraception. Situated in a New York City immigrant neighborhood, the clinic attracted primarily married working-class women. Sanger combined a genuine concern about the health of poor women exposed to too-frequent pregnancies with a eugenic belief in breeding superior, "wanted" children. At her most radical, she proclaimed that "no woman can call herself free who does not own and control her body." At her most conservative, she referred to those who were "unfit" to reproduce.[1] Whatever her motives, working women flocked to her clinic, as did British women to Marie Stopes' London clinic when it opened in 1921. As one client explained, "My mother had fourteen children and I didn't want that."[2]

Although contraception and abortion remained illegal, after 1920 taboos on discussing birth control weakened. In Protestant countries especially, liberal religious leaders gradually dropped their resistance. Some countries even decriminalized abortion. Both Sweden and Denmark liberalized their abortion laws before World War II. In addition, the Soviet Union allowed abortion from 1920 to 1936. A major impetus to changing reproductive policies was the widespread economic depression of the

1930s, which intensified acceptance of the principle of family planning. Delaying or spacing births became essential when so many families could not afford to support more children. During this era U.S. women increasingly relied on the diaphragm, fitted in doctors' offices or in the expanding number of birth control clinics sponsored by Sanger's organization, Planned Parenthood. But they also turned to patent medicines and, when these failed, illegal abortions.

Sterilization continued to provide fertility control in class- and race-specific ways, even after Nazi abuses largely discredited eugenics. In the United States hospitals discouraged married white women who wished to be sterilized by requiring that they already have several children. Yet doctors often pressured mothers who received welfare or state medical aid to consent to sterilization, which removed their choice to bear further children. The U.S. government offered free sterilization but little contraceptive information to women in the territory of Puerto Rico, more than a third of whom underwent *la operación*. Native American physicians estimate that in some tribes a quarter of American Indians of childbearing age had been sterilized by the 1970s, in part because government health services offered no other contraceptive information.

Not all of these sterilizations were voluntary. The southern sharecropper and later civil rights leader Fannie Lou Hamer did not learn of her sterilization until it was too late. In the 1960s and 1970s Mexican American women in California emerged from childbirth at public hospitals to learn they had been sterilized without their informed consent. As activist Ana Nieto Gómez recalled, doctors "saw themselves as agents of the public, saving taxpayers money," by preventing women on welfare from having more children.[3]

By the 1960s contraceptive practice had become widespread in industrialized nations. Millions of married couples were already controlling fertility when the new oral contraceptive came on the market, and many women shifted the method they used. The pill also popularized birth control among single youth, who openly embraced premarital sexual relations. Gradually courts and legislatures reversed earlier policies. By 1965 all U.S. states permitted contraception. Throughout western Europe women began to rely on the birth control pill.

By the end of the twentieth century over 60 percent of women of childbearing age in advanced industrial countries used contraception, primarily the birth control pill or the condom. Use of contraception ranges worldwide from 40 percent of Filipinas to around half of the women in Mexico and Malaysia and three-quarters of U.S. women. For the most part women have taken responsibility for limiting births. Some European men have opted for vasectomy, particularly in Britain and the Netherlands, but rates remain low elsewhere.[4] In developing countries one-fourth of women rely on intrauterine devices (IUDs) and half use sterilization to control fertility.

Abortion remained illegal far longer than contraception. During the 1950s China and the eastern European socialist states legalized abortion, and women in the Soviet bloc took it for granted. Until the 1960s, however, pregnant women in Europe and North America sought abortions only at great cost and personal risk. Because hundreds of British women died each year from illegal abortions, in 1936 the Abortion Law Reform Association began to advocate change. In the United States mortality rates were higher for abortion than for childbirth. The risks did not deter women from the procedure, however. In 1953 Alfred Kinsey estimated that 90 percent of premarital pregnancies ended in abortion and that 22 percent of married women had had an abortion. Other scholars estimate that a million women in the United States had illegal abortions each year during the 1960s and that between five hundred and a thousand of them died annually in hospitals from the complications. Because wealthier women could afford safer abortions, the death toll affected poor women disproportionately. In New York State, for example, 80 percent of the women who died from illegal abortions in the 1960s were African American and Puerto Rican.

Limited reproductive choice, combined with increasing wage earning, rallied women in the industrialized nations to press for legalized abortions. North American and European doctors, disenchanted with bureaucratic abortion restrictions, had called for reform of abortion laws since the 1950s. The feminist revival added a demand for woman's right to choose. The politics of personal experience fueled this shift. In private consciousness-raising groups women acknowledged the unspoken toll of illegal abortions. They pooled information about physicians who were willing to risk this illegal practice. In the United States a group of

Chicago women known anonymously as the Jane Collective compiled a list of safe abortion providers and shared it through word of mouth. The members then taught themselves how to perform the procedure, and between 1965 and 1973 they provided eleven thousand abortions.

In Europe and North America women increasingly spoke out publicly about abortion. In 1970 hundreds of Italian and French women, including Simone de Beauvoir, broke their silence by acknowledging that they had had illegal abortions. In Canada a caravan of women traveled across the country to demonstrate for abortion rights at the national legislature. Mass marches by women in several countries also brought the issue to public attention. The pressure contributed to the liberalization of British laws in 1967 and gradually laws throughout Europe and North America.

The key legal turning point in the United States occurred in 1973, when a suit on behalf of a woman denied an abortion reached the U.S. Supreme Court. In *Roe v. Wade* the court ruled that the state could not interfere with a woman's right to choose abortion during the first two trimesters of pregnancy. Within a year of the ruling the mortality rate for abortion fell from eighteen to three deaths per hundred thousand women, making the procedure far less risky than childbirth. France, West Germany, and Italy liberalized their abortion laws in the 1970s, as did India; Spain decriminalized abortion in 1985. By 2000 over 60 percent of the world's population lived in the sixty-four countries that permitted abortions. Where legal, abortion rates per thousand women ranged in the 1990s from a low of six or seven in the Netherlands and Belgium to around twenty-two in Australia and the United States and forty to sixty in the former Soviet Union.

Abortion remains illegal in 127 countries, with 38 percent of the world's population. Even where legally restricted, however, abortion rates can be quite high since contraception is usually not available either. In the 1990s abortions per thousand women ranged from twenty-three in Egypt to fifty in Chile. The physical costs of these illegal abortion are high. In Mexico one out of every four pregnancies ends in abortion. Of the estimated two million illegal abortions annually, the majority are for women who have already borne several children. Throughout Latin America infections and complications from unsafe illegal abortions bring peasant and working-class women into public health clinics regularly. As Nicaraguan nurse Isabel Beteta explained in 1990, "Of course it's the poorer women who suffer: the richer ones have access to decent health care."[5]

REPRODUCTIVE POLITICS

Second-wave feminist support for contraception and abortion rests upon a range of political arguments grounded in abstract rights to the body and opposition to state intervention in private issues. The insistence on reproductive choice has clear economic origins as well, for removing the risk of unplanned parenthood can reduce women's disadvantage in the labor market. Women's health also ranks high on the reproductive political agenda. In the United States activists sued drug companies that manufacture faulty contraceptives, removing from the market unsafe intrauterine devices, such as the Dalkon Shield. Double standards in world population programs also enraged feminists, including the export of the contraceptive Depo-Provera for use in developing countries before it had been deemed safe for domestic use.

Sterilization abuse is an important part of the reproductive rights agenda as well. At a 1969 rally young feminists who heard Fannie Lou Hamer talk about her experience vowed to make forced sterilization a political issue. Influenced by Puerto Rican physician Helen Rodriguez-Trias, who founded the Committee to End Sterilization Abuse, they formed the Committee for Abortion Rights and Against Sterilization Abuse (CARASA). The members pointed out the irony of the U.S. government funding 90 percent of the costs of sterilization but none of the costs of abortion. This disparity forced poor women to forfeit their ability to bear future children; because they could not afford to end an undesired pregnancy any other way, they often chose sterilization.

The Conflict over Abortion

Of all of these reproductive issues, however, a woman's right to choose an abortion has provoked the strongest controversy by far. Opinion polls conducted in a total of forty countries during the 1980s and 1990s documented the public's ambivalence. Overall, 82 percent of those questioned approved of abortion to preserve the mother's health, and 68 percent approved in the case of fetal defect. The support diminished greatly when health was not the motivation: only 31 percent approved if the mother was single and 36 percent if a married couple did not want to have additional children. Women and men had similar attitudes, but religion and class strongly influenced them. Catholics and fundamentalist Protestants opposed abortion more than liberal Protestants and Jews. Wealthier and more highly educated individuals supported abortion more than did those who were poorer and less educated. At present, support remains strong in the West. Seventy percent of those polled in Great Britain in 1996 supported legal abortion, and a 2001 poll found that over 60 percent of U.S. voters supported *Roe v. Wade.* The majority of the Americans polled defined themselves as pro-choice.

Internationally, religion has had a clear impact on abortion policy. In Catholic countries both the Church and lay organizations strongly oppose abortion. In 1983 Ireland adopted a constitutional amendment protecting the right to life of the unborn. The Irish government prosecuted abortion counseling centers and banned newspaper advertisements for clinics in England; some Irish libraries removed copies of *Our Bodies, Ourselves* to avoid legal risk. Under pressure from feminists, however, certain predominantly Catholic countries, such as Italy and Spain, have lifted their bans on abortion. After marches by tens of thousands of Italian women, in 1975 a half million women and men petitioned their government to offer a referendum on abortion.

Most Latin American countries still ban abortion. Under a Mexican law in effect in the 1990s, a woman who consented to an abortion could be imprisoned for up to five years, depending on her reputation and marital status. The abortion provider could be imprisoned for up to eight years, depending on whether or not the woman consented. Chilean women have also been prosecuted for obtaining abortions. Feminists in Latin America have protested both these laws and the risks of illegal abortions. In Bolivia, for example, women's organizations have lobbied for government services for women who have had abortions. They declared September 28, 1998, the Day for Decriminalization of Abortion in Latin American and the Caribbean.

The heated conflicts over abortion politicized women on both sides of the issue. In 1967 the liberalization of abortion in England prompted the formation of a Society for the Protection of the Unborn Child, which aligned itself with political conservatives and the Catholic Church. British feminists mobilized to stave off efforts to repeal or restrict abortion. In 1979 a hundred thousand people demonstrated in London to keep abortion legal. In the United States abortion came under attack from two powerful camps soon after the 1973 *Roe v. Wade* decision. Right-wing politicians seized on the highly charged issue to catalyze opposition to a range of liberal policies, while religious fundamentalists shifted the debate from the rights of women to the rights of the fetus. The latter group introduced the term *pro-life* instead of *antiabortion*, connoting a more positive stance of concern for children. Together these political and religious conservatives won a series of legislative victories in the 1970s and 1980s that restricted government funding for abortion. They also created bureaucratic obstacles to women's access to abortion, such as parental notification for teenagers and twenty-four-hour waiting periods.

Antiabortion politics in the United States continue to attract a core constituency of male and female voters who oppose any candidates who support the legality of abortion. As part of a broader antifeminist movement, some of the abortion opponents blame feminism for destroying the family and revive earlier rhetoric about women's selfish refusal to bear children. Others focus on the rights of the fetus. Demonstrators outside family planning clinics wave signs and shout that those seeking entrance are baby-killers. A more extreme camp of vigilantes, who are overwhelmingly male, have waged a campaign to terrorize abortion providers, bombing and burning clinics and murdering doctors who perform abortions in the United States and Canada.

In the decades after legalization, the combined force of political, religious, and social opposition has limited access to abortion. Only a third of all ob-gyn physicians were willing to perform abortions in the mid-1990s, 84 percent of American counties had no clinics or hospitals that provided abortion, and fewer than twenty states funded the procedures for poor women. In one Canadian province, less than half the general hospitals provided abortions; half the Canadian hospitals that did perform them had been harassed. To procure an abortion, a woman still needs money and the ability to travel to a provider. The attack on access also forced feminists into defensive action, protecting clinics and fighting incremental legal limitations on abortion. So successful were the threats against doctors who performed abortions that even after the U.S. government approved the widely used European drug mifepristone (RU-486), which terminates pregnancy without surgery, many American doctors were reluctant to administer it lest they become targets of protest.

Although the leadership of the pro-life movement has been largely male, almost as many women as men oppose abortion. Studies of abortion politics in the United States show that for women, the debate strikes at the meaning of motherhood as much as the protection of the fetus. Sociologist Kristen Luker found that pro-choice women were more likely to be college educated and to enjoy many more economic options than women who identified as pro-life. Less-educated women, who depended on their husbands for financial support, often felt left behind by the social changes that fostered feminism. They perceived the women's movement as inhospitable to their most valuable identity—motherhood. Because abortion seemed to undermine women's authority by denying the importance of motherhood, they were more likely to oppose it. Like increasing tolerance for divorce and homosexuality, abortion threatens the stability of family life for those who have depended on men to take care of them. In the years since Luker's study, evangelical Christians have played into these concerns, promising a more stable family life in exchange for wifely submission to husbands.

Rights and Welfare Reconsidered

Since the 1980s the staunch opposition to abortion has forced many feminists to reexamine their rhetoric and some of their reproductive politics. The initial call for "abortion on demand" insisted that women should control their own bodies. This emphasis on individual rights could, however, easily be extended to the rights of a fetus, the very argument that was gaining support among pro-life advocates. It also masked deep ambivalence among many women who chose to have abortions. As the African American poet Gwendolyn Brooks once explained, "Abortions will not let you forget / You remember the children you got that you did not get." Or in Betty Friedan's quip, "Being for abortion is like being for mastectomy."[6] Although Friedan's analogy is flawed, she did capture the sense of loss many women feel after terminating a pregnancy. While few women desire the procedure, many feel compelled to undergo it. Advocates adjusted their rhetoric accordingly. Just as the opposition coined *pro-life*, supporters of abortion rights reframed their stance as *pro-choice*. The term retains the liberal goal of self-determination, but it also recognizes that abortion, though necessary for fertility control and economic survival, can be a painful choice.

Pro-choice feminists also recognized that, aside from seeking control of their bodies, many women supported abortion in the name of child welfare. As a Central American feminist, Luz Marina Torres, put it, "It's a sin to bear an unwanted child and watch it starve to death."[7] In the 1970s Japanese reproductive rights activists convened a meeting with the title "Toward a Society Worthy of Giving Birth," signaling their concern for both social justice and women's rights. Feminists have pointed out that reproductive and children's rights correlate highly: Nations with the most liberal abortion laws also provide the most extensive child welfare systems. In contrast, many nations with restrictive abortion laws have high infant mortality and illiteracy. Similarly, spending on child welfare in the United States is lowest in those states that have enacted restrictions on abortion.

A vision of social justice has become central to many feminist arguments for choice. Social inequalities continue to extract high costs for bearing a child in societies that are neither child- nor woman-friendly. Increasing numbers of mothers raise children alone: Births to unmarried mothers have doubled or tripled in Western nations over the past generation, and divorce, desertion, or widowhood leave mothers without male economic support throughout the world. Outside of a few social democratic or socialist nations, states do not support motherhood. Moreover, given the greater need for family limitation among poor women, abortion is clearly an economic decision and not solely a moral one; therefore, it should be understood within the context of economic inequalities, not simply through arguments about rights. As one Catholic feminist explained, she supported choice "first, because we live in a society in which women are assigned final responsibility for child care without any adequate guarantee for support in the task. . . . And second, because *that lia-*

bility is then made the justification for their subservient position within that social order."[8]

On the grounds of child welfare, pro-choice and pro-life women sometimes reach across the political divide. Both groups would like to minimize the need for abortion, though social conservatives stress abstinence and parental authority while liberals favor sex education and affordable child care. Though dialogue is rare in the United States, a few European examples hint at a common ground. In Austria a Catholic lay organization dropped its opposition to liberalizing abortion laws and began to work for both public awareness of pregnant women's choices and social support for motherhood. Danish feminists who support women's right to choose have tried to lower the incidence of abortion by improving women's access to jobs, housing, and contraception. Even as they address the underlying gender inequalities that make choice so crucial, most feminists remain committed to defending legal access to both abortion and contraception.

COMMUNIST AND POSTCOMMUNIST REPRODUCTIVE POLITICS

During the period in which Western feminists struggled to achieve reproductive rights, abortion was legal in the Soviet Union, China, and many eastern European nations. The fall of the European communist states after 1989 transformed reproductive politics in the region. New patterns of usage and new forms of women's mobilization followed. In China, where reproduction continues to be controlled by the state, women's movements face unique challenges. These histories remind us that choice can have varied meanings outside of the Western context.

After World War II, women in eastern European countries took abortion for granted, often relying on it to control their fertility. Yet the availability of abortion did not necessarily signal women's reproductive control. One reason for the heavy use of abortion in the Soviet bloc was the lack of access to contraception and the poor quality of women's health care. In the USSR rates of infant and maternal mortality were three times higher than those in western Europe. Abortion itself resulted in a third of the maternal deaths. Significantly, postcommunist Russian women have eagerly embraced the oral contraceptive as an alternative, even as they continue to rely on abortion. The exception in the communist bloc, Romania, restricted abortion and placed unwanted children in inadequate state orphanages. In 1989 the new postcommunist Romanian government immediately legalized abortion.

In parts of eastern Europe, along with the emergence of market economies and democratic politics, the resurgence of Catholic political influence has influenced reproductive politics. In Poland, Catholic parliamentary deputies introduced a bill that included a five-year prison term for women who had abortions. In response, middle-class women in cities and university towns organized the Polish Feminist Association and Pro Femina, while hundreds of local committees pressured the parliament to reject the criminalization of abortion. Together these women's groups gathered 1.5 million signatures calling for a referendum on whether or not women should be punished for having abortions. The final bill enacted into law in 1993 did criminalize most abortions, but it punished the doctors who performed them rather than the women who sought them.

The Polish case is instructive for how women can respond when abortion is criminalized or recriminalized. The emergence of abortion politics in Poland helped mobilize women, as did the loss of the social services that had been available to mothers under socialism. Pro-choice forces coalesced in the Federation for Women and Family Planning. Significantly, the federation consciously avoided the term "reproductive rights" and concentrated on a variety of reproductive and health care services. They established phone banks called "trust lines" so that any woman could call anonymously and get information on contraception, rape counseling, and other health resources. An educational campaign responded to Catholic Church opposition to contraception and abortion by discussing deaths from illegal abortions and other health costs to women. Equally important, as a result of their politicization in the early 1990s, women's percentage of seats in the Polish parliament doubled.

China presents a very different set of reproductive politics. Contraceptive use is high at 83 percent. As in most developing countries, a very small percentage of women use oral contraceptives and condoms, the methods that predominate in the West. In the 1990s almost half of the birth control in China was achieved through voluntary sterilization, with intrauterine devices (IUDs) the second most frequent method. Abortion is free and available for married women who experience contraceptive failure. About ten million abortions were performed annually between 1971 and 1985.[9] Abortion was not necessarily acceptable for single women, however; given the stigma of premarital pregnancy as a sign of loss of virtue, some pregnant single women avoided state clinics and sought riskier back-alley abortions.

China has been very successful in reducing birth rates in a very short period of time. Between 1950 and 1980 urban fertility rates declined from an average of 5 children to just over 1 child; rural rates dropped from an average of almost 6 down to 2.5 children. The decline resulted in part from delayed marriages but also from contraception, abortion, and sterilization. In 1979 a one-child campaign required family planning throughout China. Families with only one child received better housing and other incentives, while those who exceeded the quota faced fines and loss of state benefits. Parents who chose sterilization enjoyed extended benefits. Difficult to enforce in the rural areas, the one-child policy was amended in 1984 to allow two children in families that would suffer from hardship with only one child (often if the first child was female) and to exempt ethnic minorities.

The Chinese approach raises questions about reproductive choice when women want to bear children but state policy penalizes them for doing so. Many women welcome government support for contraception and abortion. As one older Chinese woman lamented, "If family planning had been available earlier, my life would have been different. That is my lifelong regret."[10] To others, however, the Chinese government uses abortion to deny women the right to pregnancy in the service of its population policy. In addition, Chinese reproductive policy reflects a gender hierarchy for, as in the West, women are almost entirely responsible for contraception. Far more Chinese women than men have been sterilized because of fears that vasectomy weakens masculinity.

The meaning of reproductive choice clearly depends upon local cultural and political contexts. Given the historical importance of bearing sons to carry on Chinese lineage, the one-child policy has led some families to abort if they learn their child will be female. Anecdotal evidence suggests that husbands sometimes pressure their wives to abort against their will. A 1995 law against terminating a pregnancy on the basis of the sex of a child suggests the seriousness of this practice. Infanticide also increased under pressure to produce sons yet meet the one child quota. Taking into account the sex ratio at birth and the ratio of male to female children, as many as 2 percent of female infants may be killed. (The adult sex ratio in China is 120 males per 100 females.) Chinese orphanages now have an abundance of girls who have been abandoned by their parents.

According to economist Amartya Sen, states can achieve smaller family size without imposing coercive policies such as China's one-child rule. He points to the Indian state of Kerala. Fertility rates there have declined even faster than in China, a trend Sen attributes to the expansion of female literacy. In contrast to China, Kerala's infant mortality rate has fallen along with the fertility rate. But literacy alone does not reduce fertility or poverty. Expanding women's economic opportunities through access to credit and providing health care are also critical. Increasingly nations such as India are trying to link reproductive policy with maternal and child health services. Feminists throughout the world agree with Sen that empowering women economically and politically is more effective, and more just, than state-imposed population control.

WORLD POPULATION POLICY
AND REPRODUCTIVE HEALTH

Since the 1940s groups such as Planned Parenthood–World Population and U.S. foreign aid agencies have urged Africans, Asians, and Latin Americans to reduce their populations in order to escape poverty. The incentives these organizations offer to control global population growth have had uneven effects. Developing nations such as Kenya and Pakistan have fertility rates of four to six children per woman (See Appendix E.). As Sen points out, female literacy correlates highly with lower birth rates. Countries such as Jamaica and Brazil, which have low female illiteracy rates, had birth rates of 2.1 children per woman in the year 2000. Population reduction alone, however, does not alleviate poverty. Even as birth rates fell in Brazil, poverty rates increased.

To this criticism feminists have added concerns that, as in China, world population policy often restricts, rather than expands, women's reproductive choices. Both incentives and coercion characterize international population policy. The U.S. Agency for International Development (AID) has rewarded countries that implement long-term, sometimes irreversible contraceptive programs, such as sterilization or use of the drug Depo-Provera. In Sri Lanka, for example, a woman can receive up to a year's wages if she agrees to be sterilized. In developing nations as a whole, sterilization accounts for half of all birth control methods. Some women insist on sterilization after repeated pregnancies. As one Mexico City resident recalled, "My husband got mad but I told him I didn't care because I didn't want to get pregnant." But a 1987 survey of Mexican women found that over half of those sterilized had not formally consented. "What gives them the right to take something that doesn't belong to them?" asked one such woman after learning why she could not have any more children.[11]

The use of modern, reversible contraception has expanded in developing nations, from under 10 percent of married couples in the 1960s to over half by 1990. Nevertheless, contraceptive practice remains low in many regions, from under 20 percent in sub-Saharan Africa to under 40 percent in South Asia. Many women lack access to the health care and sex education that would increase its usage. Others fear divorce or abandonment if they remain childless. As in other regions, women remain primarily responsible for contraception. Along with female literacy, improving both men's education and communication between spouses has proven helpful in implementing contraception.

When contraception is not available or fails, women around the world continue to turn to abortion, and death rates remain high. The World Health Organization estimates that twenty million unsafe abortions are performed annually. Estimates of annual deaths range from seventy thousand to two hundred thousand. Ninety percent of these deaths occur in Asia and Africa. International policies affect these rates. When the U.S. government refuses foreign aid to agencies that provide contraceptive information, it contributes to the high numbers of risky abortions.

Along with rights to control fertility, feminist reproductive politics outside the West concentrate heavily on women's health and welfare. In the words of African health activist Adetoun Ilumoka, "I think reproductive rights, even the concept, not just the language, doesn't mean an awful lot to the average Nigerian woman. They are concerned with their health, certainly with their ability to make a living."[12] This broader economic approach to world population policies took center stage at the 1994 International Conference on Population and Development held in Cairo, Egypt. Talk of population control and family planning typically dominated such gatherings. When Gro Harlem Bruntland, the first female prime minister of Norway, addressed the opening session in Cairo, her strong advocacy of sex education and women's reproductive rights received standing ovations. "Morality becomes hypocrisy," Bruntland asserted, "if it means accepting mothers suffering or dying in connection with unwanted pregnancy and illegal abortions and unwanted children living in misery. Decriminalizing abortion should therefore be a minimum response to this reality."[13] Along with its goal of holding the world's population to 9.8 billion after the year 2050, the Cairo conference incorporated feminist proposals to improve the status of women through education and to work for greater gender equality within families. Both in Cairo and the next year in Beijing, UN action plans stressed the importance of expanding reproductive health services to include men as well as women.

These UN plans unleashed strong criticism from religious conservatives and fundamentalists who oppose sex education, contraceptive use among adolescents, and abortion. Led by the Vatican, these groups attempted to reassert parental control over sexuality and reproduction. But 126 women's groups from around the world, including 57 from Latin America, responded to the Catholic Church that the Cairo plan supported women's "just and humane development."[14] As the United Nations Population Fund concluded its 2000 report: "If women had the power to make decisions about sexual activity and its consequences, they could avoid many of the 80 million unwanted pregnancies each year,

20 million unsafe abortions, some 500,000 maternal deaths (including 78,000 as a result of unsafe abortion), and many times that number of infections and injuries."[15]

NEW REPRODUCTIVE TECHNOLOGIES

While millions of women seek the means to prevent or space pregnancies, those who cannot bear children now benefit from a range of new medical procedures. On one hand, artificial insemination and in vitro fertilization have given greater choice to infertile couples; on the other hand, depending on who makes policy, the new technologies can be used to reinforce unequal relations of gender, race, or class. Human cloning, for example, could be used eugenically to reproduce certain types of humans while subjecting others to population control.

While cloning is not an immediate option, technologies first developed by livestock breeders have been available to help produce human life since the early twentieth century. By the 1970s both artificial insemination (AI) and in vitro fertilization enabled infertile couples or women without male partners to have children. In AI, sperm donated by a fertile male is introduced directly into a woman's uterus. In vitro fertilization allows eggs taken surgically from a woman to be fertilized within a laboratory by sperm taken from a man; the fertilized egg is then implanted in the uterus of either the egg donor or another woman. Only a small percentage of efforts succeed, and the procedure is expensive and usually requires hormone injections to increase egg production. Successful but unused embryos created this way now provide a potential source of stem cells for medical research.

At first only married couples could utilize these technologies, which offered new hope for infertile women such as those who had postponed childbearing and then had difficulty conceiving in their late thirties or forties. Over time more single women, both heterosexual and lesbian, have taken advantage of AI to conceive and bear children outside heterosexual marriage. In some cases male sperm donors remain anonymous, but known donors have become involved in a range of roles. Some gay men have become coparents with lesbians, for example, creating families based on reproductive, but not sexual, relationships.

Greater control over reproduction extends to both women and men because of these new techniques. The women's self-insemination projects first established in the 1970s give single women the possibility of motherhood, a social phenomenon now accepted in most advanced industrialized nations. But artificial insemination also allows men to take more responsibility for contraception. Sexually active men can have vasectomies, first donating sperm to be used in a later, reproductive relationship. These new technologies can, of course, be applied selectively in ways that reinforce social hierarchies. Some governments, including Sweden and Denmark, have refused artificial insemination to anyone who is not married or in a heterosexual partnership. Possibilities for eugenic engineering loom, not merely in the future. At the Repository for Germinal Choice, elite men such as Nobel prize winner William Shockley have donated their sperm so that women can bear children who might reproduce their intellectual abilities (even though there is no evidence that intelligence can be transmitted selectively).

These new technologies also make possible surrogate motherhood, in which a fertile woman is paid to be inseminated and give birth by an infertile couple who will raise the child as their own. Both surrogate motherhood and egg donation have enabled infertile couples who can afford these practices to become parents, but they also introduce a range of ethical dilemmas by bringing reproductive labor into the economic marketplace. When a birth mother gives up all rights to the child, she has sold the use of her reproductive organs. Some women voluntarily give birth for sisters or other relatives who cannot do so. But when individuals who are not friends or family members enter surrogacy contracts, financial remuneration can be a prime motive. The public outcry over "Baby Cotton," the first commercial surrogacy case in England, provoked a 1985 law making all but voluntary surrogacy illegal. In the United States, however, women can contract to give birth and, unlike in all other countries, they can also legally sell eggs extracted from their ovaries to the highest bidder. Advertisements in U.S. college newspapers offer as much as $50,000 for tall, blond women with high SAT scores who will provide eggs. While the money attracts thousands of students a year, the sellers cannot know the long-term physical effects of the hormone injections and surgical procedures they undergo to earn the payment.

Custody battles over the children resulting from surrogacy contracts further illustrate problems raised by the new reproductive technologies. Some birth mothers already have children, enjoy pregnancy, and do not expect to experience psychological loss after parting with the child. Other women have learned only from painful experience that fees cannot repay them for having to relinquish a child they gestated. In most legal battles with wealthier couples, poorer birth mothers have a disadvantage. In the 1988 Baby M case in the United States the contract between birth mother Mary Beth Whitehead, a working-class woman with several children, and the Sterns, a highly educated couple, required that Whitehead not "form or attempt to form a parent-child relationship" with the baby she bore. When she did and sought custody, a U.S. court invalidated the surrogacy contract and decided that the fittest parent was the wealthier "natural father," although Whitehead won visitation rights. Since then, several U.S. states and most European nations have banned payments to surrogate mothers. China also bans all commercial surrogacy and permits but does not encourage voluntary surrogacy for infertile married couples. A 1990 British law clarified that if a voluntary surrogate mother changed her mind, she would be legally entitled to keep the child, regardless of its genetic parents.

New reproductive technologies raise further ethical questions for feminists. In the past infertile couples either remained childless or adopted children. Though many lamented their fate, some women once considered "barren" were probably relieved not to bear and raise children. Just when the stigma of choosing not to have children is lifting in Western societies, the scientific breakthroughs could make women feel inadequate if they do not become mothers. Although international and cross-racial adoptions have increased in recent years, we do not know if the promise of genetic offspring for all will discourage adoption in the future. While both surrogacy and adoption provide choices for those who cannot bear children, the reasons for their choices bear close scrutiny.

Finally, ethicists have raised questions about our social priorities. Should we invest scientific resources in costly procedures to achieve fertility when safe, inexpensive, and reliable contraception for both men and women remains an elusive goal? Given that infant mortality in the United States is four times higher among poor blacks than wealthy whites, should we be applying resources as eagerly to addressing this health disparity as we do to infertility? Feminists have no simple answers to the difficult questions posed by new reproductive technologies. The bottom line, however, is that the choice to mother or not must remain that of women themselves.

In 1968 the United Nations proclaimed that "parents have a basic human right to decide freely and responsibly on the number and spacing of their children and a right to adequate education and information in this respect."[16] In the past generation feminists have helped implement this right, but they have also taken it further to apply to all women, married or not. For some women reproductive choice means access to contraception and abortion to prevent unwanted births, a choice that is unavailable or insecure in much of the world. For other women choice means the opportunity to bear children, an option denied to millions by forced sterilization, population control policies, and state determination of family size.

Along with claiming choice as part of our human right to self-determination, feminists have increasingly insisted that women's health and children's welfare must be central to international reproductive policies. In this way, reproductive choice can help alleviate economic injustice as well as extend human rights to women. Still subject to heated political debate, however, reproductive choice is by no means guaranteed in much of the world. Because it is central to women's economic well-being as workers and as mothers, and because it is also central to the health of families and communities, feminists will continue to organize for choice. Only through continued vigilance can they ensure that no woman ever becomes one of the enforced "handmaids" of Margaret Atwood's dystopian tale, her reproductive capacity decided by male heads of state.

-ELEVEN-

SEXUALITIES, IDENTITIES, AND SELF-DETERMINATION

We think his pleasure more important than ours. . . .
We have been idiots.
—ANJA MEULENBELT, THE NETHERLANDS, 1970S

Sexuality as a term of power belongs to the empowered.
—HORTENSE SPILLERS, UNITED STATES, 1984

Like reproduction, desire is as old as humankind. The Kama Sutra of ancient India provides guidance to a variety of erotic pleasures, and ancient Greek friezes represent orgies among men. Over the past few centuries, however, a growing emphasis on nonreproductive sexuality in Western cultures has transformed sexual meanings in two important ways. First, erotic sexuality apart from reproduction has increasingly become a form of personal identity. From a term for the biology of plant reproduction, for example, the English word *sexual* came to mean "capability for sexual feelings."[1] By 1900 the new European science of sexology had coined the terms *heterosexual* and *homosexual* to classify both these feelings and individuals in terms of opposite or same-sex desire. By 2000 sexuality had become a critical marker of identity in the West. Second, for millions of women and men who live in urban, industrialized democracies, commercial economies now reinforce a quest for sexual pleasure. A sexual sell pervades Western cultures, while media representations have expanded sexuality from the private bedroom into the public spaces of billboards, movies, and radio talk shows. Both identity formation and a public sexual commerce have redefined personal happiness to include erotic pleasure apart from reproduction.

Feminists have been acutely attuned to the potential for both pleasure and danger in a sexualized world. Despite media portrayals of Western feminists as antisexual, their politics have simultaneously criticized demeaning images and demanded female sexual pleasure without shame. Rejecting the virgin/whore dichotomy and the racialized hierarchies it incorporates, feminists struggle to redefine sexuality from the varied perspectives of women's experiences. Within profit-driven consumer economies, the task of affirming female sexual agency is as tricky as efforts to balance health and beauty. As Western sexual images permeate global markets, feminists must also balance local customs against new sexual values. Feminist sexual politics currently negotiate among pleasures, dangers, identities, and commerce through a range of strategies, united by a search for female sexual self-determination.

WORLDS OF DESIRE

Preindustrial societies tend to encourage reproductive sexuality, but not to the exclusion of pleasure. In early Islamic belief men and women had equal capacity for sexual pleasure and, as in Christianity and Judaism, marriage was the legitimate place for its enjoyment. In early modern Europe a woman's sexual pleasure was considered as necessary as a man's in order for conception to take place. As the 1671 English *Midwives Book* explained, the clitoris made women "lustful and take delight in copulation" and without it they "would have no desire, nor delight, nor would they ever conceive."[2] Agricultural communities often tolerated adolescent sexual experimentation. In Puritan New England many courting couples engaged in sexual intercourse; as long as they married before the birth of a child and repented for their sins, they could remain respectable. But Judeo-Christian and Islamic ethics condemned any nonreproductive sexual acts, such as masturbation, bestiality, and sodomy.

In many religious traditions, women's sexual capacity is considered so powerful that it could distract men and undermine social order. Requirements of chastity, familial surveillance, and seclusion constrained women in order to avert sexual chaos. In Islamic countries, the institution of the *harim*, or harem, constituted a separate quarter in the home where women could avoid contact with men outside their families. Like the inner sphere of Chinese households, or the European ideal of a female domestic sphere, these segregated areas protected men from female allure as much as they protected women's virtue. The feminist Muslim scholar Fatima Mernissi criticizes Islamic views of woman as "the epitome of the uncontrollable, a living representative of the dangers of sexuality and its rampant destructive potential."[3] Similarly, Hindu religious precepts urged husbands to guard their wives carefully because women's sexual passions could lead to adultery.

Isolating women to control their sexuality preserved both male energies and male property. Fear of physical depletion underlays biblical depictions of Eve and Salome as sexually voracious temptresses, while the European myth of the *vagina dentata* imagined female genitalia devouring men. In addition, control over female sexuality has been critical to ensuring paternity. In the millennia before the availability of DNA testing, only maternity could be determined. Female sexual control reinforced male dominance in patriarchal gender systems. The fear of rape and images of female vulnerability kept women dependent upon individual male protectors and fearful of expressing sexual desires outside of these privileged relationships.

Patriarchy also condemns women's sexual pleasures with other women because they threaten the primacy of male sexual access. Yet seclusion and separate spheres can encourage female intimacy. As if to suppress its very possibility, a striking cultural silence about same-sex desire among women has characterized most of human history. The deep association of sexual relations with reproduction implicitly defined sex as involving phallic penetration. Nonetheless, historians and anthropologists have found abundant evidence of same-sex relationships among women, often coexisting with patriarchal marriage practices. As long as women's love remained surreptitious and not explicitly erotic, patriarchal societies might tolerate it.

Colonial Encounters

European, Middle Eastern, and Asian cultures have all protected the chastity of elite women by designating certain women—the poor, bad, or ruined—as sexually available. Despite religious condemnation, for example, early modern European cities tolerated brothels. Slave women in the Middle East, Africa, and the antebellum U.S. South often became their masters' concubines. During the Victorian era, middle- and upper-class men justified their visits to prostitutes in terms of preserving the purity of women of their class.

Despite similarities in sexual mores, when European colonialists encountered Asian, African, and Middle Eastern cultures they condemned the native sexual practices they observed as heathen and barbaric. Contrasting "primitive," more sexually expressive cultures to the "civilized morality" of the European middle class helped justify colonial rule. The proliferation of images of bare-breasted African women and the harems of the Middle East and Asia helped perpetuate European dominance. They also provided a means for expressing taboo sexual desires through depictions of other cultures. One African woman, Saartje Baartman, was paraded through Europe like a sideshow spectacle; billed as the "Hottentot Venus," her exposed buttocks represented an exotic, excessive sexuality. Even anthropological studies could constitute what Ann Stoler calls "scientific pornography," replete with pictures of naked native women used to illustrate "racial" difference. European fascination with the exotic East (the Middle East and Asia) characterized travel writing and fiction as well. The encounter of West and East, literary critics point out, often portrayed the Orient as a passive woman penetrated by the masculine West.

Representations aside, the social relationships between colonizers and colonized drew native women into complex sexual arrangements that enforced racial hierarchy. In the early period of encounter, single male traders, sailors, or planters often cohabited with local "temporary wives" in Southeast Asia and the East Indies. In some of these unions women helped with economic enterprises and the men recognized mixed-race children as their own. In other cases women served as concubines for early settlers, their children deemed illegitimate. European authorities in both church and state condemned the native women's "scandalous behavior" as the cause of illicit unions. As empires expanded and more men brought wives to join them, missionaries preached against the temporary liaisons. Images of modest, chaste European women constructed a racially specific feminine ideal that was passive if not asexual. Paralleling the racial supremacist views in the U.S. South, colonialists upheld the purity of upper-class wives by demonizing native men as sexual predators who had to be controlled by European authority.

Temporary unions declined over time but commercialized prostitution expanded to service single European men in the colonies. Assuming that these men needed sexual outlets, colonial officials established regulated brothels that housed native women. In Southeast Asia, French colonial law allowed prostitution for girls over age fifteen, and as early as the 1700s impoverished families in the region sold daughters into sexual service. In the 1860s the British Contagious Diseases Act instituted medical inspection of prostitutes in special "lock hospitals" to protect their soldiers and sailors from venereal disease. Stereotypes of sexually promiscuous native women both justified the spread of the sex trade and masked the exploitative aspects of prostitution, as well as the incidence of rape of native women. In short, sexuality helped enforce complex national, racial, and gender hierarchies in colonial settings, a legacy that still influences sexual ideas and practices.

THE SEXUALIZATION OF
WESTERN CULTURES

In the past two hundred years, as marital fertility rates declined and sexual commerce proliferated, sex apart from reproduction acquired greater meaning, but in different ways for men and women. The process of sexualization has strong roots in a double standard. During the Victorian era, sexual respectability required that white middle-class women remain demure, maternal figures. Upon their chastity, one British writer put it, "all property in the world depends."[4] To ensure the legitimacy of heirs, middle-class women faced social condemnation if they strayed from marital fidelity. Divorce would mean loss of respectability as well as loss of custody of any children. The price of straying from the ideal was high for middle-class women.

In the twentieth century, however, women as well as men expanded the meanings of sexuality, first within marriage and then outside it. With greater access to contraception, marital sexuality more frequently incorporated sexual pleasure as a justification for intercourse for women. An early U.S. sex survey revealed that middle-class educated women now expected the pleasures of orgasm in marital relations "as an expression of true and passionate love." As one woman reported around 1912, "even if there are no children . . . I am glad nature gave it to us." Marie Stopes' popular guide *Married Love* (1916) referred to marital sex as "a triple consummation." Along with enhancing spiritual union and creating life, it provided "a mutual, not a selfish, pleasure and profit, more calculated than anything else to draw out an unspeakable tenderness and understanding in both partakers of this sacrament."[5]

Unmarried young women also had increasing opportunities for sexual pleasures as they left their homes for work, education, or leisure pursuits. In the past, young men and women had courted near home or church; now they met at the factory or office, and after work they might visit amusement parks, dance halls, cinemas, or nightclubs. Working-class youth pioneered the new practice of dating, in which men (who earned higher wages) treated women to dining, movies, or dancing. Women often reciprocated with sexual favors ranging from kisses to touching to intercourse. These working women distinguished themselves from prostitutes, who sold sex for money, since treating involved no cash exchange and women exercised choice over the men they dated. Over time this heterosocial youth culture spread from workers to middle-class college students. By midcentury older women joined the quest for sexual pleasure as well.

Both psychology and marketing fostered this pursuit. Sigmund Freud's theories of the centrality of sexual drive to human development had enormous impact on popular ideas about sexual health. In the 1950s Alfred Kinsey's books detailing the diversity of American sexual practices intensified self-consciousness about sex. By then sex was becoming a legitimate service industry in western Europe and North America. Strip clubs, pornographic literature, and magazines such as *Playboy* enticed a predominantly male audience. For women too, popular advice literature such as *The Joy of Sex* (1972) and magazines such as *Cosmopolitan* in the United States and *Forum* in England proselytized a gospel of individual sexual pleasure apart from procreative goals.

Homosexual Identities and Lesbian Taboos

This growing separation of sexual and reproductive behavior promoted homosexual as well as heterosexual identity. Same-sex desire has always existed among individuals, many of whom found opportunities to act on those desires despite legal and religious proscriptions. Some cultures have tolerated same-sex practices, including ancient Greece and some South Pacific islands, where sex between older men and boys is considered a rite of passage. In most of these cases, however, sexual behaviors do not create lifelong identities that preclude heterosexual relations. When these identities did appear, gender reversal rather than erotic desire typically formed their basis, as when a Native American man adopted women's clothing, performed women's tasks, and as a woman could marry a man.

Women have also had opportunities for same-sex relationships, but usually not to the exclusion of reproductive ones. In Suriname the widespread institution of *mati* involves loving, sexual relations between women who may also have male partners. In Lesotho a woman who loves another woman "with her whole heart" might celebrate their relationship through a village feast, but with her husband's approval. Since sex is defined as phallic penetration, no one considers female erotic desire problematic.

In both the preindustrial West and Asia, no single legal or cultural category defined those who expressed same-sex desire or engaged in sodomy, fellatio, or nonpenetrative stimulation. The earliest categories of sexual identity, introduced in Europe and North America in the 1800s, emphasized "gender inversion." Sexologists presumed that same-sex erotic desire appeared primarily in masculine women or effeminate men who adopted the dress and speech of the other sex.

A key shift toward a more widespread sexual identity occurred when an urban commercial economy allowed wage earners to live apart from family surveillance. Able to act on same-sex desires in ways not possible in the past, men initially found others like themselves. By the 1890s they had created public homosexual subcultures in London, New York, and other metropolitan centers. Women had fewer opportunities to form these relationships because they remained economically dependent on families longer than men did. When more women could support themselves, they often kept their same-sex partnerships private. In the late 1800s both working-class and middle-class women in the United States set up households together, a phenomenon sometimes known as a Boston marriage because so many college-educated women in that city lived this way. Even life partners did not necessarily consider themselves homosexual or lesbian, no matter how emotionally or erotically charged their private relations.

In the early 1900s women did begin to claim a lesbian sexual identity. In Paris and Berlin, explicitly lesbian subcultures coalesced by the 1920s. In bars and clubs women danced, met dates, and sometimes cross-dressed as men. A literary couple such as Gertrude Stein and Alice B. Toklas could survive in this climate. Even in Europe, however, these enclaves were risky. One Berlin woman recalled that in the 1920s "lesbians were watched by the police, and from time to time lesbian clubs were raided."[6] Few women risked public exposure as lesbians.

Their caution was well founded. Medical authorities condemned same-sex relationships as pathological, and the law sanctioned persecution. According to the German sexologist Richard von Krafft-Ebing, women attracted to others of their sex were "revolting, disgusting, shameful, monstrous" inverts who suffered from a neurological disease, curable by encouraging heterosexual feelings. Because women's rights advocates transgressed male space politically, sexologists assumed they were lesbian, whatever their personal sexual practices. Even celibate women came under greater scrutiny. Historian Christina Simmons has pointed out that the creation of a "lesbian taboo" coincided with the heterosexual youth culture of the early twentieth century. Just when society legitimated heterosexual pleasure for women, same-sex intimacy became more problematic. In the past, romantic female friendships escaped stigma; now they became suspect, as did feminism. While many women experimented with sexual relationships outside of marriage, those who chose lesbianism risked social ostracism, institutionalization, and unemployment.

Over time, European and North American lesbians, like gay men, would form their own alternative cultures. They socialized in working-class bars or middle-class living rooms, and after 1950 they began to reject the medical model of pathological homosexuality in favor of a politics of sexual rights. In the United States nascent lesbian political groups such as the Daughters of Bilitis insisted on the respectability of homosexual women. In 1973 the gay rights movement helped remove homosexuality from the roster of mental illnesses. From its first successes, however, the lesbian and gay movement elicited harsh political reaction. Both victories and defeats served to intensify the identity category.

THE FEMINIST RESPONSE
TO SEXUALIZATION

Two kinds of sexual politics characterize the feminist response to sexualization in Western cultures. One draws on the ideal of female purity and emphasizes the right to say no to unwanted sex. Dominant in the nineteenth century, it remains central to feminist critiques, especially in the movement against sexual violence. The other approach explores a female-defined sexuality that is not necessarily linked to reproduction. Uniting these two approaches is a firm belief in the importance of sexual self-determination for women.

During the 1800s a protective strategy dominated feminist thought. A small minority of radicals, such as the Saint-Simonian socialists in France or Victoria Woodhull in the United States, endorsed "free love" and rejected marriage. Like most women of their time, however, early feminists believed that containing sexuality within marriage best served their interests. They associated sexuality outside of marriage with prostitution or rape and feared that if men could have sex without a commitment to supporting wives and children, women would be left economically vulnerable. Anglo-American moral reformers such as Josephine Butler campaigned to limit male access to prostitutes by condemning male seducers, procurers, and clients. Butler's campaign against compulsory examination of prostitutes succeeded in the 1886 repeal of the British Contagious Diseases Act. African American activists joined the call for a single standard of morality, not only for men and women but also for blacks and whites. When southern white women's clubs rejected black members on the grounds of "immorality," the First National Conference of Colored Women in 1895 formed "an army of organized women standing for purity" to dispute the charges.[7]

Given their insistence on purity, older feminists reacted with puzzlement and some despair when a younger generation adopted the goal of nonreproductive sexual pleasure. Although anarchist Emma Goldman insisted on sexual freedom as part of any social revolution, contemporaries such as Charlotte Perkins Gilman bemoaned the new emphasis on sex and pleasure. Women gained independence, but they remained "as much the slaves of fashion as before," Gilman wrote in her autobiography. Woman finally had the chance "to rebuild the suffering world—and the world waits while she powders her nose."[8] Margaret Sanger stressed the importance of motherhood, not sexual freedom, to justify birth control. But older feminists who voiced concerns about the exploitation of women appeared to be anachronistic sexual prudes in an era of beauty contests, romance magazines, and Hollywood films.

During the watershed decade of the 1960s, however, the contradictions surrounding female sexuality became too blatant to ignore. Young white Western women who joined the sexual revolution and rejected the doctrine of sexual purity often found their taste of liberation unfulfilling. They now experienced what women of color had long known: that a double standard persisted. Sexually active women remained at risk of pregnancy, which could force them into childbearing and child rearing; given their economic disadvantages, women and not their male sexual partners could wind up on welfare if they bore children they could not support. Not all women could afford or locate illegal abortionists, and where abortion did become available, it remained an unappealing choice.

Economic risks aside, the renewed attention to women's sexual pleasure could have unexpected consequences. While birth control pills eased the fear of pregnancy, many women felt that they lost the ability to say no, the keystone of nineteenth-century principles of both voluntary motherhood and free love. Images from the Playboy bunny to the sexy homemaker proclaimed women's duty to be sexually available and excited, even if it meant pretense to please male partners. At a Dutch feminist conference in the 1970s, for example, three-fourths of the women polled reported that they sometimes feigned orgasms. "We think his pleasure more important than ours," wrote Anja Meulenbelt. "We have been crazy. We have been idiots."[9]

These sexual contradictions helped fuel the revival of feminism in the 1960s and 1970s. Much of the consciousness raising that occurred in women's groups named intimate, sexual matters as political concerns. The term "sexual politics," coined by Kate Millett in her 1970 book with that title, suggested a power imbalance not only in gender but also in sexuality. Trying to achieve sexual equality when women lacked economic and political equality was a daunting task. To some, sex, like housework, seemed too trivial for political analysis. But feminists showed that sexual self-determination for women—the right to refuse unwanted sex and to redefine sexuality from a female standpoint—was critical to women's empowerment.

While Millett exposed the so-called sexual revolution as male-centered, other writers imagined alternatives. In *The Female Eunuch* (1970) Australian feminist Germaine Greer insisted that the pleasures of sexual liberation extend from men to women. Just what that meant inspired much feminist speculation. In her essay "The Myth of the Vaginal Orgasm," first circulated in 1968, British feminist Anne Koedt pronounced that women had "been defined sexually in terms of what pleases men." She took particular issue with the Freudian concept that a mature woman experienced orgasm vaginally and not clitorally. By recognizing the clitoral orgasm, women would be less dependent on phallic sex. French feminists, such as Hélène Cixous and Luce Irigaray, reconceptualized female sexuality as quite distinct from men's. In a revision of Lacanian psychoanalytic theory, they invoked a pre-Oedipal, pre-phallic stage of psychosexual development and linked female desire to this boundless state. Rather than being focused on one organ, they suggested, women's sexuality resembled the infantile *jouissance*, or bliss, that predated the rule of law and language. Cixous urged women to explore the "immense bodily territories which have been kept under seal."[10]

Seeking female sexual pleasure could incorporate the self-help ethic of the women's health movement. Women eagerly sought information about sexuality. Books such as *The Hite Report* (1976) and *Sexualide da*

Mulher Brasileira (Brazilian Women's Sexuality) (1983) became best-sellers in their home countries. As women took personal responsibility for sexual pleasure, self-help guides provided advice on "liberating masturbation" as one means for women to learn about their own sexual needs. Sales of personal vibrators increased as so-called preorgasmic women discovered their own joys of sex. Feminist artists such as Tee Corinne and Judy Chicago began using female genital imagery to reverse centuries of negative associations of the vagina as dirty, secret, and threatening. Writers and linguists imagined what sexual pleasure would mean if defined by women. As *Our Bodies, Ourselves* put it, "Think of [intercourse] as reciprocal. You open up to enclose him warmly. You surround him powerfully as he penetrates you."[11]

Claiming authority over female sexual imagination inspired a sex-positive movement. By the 1980s sexual manuals, sexual toys, and erotica produced by women counteracted mainstream media images of female victimization and objectification. Sex-positive feminists urged women to seize the initiative in relationships and to expect pleasure and not merely service their partners. Learning to enjoy sex boosted the business of sex therapists and pornographers alike. Along with her modeling and performance art, for example, former U.S. prostitute and self-proclaimed "leader of the Pleasure Activist Movement" Annie Sprinkle lectured on "how to be a sex goddess."

The call for female sexual self-determination resonated strongly among lesbians. Rejecting decades of moral and medical condemnation, feminism provided a political theory that validated lesbian sexuality. According to Adrienne Rich, lesbians had to transcend a system of "compulsory heterosexuality" that severely punished dissenters. Because they lived outside heterosexual institutions, she suggested, lesbians naturally resisted patriarchy. Similarly, the German physician Charlotte Wolff wrote that "the lesbian woman is a feminist by nature because she is free from emotional dependence on the male."[12] Or, in the catchphrase of radical lesbians of the 1970s, "Feminism is the theory, lesbianism is the practice."

Casting lesbians as a feminist vanguard represented a radical break with past constructions of criminal, diseased, or depraved perverts. Still culturally marginalized, lesbians created within North American and European women's movements a positive, even celebratory, alternative space in which they met, organized, and explored sexual desires. Their separate culture nourished not only lesbians but any women who felt comforted by women-only spaces.

Yet feminism provided only a partial haven for lesbians. Women's movements reflected their cultures' homophobia—the fear of erotic desire for the same sex, in oneself or in others. In the West and internationally, early feminist movements often feared that lesbians would discredit them, since most people still considered lesbians as deviants, a threat to religious values and family stability. Aligning with lesbians risked a loss of heterosexual privilege. Some heterosexual feminists felt excluded by lesbianism or fearful that they were not sufficiently feminist. But all lesbians, like gay men, risked losing their jobs, while mothers who came out as lesbians faced the additional fear of losing custody of their children. Increasingly lesbians joined forces with gay men to overturn discrimination in jobs and housing. They also extended their civil rights movement to redefine the family, working for domestic partnerships, parenting rights, and gay marriage.

By the 1990s, a younger generation that could begin to take for granted the right to sexual self-determination began to question the sexual identities formed in the past generations. Many adopted a "queer" identity that included attraction for both genders as well as a tolerance, even fascination, with those who consider gender a fluid and malleable persona that can be changed or crossed at will. Potentially a more inclusive political identity, queer could at the same time mask gender by making women less visible.

Whether lesbian, queer, or straight, third-wave feminists in the United States have built upon the gains of earlier movements to forge a more sexually adventurous politics. Comfortably pro-sex, they proclaim their desires for pleasure more publicly and with less ambivalence than their foremothers. In 1990 cultural critic Camille Paglia pointed to the pop music star Madonna as "the future of feminism," citing her sexually explicit music videos as evidence that the singer "has taught young women to be fully female and sexual while still exercising control over their lives." The question of control is by no means settled, however, and old legacies, such as the virgin/whore dichotomy, continue to challenge young women's efforts at sexual self determination. "You had to make a decision. Do you want to be a good girl or a bad girl?" a thirty-one-year-old married working-class woman explained. She "decided to be a good girl" and found that "it took years before I was able to relax myself to where I could just enjoy sex."[13] As Naomi Wolf noted in *Promiscuities*, her 1997 book about coming of age sexually in the United States, "the fear of being labeled promiscuous accompanies contemporary girls on each stage of their erotic exploration."[14]

The sexual empowerment of women has had a mixed impact. For one, conservative forces persistently attempt to shore up the marital, reproductive boundaries around female sexuality. Three decades after the new sexual politics emerged, opponents tried to censor productions of *The Vagina Monologues*, a theater piece in which women speak openly of their bodies and sexuality. In addition, the strategy of appropriating sexual pleasure has not resonated similarly for all women. The African American writer Hortense Spillers pointed out in the 1980s that the feminist discussion of sexuality largely excluded the complex historical experience of women of color. Black women, she wrote, had learned through "long experience with the brutalization of male power" how sexuality can empower some but enforce the inequality of others. She reminded feminists to keep in mind that "sexuality as a term of power belongs to the empowered."[15] Because self-determination occurs against a background of social hierarchies, one person's power can either enable or deny another's.

RESISTING AND EXPANDING WESTERN SEXUALITIES

Both the feminist insistence on sexual self-determination and the concept of sexuality as a form of personal identity rest upon historical processes that are specific to industrial, capitalist societies. The separation of reproduction and sexuality occurred during the transition from a self-sufficient agricultural economy to an interdependent commercial one. The sexualization of culture accompanied the shift to a consumer and service economy. Although global capitalism has expanded these processes beyond Europe and North America, in much of the world sexuality remains deeply embedded in reproductive, familial relationships. Subsistence agriculture and female economic dependence on men is still widespread. For many of the women who struggle for survival, basic rights to marital and reproductive choice are more pressing concerns than access to sex-positive images.

In addition to these material differences, both the colonial legacy of eroticizing Eastern women and the objectification of women in contemporary Western media raise skepticism among feminists outside Europe and North America. In Egypt, for example, Dr. Latifa Zayat told an American feminist that "women in the Third World refuse to be treated as sexual objects or as sexual experiments. We want to be liberated, we want to be emancipated, we want to be equal—but from an economic point of view, not from a sexual point of view."[16] The Lebanese scholar Evelyne Accad has taken issue with this view. Interviewing rural and urban women in the Middle East, she found that "sexuality is of the utmost concern. . . . Some women asked me to shut off the cassette recorder when they talked about sexuality, and some burst into tears when talking about intimate experiences in their lives." In public, however, she noted that even activists hesitate to discuss sexuality for fear of gossip and accusations of immorality.[17]

The search for sexual self-determination thus takes very different forms outside the West. Many cultures that affirm women's sexual pleasure in marriage, including Islam, still regulate strictly the conditions under which women may have sex. In parts of Africa, Asia, and the Middle East many women do not have the right to choose their own husbands. In South Asia women have been kidnaped and couples murdered when they marry against their parents' wishes, refuse arranged marriages, or otherwise dishonor their families. Since its founding, the United Nations has called for a woman's choice in entering or ending a marriage as a basic human right. When freely chosen, though, marital sex can still be physically dangerous for women. Without adequate contraception it may result in unwanted pregnancy. Increasingly in parts of South Asia and Africa, it may also carry infection with HIV. Restraining men's extramarital sexual relations becomes critical, as does sex education and condom distribution.

Where women's identity is deeply tied to child rearing, the Western celebration of individual sexual empowerment does not always fit social reality. As Madhu Kishwar, editor of the Indian feminist magazine *Manushi*, writes, "Indian women do not seem very enamoured of the idea of sexual liberation as it came to be understood and practiced in the West." In contrast to the individualism of Western feminism, she explains, most Indians place the family before their own interests. Relations with children can be stronger than those with husbands, a bond that helps explain the refusal of many widows to remarry. Kishwar observes that Indian women "seem to consider sexual deprivation as far less painful than being estranged from their children and family." In addition, because Indian tradition values sacrifice, voluntary sexual abstinence "bestows extraordinary powers on human beings." Thus these widows can command exceptional respect in their communities. Kishwar argues that teaching sexual restraint and emotional responsibility to men serves women's interests more than women's "emulating men's casual approach to sex." She acknowledges, however, that slowly pressuring men to become sexually responsible does not represent "full freedom and equality for women. But then," she adds, "we are not living in an ideal world."[18]

While the protective strain of sexual politics resonates in these arguments, the search for pleasure is by no means absent in international feminist movements. In Brazil, for example, a group of feminist researchers working with low-income housewives found that members of a mothers club were eager to learn about sexuality. Based on their discussions, the group created sex education booklets that the government eventually distributed widely. The information they provided ranged from basic anatomical facts to encouragement for women to accept their bodies. The project also addressed women's desires and their capacity for sexual satisfaction. Along with cartoons that tried to reduce women's shame about their bodies, a photo showed men and women at a rally holding a sign reading Pleasure for All.[19]

Women's movements in many parts of the world have also begun to adopt the rights of lesbians to be free from discrimination in work and housing and to become parents. Lesbian identity has proliferated in major cities throughout the world, as have lesbian political movements. Lesbians have mobilized in the Philippines, Brazil, Mexico, and South Africa, where the 1996 constitution guaranteed equal rights to lesbians and gay men. In Taiwan lesbians have confronted the women's movement over its homophobia. In 1995, Yuxuan Aji, the editor of the lesbian magazine *Girlfriend*, called on progressive feminist organizations in Taiwan "to challenge the existent structure of the family" and extend equality to homosexuals as well as heterosexuals.[20] Communication across cultures has brought demands for a human right to sexual choice. In Europe, the International Lesbian and Gay Association was formed to lobby world organizations to end discrimination based on sexual orientation; in 1999 it represented groups from eighty countries.

Attitudes change slowly, however. At the 1975 UN women's conference in Mexico City, lesbians felt invisible at best and unwelcome at worst. By the 1985 UN conference in Nairobi, lesbians had a vocal presence. But the subject remains taboo in countries such as Bangladesh, China, Kenya, and parts of eastern Europe. Discrimination remains legal in most of the Middle East and Latin America.

As in the West, homophobia can be a powerful antifeminist tool. One group of African feminists has been called "Lesbians, Power hungry, Emotionally deprived, Sexually frustrated, 'Beijing women,' Sexually promiscuous, Unmarriageable, Against God's plan, Castrators, Westernized, Witches, Women who want to have testicles, Elite."[21] Most of these terms denote women who deviate from an ideal of dependence on men or who aspire to male privilege; any women who do so can be charged with being sexually perverse. A similar tactic of sexual vilification has been used to thwart all feminist demands for sexual self-determination. At UN conferences in both Cairo (1994) and Beijing (1995), Rosalind Petchesky observed, an international coalition of religious conservatives of all faiths repeatedly linked reproductive and sexual rights to hedonism and pedophilia. Despite the activism of lesbians in Beijing, and in response to conservative pressures, the 1995 UN conference platform did not address sexual orientation.

PERSISTENT DANGERS:
FEMINISTS DEBATE
PORNOGRAPHY AND SEX WORK

Western feminists themselves do not always agree in their sexual politics, including the line between sexual victimization and sexual agency. Like their nineteenth-century predecessors, today's activists insist on women's right to refuse unwanted sex, and they condemn sexual violence. On the question of whether women can voluntarily consent to engage in pornography, prostitution, and sadomasochism, however, opinions differ.

In the 1980s the legal theorist Catharine MacKinnon articulated most forcefully the view that "sexual objectification is the primary process of the subjection of women." She compared sexuality in feminist theory to labor in Marxist theory, that which is "most one's own, yet most taken away."[22] Marx wrote of alienated male labor; MacKinnon wrote about the alienation of female sexuality, which occurs when it is defined by men as something that exists for their pleasure. Citing rape, incest, sexual harassment, pornography, and prostitution, she emphasized sexual coercion as a means of enforcing patriarchy.

MacKinnon's colleague Andrea Dworkin gained a certain notoriety for arguing further that heterosexual intercourse can be a form of violation, given the power imbalances between women and men. "How to separate the act of intercourse from the social reality of male power is not clear," Dworkin wrote, "especially because it is male power that constructs both the meaning and the current practice of intercourse as such."[23] In her view, because ideas about female sexuality had been constructed by men, women's bodies represent an occupied territory. Similarly, Adrienne Rich's concept of "compulsory heterosexuality" suggested that given the economic and political constraints that prevent women from living independently of men, we cannot know if heterosexuality is always a free choice.

The debates over women's sexual choice grew most heated in discussions of pornography. By the 1970s pornography flourished as a multibillion-dollar industry marketing hard-core images at one extreme and softer porn, advertising, sex advice books, and television talk shows at the other. Some feminists suggested that women seize control of the means of cultural production to create their own women-centered representations of sexuality. Women, they insisted, could enjoy the pleasures of the body without accepting the male gaze or the structures of male dominance. In contrast, a vocal camp insisted that all pornographic images were degrading, even dangerous, to women. In Susan Brownmiller's view, because pornography "is a male invention, designed to dehumanize women," there "can be no 'equality' in porn, no female equivalent."[24] Reflecting on the commoditization of woman in Japanese erotic comic magazines, advertisements, and adult videos, Kuniko Funabashi declared that "pornography destroys her dignity as a human being and does injury to her identity and self-respect; it represents violence committed against her."[25]

In the United States what began as an intellectual debate shifted in the 1980s to a contest over state authority to regulate pornography. Dworkin and MacKinnon drafted an innovative legal ordinance that treated pornography as an infringement on women's civil rights because of its offensive and threatening nature. Legislation introduced in several cities allowed any woman to sue the makers, distributors, and dealers of pornography. In Great Britain too, critics of pornography introduced new laws. Several female members of Parliament tried to ban nudity in certain publications. U.S. courts overturned the antipornography civil rights ordinances in 1986, but a few years later the supreme court of Canada upheld an obscenity provision that allowed an antipornography law opposed by many feminists. Canadian prosecutions soon realized the fears of feminists and civil libertarians that the law would limit the availability of sexually explicit feminist writing, including lesbian and gay literature that was turned away at the border.

Marking a public split within the movement, prominent U.S. feminists joined book sellers and other civil libertarians who opposed the constitutionality of these antipornography laws on the grounds that they infringed on free-speech rights. British feminists warned that censorship would undermine the "non-moralistic exploration of women's sexual fantasy and desire."[26] MacKinnon and Dworkin countered the free-speech argument by contending that in an unequal society, the speech of the powerful is so dominant that free-speech rights will never accord feminism a fair hearing. Since men monopolize the construction of sexuality, obscenity is defined as that which makes men uncomfortable. For opponents of censorship such as Ellen Willis, however, suppressing pornography affected only superficial evidence of male dominance. Even if the hard-core *Hustler* magazine were to vanish immediately, Willis pointed out, rape and battery would not decline, since deeper structural inequalities sustained them.

The difficulty of drawing the line between dangerous pornography and sexually empowering images is illustrated by the efforts to censor feminist representations. In the United States right-wing politicians rescinded public funding for performance artists, such as Holly Hughes, who openly explore lesbian sexuality. In India the 1996 film *Fire* provoked widespread protests, vandalism, and death threats against filmmaker Deepa Mehta. Her story of two unhappily married sisters-in-law in urban India who fall in love with each other exposed men's sexual double standard and portrayed women's sexual passion. In Mehta's view the source of the protests was less the film's sexual imagery than its critique of patriarchal power relations: "It would invariably emerge that it was not the lesbian relationship that so offended middle-aged Indian men . . . it was the fear that *Fire* might shift the status quo of husbands."[27]

Sex Workers as Victims or Agents

In contrast to the antiporn movement's portrayal of them as the victims of men, some porn stars claimed that they choose their jobs, one of the few in which women earn more than men. As Chicana writer Cherríe Moraga commented, "Plainly put, it is our sisters working in the sex industry."[28] Some women prefer sex work, finding it no more degrading than other labor performed by women. As a topless dancer in the United States explained, "The money was lots better than I'd been making." A former prostitute recalled that when she left the trade to become a secretary, she became depressed. As a sex worker, she found that "life was rarely predictable," but as an office worker, she explained, "I was invisible." Moreover, it took two weeks to make what had been one evening's earnings.[29]

To feminists such as Kathleen Barry, however, these jobs represent a form of sexual slavery. Disclosures by sex workers such as Linda Lovelace that they had been coerced into performing in porn films support this argument. Studies of the international sex industry document the sale of women into prostitution. Whether South Asian daughters sold by kin into brothels or European teenage runaways lured into the trade or exploited by pimps and drug dealers, we have abundant evidence of cases in which no truly free choice has been made. Young women from the former communist nations have been promised jobs abroad only to find themselves confined in makeshift brothels, forced to have sex, and beaten if they try to escape. In India and Thailand, the UN estimates, up to a hundred thousand children are sex workers. As many as two-thirds of those in India entered the trade as the result of rape, gang rape, or kidnapping.

Both sides in this argument can muster supporting data because the burgeoning sex industry includes such a wide range of participants. Some of them are more, and some less, consensual workers. When destitution, dependency, or violence induce women or men to enter sex work, the choice may be illusory. To prevent exploitation, feminists address these underlying inequalities and provide social services for those affected. When adults weigh their options without compulsion and prefer topless dancing, sexual massage, or prostitution, feminists insist on respect and decent working conditions. The proliferation of sex workers' organizations, such as the International Committee for Prostitutes' Rights, champions the concept of self-empowerment for these women.

All sides to the debate now agree that condemning and incarcerating sex workers perpetuates rather than eliminates inequality. By making criminals of prostitutes, the law leaves male clients free to find other women for paid sex and disproportionately punishes women of color. In the 1970s the National Organization for Women called for decriminalization in the belief that legalized prostitution would undermine the control of pimps by making women less vulnerable to the police. Prostitutes' organizations in the United States and Europe also favor deregulation to allow greater control and better working conditions.

These legal reforms reflect the liberal origins of feminism, with its emphasis on the right to labor, and their accomplishments illustrate both the strengths and limits of liberalism. Optional deregulation in one U.S. state, Nevada, created a disciplined workforce of prostitutes who put in long hours to net large profits for male brothel owners. In the Netherlands, where prostitution itself is not illegal (but trafficking in women and pimping are punishable), sex workers pay taxes but do not enjoy unemployment insurance or sick leave. The fact that an increasing proportion of the twenty thousand prostitutes in the Netherlands come from Latin America and Southeast Asia suggests that prostitution is both racialized and the choice of women who have few economic options. In 2001 a member of the Dutch parliament who had supported legalization of brothels wondered "whether we did the right thing."[30]

Feminists outside the West bring other political traditions to bear on the question of prostitution, rejecting both exploitation and legalization. In the 1990s, when men tried to evict prostitutes from urban red-light districts in Bangladesh in the name of resisting "un-Islamic activities," women's groups organized humanitarian sympathy for the prostitutes. In cooperation with prostitutes they stopped the evictions that would have left these women homeless, tried to discourage police harassment, and called for the identification of male clients. In the Philippines women's groups helped relocate prostitutes after the departure of the U.S. military, which had tolerated the trade around its bases.

Feminist responses to prostitution complicate the international movement for sexual self-determination. For one, the legacy of colonialism includes both the sexual objectification of women from developing countries and the impoverishment that induces young women to enter prostitution. It is harder to locate sexual agency in the complex mix of racial, national, and economic relationships in the international sex trade. Sexual self-determination is intricately connected to local and global economies. The factories where young women endure long hours of demanding manual labor provide an alternative to sex work. Their wages may provide leverage within the family that allows daughters to select their own marital partners. Whether women choose to work in sex tourism or on the global assembly line, they may spend their wages to purchase consumer goods, such as cosmetics and fashionable clothing, that may or may not empower women sexually.

Sexuality as both a form of identity and a component of commercial life has become entrenched in Western societies. While religious states and conservative movements attempt to restore an older, patriarchal control of female sexuality, they are unlikely to succeed where free choice prevails. Yet the sexualization of culture is by no means a feminist accomplishment. To transform sexuality from a mere commodity to a source of personal pleasure, women in every culture need more positive images of their sexual choices than have been available in the past. At the same time, without financial options and the right to determine their reproductive lives, sexualization will not free women. In short, only when women have economic and political self-determination will sexuality provide a clear source of empowerment. Until then, feminist sexual politics will attempt to distinguish between the pleasures and dangers that continue to define women's sexuality.

-TWELVE-
GENDER AND VIOLENCE

*I, like most women, have thought of rape as part of my natural
environment—something to be feared and prayed against like fire
or lightning. I never asked why men raped.*
—SUSAN GRIFFIN, UNITED STATES, 1971

*It is important for men to . . . identify a new man within
themselves whose identity does not thrive on conquest or on the use
of violence against women.*
—JONAH GOKOVA, ZIMBABWE, 1997

In February 2001 Justice Florence Mumba of Zambia handed down a
historic guilty verdict at the International Criminal Court in The
Hague. She sentenced three Bosnian Serb soldiers to a total of sixty years
in jail for the 1992 systematic rape, torture, and enslavement of Muslim
women. As part of the ethnic cleansing campaigns in the Balkans, the
defendants had personally confined and tortured girls as young as twelve
years old in "rape houses." The three convicted men had committed only
a small proportion of the twenty thousand to fifty thousand assaults on
Muslim women intended to humiliate and force them to bear "Serb"
children. Sexual violence as an instrument of war has not been limited to
the Balkans. The United Nations has documented mass rapes in Cambo-
dia, Liberia, Peru, Somalia, and Uganda. In 1994 up to half a million
women in Rwanda endured rape, torture, and sexual slavery during the
genocidal campaign against the Tutsi. In 2001, however, for the first
time an international criminal court had the authority to prosecute
wartime gender violence.

In the past gender violence has been tolerated, even expected, in wartime. While nations mourned the deaths of male soldiers and honored their valor, women raped in wartime usually hid their shame. Some of the women raped by soldiers in Kosovo in 1999 committed suicide because they knew that revealing their plight would bring ostracism, divorce, and lifelong shame. Even though post–World War II international law had established humanitarian standards for war, the protocols did not cover sexual violence specifically.

Only after an international women's movement lobbied the United Nations did the International Criminal Court include wartime rape in its jurisdiction. In 1997 two hundred organizations from around the world formed the Women's Caucus for Gender Justice to insist that international law condemn gender-based violence in wartime. They built upon earlier, nonbinding human rights provisions, including the 1995 Beijing Platform for Action. Despite strong opposition, their effort succeeded when the 1998 Rome Statute of the International Criminal Court outlawed not only rape but also sexual slavery, enforced prostitution, forced pregnancy, and enforced sterilization. In addition, it required that the court include both female and male judges with expertise on violence against women or children. Because of this international women's movement, Justice Mumba was able to set a precedent that resonated throughout the world: Rape in wartime is a crime against humanity and will be prosecuted and punished.

RAPE: FROM FORCE TO RIGHTS

Changing ideas about violence, individual rights, and gender relations all contributed to this historic ruling. In the past, few men or women questioned the legitimacy of physical force in war or peace. In hierarchical societies, masters both confined and beat slaves, husbands could physically chastise their wives, and parents hit children. Even murder could be acceptable if a family or clan sought revenge for an insult to its honor, a practice that still occurs in parts of the world. Rulers could also use force, including the corporal and capital punishment of criminals. Wartime legitimated not only the murder of enemy soldiers but also the rape of civilian women. All of these forms of violence induced anger, grief, and long-standing animosities. Until very recently, however, they did not trigger protests against the use of force per se.

Although masters, husbands, parents, and soldiers continue to exercise physical force, over the past two centuries the line between legitimate force and unacceptable violence has shifted. Along with liberal ideas about individual rights, the economic transition to free markets undermined earlier labor systems that rested upon physical force. The emancipation of serfs and slaves, the organization of workers, and the overthrow of colonial rule all rejected the imposition of hierarchies through force in favor of contractual relations that rested on individual rights. Within the family, the principle of "spare the rod and spoil the child" gradually fell into disfavor among those who championed the rights of children. Industrialized nations, though notably not the United States, have eliminated capital punishment as an inhumane practice.

Like other democratic principles, the individual right to freedom from force applies unevenly. Those whose age, gender, nation, race, or class most advantage them enjoy more leeway in exercising force without paying the legal penalties. The disproportionate execution of African American men in the United States attests to the differential application of justice. Children, women, minorities, and the poor are more likely to be legitimate targets of force, even though they may also perpetrate violence themselves. Gender has a particularly powerful role in shaping the history of violence. Given human physiology, greater bodily strength has advantaged men who assault women. The social inequality that results from privileging males over females exacerbates this physical disparity. Men who use force often act within their rights (as husbands, for example); women have had fewer claims on the right to use force or to protect themselves physically. Furthermore, fears of the female body and efforts to control female sexuality create volatile settings for expressing violence as part of sexual relations.

All of these factors can also make men vulnerable to gender-related violence: if they have smaller bodies (as boys, particularly); if they do not assert male privilege (as when men are accused of being wimps or sissies); or when men assume female gender or sexual identities (effeminate, gay, or transgender males). Historically, however, men have more often perpetrated physical and sexual violence than women. When ideas of individual rights overturned feudal obligations and nations outlawed slavery and serfdom, men maintained the right to discipline women and children.

In the 1800s, just as voluntary groups took up the cause of protecting children from physical abuse, feminists challenged the legitimacy of men's violence against women. After 1850 the women's rights movement in England and the United States exposed the problem of abusive husbands. Only since the 1970s, however, have feminist efforts had a mass impact. Second-wave feminists expanded the critique of violence, beginning with a campaign to redefine rape to include not only attacks by strangers but also those by acquaintances and husbands. They coined the terms "marital rape," "date rape," "sexual harassment," and "domestic violence." Breaking down the distinction between public and private, they rejected men's customary use of force within the family.

The antiviolence movement insists that women's right to control their bodies includes resistance to forced sex and physical abuse. It also champions children's right to a life free from violence. Not all feminists agree about definitions and tactics, but three elements characterize the antiviolence movement: the importance of naming all forms of violence against women as illegitimate practices, the provision of services to heal and empower survivors of violence and change male behaviors, and the obligation of the state to enforce laws that both criminalize male violence and protect women and children from abuse.

Historical Constructions of Rape

Like gender and sexuality, rape has a history that is both complex and changing. Its meaning as an act of forced sexual relations differs according to the social context in which it occurs. In patriarchal societies, rape has often been understood as a crime against family property, not against women, while in liberal societies, rape tends to be viewed as a crime motivated by individual sexual desire. In contrast, feminist analysis has reconceptualized rape as a crime of power enacted by men to control women. In fact, all of these meanings coexist in the contemporary world and affect both individual behavior and social policy.

The notion of rape as a crime against property is a legacy of patriarchal societies that contained women's sexuality within the family for the purpose of producing legitimate heirs. Virginity determined a woman's worth in the marriage market; it increased the bride-price in some cultures and was necessary for betrothal in others. Parents therefore attempted to protect their daughters to keep them pure for future husbands. Biblical law held that a man convicted of raping an unmarried woman had to pay the bride-price and marry her, since no one else would accept damaged goods. In medieval France and England, a convicted rapist could achieve "grace by marriage," avoiding punishment if the woman agreed to the wedding. If a woman was not a virgin, however, she did not merit protection.

Once marriage had taken place, a wife's fidelity ensured the legitimacy of heirs, so her husband protected her honor. Biblical law called for stoning to death the rapist of a married woman. Because the theft of a woman's virginity before marriage or her reproductive capacity after marriage constituted crimes against men's property, under medieval English law a father or husband pressed charges when a woman was raped. Moreover, for the charge of rape to hold, the woman had to be beyond moral reproach—a virgin or a chaste wife. A husband could not rape his own wife, since he owned the rights to her sexual and reproductive labor. Until at least the 1600s, this view of women's sexual body as male property both protected women within European families and denied them entitlement to either self-protection or the sexual expression enjoyed by men.

A second framework for understanding rape emphasizes sexual desire rather than property rights. Many cultures believe that men have irrepressible carnal lusts that women can easily excite by their very presence. The seclusion of women is partly intended to protect them from men's desire. The biblical story of Potiphar's wife, who tried to seduce Joseph and then claimed rape when he rejected her, illustrates another Western cultural belief that the accused man is often the victim of female allure and deception.

In the early twentieth century, psychologists elaborated on the theme of men's uncontrolled desires in their concept of a "sexual psychopath." Depictions of a crazed stranger rapist who stalked unsuspecting women proliferated in popular culture. More recently, *A Natural History of Rape* argues from animal studies that the rapist is not an anomaly but rather an everyman compelled by evolution to spread his genes. Its theory of a sociobiological male urge for sexual coercion overlooks close evolutionary relatives of humans such as the bonobos, for whom sex is non-violent and a frequent pleasure initiated by females.

The view of rape as a sexual act incited by male desire requires proof that a woman neither incited nor consented to sexual relations. In the Bible, if no witness heard a married woman cry out, she was stoned to death for presumed adultery. A 1646 Chinese statute required evidence that a woman had struggled during the entire rape. Anglo-American law called for corroboration by witnesses who could attest that a woman had tried to resist male assault by calling for help or struggling.

These historical constructions of rape placed women in a precarious position. Any past expression of sexual desire on a woman's part could discredit her if she later accused a man of sexual assault. At the same time, presumptions of sexual availability entitled elite men to engage in nonconsensual sex with working-class, slave, and native women without fear of prosecution for rape. In recent history medicine and marketing have increasingly sexualized women of all classes, which makes female resistance more problematic. If a woman initiates a meeting or expresses sexual attraction for a man, can she still be raped, or has she implicitly consented to have sexual relations? For women raised in the sexual liberalism of post–World War II Western cultures, sexual freedom can mean losing the right to say no.

Feminists on Rape

Early feminists recognized rape as a criminal use of male power against women. In the 1870s *Woman's Journal* editor Lucy Stone and her husband Henry Blackwell publicized "crimes against women," including rape, and urged reforms such as temperance to prevent them. Free-love advocates identified unwanted sexual relations in marriage as a form of rape. For the most part, however, these early women's rights activists concentrated on wife abuse rather than rape. During World War I the international women's movement did document rape in the Balkans, Germany, and Turkey. Although they protested "the horrible violation of womanhood that attends all war," no movement to oppose rape or reform the law took hold.[1]

After the 1960s, however, second-wave feminists seized upon the critique of rape and made violence against women a central concern. Both consciousness-raising and the theoretical turn to the politics of personal life inspired a mass antirape movement. In the United States, for example, several pivotal feminist analyses of rape publicized its extent, the daily fears women internalized, and the influence of race and class on the meaning and prosecution of rape.

Susan Brownmiller's 1975 book *Against Our Will: Men, Women, and Rape* reconceptualized sexual violence and helped spark the antirape movement. Brownmiller insisted that rape is not merely an individual act committed by deviant men motivated by sexual desire. "From prehistoric times to the present," she wrote, rape has been "nothing more or less than a conscious process of intimidation by which *all men* keep *all women* in a state of fear."[2] This fear sustained female subordination in economic, political, and personal life. Rape, she showed, has also been a powerful political tool used in the act of conquest, accepted as part of the "spoils of war" since at least the time of the Sabine women in Rome. In U.S. history she cited the enforcement of slavery through rape and the assault of native women by soldiers and settlers in the West. During the Russian and Polish pogroms against Jews and the Turkish efforts to annihilate Armenians, rape served as a weapon of retaliation.

While Brownmiller insisted that rape is endemic rather than isolated in Western culture, Susan Griffin elaborated further on the ways that the politics of rape affected women's daily lives. Girls grew up learning that "the world is not safe for women." As Griffin explained, "I have never been free of the fear of rape. From a very early age I, like most women, have thought of rape as part of my natural environment— something to be feared and prayed against like fire or lightning. I never asked why men raped; I simply thought it one of the many mysteries of human nature." To protect herself she learned "not to walk on dark streets, not to talk to strangers or get into strange cars, to lock doors, and to be modest."[3]

Griffin's description of learning to live with rape rests upon the historical construction of the irrepressible male violence that women can ignite. The impact of this legacy is twofold. First, fear remains part of women's daily consciousness. Even three decades after Griffin wrote, for example, half the women in England report that they still do not feel safe walking home at night. Second, since women have responsibility for avoiding assault, their behavior bears close scrutiny. Courts often place rape victims on trial, interrogating them about why they walked at night or ventured into certain neighborhoods. Questions about a woman's clothing or sexual history suggested that the victim had invited sex.

Brownmiller and Griffin each acknowledged that class and race influenced the politics of rape, but the African American scholar Angela Davis took the analysis further. She rejected echoes of the myth of the black rapist in early feminist works on rape, including Brownmiller's. That myth obscured the higher frequency of rape by white males, whose race and class privilege granted them immunity from prosecution. In early America, African and Native American men accused of rape were more likely to be convicted than accused white men. In the late nineteenth century southern black men who stood up for their economic or political rights risked being accused of rape and lynched. In the twentieth century the majority of men convicted and executed for rape were black (405 of the 455 men executed for rape between 1930 and 1967 were African American). Rape myths helped justify racial segregation in the United States by inciting fear of assault by African American men.

This cultural construction of the rapist as a black male drew attention away from other kinds of rape. Although 90 percent of rape in the United States is intraracial, it is interracial rape that has long obsessed the nation. In the slave South rape was once defined as an act of forced sex perpetrated against a white woman, denying legal recourse to all African American women. In the twentieth century the rape of black women continued to be underreported, and when it was prosecuted, the penalties did not equal those in the cases of white victims. In 1974, Davis noted, when ten white policemen gang-raped a seventeen-year-old black woman, only a few of them were reprimanded by suspension from the force.

For a generation feminists have insisted that the greatest threats to women's safety do not come from interracial relations or crazed strangers but from the defense of male privilege, taken to its extreme. Rape or its threat has explicitly terrorized women who try to break away from patriarchal authority. During the 1920s, for example, local men in the Islamic communities of Uzbekistan raped Russian Jewish and communist women who came into the region to urge women to remove their veils, go to school, and become politically active. Rape continues to target women who deviate from heterosexual norms. In South Africa in 1997 a gunman accosted a lesbian couple and told one of the women that "he knew who I was, and he was going to rape my girlfriend in front of me to teach us what happens to people like us."4 An off-duty police officer, the woman successfully fought off the assailant.

A culture of male entitlement allows men to act out this extreme form of gender privilege. In the notorious Glen Ridge, New Jersey, gang rape case of 1989, for example, a group of star athletes from a local high school selected a developmentally disabled girl and brutally raped her. The community struggled to understand how its favorite sons could have behaved so cruelly. These young men were not completely anomalous. In studies of male college students in the United States one-third admitted that they would commit violent rape if they knew that they could get away with it. When a 1998 survey asked young British men whether they would force a woman to have sex, one in eight said they might in a long-term relationship, while one in sixteen would if they had "spent a lot of money on her" or if she had "slept with loads of men."5 Portraying rape as an isolated act cannot address the extent to which gender relations create this feeling of entitlement.

Organizing Against Rape

Drawing on these analyses of rape, second-wave feminists built an anti-rape movement dedicated to naming the problem, providing services, and fighting back against sexual violence. Simply naming rape provided an initial break with past silence, shame, and the denial of racial violence against women. In the 1990s, for example, hundreds of Korean women who had been forced to have sex with Japanese soldiers during World War II finally began to reveal their painful histories of rape and gang rape. Silenced by shame for decades, their stories led to investigations into the use of "comfort women" in war, a lawsuit against the Japanese government, and the testimony of Dutch and Filipina women forced into sexual slavery during World War II.

The shame women have endured at the hands of police and family members who blame them for their plight has discouraged the reporting of peacetime rape. Estimates of the percentage of rapes reported to police are very low: 5 percent in South Africa, under 10 percent in the United States, and 12 percent in England. If fully reported, however, rape appears to be more common than rare. In the United States a rape occurred every five or six minutes during the 1990s; the Centers for Disease Control and Prevention found that one in five women had experienced a rape or attempted rape at some point in her life. Reported rape rates are lower in other industrialized nations, conspicuously so in Japan, Italy, and Spain, and slightly so in Scandinavia and England. Rates are extremely high in South Africa, and a women's rights group in Zimbabwe reports that one in three women surveyed in 1997 had been sexually assaulted, abused, or harassed.

Breaking silence and naming the experience of rape has contributed to fuller police reporting and helps remove the social stigma attached to women who have been sexually assaulted. Rather than blaming themselves for allowing the rape to occur, women began to recognize that such a widespread problem could not be their own faults. Renaming women as rape "survivors" rather than rape "victims" rejected the implied helplessness and need for protection in favor of emphasizing that women had lived to tell the tale of rape and pass on this reality so that others might escape it.

The process of naming has identified as crimes certain acts once accepted as the price of female existence. These include acquaintance rape (when a date or friend uses force to have sex without a woman's consent) and marital rape (when a wife's refusal to have sexual intercourse is not honored by her husband). In more than half of reported rapes in the United States the assailant knew the victim. The pattern of known assailants is widespread: 75 percent of Swedish women and 80 percent of Colombian women reporting rape knew their assailant. A South African woman attested to the practice in her community: "They find you on the street and they force you to go home with them so that they can have sex with you. It is rape but we do not call it rape because they are our boyfriends."[6]

Feminists pioneered services for rape survivors. In Europe and North America they set up hotlines where women could call to get medical and legal advice. They also instituted support groups where survivors could begin to heal from their trauma. Rape crisis centers opened in London in 1976 and in South Africa in 1979. The movement spread rapidly in thousands of community-based rape hotlines and service centers in the United States, Europe, Latin America, and Asia. In 2000 the Rape and Sexual Assault Support Centre in London took five hundred calls a month from all over the country, advising both women and men who experience sexual abuse.

Preventing rape takes many forms. Feminists began to reject earlier advice to submit to rape in order to avoid further injury. Defying stereotypes of female passivity and dependence, women's movements encouraged fighting back. Since the 1970s a self-defense movement for women and girls has burgeoned in Europe and North America. For some women, traditional martial arts provide the training to assert themselves both on the streets and in their personal lives; others enroll in women's self-defense classes. Through them women have learned how to walk safely on urban streets, how to discourage attack, and how to reclaim public space. In personal life, women who had been taught to acquiesce to male demands now practiced saying no as a form of empowerment. Forced into an alley by a man, one woman in the United States tried kicking and then "took a long, deep breath" and let out "a loud, clear scream." As she recalled: "It was something he hadn't counted on. 'Okay, lady, okay,' he responded. 'Lighten up. I'm leaving.' "[7]

In a collective method of reclaiming public life, Take Back the Night marches, women refuse the fear of going out after dark by walking together through city streets at night. Inspired by a candlelight march at a 1976 international feminist conference held in Belgium, the march has become an annual ritual on college campuses throughout North America. Marchers may walk silently with candles or carry banners and shout slogans such as "Survivors unite, take back the night." Colleges organize rape awareness projects in conjunction with the marches to educate students about the legal and moral importance of mutual consent in sexual relations.

The feminist antirape movement has called on men to become allies to women by respecting their right to say no and refusing to participate in the objectification or stereotyping of women. In response, men have formed their own antiviolence projects. In Zimbabwe Padare (Men's Forum on Gender) opposes violence against women. "We condemn rape," explained Jonah Gokova. "It is important for men to sit down and interrogate themselves and identify a new man within themselves whose identity does not thrive on conquest or on the use of violence against women." Gokova is also active in the Global Network of Men, organized in 2000 through the YMCA and the World Council of Churches. In the United States former athletes established the group MVP (Mentors on Violence Prevention), which urged teachers to rethink male socialization. As founder Jackson Katz explained, "We need to redefine strength. When a boy expresses pain or sadness, we need to support him by acknowledging the strength it takes to do such a thing." Asked if doing so would feminize boys, he replied: "The charge itself is sexist. It suggests that feminizing boys diminishes them, that girls are less than boys. In fact, it's a good thing to feminize boys and to masculinize girls, to break down rigid categories of gender."[8]

Legal Reform and Its Limits

The most important target of the feminist antirape movement has been the legal system. The treatment of rape by police and courts long resembled a second form of violence against women. Intrusive, suspicious questioning of women about their sexual pasts, along with the insensitivity of police officers, discouraged many women from reporting assaults. In response, feminists called for training police, emergency room staff, and court personnel to make them more sympathetic to women reporting rape. As a result, police have adopted a variety of new procedures. In the Philippines special women's desks at police stations make it easier to report sexual assault. In the United States women officers are now available, and both male and female police train to respond sensitively in sexual assault cases. Health care and psychological counseling have become standard in many departments. The Portland, Oregon, police department created a WomenStrength Web page with suggestions for healing and recovery from assault and readings on self-defense. The British government has encouraged comprehensive medical and legal services for victims of assault, including the choice of women doctors and support services for women who testify in court against assailants.

Feminists have insisted on the reform of legal procedures as well.

These include rejecting questions about a woman's prior sexual history, the kinds of clothing she wore, and whether or not she knew the accused rapist. Many states have redefined consent so that a woman no longer has to show that she resisted to prove assault. Although the requirement of corroborating witnesses has been dropped in most laws, adult male witnesses are still required for conviction in some countries. (In Sudan, for example, a 1991 law required four male Muslim witnesses to testify that a rape occurred.) Some states have redefined rape to include forcible sex without complete penetration. While sentencing still varies widely, new laws provide mandatory jail sentences for repeat offenders.

The impact of feminism on the law is illustrated by the concept of marital rape. In the 1970s women in the United States began to file legal suits establishing the right to say no to sex in marriage—a right that nineteenth-century feminists had argued for in their campaign for voluntary motherhood. This legal change overturned the traditional marriage contract, in which a wife owed sexual services to her husband. By the 1980s twenty-three U.S. states had enacted laws against marital rape. By 1996 all U.S. states allowed prosecution, although with extensive exceptions. Internationally, however, only seventeen countries considered marital rape a crime in 1998.

Although rape is not universally seen as a denial of women's rights, the United Nations now defines it this way. After lobbying by feminist NGOs, the Vienna Declaration and Program of Action at the fourth World Human Rights Conference in 1993 adopted the statement "Gender-based violence and all forms of sexual exploitation are incompatible with the dignity and worth of the human person, and must be eliminated." The 1995 Beijing Platform of Action declared violence against women "an obstacle to the achievement of the objectives of equality, development and peace."[9] It named marital rape specifically and included within the rubric of violence against women a range of practices, from female genital cutting to forced sterilization.

Despite the legal reforms achieved by feminists, "there's still a long way to go," British detective chief inspector Sue Hill reported in 2000. "To get a conviction, the victim should be preferably a virgin, preferably white, respectable, middle class, not been drinking, be traumatised, have given up on life, given up her job."[10] Individual judges continue to blame the victim of assault. In the 1990s a judge in Florida sympathized with a male defendant by commenting on the way a woman's clothing had provoked rape, while an Italian judge accepted a "denim defense" that argued that a woman who wore tight jeans could not be raped, since "it is impossible to pull them off if the victim is fighting against her attacker with all her force."[11] In response to his ruling, female legislators from Italy to California protested by wearing jeans to their jobs.

Nor do all feminists agree with the direction of the antirape movement. Some critics claim that the concept of date rape overemphasizes the victimization of women by men. In the U.S., Katie Roiphe and Camille Paglia objected to blaming men for having sex with women who chose to drink heavily or engage in otherwise risky behaviors. "Every woman must take personal responsibility for her sexuality," Paglia wrote. "When she makes a mistake, she must accept the consequences." Many sexual conservatives might agree with her solution to date rape: "female self-awareness and self-control." But male and female feminists alike reject her views that rape is "one of the risk factors in getting involved with men" and that male sexuality is naturally aggressive, "uncontrollable," and thus highly erotic.[12] In contrast, feminists who stress the cultural construction of sexuality envision an eroticism that rests on full consent and minimizes the risks that have been borne disproportionately by women in the past.

Given this cultural construction, legal reforms alone cannot reduce the extent of sexual assault. If rape is embedded in power imbalances between men and women and across classes and races, we need to address these social inequalities. To do so requires breaking the cycle of male entitlement to women, the sexual objectification of women, and the structural obstacles to gender and race equality. We also need to rethink the cultural associations of sexuality with aggression and women as objects of acquisition. Boys still learn to speak of "scoring" with girls, men to measure their worth by sexual conquests. Achieving such cultural change requires innovative, widespread community mobilization, such as the Zero Tolerance media campaigns sponsored by dozens of British communities to dispel myths about rape and "convey the message that violence against women and children is a crime."[13]

Finally, the historical links between race and sexual violence remind us that addressing gender alone cannot explain the persistence of rape. In South Africa only the rape of white women was prosecuted under apartheid. In the 1980s a predominantly white feminist group, Rape Crisis, discovered the limitation of this definition. Attending to the needs of victims of assault, they learned that political violence led to the rape of black women detained in jail by the white government. In response to this racially specific sexual violence, the members of Rape Crisis joined the multiracial antiapartheid movement. Only by seeking racial and social justice, as well as gender justice, can feminism undermine all sexual violence.

EXPANDING THE DEFINITION: SEXUAL HARASSMENT AND DOMESTIC VIOLENCE

Feminists have named all forms of unwanted sexual and physical acts as a source of gender inequality, including behaviors once taken for granted as woman's lot to suffer. In 1974, for example, Carmita Wood, a U.S. wage-earning mother of four, resigned from her job after her supervisor made repeated sexual advances toward her. In her claim for unemployment benefits, she used the phrase "sexual harassment." Courts had never ruled on this concept, but at least half of all working women had experienced it. The phrase would soon come to national and then international attention. In 1979 feminist legal theorist Catharine MacKinnon argued in *The Sexual Harassment of Working Women* that sexual pressures on women workers enforced women's economic disadvantage in the labor market. Sexual harassment, she held, was therefore a form of sex discrimination prohibited under Title VII of the U.S. Civil Rights Act of 1964. Serving as cocounsel before the U.S. Supreme Court, MacKinnon contributed to a 1986 ruling that made sexual harassment illegal in the United States. The court's narrow ruling, however, permitted a woman's speech or dress to be cited as relevant "sexual provocation."

In her book MacKinnon identified two ways in which the imposition of unwanted sexual requirements in the context of a relationship of unequal power could disadvantage women at work or in school. The first, quid pro quo, involved the promise of some form of advancement, such as a job, a raise, or better grades, in exchange for sex. The second, a hostile work environment, meant that sexual advances made the workplace or classroom unbearable, even if the worker refused the advances and no exchange of favors occurred. Both forms left psychological scars and undermined job or academic performance. While women who have advanced professionally can also harass their subordinates, as many as 90 percent of reported cases involve male workers who use sexual language and gestures to harass women. According to MacKinnon, sexual harassment is not simply about sex; rather, it rests at the intersection of the economic and the sexual control of women. Harassment often dissuades women from persisting in higher-paying blue-collar or managerial jobs or in professional education.

Like women who report rape, those who name sexual harassment often face disbelief and questioning about their sexual histories, as former Equal Employment Opportunity Commission employee Anita Hill learned in 1991 when she testified about harassment at the confirmation hearings for Supreme Court justice nominee Clarence Thomas. Commentators discredited her testimony because she had remained in her job despite the offensive behavior of her supervisor, even though Hill explained that she had feared retribution in her career if she revealed his unwanted advances and crude comments. Moreover, her status as a single African American woman made his behavior seem acceptable to some.

Anita Hill's painful testimony riveted the American public and the hostile response of male legislators unleashed a powerful female political force. African American women organized a defense of Hill in the press; after the hearings, sexual harassment complaints increased by 50 percent at the EEOC; membership in the National Organization for Women surged the following year; and 1992 became known as the Year of the Woman in U.S. politics, with 117 women candidates for congress. During the 1990s more women took employers and schools to court for not controlling sexual harassment, with major victories won by U.S. workers at Mitsubishi Motors and by public school students in Georgia and Texas who demanded protection from harassment by peers or teachers.

Tolerance for sexual harassment has declined outside the United States as well. In 1989, for example, Spain outlawed sexual harassment, while lawyers in Japan organized a hotline for women workers who felt they had been harassed. By the end of the 1990s countries such as Israel, Korea, and Venezuela had outlawed the practice, and the Indian Supreme Court ruled that sexual harassment violated a woman's right not only when manifested by physical touching but also through verbal offenses. As with rape, legal reform could achieve only limited progress toward changing cultural practices. Feminists have insisted on broader measures, including educational workshops for teachers and managers to explain the costs of inappropriate sexual advances and the procedures for complaining of them.

While institutions struggle to change practices that once intimidated women, feminists have disagreed about the extent and importance of sexual harassment. Some fear that highlighting sex as the source of a hostile work environment could produce a climate that constrains free speech about sexuality in the name of protecting women. For instance, a teacher or worker could elicit charges of sexual harassment for discussing sex in any form. In addition, the law itself is vulnerable to abuse through false charges. In the "he said/she said" scenarios, one party claims that the other either misunderstood or misrepresented the encounter, finding hostile intent in allegedly innocent behaviors. Like the controversy over date rape, the line between sexual play and sexual harassment creates a blurred legal and ethical space that fosters dissent among feminists. Most can agree, however, that learning to communicate clearly about sexual desire and respect for women's right to say no are common goals.

Domestic Violence

Sexual harassment occurs in public work and educational settings, so it is subject to antidiscrimination laws. In contrast, violence against women in the home has long been protected by the privacy accorded to the family and the implicit right permitted to husbands to rule over their wives and children. Behind closed doors, battery, verbal abuse, and life-threatening assaults take place regularly. "I can't remember a time when my mother wasn't physically abused by my father," a woman recalled in 1991. "I learned at an early age," another woman wrote, "that a man has the right to beat his wife and if he abstains, she should be grateful."[14]

In patriarchal cultures, husbands had the right to chastise their wives physically. From the Greeks through the Reformation, European husbands ruled over their wives and children and could correct them, as St. Augustine wrote, "by word or blow." The "rule of thumb" in Anglo-American law held that a husband could beat his wife as long as he used a stick that was no thicker than his thumb. The legitimacy of the practice persisted in the English-speaking world even after courts began to reject the legality of wife beating in the 1800s. In other cultures, husbands meted out physical punishment of wives, whether in China (where mothers-in-law also beat daughters-in-law), Africa, or the Middle East.

Early European feminists challenged the right of husbands to punish their wives. In England, Harriet Martineau and John Stuart Mill fought for the right to divorce in part so that wives could leave abusive husbands. In the United States social purity reformers and the Women's Christian Temperance Union blamed liquor for making men brutish husbands. Historian Elizabeth Pleck has shown that by the 1890s women's organizations provided social services, encouraged victims to bring charges in court, and established the first safe houses for abused wives. By the twentieth century a new legal concept of marital cruelty provided grounds for divorce. For mothers, however, it was difficult to apply these grounds if divorce left women either without custody of their children or economically unable to support them.

Although abuse of wives in Europe and the Americas has been publicly portrayed as a lower-class phenomenon, estimates of its incidence reveal a more extensive social problem. At the end of the twentieth century, each year between 10 and 20 percent of North American women were beaten by a man with whom they had an intimate relationship. One-fourth to one-half of all North American women could expect to experience domestic violence at some point in their lives. In the United States a woman is battered every fifteen seconds, and domestic violence is a major cause of injuries to women, including one-third of their murders. The Federal Bureau of Investigation notes that four women die every day in the United States from domestic assaults. In one Canadian study 62 percent of the murderers of women had been their intimate partners. One-third of all U.S. calls for police assistance concern domestic violence, yet until recently no police training existed and police departments typically advised officers not to interfere with private family matters. For years a "stitch rule" held that perpetrators should be charged with a crime only if the violence required stitches.

Internationally, the figures are equally disturbing. A 1985 survey in Thailand found that 50 percent of respondents had experienced domestic abuse. While the figures emphasized lower-class violence, they probably reflected underreporting among other social groups. United Nations figures for the proportion of adult women who had been physically assaulted by an intimate partner ranged in 1995 from about one-fourth in northern Europe and some Latin American countries, such as Chile, to three-fourths of the lower-caste women in Indian villages. An Egyptian study found that domestic violence was the major reason women were treated for physical trauma. Unique forms of family violence lead to injury and death in India. Dowry deaths and dowry burnings refer to the harassment of a wife who is either pressured to commit suicide or murdered so that her husband's family can extract and keep her dowry, the price paid at marriage. During the 1980s one or two women were burned to death a day in each of several Indian cities. Estimates during the 1990s ranged from five thousand to fifteen thousand Indian women killed annually in dowry-related incidents.

Contemporary feminists analyze domestic violence as a problem shared by women across class, race, and national lines. While social science studies show that patterns of abuse are passed from parents to children in families of any background, feminists move beyond a purely psychological argument based on family dynamics. Rather, they emphasize the economic problem of female dependency as a contributing factor to domestic violence. As Zimbabwe's deputy health minister, Tsungirirai Hungwe, explains, "Those leaving violent relationships often have limited options to support themselves and their children, and face poverty and isolation. Each year, a number of women try to commit suicide to escape such difficult situations."[15] A survey of Thai women found that those who worked in the low-paid informal sector and those who considered divorce a stigma for their families often remained in abusive relationship. Women who cannot be economically self-supporting may become trapped in cycles of "learned helplessness." Most battered women in North America are homemakers, many of whom have internalized blame for a husband's violence. When a wife depends on her husband for economic support she may feel both financially and psychologically dependent. Whether in Africa, India, Iran, or the United States, women who feel trapped within their families fear that they may be beaten or killed if they attempt to leave.

Throughout the world feminists have responded to domestic violence by naming the problem, providing services, and empowering women to claim their rights. In India protest marches began in 1979 to call attention to dowry burnings, making the once-personal issue a public one. Refusing the stories that deaths by fire were suicides, Indian women rallied with signs reading Down with Dowry. They also demanded police investigations and pressed for laws to punish cruelty to wives. In Latin America Brazilian women formed the Committee on Violence Against Women, which became the most active feminist organization in the country at the end of the 1970s. After a series of murders of Brazilian women, feminists staged public demonstrations that paralleled the Take Back the Night marches that protested rape.

Along with protests and services feminists insist on adequate police protection from domestic violence. Pop singer Tracy Chapman captured well the way law enforcement once handled domestic disputes: "The police always come too late if they come at all." In 1976 feminist lawyers brought a class action suit against the Oakland, California, police department because of its weak response to calls about domestic violence. A court settlement required special training for officers who intervene in domestic disputes. By 1986 almost half of the large urban police departments in the United States had adopted the policy of arresting perpetrators of domestic violence, compared to only 10 percent just two years earlier. Laws mandating the arrest of batterers have also become more common—twenty-six U.S. states had enacted them by 1994. The process of obtaining a judicial restraining order against an abusive partner has been simplified in the United States, and hospitals have also changed their responses. Since the American Medical Association declared the physical abuse of women a major health issue in 1991, emergency room staff have become more sensitive to the signs of domestic abuse.

International movements to protect women from abuse and to prosecute batterers expanded rapidly after 1980. Between 1985 and 1995 a hundred special police stations for women opened in Brazil, with feminist monitoring so that women could report violence and find their way to shelters. Women's courts hear cases of abuse in the Indian capital, New Delhi. In 1995 the Association of Women's Organizations in Jamaica succeeded in obtaining the passage of the Domestic Violence Act, which allows courts to remove abusive partners.

Feminists around the world have established shelters for battered women. First founded in England, the movement spread internationally after 1970. By 1990 there were over 1,250 shelters in the United States and Canada. The Women's Shelter Programme in Bangkok, founded in the 1980s, serves poor women in a neighborhood where up to half of them had been attacked by husbands. Some of these women fought back; some had killed their attackers. The founders of the shelter recognized that "the issue of battered women is not merely one of 'bad Karma' or a 'private matter' of each individual woman. We see it as a problem embedded in our social structure, which neglects the fundamental rights of women." In response they provided a temporary refuge from abuse, group therapy for residents, and a campaign to raise public consciousness "of battered wives as another form of violence which any woman, regardless of status or class, can fall prey to."[16] Run by volunteers who have survived abuse themselves, the Ambassador One-Stop Drop-in Advice Centre in England, established in 1998, provides a range of services to women fleeing domestic violence. In both Great Britain and the United States law enforcement agencies sometimes cooperate with shelters, directing women to them when they report abuse. By the 1990s specialized agencies reached out to immigrants. South Asian women living in the United States had organized shelters in New York, New Jersey, and California.

Most of these shelters rely on private funding, although some governments have provided help. The Netherlands, for example, subsidized forty-eight shelters in the 1990s, while Spain offered a toll-free hotline advising women about shelters. To fund its shelter, one city used a marriage license tax, while in the Basque area of Spain, battered women receive a "salary" to encourage them to leave their abusers. In 1994 the U.S. Violence Against Women Act provided funding for grants to shelters, as well as for research on violence and its prevention. Despite conservative opposition, the funding was renewed in 2000. Much of the funding for shelters continues to be raised by the feminist community, however. In the United States young women take wilderness hikes to raise funds for the Elizabeth Stone House in Boston, founded in 1974. In California a shelter solicits funds by sending Mother's Day cards created by children who reside there with their mothers.

Shelters offer a variety of services, including a safe house (a location kept secret from an abusive husband), group therapy, child care, and legal counseling to let women know their rights and options. In some cases consciousness-raising or support groups are critical elements. As one woman explained, the shelter helped her forget her husband and her fears. "They listened when I told my story . . . I felt safe."[17] As in the cases of rape and incest, part of the resistance to violence is to break down silence and isolation.

Shelters and restraining orders cannot always protect women, some of whom have been murdered while under court protection. Fear of continued abuse has driven some women to strike back. A large proportion of women serving prison sentences for murder in the United States have killed their batterers, often in self-defense. Lawyers have turned to the psychological theory of "battered woman syndrome" to explain why these women remained in abusive relationships to the point that they became violent themselves.

Women can be violent against partners or children as well as in response to abusive husbands. Studies of violence suggest that those who feel most entitled to social power are most likely to use violence to achieve or enforce it. Since power, not simply masculinity, produces violence, the solution is not just for women to achieve greater power. Rather, as theorists such as Nancy Hartsock have argued, feminists must reexamine the very concept of power. One kind of power, self-determination, is critical to full citizenship in democratic societies; another form, power over others, can legitimate violence as a means to enforce it. Thus, for African American feminist bell hooks, "Feminist efforts to end male violence against women must be expanded into a movement to end all forms of violence."[18]

THE SEXUAL ABUSE OF CHILDREN

In a 1980 book Florence Rush referred to incest as "the best-kept secret." Her phrase is significant on several counts. Rape has been a serious
crime, a matter of public record, a subject of warning for girls and women.
Though fear of shame, blame, and rejection have silenced many women
from revealing rape, some sexual experiences are even harder to talk about.
Nonconsensual sex between adults and children within families, or between older and younger siblings, has been so taboo that language and
law generally evade it. Sexual relations with children under the "age of
consent" (which can range from ten to eighteen years of age) constitute
statutory rape, but the law usually applies this term to individuals outside
the family. Marriage laws forbid incest, an anthropological and legal term
for marriage among close relatives that implies consenting partners. Thus
the very term *incest* obscures the abuse of power that lies at the heart of the
sexual violation of children.

Though silenced in most cultures, the sexual abuse of children may
be as extensive as domestic violence and rape. According to a 1995 UN
report, between one-fourth and one-third of the women in Barbados,
Canada, the Netherlands, New Zealand, Norway, and the United States
reported sexual abuse as children or adolescents. Other U.S. studies place
the figure somewhere between 12 and 20 percent. In India one-fourth of
a sample of students reported abuse before the age of twelve, and over
half of one sample of Canadian women reported assaults by age sixteen.
Across the world assaults are usually committed against girls under age
fifteen. A study of women inmates of U.S. prisons found that twice as
many had been physically or sexually abused as children than in the overall female population, and those who had been abused were more likely
to have committed violent crimes.

In the United States over 90 percent of adults who report having experienced child sexual abuse are female, but the data may be biased by a
reticence to speak that may be even stronger for men than women. A
1999 survey of studies in nineteen countries revealed that between 7 and

34 percent of girls, and between 3 and 29 percent of boys, had been sexually abused. Recent estimates that one out of six boys in the United States has been sexually assaulted may eventually be revised upward. Of those boys affected, approximately 80 percent had been abused by men. Assaults sometimes took place in the home but also in institutions such as churches or the boarding schools to which many Native American children were sent in Canada and the United States. Like women, men are more likely to commit violent crimes if they were abused as children.

While both girls and boys are vulnerable to physical and sexual abuse, the perpetrators are overwhelmingly male. According to the American Psychological Association, fathers commit about one-fourth of the sexual abuse of girls, stepfathers commit another one-fourth, and most of the remaining perpetrators are adoptive fathers and other male relatives. When women abuse children (about 5 percent of the female children and 20 percent of the male children abused), they are less likely to use physical force, which may lead to underreporting.

Given the extent of child sexual abuse—and the enormous social costs in crime, violence, depression, suicide, and the passing on of abuse through children—why did this crime remain "the best-kept secret" until the feminist movement exposed it? One answer lies in the patriarchal family, which invested in fathers the power over their children. Freudian theory also contributed to this silence. At a critical point in his thinking Sigmund Freud decided that there could not be as much fondling and sexual intercourse with fathers, brothers, and uncles as his female patients reported. He suggested that instead of memories, these reports could be imagined fantasies representing unfulfilled desires for the sexual attention of fathers. Because this influential Freudian view pervaded psychoanalytic and social work practice for decades, even children with behavioral symptoms of abuse could be diagnosed as promiscuous or hypersexual.

In addition, children have a difficult time naming sexual abuse themselves. They rarely have words to describe what feels wrong about unwanted fondling, especially if perpetrated by a parent or relative who may also provide love, affection, recreation, and material support. When children do name unwanted acts, they risk either being blamed for them or not believed by adults. As the novelist Dorothy Allison recalled, "I had been repeatedly warned throughout my childhood that if I ever revealed what went on in our home, they would take me away. I would wind up in juvenile detention and spend the rest of my life in and out of jail."[19] In reporting abuse, the child also risks the loss of the parent or other relative who is prosecuted. Thus many children remain silent as unwanted sex continues. The UN cites a reporting figure of only 2 percent of all child sex abuse cases.

Some children choose silence strategically, while others suppress the memories of unwanted sex as a mechanism for surviving the ordeal. Approximately three-quarters of women reporting incest as adults experienced blocked memories for a time. Charges of "false memory syndrome," reminiscent of Freud's views, raise questions about the filters through which childhood abuse is recalled. As feminist therapist Janice Haaken argues, authorities must listen carefully to understand the impact of past experience, neither rejecting out of hand nor accepting uncritically the memories that emerge years after the fact. But recognizing the malleability of memory should not reimpose silence on those who have experienced sexual assault in childhood.

Feminists have redefined incest as an abuse of power historically exercised by more powerful adults, usually males, upon children of both sexes. According to Judith Herman, the greater the paternal dominance in a family, the more likely it is that abuse will occur. In contrast to Freudian theories of imagined, and desirable, father-daughter incest, Herman found that most girls experience sexual relations with their fathers as coercive and assaultive. She also looked at the controversial role of mothers in abusive families. Often the victims of violence themselves, those who have been immobilized either by illness or by their own experiences are more likely to cede power to fathers who then abuse it. "Maternal collusion in incest," Herman concluded, "is a measure of maternal powerlessness."[20]

The family, however, is not the sole focus of feminist analysis. Cultures at large eroticize children, tolerate sexual abuse, and contribute to silence by incriminating the child who reports sexual contact. Fairy tales caution little girls to obey their fathers, while the coquetry of child film stars celebrate seductive young females. Other critics note the sexualization of children in advertisements and the growth of child pornography on the Internet. Since girls and boys lack power by virtue of their age, these cultural messages make children particularly vulnerable.

Children who are sexually abused do not become entirely powerless, as myriad stories of survival reveal. Some resist physically or learn how to avoid the offending adult; some negotiate to lessen the abuse for themselves or for younger siblings. An older sister agrees to have sex with her father on the condition that he leave her younger sister alone. In a middle-class family, two older siblings who remained silent about the long-term physical or sexual abuse they suffered at the hands of their father break silence when their younger sister enters puberty, revealing their ordeals to authorities to prevent her from sharing them. One daughter resisted her father by telling him "that the priest told her not to." Her sister, forced to perform oral sex with their father from age twelve, decided when she was sixteen that "I wasn't going to do it anymore. . . . I was afraid when I told him, but he just said, 'O.K.' "[21]

Feminists have insisted on naming the problem of child sexual abuse and renaming the victims as survivors. They have called on social agencies to become sensitive to evidence of physical or sexual abuse, and they have insisted that children should learn about their rights to say no to unwanted sex. The latter strategy requires the lifting of taboos on early sex education, and it has not gone unopposed. Along with educators and parents, feminists have embarked on proactive campaigns to teach girls as well as boys that they can resist unwanted touching.

Given how recently feminists have waged their campaigns, it is heartening that so much has changed already. From shelters and hotlines to the International Criminal Court, feminists have named sexual and physical abuse as both morally and legally unacceptable. Though millions of women remain vulnerable, many are healing from abuse. Instead of living in constant fear, they are reclaiming their lives in the face of a history of sexual and racial violence. The Native American poet Joy Harjo provides a glimpse of this process. Even as she recounts the violence committed against native peoples and against women and children, she rejects the internal hold of terror. "I release you fear . . . I release you," Harjo repeats in affirmation. "I take myself back, fear. You are not my shadow any longer."[22] Through creative voices like hers, along with the continued political activism of women and their male allies, the movement against violence is poised to extend the right to bodily self-determination to women around the world.

PART V

FEMINIST VISIONS AND STRATEGIES

THIRTEEN

NEW WORDS AND IMAGES: WOMEN'S CREATIVITY AS FEMINIST PRACTICE

{N}ew words, to express new values, are much to be desired.
— VIRGINIA WOOLF, ENGLAND, 1938

*Woman must write her self: must write about women and
bring women to writing.*
— HÉLÈNE CIXOUS, FRANCE, 1976

*When Sexism & Racism Are No Longer Fashionable,
What Will Your Art Collection Be Worth?*
— GUERRILLA GIRLS, UNITED STATES, 1989

In 1974 four women in Boston, Massachusetts, decided to open a bookstore devoted to writing by, for, and about women. At the time the concept seemed radical. Why a *women's* bookstore? Could it fill its shelves? Would customers support it? In a one-room Cambridge storefront the founders established their shop, stocked with five hundred titles. They called the store New Words, a conscious tribute to Virginia Woolf's observation about the desirability of providing language to match changing values.[1] In creating a space for women's writing, New Words announced the connection between literature and the larger feminist political movement.

Throughout the United States and in other countries as well, women's bookstores proliferated. Since the 1970s they have served a

growing audience of readers in search of new images to support their
politics. "Some women walked around the block many times before they
found the courage to enter," wrote Carol Seajay, who helped found the
Old Wives' Tales bookstore in San Francisco. "Once they made it
through the doorway, they took what they found and changed their
lives—left abusive relationships, found new self-images, came out, found
sisterhood and community." Comedian Roseanne, for example, "got the
boost she needed working in a large collective bookstore, Denver's
Woman to Woman Bookcenter, where her humor was understood and
supported."[2] Not all of these new cultural spaces survived economically,
but many, including New Words, continue to thrive. By 2000 New
Words stocked ten thousand titles in an expanded space that housed
rooms for children's books, arts books, author readings, and periodicals.
Similar shops—from Mother Tongue Books/Femmes de Parole in Ottawa
to Las Sirenas in Mexico City to the Binti Legacy Feminist Bookstore in
Nairobi—sustain an international network of women's cultural spaces
that in turn invigorates women's movements. Besides the thousands of
titles by women from mainstream publishers—far more than in the
past—these stores carry books from feminist presses, such as Virago in
England and Kali for Women in India.

The growth of bookstores and publishers, along with art galleries,
museum exhibitions, and concerts featuring the creative works of women,
parallels the reclamation of the body as a means of feminist empowerment. Women's creativity encompasses strategies based on both female
difference and human equality. Feminist artists launched their own alternative cultural spaces and demanded access to institutions that previously excluded them: the theater, the museum, the concert hall. Once
admitted to these public cultural spaces, feminists bring to their arts not
only an exploration of women's experiences, such as motherhood and
sexual violence, but also the complex politics of race, nationality, and
sexuality.

LANGUAGE AND GENDER

New words require a fresh look at language, beginning with spoken
language. Many cultures admonish girls and women to remain silent but

encourage boys and men to express themselves. In early modern England, for example, for a respectable lady, public silence was as important as chastity. Historically, Japanese women were not supposed to speak as much as men. Such discouragement can affect women's creative capacity by suppressing the female voice, as speaker or as author.

While not all cultures value women's silence, the tradition still influences much of the English-speaking world. In the United States, for example, boys and men still speak more often than do girls and women. Scholars who observe and quantify conversations find that men talk more often than women. Although women speak more in informal settings, such as with friends or at home, men are more likely to dominate formal conversations, at school or at work.[3]

Training in female silence can begin in the classroom. From kindergarten to college, social scientists have observed, both male and female teachers call on boys more frequently in class. Writing in 1994 about a California middle school, Peggy Orenstein discovered a "hidden curriculum" in gender relations and called it "Learning Silence." Boys flailed their hands in the air to be called on, whether they knew the answers or not, while girls politely waited their turns. When an eighth-grader named Amy finally had a chance to speak but gave a wrong answer, she resigned herself to silence: "That's about the only time I ever talked in there. I'll never do that again."[4]

The English language itself silences women when it makes them invisible. According to Laurel Richardson, English usage marks the male as the human, the female as other. A term such as *mankind* may stand for both sexes, but it reinforces the cultural importance of the male. When academics use concepts such as "the ascent of man," "political man," or "modern man," they implicitly exclude women from society and history. The words *author*, *poet*, or *artist* once presumed a male subject and marked the female who engaged in these pursuits as an *authoress*, *poetess*, or *woman artist*.

Language can also make women seem dependent and invisible. Historically, the personal titles used in many languages have denied women's personal identity, emphasizing instead their relationships to males. For men, the English courtesy title *Mr.* refers to all adult males, while adult women are defined by the relationship of marriage as either *Miss* or *Mrs.*

In the past marriage erased a woman's individual identity entirely by using both her husband's first and last names; we know only that Mrs. Henry Jones is a married woman, with a husband named Henry Jones.

Changing Language

Since the nineteenth century, feminists have tried to transform language use that makes women invisible. Instead of becoming Mrs. Henry Stanton, the American women's rights activist proclaimed herself Elizabeth Cady Stanton. When Lucy Stone and Henry Blackwell married in 1855 they went a step further by insisting that she keep her "maiden name" and not take his at all, an innovation rarely followed in English-speaking cultures until the late twentieth century. Today more women follow this practice, while many couples either hyphenate their family names or choose new ones. The term *Ms.* gradually took root in English as the equivalent of *Mr.*, referring to an adult woman without highlighting her marital status. Though *Ms.* endured ridicule when first introduced in the 1970s, within a decade the *New York Times* had adopted the usage, as did most business, educational, and U.S. government forms by the end of the century. American feminists also insisted on using *woman* rather than *girl* as the equivalent of *man*, indicating that females do grow up and become adults. Just as calling adult black males or colonial subjects *boy* instead of *man* once enforced white and European dominance, so too reducing adult women to childlike status enforced male dominance. References to forty-year-old female employees as the "girls in the office," for example, subtly supported their low wages and low status.

The language used to describe workers has inspired a range of new words in the past generation. To shift attention away from sex-based qualifications for jobs, gender-neutral terms, such as *waiter* and *actor*, can describe both men and women, instead of marking one sex with diminutive forms such as *waitress* and *actress*. Amending an older term sometimes does the trick; thus either *chair* or *chairperson* can replace *chairman*. New terms such as *mail carrier*, *flight attendant*, and *police officer* have replaced the gender-specific terms *mailman*, *stewardess*, and *policeman*.

English is not the only language for which feminists have sought new words. In the 1940s Arab feminists called for the elimination of feminine endings in Arabic. Today Spanish-speaking women in the

United States experiment with language to reflect new social relationships. Mexican American writer Gloria Anzaldúa recalled her initial shock upon hearing women use the term *nosostras* as the third person (feminine) plural, rather than the generic masculine plural *nosostros*. Emma Pérez recounts the "transgressive connotations" of the term that Chicana lesbians invented to replace *chingar* (fuck), drawing on the Nahuatl root *panocha*, a slang term for vagina: "Instead of using *chingón*, which implies a Herculean man, we invented *panochear*, representing a formidable, impressive, woman, whether lesbian or straight."[5]

Those who recognize the power of language as a tool for social change have reacted fiercely to these innovations. The opponents of feminist language reform either trivialized the effort, asking, "What difference do words make?" or painted all feminists as extremists obsessed with "political correctness." Thus right-wing radio commentator Rush Limbaugh popularized the term *feminazis*. This defensive venom tells us just how high the stakes can be when it comes to language use. As author Toni Morrison put it, "The political correctness debate is really about . . . the power to be able to define. The definers want the power to name. And the defined are now taking that power away from them."[6]

RECLAIMING LANGUAGE: TOWARD A FEMINIST VOICE

The politics of language represent one step in a larger movement to encourage women to speak, to value what they have to say, and to envision a female creative voice. That voice is not new. For millennia human cultures valued women's storytelling and their lullabies. We know that since pre-Islamic times Arab women have composed poetry and songs that are central to their cultural life. Elite women participated in the rise of national literary cultures. They circulated their poems as early as the T'ang Dynasty in China during the 700s and 800s. Lady Murasaki's *The Tale of Genji*, written circa 1000 CE, remains a classic of Japanese literature. Even when men dominated the arts, some women managed to write, as did Aphra Behn, the seventeenth-century British playwright and novelist.

In the early modern West, however, the spread of literacy and the commercialization of art initially widened the cultural gender gap. Until the 1800s more men than women learned to read and write. Popular and religious beliefs about women's intellectual and spiritual inferiority could discourage even literate women. The woman writer had to overcome accusations that she was sinful, offensive, or even crazed for stepping outside of her domestic sphere. In 1650 the Puritan poet Anne Bradstreet wrote, "I am obnoxious to each carping tongue / Who says my hand a needle better fits." In 1837 poet Robert Southey told British novelist Charlotte Brontë that "literature cannot be the business of a woman's life and it ought not to be."[7] With such advice it is not surprising that so many women writers of Brontë's time, including George Eliot, published under male pseudonyms. In 1978 Tillie Olsen chose an apt title for her book about women's literature over the previous century: *Silences.* Despite the exceptional women who wrote, painted, or composed music, expectations of female silence remained powerful.

Every feminist movement has created a literature that voices women's protests and hopes. In the early twentieth century the utopian tales of Charlotte Perkins Gilman in the United States and Rokeya Sakhawat Hossain in South Asia imagined women in charge of peaceful and productive societies. Second-wave feminism inspired poets, novelists, and playwrights. A growing school of feminist writers addressed the importance of women's consciousness and women's language to their political awakening.

In an influential essay, "When We Dead Awaken," Adrienne Rich recalled her training in the formal techniques of poetry, her early successes as a writer, and the feeling of being creatively paralyzed during the years she raised three children. After the 1950s, her approach to writing changed. "I had been taught that poetry should be 'universal,' which meant, of course non-female," she explained. Eventually, the woman in her poems shifted from "she" to "I," as Rich rejected a distinction between herself as a woman and as a poet.[8] Other writers also grappled with the gender divide that required poets to reject the world and the language of women. In her 1972 poem "In the men's room(s)," Marge Piercy recalled that "when I was young I believed in intellectual conversation," including a desire "to be certified worthy of high masculine discourse."

In contrast, other women simply

. . . ran out for six-packs and had abortions
in the kitchen and fed the children and were auctioned off.

Piercy too eventually questioned rather than quested for men's approval:

Now I get coarse when the abstract nouns start flashing.
I go out to the kitchen to talk cabbages and habits.[9]

Science fiction writer Ursula LeGuin echoed these themes in her 1986 commencement address at Bryn Mawr College, when she urged the young women graduates to reconsider their "mother tongue." They had been well trained to speak the abstract, analytical, academic "father tongue," but what of women's speech—the cooing of mothers to their infants, the litanies of everyday life, the vernacular learned within the family? "Our schools and colleges, institutions of the patriarchy, generally teach us to listen to people in power, men or women speaking the father tongue," LeGuin explained, "and so they teach us not to listen to the mother tongue, to what the powerless say: poor men, women, children, not to hear that as valid discourse. I am trying to unlearn these lessons."[10]

For immigrant and migrant women who are nonnative speakers, the mother tongue is even more complex. Colonial schools in Africa, Latin America, and Asia regularly suppressed native languages. Similarly, U.S. schools have imposed English, whether upon Native Americans in the 1800s, Yiddish-speaking European immigrants in 1900, or Spanish-speaking Mexican migrants in 2000. Silencing language enforces social dominance of race, religion, and ethnicity as much as gender. As Gloria Anzaldúa explains, "If a person . . . has a low estimation of my native tongue, she also has a low estimation of me."[11] Anzaldúa and other Latinas in the United States have experimented with bilingual writing as a means of breaking both kinds of silence.

Writing as Women

Addressing female consciousness in writing has been critical to the process of breaking silence. Like the consciousness-raising groups of the 1960s and 1970s, the feminist literature of that era revealed parts of women's inner lives once kept secret: the abortions, rapes, and childhood sexual assaults; the unstated love for other women; the desire to create art as well as children; the pain of racial discrimination and class exclusion. Dilemmas once assumed to be personal problems came to light as the product of social constraints.

In Muriel Rukeyser's 1968 poem about the German artist Käthe Kollwitz, she wrote prophetically: "What would happen if one woman told the truth about her life? / The world would split open."[12] Indeed, the literature that poured forth in the second wave of feminism put a lie to the old divide between domestic and public, placing women's personal experience within political discourse. From personal journal writing, novels, and memoirs to exposés of abuse with titles such as *I Never Told Anyone*, women named what had been silenced. Nor was this literature limited to Western writers. When authors such as Nawal El Saadawi of Egypt wrote about female circumcision and Buchi Emecheta of Nigeria explored the impact of colonialism on motherhood, they challenged not only gender relations but also Western feminist assumptions that other women could not speak for themselves.

French feminists articulated a theory of women's writing that insisted on the centrality of the act of writing as a woman to both breaking silence and undermining patriarchy. If discourse constructed gender, Luce Irigaray explained, language enabled women to create a "female imaginary" that would displace the phallocentric word, particularly through a language of female pleasure. "Woman must write woman," declared Hélène Cixous in 1976. "Write, let no one hold you back, let nothing stop you: not man; not the imbecilic capitalist machinery . . . ; and not *yourself*." For Cixous and other feminists, writing represents a forum for "women *seizing* the occasion to speak, hence her shattering entry *into history*."[13]

Not only through words but also in their images, performances, and crafts, women throughout the world are reclaiming a heritage of creativity, exploring the "female imaginary" in all its forms. A good example of this release of "woman writing woman" is the renaissance of women's autobiographical literature in English. For two centuries the European literary tradition included the *Bildungsroman*, or coming-of-age story. Through these tales of self-emancipation, young men established their positions as modern subjects, freed from constraints and in charge of their lives. But where were the female coming-of-age narratives? The marriage plot preoccupied many women writers; finding a suitable husband seemed to seal the fate of female subjects, although hints of subversion appeared regularly. In the 1970s a spate of consciousness-raising novels explored women's struggles to come of age. In the United States the popularity of Piercy's *Small Changes* (1973), Rita Mae Brown's *Rubyfruit Jungle* (1973), and Marilyn French's *The Women's Room* (1977) suggested that female readers were hungry for these narratives. Variations on this theme employed historical settings to confront the legacy of both racial and gender limitations. Books such as Maxine Hong Kingston's *The Woman Warrior* (1976), Alice Walker's *The Color Purple* (1982), and Toni Morrison's *Beloved* (1987) portrayed women not only as victims but also as complex heroines.

Breaking silence and coming of age recurs in women's literature wherever feminist movements revived in the late twentieth century. The Egyptian writer Ahdaf Soueif's 1992 novel *In the Eye of the Sun* recalls modern Egyptian history through the coming of age of a young woman. In 1997 the Indian writer Arundhati Roy's *The God of Small Things* broke silence about gender, sexuality, and caste to earn both the anger of traditionalists and the praise of feminists. Novels such as *A Matter of Time* (1996), by Shashi Deshpande, explore the inner and outer struggles of Indian women's quest for self-expression. The public recognition of women's literary achievements—from the Nobel prizes for literature awarded to Nadine Gordimer in 1991 and Toni Morrison in 1993 to the Booker Prizes given to Arundhati Roy in 1997 and Margaret Atwood in 2000—attests to the quality and broad impact of this renaissance of women's writing. Not all obstacles have fallen, by any means. An eager audience now reads fiction by women, but as Francine Prose noted in a 1998 tally of major book reviews and prizes in the United States, male novelists receive far more than their share of each.

HAVE THERE BEEN NO GREAT
WOMEN ARTISTS?

The explosion of feminist memoirs, fiction, and poetry in our own time raises questions about what has limited or encouraged women's creativity in the past. In her 1971 essay, art historian Linda Nochlin provocatively phrased the question "Why have there been no great women artists?" Assuming that women had not in fact produced great art, Nochlin concluded that "the fault lies not in our stars, our hormones, our menstrual cycles, or our empty internal spaces, but in our institutions and our education—education understood to include everything that happens to us from the moment we enter this world of meaningful symbols, signs, and signals."[14]

It is not difficult to find evidence to support her argument. Art academies once rejected students because they were female, and painting genres have objectified women's bodies. Even when women created art they were deemed exceptional or not taken seriously. In 1521, for example, the artist Albrecht Dürer so admired a picture of Jesus made by a young illuminator named Susanna Horenbout that he bought it, yet he commented that he was surprised "that a woman can do so much." In 1820, Fanny Mendelssohn's father told her that music "must be an ornament, never the root of your being and doing," as it could be for her brother Felix.[15] For centuries marriage and motherhood have preoccupied many women who would be artists. Nawal El Saadawi reflects that her mother would have been a "poet, painter, or surgeon," but instead had to leave school at age seventeen to marry. While the tasks of daily survival discourage most people from making art, when working women have a double duty they have even less time to write or paint.

Virginia Woolf offered the classic feminist argument about women's historical exclusion from the arts in her 1929 essay *A Room of One's Own*. Woolf asked her readers to imagine that William Shakespeare had a sister named Judith. While he went to grammar school, ran wild in the woods, worked in the theater, and gained access to royalty, "his extraordinarily gifted sister remained at home." Judith Shakespeare was not sent to school. Her parents told her that reading books would ruin her, that she should mind the mending and the stew, so she hid or burned her scribbling. Betrothed at a young age, beaten by her father when she resisted the idea of marriage, Judith Shakespeare ran away from home at age seventeen to join the theater. But women were not permitted to act. She became pregnant by an actor and, Woolf imagines, she "killed herself one winter's night and lies buried at some crossroads where the omnibuses now stop outside Elephant and Castle."[16]

Women Have Produced Great Art

Exclusion, however, is far from the whole story. Another direction in feminist criticism recognizes that women have in fact created great art throughout the centuries. Sometimes they simply did not get credit for it. Anonymous Was a Woman, proclaims a feminist bumper sticker. Other works went out of print for generations. A major project of feminist scholarship has been the recovery of "lost texts" by women, such as Harriet Wilson's *Our Nig, or Sketches from the Life of a Free Black* (1859). The first novel published by an African American in the United States, *Our Nig* depicted northern racism on the part of both women and men, as experienced by a young female servant. In Britain, Germany, and Scandinavia, feminists have restored "great" works by women to the canon of Western culture. Feminist art historians coined the term "Old Mistresses" to refer to these female equivalents of the Old Masters of European painting. Those artists resurrected by feminist critics include the seventeenth-century Italian painter Artemisia Gentileschi, the nineteenth-century German composer Fanny Mendelssohn Hensel, and the African American sculptor Edmonia Lewis. Clearly, their work declares, some women overcame the obstacles that defeated Judith Shakespeare.

Do the exceptions, however, prove the rule? Until very recently in the West and in much of the world today, rural and poor women do not have the luxury to learn to read and write or the tools to paint and sculpt. Even among the literate, women's work in the home has often precluded formal artistic practice. In the 1800s Clara Wieck felt that "there is nothing greater than the joy of composing something oneself, and then listening to it," but after marriage she devoted herself to raising eight children and caring for her husband, composer Robert Schumann.[17] As the German Jewish poet Mascha Kaléko explained, "Wagner had his Cosima / And Heine his Mathilde / . . . We women, though, have no 'artist's wife.' "[18]

The conflict between the roles of artist and wife/mother has haunted creative women for centuries. Contemplating women who wrote in English, Tillie Olsen pointed out how often those women whose work gained public notice happened not to have children, whether single or married. Her list included Jane Austen, Emily Brontë, Emily Dickinson, Christina Rossetti, Willa Cather, Ellen Glasgow, Gertrude Stein, Edith Wharton, Virginia Woolf, Isak Dinesen, Lillian Hellman, Dorothy Parker, and Eudora Welty. We can add as well Djuna Barnes, Anaïs Nin, Zora Neale Hurston, Simone de Beauvoir, Janet Frame, Lillian Smith, Iris Murdoch, Joyce Carol Oates, and Lorraine Hansberry. By the late twentieth century, however, Olsen noted an expanding list of writers in English who did raise children, including Doris Lessing, Nadine Gordimer, Grace Paley, Cynthia Ozick, Joan Didion, Maxine Kumin, Alice Walker, Ursula LeGuin, and Ruth Prawler Jhabvala. To these we can add Buchi Emecheta, Nawal El Saadawi, Isabel Allende, Simone Schwartz-Bart, and a growing generation of artists and writers who find a balance between motherhood and creative careers.

What's Wrong with the Question?

By whose standards does art become great? In European history, growing capitalist wealth helped create a hierarchy of art forms that deemed painting more valuable than domestic crafts. In the process, women ceased to be identified with the emerging fine arts. The aesthetic values of elites may, by definition, exclude the arts of women and the poor. If we reject the distinctions between fine art and crafts, between high culture and popular culture, we find many more great women artists. Abundant female voices and creative visions filled the realm of everyday, vernacular culture. Mexican American female singers wrote their own *corridos* (ballads) recalling historic or family events. African American blues singers, such as Bessie Smith and Gertrude "Ma" Rainey, voiced their complaints about no-good men who drank and abandoned them while they insisted that they deserved better. As Bessie Smith put it in "Young Woman's Blues," "See that long lonesome road, Lord, you know it's gotta end / And I'm a good woman and I can get plenty men."[19]

Poor women regularly tap into their creativity to produce great art that is part of everyday life. In parts of China, for example, women highly value the domestic needlework they produce; in southern Africa, Ndebele women still pass on the secrets of their magnificent beadwork and wall paintings during girls' initiation; in Central America villagers take pride in the colorful cloth woven specially by the women. Domestic crafts have provided an important source of female creativity in the United States, as well. In her essay "In Search of Our Mothers' Gardens," Alice Walker explored her own mother's "creativity with her flowers." Only while working in her garden did Walker's mother become "radiant." Viewing an original quilt made by "an anonymous Black woman in Alabama," Walker wondered if its maker could be "one of our grandmothers—an artist who left her mark in the only materials she could afford, and in the only medium her position in society allowed her to use."[20]

Quilts provide a good example of the ingenuity of women's creativity. In America from the eighteenth through the twentieth centuries, women of all classes and races designed and sewed quilts. Art historian Pat Mainardi once called quilts "the great American art form." These practical items for daily use, handed down through generations, included magnificent patterns and colors, often patched together from scrap. Women quilted not only to supply warmth on cold nights but also to encode their personal and family stories, as well as historical phenomena such as the Underground Railroad, the Civil War, the migration west, or the suffrage movement. Like the pottery made by native Pueblo or Peruvian women, quilts allowed their creators to both express aesthetic visions and engage in skilled handiwork. Both pots and quilts became highly valued art forms in the late twentieth century, adopted by men as well as women. The political heritage of quilting lives on as well. During the 1980s, for example, the AIDS quilt in the United States poignantly and creatively broke public silence about the human costs of the epidemic.

IN SEARCH OF
FEMINIST AESTHETICS

The elevation of the quilt from domestic art to high culture stood in stark contrast to the highly masculinist tone of Western art in the period after World War II. In the United States the popularity of abstract expressionism, heroic male artists, and novels that demeaned or sexually objectified women set the stage for the harsh criticisms of second-wave feminists. For example, to introduce her critique of "power and dominance" in modern literature, Kate Millett detailed a scene from a Norman Mailer novel in which the hero murders his wife and then sodomizes the maid. The place of women in this art, she and others suggested, was dangerously demeaning. Even without violence and sexual objectification, most arts represented women from a male point of view, and feminist criticism initially tried to expose the bias of that perspective. Film theorists such as Laura Mulvey wrote about the "male gaze," arguing that Hollywood's portrayals of women provided a kind of voyeuristic pleasure for male spectators. Later critics complicated the picture by questioning whether women simply internalized the negative images offered by film. For example, literary critic Janice Radway proposed that readers used romance novels for their own ends, including escape from patriarchy through fantasy.

Moving beyond critiques of male representations of women, the creation of new forms of art that reflect women's lives and imaginations has become critical to feminist politics. Literary scholar Rita Felski explains the importance of this artistic endeavor in terms of women's public space. Since the 1600s a public sphere apart from the state has helped to produce Western culture and politics; feminism responds to women's exclusion from that sphere. The arts contribute importantly to creating a public space in which to criticize unexamined gender relations and articulate women's particular perspectives.

Creating Space for Women Artists

At the beginning of the second wave of Western feminism, the public arena for women's arts remained minimal. In 1970, for example, only 5 percent of the artists represented at New York's Whitney Museum were female. That year a group called Women Artists in Revolution, or WAR, formed to protest this exclusion. Over the next three decades women throughout the world created alternative spaces to support their arts. In New York and San Francisco they founded women's workshops and galleries; all-women art shows opened in London and The Hague in the 1980s; a 1983 New York exhibit was titled "The Revolutionary Power of Women's Laughter." In Korea a "Women and Reality" exhibit in 1987 helped launch feminist art within a social realist movement concerned with injustices of class as well as of gender. By the 1990s women's galleries had opened in countries around the world, including the Seniwati Gallery of Art by Women on the Indonesian island of Bali, which soon represented over forty Balinese women artists.

The growth of art spaces for women of color in the West illustrates the impact of the feminist art movement. In England artists Lubaina Himid from Tanzania and Maud Sulter from Scotland founded the Black Women's Creativity Project to showcase the works of women from Africa, the Caribbean, and Great Britain. In the United States Faith Ringgold has been critical to the development of African American women's art. She organized Women Students and Artists for Black Art Liberation and helped plan the 1976 Sojourner Truth Festival of the Arts at New York's Women's Interarts Center. There Ntozake Shange read from her brilliant 'choreopoem' *for colored girls who have considered suicide when the rainbow is enuf . . .* , which had been nurtured in women's cultural spaces in the San Francisco Bay Area. By then, Shange's moving portrayal of the travails and spiritual survival of African American women had reached large, appreciative mainstream audiences in New York theaters.

The success of Shange's play implies that this separatist approach in turn infiltrated established institutions, but the glass remains more than half empty. In 1995, for example, a generation after WAR protested the underrepresentation of women artists, New York's Whitney Museum had increased the proportion of women's art to only one-third of those exhibited. That was not good enough for activists like the Guerrilla Girls, who have kept up the pressure to do better since the 1980s. This anonymous group of women dressed in gorilla suits exposes "sexism and racism in the art world and the culture at large." In performance art and posters they proclaim "When Sexism & Racism Are No Longer Fashionable, What Will Your Art Collection Be Worth?" and "Guerrilla Girls Proclaim Internet Too Pale, Too Male!"[21]

Public Art, Private Themes

As women gained access to the arts they experimented with both subjects and materials grounded in female lives, including the female body and domestic images. Turning inward to women's spaces but outward to public audiences, feminist artists paralleled the explorations of the mother tongue in language. During 1971–72, for example, feminist art program founders Judy Chicago and Miriam Schapiro helped create the project *Womanhouse* at the California Institute of the Arts. Students remodeled a large house, with each room making a creative statement about women's lives. Schapiro's *Menstrual Bathroom* overflowed with bloody tampons and other menstrual supplies. According to art critic Peggy Phelan, "*Womanhouse* celebrated what had been considered trivial: cosmetics, tampons, linens, shower caps and underwear became the material for high art."[22] A similar project in England, *A Woman's Place* (1974), included "a nightmare kitchen, oppressive and cluttered. Footsteps on the floor marked an endless, persistent circle from fridge to basin to stove and back again."[23]

The kitchen as metaphor and medium would recur in feminist art in the 1990s, as illustrated by Las Comadres, a women's art collective on the U.S.–Mexican border. In response to a local exhibit that had stereotyped Mexicans as aliens, these politically committed women artists created a multimedia installation that celebrated the diversity of border life. They included *The Kitchen*, a room that combined folk art and humor, such as a kitchen table that was itself a large open book. Their performance piece, *Border Boda,* also incorporated the kitchen as a space in which a female heritage persists over the generations.

Thanks in part to efforts of feminist artists such as Judy Chicago and

Faith Ringgold, domestic arts began to command high status. Chicago's installation *The Dinner Party*, perhaps best known for the genital imagery on the ceramic plates that celebrated famous women, also included intricate place mats and runners honoring the history of fine needlework and embroidery. Ringgold adopted the quilt form to painting, combining it with texts to tell historical and autobiographical stories of African American experience. In addition, the "found objects" of domestic life, such as artifacts from kitchens and child care, gained new meaning when appropriated by feminist artists. One of the most controversial projects, the London exhibit of Mary Kelly's *Post Partum Document*, incorporated both her son's used diapers and extensive theoretical "footnotes" that explored the psychological effect of motherhood on femininity.

Two further examples from art illustrate the feminist strategies of reshaping once-negative images, integrating domestic materials, and subverting gender, race, and national boundaries. In the United States, Betye Saar responded creatively to the historical stereotype of the black mammy in her 1972 work *The Liberation of Aunt Jemima*, in which a pancake-mix Aunt Jemima figure holding a white baby is enclosed by a larger mammy image holding not only a broom but also a revolver and a rifle. Another subversive use of traditional female imagery appeared in the work of Sutapa Biswas in England in the 1980s. Biswas combined Western and Eastern motifs in *Housewives with Steak-Knives*, which depicts the Hindu goddess Kali, who mythically destroyed but also embodied evil. Biswas created a multiarmed, dark-skinned housewife/goddess who holds flowers in one hand but with another hand raises a kitchen knife threateningly. Yet another hand grasps a copy of a painting by Artemisia Gentileschi depicting the decapitated head of a man, one of those "lost" works recovered in the canonization of European Old Mistresses. For art historian Griselda Pollock, this "powerful image of an active, divine, and politically insurgent femininity from Hindu culture functioned equally to displace racist stereotypes that currently represent Asian women as passive."[24]

The feminist appropriation of myth recurs in literature, as well, particularly the reclamation of women once demonized in popular culture. In the United States a generation of Mexican American feminists have retold the story of Malintzin Tenépal, the native translator for the Spanish conqueror Hernán Cortés, who had been condemned in myth and men's texts as La Malinche. Rather than a traitor to her people or a victim of rape, she becomes a feminist heroine in the works of writers such as Ana Villanueva or Carmen Tafolla. In "Trilogy," Naomi Quiñonez memorialized not only La Malinche but also Eve and Helen of Troy. In Italy playwright Franca Rame updated *Medea* from a feminist perspective, and in Germany Christa Wolf has reworked the tales of both Cassandra and Medea. Jewish feminist writers have revised the myth of Lilith, the apocryphal first woman created by the Hebrew God, who replaced her with the more submissive Eve because Lilith had demanded equality with Adam. Once feared as a demon who killed newborn babies, poet Lynn Gottlieb reclaims her as a model: "Lilith, / we are your children / Help us recover our wings of fire / so we can come together / woman and man / as intended by God / in the beginning of creation."[25]

THE POLITICS OF CREATIVITY

By the end of the century, feminist art movements had expanded women's creative repertoire by reclaiming lost works, reevaluating female aesthetics, and revising negative myths. In addition to these implicitly political projects, feminist artists and writers used their skills to advance specific political movements. A recurrent theme has been finding a voice for women's protests against injustice. In South Africa, for example, women in the African National Congress insisted that women, as well as men, should express their opposition to the apartheid system of white supremacy. Lindiwe Mabuza solicited poems from women who had never published, and she helped produce the anthology *Malibongwe: ANC Women: Poetry Is Also Their Weapon*.[26] In the visual arts, collectives of women muralists have painted scenes depicting the lives of women, such as New York City's Lower East Side Collective, which created the Wall of Respect for Women. The mural portrayed women from a variety of ethnic cultures engaged in the work of laundry, sewing, child care, street peddling, and clerking, as well as carrying picket signs while on strike.

A final example of the political message of feminist art comes from the theater, a world that once excluded women both onstage and as writers. In the United States and Europe a generation of female playwrights and performers has translated women's lives into challenging theater. Since the 1980s experimental performance artists such as Karen Finley have enraged conservative politicians with their explorations of female sexuality. More conventional plays, such as Paula Vogel's *How I Learned to Drive* (1998), reveal the unwanted sexual advances that girls and women have long endured. In *The Vagina Monologues* (1998), based on interviews with women, Eve Ensler broke silence not only by naming women's genitals but also by vividly describing the trauma of rape. Performances of the play have become both feminist cultural ritual and political organizing tool. Produced annually on Valentine's Day around the United States, proceeds from benefit performances of *The Vagina Monologues* help fund women's shelters and antiviolence campaigns.

Is It Feminism?

In the past thirty years feminism has greatly expanded the space for women artists, yet not all women artists consider themselves feminists. For some, art must have no sex or gender, lest the particularities of identity limit the subject matter of the artist. Calling attention to female difference still provokes fears of exclusion. Centuries of devaluing certain arts as *merely* women's crafts has also had a lasting impact. However, many artists have come to acknowledge that feminism makes a difference to their work. Choreographer and filmmaker Yvonne Ranier recalled that "It wasn't until 1975, when Mimi Schapiro convinced me that feminism is as much a state of mind as a matter of activist alliances, that I dared to use the term self-referentially."[27] Pulitzer Prize–winning playwright Wendy Wasserstein explains, "Feminism gave me the right to find my own voice . . . the perspective to see that there weren't enough women's voices being heard."[28] In response to critics who reject the term, South African writer Lindiwe Mabuza counters that "if feminism means recognition of my fullest capacities, welcome feminism. If it means staving off the hand that wants to destroy me, I say all power to feminism."[29]

Feminist artists themselves worry about essentializing gender, as if all women have a common experience or a common aesthetic. By the 1980s the postmodernist questioning of the stability of identity raised questions about the second-wave emphasis on a unique, often bodily, female experience. If gender itself is historically constructed, a kind of performance that can be transformed and interrupted, is there any basis for a distinctively *women*'s art? The Vietnamese American filmmaker and critic Trinh Minh-ha has addressed this concern directly. When asked how she viewed her work in relation to feminism, Trinh replied: "As long as Difference is not *given* to us, the coast is clear. We should be the ones to define this difference." Reducing either gender or race to an essential type ignores their complexities. For this reason, she argues, "a feminist always has at least two gestures at the same time: that of pointing insistently to difference, and that of unsettling every definition of woman arrived at."[30]

Since the 1990s third-wave feminists have contributed to the task of unsettling our definitions. A queer performance group called the Five Lesbian Brothers makes us think twice about gender and sexual categories. So does the reclamation of language in third-wave magazines such as *Bust* and *Bitch*. ("If being opinionated makes me a bitch, then bring it on!" says cofounder Lisa Miya-Jervis).[31] In contrast to the second-wave insistence on the term *woman*, this generation is transforming the meaning of *girl*. Feminist punk rock musicians inspired a "riot grrrl" movement that celebrates a sexy, defiant female stance and refuses the good girl/bad girl divide. As one manifesto from a riot grrrl band proclaims: "We are angry at a society that tells us Girl = Dumb, Girl = Bad, Girl = Weak . . . we are unwilling to let our real and valid anger be diffused . . . I believe with my wholeheartmindbody that girls constitute a revolutionary soul force that can, and will, change the world for real."[32] Not to be confused with the marketing of "girl power" in popular culture, the young feminists who produce their own underground 'zines such as *Annoying Girl* and *Girlwize* voice a militant critique of racial and sexual boundaries.

A refusal to be "nice" resonates throughout third-wave creativity. In cyberspace an emerging feminist subculture recently dubbed "Surfergrrrls," provides "a counter to the 'nice girls don't hack around with computers' message."[33] From the all-woman Beijing rock band Cobra to Ani DiFranco's Righteous Babe records in the United States, musicians press upon the boundaries of what women can sing and play. When DiFranco demands freedom of choice, refuses to be a commodity, and declares herself "more than a pretty girl" for men to rescue, she expresses the longings of a generation. While their style is hard-hitting, these musicians reject the violence of male-dominated popular culture. In contrast to the objectification of women in rap music, Queen Latifah's "Ladies First" video celebrates heroines such as Sojourner Truth. Refusing the standards of "great" rap, rock, and punk music, the band Sleater-Kinney sings, "I've been crawling up so long on your stairway to heaven / And now I no longer wanna get in."[34]

At the beginning of the twenty-first century, "new words" echo across venues and cultures. Women both demand access to the art establishment and seek to transform its subjects and genres. Whether exhibiting in museums or performing on village streets, women have incorporated their experiences of motherhood, sexuality, and violence in their own creative words and images. Simultaneously, older forms of women's arts such as pottery, rugs, and quilts continue to grace private homes and, increasingly, public space across cultures. Today some of the most impoverished women in the world are reviving domestic crafts to help sustain their families, such as the poor rural women in eastern India who sew *sujuni kanthas*, embroidered quilts, that incorporate political messages condemning domestic violence and rape and celebrating women's friendships and the education of girls.

A final example from this crafts revival reminds of us the links between art and politics, beauty and survival. Outside Lima, Peru, displaced shantytown residents have created workshops to produce *arpilleras*, appliquéd scenes sewn onto sweaters or other garments. This art form originated in Chile, where women political prisoners could smuggle notes to the outside in the appliqué, since guards ignored women's handiwork. Today, regional artisans' organizations help Peruvian women market these bright, colorful works of art throughout the world. Though far removed from the cosmopolitan museums and theaters now open to women, these artists have much in common. "The more we work, the more creativity we find in ourselves," *arpillera* maker Rita Serapión explains. "We all have a little art in our minds and in our hands; we will leave something as a legacy for society. It will stay behind us, in another place, in another time."[35]

FOURTEEN

NO TURNING BACK: WOMEN AND POLITICS

Women had to break the separation between the private and the public and make their concerns a public issue.
—María Suárez, Costa Rica, 1993

A revolution has begun and there is no going back.
—Gertrude Mongella, Tanzania, 1995

In the centuries before feminism, wherever women lived under patriarchy they found ways to exercise their own authority. Where reproduction empowered them, women seized upon identities as mothers. Where kinship provided protection, women fostered strong relationships with male relatives. Where class, race, or nationality bestowed privilege, elite women exercised these powers. Where religion defined social authority, women elaborated upon female figures such as the Virgin Mary or the goddess Guan Yin. When education opened new worlds, women asserted their God-given rights to learn and to voice their ideas. When their wage labor became economically critical, women forged alliances with other workers. When monarchies succumbed to democratic governments, women claimed the full rights of citizens.

Why, then, do we hear about the relatively recent entry of women into politics? Women's political involvement did not begin with the passage of suffrage measures in Western democracies, nor can it be measured solely by the percentage of women winning elective office.

Electoral success is only one route to political authority, albeit a highly significant one. All of the other means by which women resisted or re-shaped patriarchy—whether familial, maternal, religious, economic, or educational—also involved them in politics when that term is defined as the "acquisition or exercise of authority" and not merely "the art or sci-ence of government."[1] Until recently, however, the Western definition of *political* has been quite gender-specific. It referred to the formal, public arena in which men vied for power over others. Like its Greek an-tecedent, modern Western democracy initially applied only to the public sphere. Even after citizens acquired rights, the private family could remain an undemocratic hierarchy ruled by men.

One of the most important contributions of twentieth-century femi-nist theory has been the redefinition of the political to include both public and private realms, both male and female concerns. Scholars such as Carole Pateman and Susan Okin exposed the false dichotomy of public/private to show the deep interdependence of these two realms. The lib-eral ideal of an autonomous male citizen, Pateman argued, ignored the dependence of men upon familial care. The Western social contract, in which men became citizens, rested upon an unstated sexual contract, in which women served the interests of men. The Western ideal of the unified family that is represented politically by a male citizen, Okin ex-plains, "is founded on the refusal to cede to women any independent exis-tence at all."[2]

These political theorists echoed the popular dictum of the 1960s that "the personal is political." Through the process of consciousness rais-ing, second-wave feminists politicized the dilemmas of women's private lives. The blurring of the public/private divide redefined the political to include power relations between men and women. By the end of the twentieth century, formal politics in nations on every continent had to take into account once-private issues such as abortion, domestic violence, and lesbian rights.

Just as important as this interdependence of public and private is the recognition that feminism incorporates a large repertoire of over-lapping political strategies. Today, as in the world before feminism, women continue to resist patriarchal dominance by affirming their authority within families as mothers. At the same time, feminist movements continue to demand full citizenship, independent of family relations. International agencies and transnational feminist organizations increasingly promote equal education, property rights, marital choice, and suffrage where women still lack these basic rights. Where women can exercise political rights, they have affected powerful public institutions such as legislatures, courts, and the military. These multiple feminist challenges to male dominance have irrevocably infiltrated world politics.

FEMALE CONSCIOUSNESS AND THE PERSISTENCE OF MATERNALISM

Like maternalists of the early women's movement, contemporary women draw on their identities as mothers to protect the interests of their families. Historian Temma Kaplan has called such maternal authority "female consciousness" to distinguish it from feminist consciousness. When women act in the name of their assigned gender identity to improve their lives and protect their families, they do not necessarily demand privileges enjoyed by men. Political scientist Maxine Molyneux applies the label "practical gender interest" to describe the agenda of those who accept gender hierarchy but attempt to solve specific problems by making moral claims as mothers. Other scholars argue that these "ameliorative" movements flourish when middle-class women gain access to education but have not yet entered the wage labor force.

Whatever the label, women's efforts to achieve justice as mothers and nurturers can be found today from Peruvian towns, where churchwomen provide free meals for those in need, to Mexican barrios in U.S. cities, where the Mothers of East Los Angeles organize to oppose prison construction. One of these mothers, Juana Gutiérrez of Los Angeles, captured well the theme of female consciousness. Even though she organized other women and lobbied politicians, Gutiérrez explained in 1986, "I don't consider myself political. I'm just someone looking out for the community, for the youth."[3]

Many of these grassroots activists who do not identify as political show themselves to be, in Kaplan's phrase, "crazy for democracy." In the

United States women founded the Love Canal Homeowners Association and the Citizens Clearinghouse for Hazardous Waste to protect their homes from toxic dumping. In South Africa they resisted removal from their houses with the claim that "housing is a human right." Although they speak as citizen-mothers rather than as feminists, their work in defense of their families can be politically transformative. In the words of Costa Rican feminist María Suárez, women "had to break the separation between the private and the public and make their concerns a public issue . . . what happened in the house stopped being a private issue."[4] Both the women's peace movement and Latin American mothers' movements illustrate her point.

Another Mother for Peace

The association of women and pacifism runs deep in Western culture. In the Greek drama *Lysistrata* women withheld sex from their husbands to pressure them to end their warfare. In the twentieth century maternalist reformers such as Jane Addams and Emily Greene Balch explicitly linked pacifism to feminism in the Women's Peace Party; each woman won a Nobel Prize for her efforts. From Virginia Woolf's critique of war as the product of masculinist culture to the grassroots activism of the Women's International League for Peace and Freedom, women helped shaped pacifist politics.

Since World War II, women have repeatedly protested militarism. In 1961, when Women Strike for Peace called for a one-day housewives' strike to protest nuclear proliferation, over fifty thousand women in sixty U.S. cities participated. During the 1980s dozens of women's peace camps linked feminism, spirituality, and environmentalism, starting with the Greenham Common peace encampment in England. Women camped out at military bases, where they protested nuclear war and militarism; no sooner did police arrest them than another group of women would join the ongoing encampment. In Denmark housewives organized a campaign that eventually gathered the signatures of half a million women on petitions to ban cruise missiles in their country. In the 1990s the Israeli group Four Mothers (Leave Lebanon in Peace) protested the Israeli occupation of southern Lebanon by picketing the defense ministry, writing letters to legislators, and memorializing every dead soldier. "Why should we send our children to die because our leaders can't solve our problems by talking?" asked founder Rachel Ben Dor.[5]

The desire to protect their children has also propelled Latin American mothers into politics. Alongside movements for women rights, Latin American women have drawn upon a tradition of *marianismo*, or self-sacrificing motherhood, that contrasts women's moral superiority to the corrupt world of machismo politics. Despite the element of subservience to men within this gender system, women have adapted marianismo to create what Sonia E. Alvarez has termed "militant motherhood." Particularly in the face of threats to their children, mothers have demanded accountability from some of the most repressive political regimes in the region.

A prime example of militant mothers confronting powerful states took place during the "dirty war" of Argentine military rule (1976–83). Thousands of people taken to detention camps simply disappeared, presumably killed by the military. In response, *Las Madres del Plaza de Mayo* (Mothers of the Plaza de Mayo) formed in Buenos Aires. At a time when political terror had silenced most critics and journalists, these mothers spoke out silently by demonstrating in the plaza outside the presidential palace to demand the return of their missing children. The military junta called them *las locas* (the crazy ones), but the mothers continued to demand information about their lost relatives. After the restoration of democracy in 1983 Las Madres insisted on the prosecution of the killers, despite repeated threats to their lives. By then, many of their own lives had been transformed. As Hebe de Bonafini explained, "The women of my generation in Latin America have been taught that the man is always in charge and the woman is silent even in the face of injustice." Over time, however, the protests affected their consciousness as women. "Now I know that we have to speak out about the injustices publicly," Bonafini reported in 1992. "If not, we are accomplices."[6]

The Mixed Blessings of Maternalism

Feminists have had mixed reactions to maternal politics. Some embrace an essentialist view that women are naturally more peaceful and less militarist than men. According to Tatyana Mamonova, a Russian feminist who left the former Soviet Union to live in the United States, "woman is altruistic. She gives life and appreciates life. I think the woman is organically against war." Similarly, Australian physician Helen Caldicott, founder of the Women's Action for Nuclear Disarmament and the Women's Party for Survival, believes that "a typical woman . . . innately understands the basic principles of conflict resolution" because female bodies "are built anatomically and physiologically to nurture life."7 Without accepting such biological arguments, feminist philosopher Sarah Ruddick suggests that women's experiences of motherhood may lead to "maternal thinking" that is more responsive to others and more interested in resolution than in conflict. These beliefs echo the contrast drawn by psychologist Carol Gilligan between women's "morality of responsibility" and men's more hierarchical moral frameworks.

Other feminists cringe at these essentialist elaborations of sex difference. Simone de Beauvoir told an interviewer in 1983 that "women should desire peace as human beings, not as women!" If women were "being encouraged to be pacifists in the name of motherhood, that's just a ruse by men who are trying to lead women back to the womb. Beside, it's quite obvious that once they are in power, women are exactly like men."8 Furthermore, governments can appeal to patriotic motherhood to support war, not peace, and mothers have demonstrated in favor of as well as against militarist and authoritarian regimes. Maternal politics have had practical limits too. Although mothers in Argentina and Venezuela found space to protest authoritarian regimes that suppressed male-dominated political parties, the restoration of democracy paradoxically undermined women's authority. Men easily dismissed mothers as private, nonpolitical actors. As Elia Borges de Tapia of Venezuela lamented, "There are talented women, with vast training, with a serious political conscience, and they are relegated to the women's organization within the parties or attending to household duties."9

Both advocates and critics of female consciousness must take into account that the majority of women in the world continue to perform familial duties, many of them in societies that have not adopted fully the liberal democratic politics that gave rise to Western feminism. For many of these women, social authority still rests largely upon their maternal identities. In liberal democracies too, women who choose to work full-time in their homes have insisted on political identities as mothers or housewives. In Japan, for example, a "housewives' movement" in the 1980s called on women to reject the cultural subordination of mothers, not by becoming financially independent of husbands but rather by asserting their own worth.

Whether they live in Japan, North America, Europe, or urban centers of Latin America, some women continue to call on their societies to value maternal labor even after they gain access to education, income, property, and suffrage. It is worth remembering that the earliest feminist movements used maternalist claims to win these rights. These claims still resonate throughout the world. Like the craftswomen and peasant entrepreneurs whose goal is to earn enough to educate their daughters, militant mothers challenge gender hierarchy through their self-empowerment. They also remind us that women's politics have strong links to broader social justice concerns, such as environmentalism, pacifism, and democratic government.

GENDER CONSCIOUSNESS AND FEMINIST MOVEMENTS

Just as democratic revolutions inspired the early feminist movements in Europe and the Americas, struggles for democratization in the twentieth century provided catalysts for women's politicization. In the Philippines women joined peasant organizations during the 1930s and workers movements during the 1950s and 1960s. In the 1980s they helped elect President Corazon Aquino, and in return they called for and gained legislation on health care, maternity leave, and equal pay. The Chilean women's movement coined the slogan "Democracy in the country and in the home," a phrase echoed after the fall of communism by women in eastern Europe, who proclaimed that "democracy without women is not democracy." In the Taiwanese democracy movement, women insisted that they had "to be human before they can be women."

By calling for democratic rights as citizens, these movements helped produce feminist consciousness, which questions gender hierarchy rather than maneuvers within it. Feminist movements seek to restructure society to end legal discrimination and to expand economic, reproductive, and political rights. Molyneux labels these goals "strategic gender interests," in contrast to the practical gender interests of maternalists. Feminist consciousness originated among middle-class women in industrializing nations with strong democratic movements; it revived during women's massive entry into the wage labor force. Today, however, international communication among feminists spreads ideals of gender equality even where democratic rule is incomplete, where women's labor force participation rates remain low, or where democratization is accompanied by a decline in women's paid labor, as in the former Soviet bloc.

Islamic Women's Rights

In Asia and the Middle East, movements to achieve basic women's rights remain controversial. Both international organizations and male reformers help sustain the quest for rights that are often opposed by Islamic fundamentalists of both sexes. One of the most fiercely fought battles concerns family law. In the opinion of Amira El Azhary Sonbol, "Nothing exemplifies more the contradictions of modern state patriarchy than the fact that today Muslim women can aspire to becoming the heads of governments, yet they face often insurmountable difficulties in divorcing their husbands."[10] Women in many Islamic societies seek basic rights to choose whom they marry and whether to divorce. They often invoke Islamic law to support these rights, rather than rejecting Islam, and they provide practical services along with arguments for rights.

The most extreme case has been Afghanistan, where in the 1990s the Taliban imposed a strict patriarchal state. Women could not appear in public without a male relative or work for wages. Widows and women who had no male relatives to provide for them had to beg. An underground within and outside the country kindled the movement for women's rights. The Revolutionary Association of the Women of Afghanistan, based in Pakistan, opposed fundamentalists while it provided education and health care for refugees from the Taliban. The group Women Living Under Muslim Laws, based in France, also created links among women from Muslim countries to publicize discriminatory treatment of women and to send protests when states such as Afghanistan allow these practices.

In Pakistan, Egypt, and Kuwait feminists and male reformers struggle against efforts to impose fundamentalist interpretations of Islam. In Pakistan liberal efforts to empower women as citizens abruptly ended in 1977 when a new regime implemented Islamic personal law, claiming that the Qu'ran supported the patriarchal authority of men. Along with enforcing modest dress, harsh laws restricted women's personal choices. In parts of the country, women were killed for marrying against the wishes of their parents. A law allowing the death penalty for sex outside marriage could have been applied to a woman who had been raped. Pakistani feminists responded by providing legal aid and practical services, such as a shelter for women threatened with murder for dishonoring their families. They also created the Women's Action Forum, which demonstrated for marital rights. When police arrested demonstrators, a women's movement crystallized and became critical to the larger democratization movement. Pakistani feminists coordinated with international NGOs and invoked the UN Convention to End Discrimination Against Women (CEDAW) in their campaign. During a restoration of democratic government, Pakistan elected Benazir Bhutto as prime minister in 1988, the first woman to head an Islamic state. Pakistan then signed on to CEDAW, although, as in other countries, it has not been implemented fully.

In Egypt feminists who had recently participated in the UN Women's Forum helped secure the reinstatement of a 1979 presidential decree expanding women's ability to divorce. The international conferences, Suzanne Mubarak explained in 1999, helped Egyptian feminists "come a long way both on the national and international level in bringing women's issues to the forefront."[11] That year her husband, Egyptian president Hosni Mubarak, extended to women the right to divorce without a spouse's assent and ensured economic support for divorced women. He also repealed an older ruling that women could not leave abusive husbands. Male lawyers and judges, as well as women's rights advocates, supported these reforms, which could be enacted because moderate Muslim clergy offered assurances that they represent a proper interpretation of Islamic principles.

Along with family law reform, Islamic feminists seek rights to full political participation. Twenty years after the Iranian revolution imposed Islamic law, a generation of highly educated women have become gender-conscious voters who have elected women candidates to local and national office. By 2000 women held 5 percent of the national legislative seats in Iran, and their votes had become critical to the national reform party. By then Kuwait remained the only parliamentary government in the world that denied women the right to vote and to run for office. In 1999 the emir of Kuwait decreed that women would gain voting rights, pending parliamentary approval. Despite the support of moderate male legislators, a coalition of religious and social conservatives rejected the bill. As one male legislator predicted, "The day will surely come when women will get political rights."[12]

In the meantime, women's rights evoke strong political sentiments, as captured in March 2000 by a poignant set of images. When the Moroccan government announced programs to expand female literacy and enact equal rights to divorce for both spouses, between two hundred thousand and three hundred thousand women and men, including politicians and government officials, rallied in the capital city of Rabat in support of the plans. At the same time, however, two hundred thousand women and men marched in the streets of Casablanca to oppose these programs, vowing to "defend Islam with our bodies and souls." From their separate male and female marching lines they chanted the Islamic principle that "men and women are equal before God."[13] Newspapers juxtaposed photos from each city, one showing a woman holding up the Qu'ran to oppose change, the other a woman cheering in support of reform. Like women in the United States who face off at clinics over access to abortion, these Moroccan women attest to the historic transformation that feminism has wrought. Even opponents of women's rights march in the streets, lobby politicians, vote, and speak publicly about their views. From a long historical perspective, both sides in these rallies are participants in a movement toward full citizenship for women.

Women's Rights as Human Rights

The importance of both marital and civic reforms in Islamic women's movements reflects the expanding definition of rights in the past century.

When second-wave Western feminists insisted that personal relations are also political, they added reproductive and sexual rights to the political agenda. Today European and North American feminists defend reproductive choice, while African feminists seek to eliminate female genital cutting and Indian feminists target dowry deaths and domestic violence. In each case achieving legal reform represents only one step in the process of changing long-standing attitudes about women's maternal, domestic, and sexual lives.

Beyond defending these rights on the national level, feminists are redefining international human rights movements to include them. Watchdog agencies such as Amnesty International and Human Rights Watch initially worked to protect political prisoners from torture and prevent state intrusions on rights to free speech, public assembly, and due process of law. But private abuses such as domestic violence, female genital cutting, rape, and forced sterilization also violate human rights. After the 1985 UN women's conference in Nairobi, groups such as International Women's Rights Action Watch trained local activists to report such abuses, as did regional networks in Latin America, Asia and the Pacific, and Africa.

Governments violate women's human rights whenever their laws allow husbands to beat or kill their wives because of alleged adultery. When states outlaw these practices but prosecutors and judges dismiss the charges or treat abusers leniently, they empower men to continue to abuse women. In Brazil, for example, women activists documented that courts consistently condoned domestic violence if a man claimed he was defending his honor. They convinced Human Rights Watch to explore this injustice through its Women's Rights Project. Amnesty International recognized rape and sexual torture as human rights violations. In a campaign leading up to the Beijing women's conference in 1995 the group also cited state persecution based on sexual orientation. Feminist foundations such as *Semillas* (Seeds) in Mexico and the Global Fund for Women in the United States support international human rights through grants that help train women's human rights workers in Mexico and Brazil. They also support hundreds of local shelters for survivors of domestic violence around the world and both disability and lesbian rights organizations.

A major human rights battle is still being fought over extending political asylum to women seeking refuge from gender-specific abuses. In 1993 the Canadian Immigration and Refugee Board recognized the claim to asylum of women fleeing forced sterilization. Two years later an Iranian lesbian who could have faced a death sentence at home won asylum in the United States. In 1996 the U.S. Immigration and Naturalization Service recognized female genital cutting as a form of persecution, although judges were not obliged to accept the ruling. In 1998, Rodi Alvarado of Guatemala won temporary asylum after a decade of brutal torture by her husband, a former soldier. Though the precedents are few and very recent, at the UN's Beijing Plus Five conference in June 2000 delegates called for the inclusion of marital rape and domestic violence as grounds for international asylum.

WHEN WOMEN HAVE RIGHTS: INTEGRATING AND CHALLENGING POLITICAL SYSTEMS

Once women establish a foothold in political institutions through full citizenship, they can have a transformative effect on national and world politics. Women citizens bring to the political arena many substantive issues overlooked because of the public/private divide. These include reproduction and violence as well as the child welfare agenda long supported by maternalists. Women's participation can reshape the political landscape not only by electing women to office but also through innovative electoral procedures to achieve more representative government.

Political Representation

More women lead governments than ever before—twenty-three states had female heads during the 1990s—and fewer than a dozen countries have no women representatives in government. Some of them have moved into leadership within the United Nations. Norway's first woman prime minister, Dr. Gro Harlem Bruntland, later became the first woman to direct the UN's World Health Organization; Mary Robinson, former president of Ireland, became UN High Commissioner for Human Rights. Other women lead opposition movements, such as Aung San Suu Kyi of Burma, or indigenous nations, such as Wilma Mankiller, former principal chief of the Cherokee Nation.

Despite real progress toward political representation, in 1995 there were no women in cabinet positions in fifty-nine countries, and in only fifteen countries did women hold more than one-fifth of these offices. Only 5 to 10 percent of the formal decision makers in the world were female. Women's share of national legislative seats ranged from under 5 percent in Ecuador, Mali, and Ukraine to around 25 percent in Germany, Iceland, and Mozambique, to over a third in Sweden, Norway, Finland, and Denmark. (See Appendix F.) As geographer Joni Seager found in mapping women's elected and appointed offices, "nowhere in the world are women represented in proportion to their population."[14] The 1995 Beijing Platform of Action set a target of achieving 30 percent of parliamentary seats for women by the year 2005, but as of 1999 only eight countries, mostly in Scandinavia, had met the goal.

The legacy of men's monopoly on political office holding contributes to the underrepresentation of women in national positions. Attitudes change slowly, and both men and women are used to electing men to office. In addition, in many countries women have not had the educational opportunities enjoyed by men, nor do they have the same personal wealth or financial support of political parties. Running for office as a woman has been challenging for many of the same reasons that women have had difficulty advancing in other male-dominated jobs and professions. Entrenched male networks may resist female candidates, while women's double duty as caregivers and political candidates can prove burdensome. Yet subtle changes in attitudes and in office holding suggest that women are poised to assume a much greater share of government offices in the next century.

Voting and Running as Women

Although women gained the right to vote in most of the world during the twentieth century, enfranchisement did not necessarily produce gender-conscious voting. In the United States, for example, when women first went to the polls in the 1920s they split along party lines rather than forming the voting bloc many expected. Decades later, the revival of feminism and heightened public consciousness of issues such as sexual harassment provoked a "gender gap" in voting. In the 1990s voting patterns of women and men began to diverge, with women's votes helping to elect more liberal local and national politicians. By the 2000 election both major parties recognized that they had to court the "women's vote" to win.

The U.S. case also suggests that concerted efforts to field women candidates can shift electoral patterns. In the 1980s and 1990s organizations such as the National Women's Political Caucus and EMILY's List (the acronym stands for "Early Money Is Like Yeast") urged women to run for office and contributed funds to jump-start their campaigns. To counter voter apathy, the Third Wave Foundation launched a voter registration campaign among young women. For multiple reasons, the proportion of women in the U.S. Congress tripled between 1980 and 2000, from 4 to 12 percent. Women hold more offices in U.S. state legislatures, where their share increased from 10.5 percent in 1980 to 28.5 percent in 2000. In that year 20 percent of the mayors of major cities and 28.5 percent of the state executives in the United States were female. (See Appendix G.)

In Japan a handful of pioneering women won elections to city assemblies in the 1980s, including Aokage Takako, who had the support of a network of housewives' cooperatives. These early successes inspired other Japanese women to run for office. In 1989 a record twenty-two women won, occupying 9 percent of the seats in the national legislature. To increase women's representation further, in 1999 several wealthy business and professional women created a group called WIN WIN. Following the U.S. fund-raising model, they provided money for women candidates who supported issues such as child care, health care, and the environment. The initial results were impressive: Three of the four candidates they endorsed won their races. Overall, in 1999 Japanese women won in over one thousand local elections, or 10 percent of the total races.

In the past, women elected to office rarely represented women's interests, particularly if they were heads of states. In order to get political support, pioneering women politicians often had to prove not only that they were uninterested in gender issues but also that they were willing to wage war, as did Golda Meir of Israel, Indira Gandhi of India, and Margaret Thatcher of England. The recent surge in women's political participation points toward self-identified feminists taking office. In 2000, for example, Taiwan elected as its vice president Annette Lu, a founder of the Taiwanese women's movement. An outspoken feminist, in the 1970s Lu established a women's coffeehouse and hotline as well as a feminist publishing house. After serving six years of a prison sentence for speaking out against authoritarian rule, she first won election to the national legislature on a reform party platform. Once elected vice president, she continued to press for women's rights.

In the United States women officeholders increasingly support feminist issues. A good example is former representative Patricia Schroeder's successful effort to enact the Family and Medical Leave Act. Although all legislators tend to vote along party lines on fiscal matters, women in both major U.S. parties are more likely than their male colleagues to sponsor legislation on issues of concern to women, such as child care and domestic violence. In 1999 all U.S. legislators agreed that education was a top priority, but a gender gap appeared in their second priority: Men named taxes, while women cited health care. Similarly, a U.S. survey conducted in 2000 showed that when asked about their priorities for foreign policy, women were more likely than men to include social concerns such as health, education, fair labor practices, and birth control.

Changing the System

Throughout the world, women have developed new ways to boost their representation in government by building upon gender-conscious voters and contributors. A concept known in France as *parité* tries to achieve "equal access to elective functions for men and women." Since women make up half of the population, advocates reason, they should have at least a 50–50 chance of election to office. The French state provides funding for political parties, so supporters of *parité* recommended a reduction of funds to parties that failed to field equal numbers of women and men as candidates for office.

Some feminists disliked *parité*'s emphasis on sex, rather than the neutral category of citizenship, as a qualification for office. According to feminist philosopher Sylviane Agacinski, however, the gross imbalance in elected officeholders (men held 90 percent of National Assembly seats) showed that sex clearly makes a difference, and *parité* tries to make political sense out of that difference. Socialist prime minister Lionel Jospin (Agacinski's husband) adopted *parité* in his 1997 campaign, and the measure passed the National Assembly to become law in 2000. In 2001, the year municipal elections were first held under the plan, women won 47.5 percent of city government seats, over twice their previous level.

France is not the only nation to institute some form of political quota system. Over a dozen countries, including Sweden, Germany, Israel, and Venezuela, now provide for at least minimal representation of women. In 1991 Argentina called on its political parties to achieve a minimum of 30 percent participation by women. Tanzania passed a law in 1992 requiring that women constitute at least 15 percent of the members of the parliament. Even where countries have not adopted quotas, simply raising the issue of women's underrepresentation can affect electoral outcomes. In 1997, one year after the European Community issued a nonbinding recommendation of affirmative action for political candidates, the proportion of women elected to national legislatures increased from 5.9 to 10.9 percent in France and from 7.5 to 18.2 percent in Great Britain.

In India a system for bringing both women and members of lower castes into village political leadership is surprising skeptics by empowering some of the least powerful women in the world. Indian women's groups first called on the national legislature to set aside seats for women in the 1970s. Although that plan never materialized, during the 1980s some Indian states did reserve local council seats. By convincing their male allies in the farmers' movement to support all-women slates for district council elections, the Alliance of Women Farmers in one Indian state succeeded in electing the female candidates in nine villages. These victories demonstrated both women's desire for political office and the usefulness of gaining support from respected village elders and politically active men. Prime Minister Rajiv Gandhi later extended the principle by calling for an electoral affirmative action policy that would reserve one-third of all village council seats for women and those from the lowest castes. A 1993 constitutional amendment put the plan into effect.

As a result of this electoral reservation policy, nearly a million women now serve on village councils or as village heads in India. The impact has been both personal and societal. Simply running for office increased some women's horizons. As one candidate explained, "I had been married twenty years but had never seen the whole village."[15] Despite the resistance of some local men, most of the new officials have been successful in exercising authority, especially in those regions where women already had access to education. They have lightened the heavy burdens of rural women with better water, sewer, and transportation systems. As a result, more girls have time to go to school, further improving female literacy. Empowered politically, women are more likely to get the health care they need and to report domestic violence. Even so, council members' household duties are not completely lightened by their political labors. "Even the village head goes to fetch firewood," one woman council member pointed out. "Do you think a male village head would work in the fields?"[16]

Fund-raising, *parité*, and reserving local seats have all helped increase women's political representation in some countries, but in other parts of the world women's office holding has declined. In eastern Europe single-party communist governments used to ensure that women held a quota of political offices. Since these legislatures had much less power than the Communist Party, office holding did not necessarily enhance women's authority. After the fall of communism in 1989, electorates in eastern Europe rejected the "state feminism" that had prescribed women legislators by electing predominantly male officials to serve in the newly empowered legislatures. In communist Romania, for example, women held a third of the national assembly seats, but after democratic elections they could claim under 4 percent of them. In Hungary the proportion of women legislators declined from 21 percent in 1987 to 8 percent in 1999. Even with their reduced numbers, however, women had more political strength in some of the former Soviet bloc countries than in many long-standing democracies. In 1995 women held 13 percent of the seats in the Russian and Polish legislatures, compared to 11 percent in the United States and 9.5 percent in the United Kingdom. Where Communist Parties still rule, the figures remain higher: 21 percent in China, 23 percent in Cuba.

POLITICS BEYOND GOVERNMENT

Elected office is not the only measure of political influence. Democratic governments rely in part on NGOs that foster debate or take action to shape public policy in what has been called "civil society." Western democracies provide abundant examples, from explicitly political groups such as the National Organization for Women to service organizations such as rape crisis hotlines and women's health centers. These NGOs now flourish internationally as well.

In postcommunist eastern European countries, for example, although men increased their share of state legislative seats, women increased their leadership of nongovernmental organizations. NGOs provide services and pressure the state to respond to women's needs. A new women's activism in Russia is "directed not by the party or the state but by women themselves."[17] As state-supported child and health care declined, voluntary women's groups formed to help. Other NGOs combine service with political pressure. The GAIA Women's Center in Moscow provides a forum for consciousness raising, social services, and job training, while members also lobby politicians to act on women's interests. In 1994 the Feminist League was formed in the former Soviet central Asian state of Kazakstan, with the goal of eliminating sexism in mass media and supporting feminist education.

In Poland, while women's share of parliamentary seats dropped from 20 percent in the late 1980s to 13 percent in the late 1990s, women's organizations have proliferated. Service organizations help battered wives and single mothers. Business and professional women meet to further their careers. Groups supporting women's rights and the right to abortion keep these issues visible. Similarly, in postcommunist Romania, urban women have created dozens of NGOs. Most of their members neither identify as feminists nor exhibit gender consciousness, but some of them do address women's rights to work, education, and contraception. Given postcommunist distrust of state solutions, it is not surprising that many eastern European women's groups rely on voluntarism and at times invoke the maternalist principles that have historically appealed to women who remain outside of formal politics.

NGOs also help create space for women's movements in China, where the Communist Party still maintains political power, even as it allows a mixed socialist and capitalist economy. In contrast to the official state-sponsored women's federation, new organizations have emerged that explicitly address women's rights. In 1988 cofounder Wang Xingjuan explained at the opening of the Women's Research Institute that its goals were "to help women gain their own rights, to develop their own abilities, and to not only adapt to, but also succeed in the face of the rapidly developing society."[18] In 1992 the institute created the first national hotline for women, where trained volunteers responded to legal, economic, sexual, and health questions. By legitimating discussion of problems once considered personal, the hotline draws women's issues into the public sphere.

NGOs have a limited capacity to enforce women's rights. In some contexts service organizations can become substitutes for state support for women. In a speech to the 1998 African Women's Leadership Institute, Patricia McFadden of Zimbabwe expressed concern that women's groups were "taking over the civic responsibilities which the state should be shouldering."[19] In contrast, some critics worry that NGOs succeed too well when they create state-funded women's projects that compromise feminism and discourage activism. When a reunified Germany established women's bureaus and affirmative-action plans in the 1990s, Sabine Lang argues, "institutional feminism and femocracy" blossomed but "the visibility of women's movement politics in East and West Germany declined."[20] In the German case the price of successful implementation of feminist policies could be indifference in the next generation.

Similar claims surfaced in the United States after the enactment of woman suffrage in 1920, when many youth presumed that equality had been achieved. In fact, however, women in maternalist, liberal, and labor organizations kept women's movements alive for decades until the broad revival of feminism after the 1960s. Just as observers tried to declare feminism dead after suffrage and again during the peak of the second wave, many today fail to see the deeper currents of women's history that propel the feminist revolution.

Today feminism takes many forms, some more vocal than others. Where Western governments now provide services such as women's shelters, more feminists are turning their attention to electoral politics. Throughout North America and Europe feminists contribute to labor and environmental movements. In Africa, Asia, and the Middle East women continue to press for educational, health, and reproductive rights. Transnational organizations stimulate all of these efforts. As long as these diverse activists continue to question gender inequalities, they sow the seeds of future political change that we cannot even imagine at present.

NO TURNING BACK

At the beginning of the twenty-first century the unifying forces of economic globalization, the communications revolution, and international networks of NGOs encourage both local feminist politics and international alliances. Just as the suffrage movement of the last century spread across the world, today transnational feminist politics help sustain diverse movements in their quest for full economic, reproductive, and sexual justice for women.

Despite the persistence of inequality, and despite formidable backlash, we live in a period of unprecedented attention to gender relations, marked by visible changes in women's status worldwide. Whether measured by the grassroots protests that draw on maternal authority or the flourishing of women's art and literature, by women's participation in athletics or their election to legislatures around the world, or by the international movement to outlaw discrimination against women, the past generation has expanded the reach of feminism enormously. The future of women will be in large part determined by this ongoing political force.

The case for the future of feminist politics is strong. Throughout the world national economies now depend on women's paid labor as much as families have historically. The contradictions of women's double day and lower pay continually mobilize working women, whether they are domestics or professionals. Women and men are demanding new social policies that can allow them to choose both caring and breadwinning rather than choose between them. The demands of our labor system, as well as the limits of our planet's resources, now require reproductive choice and family planning. And while motherhood will remain critical to women's identities, sexual self-determination has become equally important around the world. For some women that means the choice to marry or divorce; for others it means the choice of sexual partners and pleasures. Throughout the world women are saying no to unwanted sex, violence, and degrading cultural images; throughout the world women are creating alternative visions of beauty, power, and justice.

The historic changes in labor, reproduction, and culture provide a momentum powerful enough to survive recurrent antifeminism. Both external opposition and internal conflicts will undoubtedly continue in the future, as they have since the origins of feminism. In the past, feminism grew and thrived because of its flexibility and adaptability; by listening to the voices of all women, it will continue to redefine its politics and broaden its reach. Along with their strong historical commitment to individual rights, feminists have recognized that interdependence can be as important as autonomy; along with their insistence on naming gender injustice, feminists have recognized how gender is intertwined with and inseparable from inequalities of race, class, and nation.

Not all participants will claim the label *feminist*, though many activists would like them to. When women in her native Dominican Republic "shake their heads disapprovingly and say, '*Yo no soy feminista, pero, si, creo . . .*'" (I'm not a feminist, but I believe . . .), novelist Julia Alvarez feels "that by refusing to claim their feminism openly, these women make the burden all the harder for the rest of us who are willing to pay the price."[21] Yet those who still fear feminism as a political identity are living and breathing its politics whenever they stand up for themselves, their families, their rights. As in the past, some women will pay the price; many more will ultimately be grateful for their willingness to do so.

Ever malleable, sometimes contradictory, feminism itself is not likely to disappear. Rather, this varied movement to recognize all women as fully human and fully citizens, to value women's labors as much as men's, and to honor women's physical integrity is now poised to expand. It will undoubtedly be central to the future of women. As Gertrude Mongella, secretary general of the Fourth World Conference on Women, held in Beijing in 1995, told the planning commission: "A revolution has begun and there is no going back. There will be no unraveling of commitments—not today's commitments, not last year's commitments, and not the last decade's commitments. This revolution is too just, too important, and too long overdue."[22] Understanding the complex history of women's movements can help ensure that the feminist revolution will succeed.

NOTES

-ONE-

1. Madhu Kishwar, "Why I Do Not Call Myself a Feminist," *Manushi* 61 (1991), 2–8.

2. Alice Walker, *In Search of Our Mothers' Gardens: Womanist Prose* (New York: Harcourt, Brace, Jovanovich, 1983), xi; Rebecca Walker, "Becoming the Third Wave," *Ms.* 2:4 (1992), 39–41.

3. Muriel Rukeyser, "Myth," *The Norton Anthology of Literature by Women: The Tradition in English*, eds. Sandra M. Gilbert and Susan Gubar (New York: W. W. Norton, 1985), 1777–8.

4. Suneeta Adar, "Commitment to the Future, Regional Action Plans: Asia & the Pacific," NGO Forum Beijing, 7 September 1995, quoted in "Beijing Report 3," September 7, 1995.

5. In April 2000 a Gallup poll asked if respondents personally agree or disagree with the goals of the women's rights movement; 45 percent strongly agreed and another 40 percent somewhat agreed. An NBC News/*Wall Street Journal* poll in June 2000 asked "whether you consider yourself a feminist," and 29 percent responded yes.

6. Jennifer Pozner, "False Feminist Death Syndrome," *Sojourner* 23:12 (1998), 2.

-TWO-

1. "Declaration of Sentiments," from *The History of Woman Suffrage*, in *The Feminist Papers*, ed. Alice Rossi (New York: Bantam, 1973), 415–18.

2. Gerda Lerner, *The Creation of Patriarchy* (New York: Oxford University Press, 1986), 6.

3. For proverbs and son preference, see Neera Kuckreja Sohoni, *The Burden of Girlhood: A Global Inquiry Into the Status of Girls* (Oakland: Third Party Publishing, 1995), and Leviticus 27:1–4; and Joni Seager, *The State of Women in the World Atlas* (London: Penguin, 1997), 34–35. Parents in Venezuela and Jamaica had daughter preferences.

4. Quoted in Haruko Okano, "Women's Image and Place in Japanese Buddhism," in *Japanese Women: New Feminist Perspectives on the Past, Present, and Future*, eds. Kumiko Fujimura-Fanselow and Atsuko Kameda (New York: Feminist Press, 1995), 16.

5. Quoted in Joan Jensen, "Native American Women and Agriculture: A Seneca Case Study," in *Unequal Sisters: A Multi-Cultural Reader in U.S. Women's History*, eds. Ellen Carol DuBois and Vicki L. Ruiz (New York: Routledge, 1990), 57, 73.

6. Friedrich Engels, *The Origin of the Family, Private Property, and the State* (New York: International Publishers, 1942), 50.

7. Lerner, *Creation of Patriarchy*, 216.

8. Tani Barlow, "Theorizing Woman: Funü, Guojia, Jiating (Chinese Women, Chinese State, Chinese Family)," in *Scattered Hegemonies: Postmodernity and Transnational Feminist Practices*, eds. Inderpal Grewal and Caren Kaplan (Minneapolis: University of Minnesota Press, 1994), 173–96.

9. Buchi Emecheta, *The Joys of Motherhood* (London: Allison & Busby Ltd.; New York: George Braziller, 1979), 186.

10. Fu Xuan, "Woman," in *Chinese Poems*, ed. Arthur Waley (London: G. Allen and Unwin, 1946), 84–85.

11. Bonnie S. Anderson and Judith P. Zinsser, *A History of Their Own: Women in Europe from Prehistory to the Present* (New York: Harper and Row, 1988), vol. I, 88.

12. Ibid., vol. I, 149.

13. Quoted in Dorothy Ko, *Teachers of the Inner Chambers: Women and Culture in Seventeenth-Century China* (Stanford: Stanford University Press, 1994), 164–66.

14. Aristotle, *Politics*, Book I, Ch. 13, 22, in *Women: From the Greeks to the French Revolution*, ed. Susan Groag Bell (Belmont, Calif: Wadsworth, 1973), 20.

15. Quoted in Norma Basch, *In the Eyes of the Law: Women, Marriage, and Property in Nineteenth-Century New York* (Ithaca: Cornell University Press, 1982), 48.

16. "The Princess," in Alfred Tennyson, *Tennyson: A Selected Edition* (Essex, England: Longman Group UK Limited, 1989), section V, lines 437–41, p. 298.

17. Charles Darwin, *The Descent of Man and Selection in Relation to Sex* (New York: D. Appleton and Company, 1871), 301, 311.

18. Quoted in Rosalind Rosenberg, *Beyond Separate Spheres: Intellectual Roots of Modern Feminism* (New Haven: Yale University Press, 1982), 9.

19. Quoted in Susan Mann, *Precious Records: Women in China's Long Eighteenth Century* (Stanford: Stanford University Press, 1997), 108. The poet is quoting her grandfather's advice, which enabled her to become a writer.

-THREE-

1. Jeanne Deroin and Anne Knight, quoted in Bonnie S. Anderson, *Joyous Greetings: The First International Women's Movement, 1830–1860* (New York: Oxford University Press, 2000), 156.

2. Ibid., 158.

3. Jean-Jacques Rousseau, quoted in *Women of the Republic: Intellect and Ideology in Revolutionary America*, ed. Linda K. Kerber (Chapel Hill: University of North Carolina Press, 1980), 23–26.

4. Nina M. Scott, " 'If You Are Not Pleased to Favor Me, Put Me Out of Your

Mind . . .': Gender and Authority in Sor Juana Inés de la Cruz and the Translation of the Letter to the Reverend Father Maestro Antonio Núñez of the Society of Jesus," *Women's Studies International Forum* 11:5 (1988), 435–36.

5. *A Serious Proposal to the Ladies*, ed. Patricia Springborg (London: Pickering & Chatto, 1997), 22.

6. Bonnie S. Anderson and Judith P. Zinsser, *A History of Their Own: Women in Europe from Prehistory to the Present* (New York: Harper & Row, 1988), vol. II, 110.

7. Quoted in Anderson, *Joyous Greetings*, 16.

8. Mary Wollstonecraft, *A Vindication of the Rights of Women*, excerpted in *Women, the Family, and Freedom: The Debate in Documents, Volume I: 1750–1880*, eds. Susan Groag Bell and Karen M. Offen (Stanford: Stanford University Press, 1983), 62.

9. John Stuart Mill, *The Subjection of Women*, ed. Susan M. Okin (Indianapolis: Hackett Publishing Company, 1988), 19.

10. John Stuart Mill, speech before the House of Commons, 20 May 1867, reprinted in Bell and Offen, *Women, the Family, and Freedom*, vol. I, 487.

11. Quoted in Anderson, *Joyous Greetings*, 8.

12. June Hahner, *Emancipating the Female Sex: The Struggle for Women's Rights in Brazil, 1850–1940* (Durham: Duke University Press, 1990), 26–27; Francisca Senhorinha da Motta Diniz, "Equality of Rights," *O Quinze de Novembro do Sexo Feminino*, 6 April 1890, Appendix B, 214–15; and Josefina Alvares de Azevdo, "Our Anniversary," *A Familia*, 31 December 1889, Appendix C, 216, reprinted in Hahner.

13. Quoted in Sharon Sievers, *Flowers in Salt: The Beginnings of Feminist Consciousness in Modern Japan* (Stanford: Stanford University Press, 1983), 41.

14. Charles Fourier, quoted in Bell and Offen, *Women, the Family and Freedom*, vol. I, 41; *The Free Woman* (1832) quoted in Anderson and Zinsser, *A History of Their Own*, vol. II, 377.

15. Tristan, *L'Union Ouvrière* in Bell and Offen, *Women, the Family, and Freedom*, vol. I, 212–15.

16. Quoted in Anderson and Zinsser, *A History of Their Own*, vol. II, 387.

17. Alexandra Kollontai, *The Social Basis of the Woman Question*, in *Women Imagine Change: A Global Anthology of Women's Resistance from 600 B.C.E. to Present*, eds. Eugenia Delamotte, Natania Meeker, and Jean O'Barr (New York: Routledge, 1997), 258–59.

18. Quoted in Judith Stacey, "When Patriarchy Kowtows: The Significance of the Chinese Family Revolution for Feminist Theory," *Feminist Studies* 2:2–3 (1975), 83.

19. Quoted in Alice Schwartzer, "The Radicalization of Simone de Beauvoir," trans. by Helen Eustis, *Ms.* 1:1 (1972), 60–61.

20. Quoted in Evelyn Brooks Higginbotham, *Righteous Discontent: The Women's Movement in the Black Baptist Church, 1880–1920* (Cambridge: Harvard University Press, 1993), 192.

21. Francisca Diniz, "Equality of Rights" (1890), in June E. Hahner, *Emancipating the Female Sex: The Struggle for Women's Rights in Brazil, 1850–1940* (Durham: Duke University Press, 1990), Appendix B, 214.

22. Quoted in Corinne A. Pernet, "Chilean Feminists, The International Women's Movement, and Suffrage, 1915–1950," *Pacific Historical Review* 69:4 (2000), 668–69.

23. Quoted in Gail Bederman, *Manliness and Civilization: A Cultural History of Gender and Race in the United States, 1880–1917* (Chicago: University of Chicago Press, 1995), 151.

24. Charlotte Perkins Gilman, *The Living of Charlotte Perkins Gilman: An Autobiography* (New York: Harper & Row, 1935), 331.

25. Virginia Woolf, *Three Guineas* (New York: Harcourt Brace, 1938, repr. 1966), 60, 66, 102, 109.

26. Alison M. Jaggar, *Feminist Politics and Human Nature* (Totowa, N.J.: Rowman & Allanheld, 1983), 132.

-FOUR-

1. Charlotte Hawkins Brown, October 8, 1920, in *Black Women in White America: A Documentary History*, ed. Gerda Lerner (New York: Vintage Books, 1973), 467–72.

2. Elsa Barkley Brown, "African-American Women's Quilting: A Framework for Conceptualizing and Teaching African-American Women's History," *Signs* 14:4 (1989), 922. Brown credits Bettina Aptheker with this phrase (*Tapestries of Life: Women's Work, Women's Consciousness and the Meaning of Daily Life* [Amherst: University of Massachusetts Press, 1989]); it is also adopted by Patricia Hill Collins, *Black Feminist Thought: Knowledge, Consciousness, and the Politics of Empowerment* (Boston: Unwin Hyman, 1990), 236–37.

3. "Mrs. Stewart's Farewell Address to Her Friends in the City of Boston. Delivered September 21, 1833," excerpted in Lerner *Black Women in White America*: 565–66.

4. Angelina Grimké to Catharine Beecher, Letter XII in Alice S. Rossi, *The Feminist Papers: From Adams to de Beauvoir* (New York: Columbia University Press, 1973), 320.

5. Quoted in Gerda Lerner, *The Grimké Sisters from South Carolina: Pioneers for Woman's Rights and Abolition* (New York: Schocken Books, 1971), 187.

6. Quoted in Nell Painter, *Sojourner Truth: A Life, a Symbol* (New York: W. W. Norton, 1996), 125.

7. "The Akron Convention," in *History of Woman Suffrage*, eds. Elizabeth Cady Stanton, Susan B. Anthony, and Matilda Joslyn Gage, reprinted in Rossi, *Feminist Papers*, 428.

8. Convention of the American Equal Rights Association, New York City, 1867, excerpted in Lerner, *Black Women in White America: A Documentary History*, 568.

9. Higginbotham, *Righteous Discontent: The Women's Movement in the Black Baptist Church, 1880–1920* (Cambridge: Harvard University Press, 1993), 91–105.

10. Quoted in Bettina Aptheker, *Women's Legacy: Essays on Race, Sex, and Class in American History* (Amherst: University of Massachusetts Press, 1982), 65.

11. Anna Julia Cooper, *A Voice From the South, by a Black Woman of the South* (Xenia, OH.: Aldine Printing House, 1892; repr., New York: Oxford University Press, 1988), 32.

12. Elinor Lerner, "American Feminism and the Jewish Question, 1890–1940," in *Anti-Semitism in American History*, ed. David Gerber (Urbana: University of Illinois Press, 1986), 305–28.

13. Quoted in Jacquelyn Dowd Hall, *Revolt Against Chivalry: Jessie Daniel Ames and the Women's Campaign Against Lynching* (New York: Columbia University Press, 1979), 164.

14. Moreno quoted in Vicki L. Ruiz, *From Out of the Shadows: Mexican Women in Twentieth-Century America* (New York: Oxford University Press, 1998), 101.

15. Baker quoted in Karen Anderson, *Changing Woman: A History of Racial Ethnic Women in Modern America* (New York: Oxford University Press, 1996), 211.

16. NOW mission statement in Miriam Schneir, *Feminism in Our Time* (New York: Vintage Books, 1994), 96.

17. Quoted in Susan Hartmann, *The Other Feminists: Activists in the Liberal Establishment* (New Haven: Yale University Press, 1998), 191.

18. Dorothy Dawson Burlage, quoted in Sara Evans, *Personal Politics: The Roots of Women's Liberation in the Civil Rights Movement and the New Left* (New York: Knopf, 1979), 51.

19. Casey Hayden and Mary King, "Sex and Caste," November 18, 1965, reprinted in Evans, *Personal Politics*, 236.

20. "Liberation of Women: New Left Notes, July 10, 1967," reprinted in Evans, *Personal Politics*, 241.

21. Kreps, "Radical Feminism 1," in *Radical Feminism*, eds. Anne Koedt, Ellen Levine, and Anita Rapone (New York: Quadrangle Books, 1973), 239.

22. Ibid., 245.

23. Enriqueta Longeaux y Vásquez, "The Woman of La Raza," in *Chicana Feminist Thought: The Basic Historical Writings*, ed. Alma García (New York: Routledge, 1997), 31.

24. Elizabeth (Betita) Martinez, "History Makes Us, We Make History," in *The Feminist Memoir Project: Voices from Women's Liberation*, eds. Rachel Blau Duplessis and Ann Snitow (New York: Crown Publishing, 1998), 118–20.

25. Lynet Uttal, "Inclusion Without Influence: The Continuing Tokenism of Women of Color," in Gloria Anzaldúa, ed., *Making Face, Making Soul/Haciendo Caras: Creative and Critical Perspectives by Women of Color* (San Francisco: Aunt Lute Foundation, 1990), 42; Bernice Johnson Reagon, "Coalition Politics: Turning the Century," in *Homegirls: A Black Feminist Anthology*, ed. Barbara Smith (Brooklyn: Kitchen Table/Women of Color Press, 1983), 359.

26. Quoted in Hartmann, *The Other Feminists*, 205.

27. Del Castillo quoted in Ramón A. Gutiérrez, "Community, Patriarchy, and Individualism: The Politics of Chicano History and the Dream of Equality," in Vicki L.

Ruiz and Ellen Carol DuBois, *Unequal Sisters: A Multicultural Reader in U.S. Women's History* (New York: Routledge, 2000), 3d ed., 591.

28. Combahee River Collective, "Black Feminist Statement," in *Capitalist Patriarchy and Socialist Feminism*, Zillah Eisenstein, ed. (New York: Monthly Review Press, 1979), 366.

29. "How to Tame a Wild Tongue," in Gloria Anzaldúa, *Borderlands/La Frontera: The New Mestiza* (San Francisco: Spinsters/Aunt Lute, 1987), 59.

30. Cherríe Moraga, "Preface," *This Bridge Called My Back: Writings by Radical Women of Color* (Watertown, Mass.: Persephone Press, 1981; repr., New York: Kitchen Table/Women of Color Press, 1983), xv.

31. Smith, "Racism and Women's Studies," in *The Truth That Never Hurts* (New Brunswick, N.J.: Rutgers University Press, 1998), 96.

32. Ruth Frankenberg, *White Women, Race Matters: The Social Construction of Whiteness* (Minneapolis: University of Minnesota Press, 1993), 6.

33. Gloria Yamato, "Something About the Subject Makes It Hard to Name," in Anzaldúa, *Haciendo Caras*, 23–24.

34. Reagon, "Coalition Politics," 359.

35. Maxine Baca Zinn and Bonnie Thornton Dill, "Theorizing Difference from Multiracial Feminism," *Feminist Studies* 22:2 (1996), 321; Collins, *Black Feminist Thought*, 326; Barkley Brown, "African American Women," 921.

36. Donna Haraway, "A Cyborg Manifesto: Science, Technology, and Socialist-Feminism in the Late Twentieth Century," in *Simians, Cyborgs, and Women* (New York: Routledge, 1991), 150, 155.

37. Chela Sandoval, "U.S. Third World Feminism: The Theory and Method of Oppositional Consciousness in the Postmodern World," *Genders* 10 (spring 1991), 1–24; Paula M. L. Moya, "Postmodernism, 'Realism' and the Politics of Identity: Cherríe Moraga and Chicana Feminism," in *Feminist Genealogies, Colonial Legacies, Democratic Futures*, eds. M. Jacqui Alexander and Chandra Talpade Mohanty (New York: Routledge, 1997), 125–50.

38. Audre Lorde, "The Master's Tools Will Never Dismantle the Master's House," *Sister Outsider* (Freedom, Calif.: Crossing Press, 1984), 112.

–FIVE–

1. Adrienne Rich, "Notes Towards a Politics of Location," *Blood, Bread, and Poetry* (New York: W. W. Norton, 1986), 210–31.

2. Chandra Mohanty, "Under Western Eyes: Feminist Scholarship and Colonial Discourses," *Feminist Review* 30 (1988), 61–85.

3. Quoted in Mary Louise Pratt, *Imperial Eyes: Travel Writing and Transculturation* (New York: Routledge, 1992), 167–68.

4. Radha Kumar, *The History of Doing: An Illustrated Account of Movements for Women's Rights and Feminism in India, 1800–1990* (London: Verso, 1993), 2.

5. Bahithat al-Badiyah [pen name of Malak Hifni Nasif], "A Lecture in the Club

of the Umma Party, 1909," in *Opening the Gates: A Century of Arab Feminist Writing*, eds. Margot Badran and Miriam Cooke (London: Virago, 1990), 230.

6. Petition reprinted in Elizabeth Warnock Fernea and Basima Qattan Bezirgan, eds., *Middle Eastern Muslim Women Speak* (Austin: University of Texas Press, 1977), 196.

7. Quoted in Badran and Cooke, *Opening the Gates*, 355.

8. Quoted in Anne McClintock, *Imperial Leather: Race, Gender and Sexuality in the Colonial Conquest* (New York: Routledge, 1994), 381.

9. Marie Aimée Hélie-Lucas, "Women, Nationalism and Religion in the Algerian Liberation Struggle," (1987), in Badran and Cooke, *Opening the Gates*, 110.

10. Joyce Zonana, "The Sultan and the Slave: Feminist Orientalism and the Structure of *Jane Eyre*," *Signs* 18:3 (1993), 592–617; Leila Rupp, *Worlds of Women: The Making of an International Women's Movement* (Princeton, N.J.: Princeton University Press, 1997), 75ff.

11. Quoted in Rupp, *Worlds of Women*, 80.

12. Ibid., 77.

13. Ibid., 224–25; "Universal Declaration of Human Rights," in *Human Rights Documents* (Washington, D.C.: U.S. Government Printing Office, 1983), 61–67.

14. Quoted in Barry Schlachter, "International News," Associated Press, Nairobi, Kenya, July 15, 1985.

15. NGO *Forum '80* newsletter (Copenhagen), quoted in Charlotte Bunch, *Passionate Politics: Feminist Theory in Action* (New York: St. Martin's Press, 1987), 299.

16. Charlotte Bunch, "U.N. World Conference in Nairobi: A View from the West," *Ms.* 13:12 (1985), 79–82, reprinted in Bunch, *Passionate Politics*, 325.

17. Quoted in Arvonne S. Fraser, *The U.N. Decade for Women: Documents and Dialogue* (Boulder: Westview Press, 1987), 155.

18. Quoted in Bunch, *Passionate Politics*, 300.

19. Cheryl Johnson-Odim, "Common Themes, Different Contexts: Third World Women and Feminism," in *Third World Women and the Politics of Feminism*, Chandra Talpade Mohanty, Ann Russo, and Lourdes Torres, eds., (Bloomington: Indiana University Press, 1991), 317.

20. "Convention on the Elimination of All Forms of Discrimination Against Women," in *Human Rights Documents*, 139–40.

21. "Eagle Letters to Congressmen," Phyllis Schafly Eagle Forum, accessed at http://www.eagleforum.org/conglet/1997/unwomen.html, 26 August 2001. The U.S. Senate has never ratified CEDAW, although President Carter signed the treaty for the United States in 1980.

22. Ester Boserup, *Woman's Role in Economic Development* (New York: St. Martin's Press, 1970), 56.

23. Naila Kabeer, *Reversed Realities: Gender Hierarchies in Development Thought* (London: W. W. Norton, 1994), 27.

24. Aihwa Ong, *Spirits of Resistance and Capitalist Discipline* (New York: State University of New York Press, 1999), 163–68.

25. "The 25 Year Life Story of the Institute for Women's Studies in the Arab World," *Al-Raida* 57 (1998), 83–84. See also Helen Zweifel, "The Gendered Nature of Biodiversity Conservation," *National Women's Studies Association Journal* 9:3 (1997), 106–16.

26. The term comes from Amrita Basu, ed., *The Challenge of Local Feminisms: Women's Movements in Global Perspective* (Boulder: Westview Press, 1995).

27. Association of African Women for Research and Development, "A Statement on Genital Mutilation," in *Third World, Second Sex: Women's Struggle and National Liberation/Third World Women Speak Out*, ed. Miranda Davies (London: Zed Books, 1983), vol. 2, 217–19.

28. Domitila Barrios de Chungara, "Women and Organization," in Davies, *Third World, Second Sex*, 39–59.

29. Nilufer Cagatay, Caren Grown, and Aida Santiago, "Nairobi Women's Conference: Toward a Global Feminism?" (1986), quoted in Johnson-Odim, "Common Themes," 325.

30. Dr. Bene Madunagu, quoted in Hussaina Abdullah, "Wifeism and Activism: The Nigerian Women's Movement," in Basu, *The Challenge of Local Feminisms*, 212.

31. Quoted in McClintock, *Imperial Leather*, 384 and Gwendolyn Mikell, "African Feminism: Toward a New Politics of Representation," *Feminist Studies* 21:2 (1995), 419.

32. Statement by Network of African Rural Women Associations, 13 September 1995, reprinted in Bisi Ogunleye, "No Longer Invisible and Voiceless," *Women's Studies Quarterly* 24:1–2 (1996), 57.

-SIX-

1. Lenore J. Weitzman, *The Marriage Contract: Spouses, Lovers, and the Law* (New York: Free Press, 1981), 67–68.

2. Mary Collier, "The Woman's Labour" (1739), reprinted in *Women Imagine Change: A Global Anthology of Women's Resistance from 600 B.C.E. to Present*, eds. Eugenia Delamotte, Natania Meeker, and Jean O'Barr (New York: Routledge, 1997), 135–36.

3. Frances E. W. Harper, "Coloured Women of America," *Englishwoman's Review*, 15 January 1878, in *Black Women in White America: A Documentary History*, ed. Gerda Lerner (New York: Vintage Books, 1973), 247.

4. Om Naeema, "Fisherwoman," in *Five Egyptian Women Tell their Stories*, ed. Nayra Atiya (Syracuse: Syracuse University Press, 1982), 141.

5. *Mrs. Beeton's Book of Household Management*, quoted in *Victorian Women: A Documentary Account of Women's Lives in Nineteenth-Century England, France and the United States*, eds. Erna Olafson Hellerstein, Leslie Parker Hume, and Karen M. Offen; associate eds. Estelle Freedman, Barbara Gelpi, and Marilyn Yalom (Stanford: Stanford University Press, 1981), 294–95.

6. Buchi Emecheta in *Women: A World Report* (London: Oxford University Press, 1985), 217.

7. Alva Myrdal, *Nation and Family: The Swedish Experiment in Democratic Family and Population Policy* (London: K. Paul, Trench, Trubner & Co., Ltd., 1945), 419.

8. Linda Kerber, *No Constitutional Right to Be Ladies: Women and the Obligations of Citizenship* (New York: Hill and Wang, 1998), 174, 181.

9. Quoted in Maria Mies, "The Dynamics of the Sexual Division of Labor and Integration of Rural Women Into the World Market," in *Women and Development: The Sexual Division of Labor in Rural Societies*, ed. Lourdes Beneria (New York: Praeger, 1982), 20.

10. Joni Seager, *The State of Women in the World Atlas* (London: Penguin, 1997), 60.

11. Pat Mainardi, "The Politics of Housework," in *Sisterhood is Powerful: An Anthology of Writings from the Women's Liberation Movement*, ed. Robin Morgan (New York: Random House, 1970), 503.

12. Joy Kogawa, *Obasan* (New York: Penguin Books, 1981), 56.

13. June Jordan (lyrics) and Bernice Johnson Reagon (music), "Oughta Be a Woman," Songtalk Publishing Co. 1980, recorded by Sweet Honey in the Rock, *Good News* (Flying Fish Records 1981).

14. Quoted in David M. Katzman, *Seven Days a Week: Women and Domestic Service in Industrializing America* (Urbana: University of Illinois Press, 1981), 3–4.

15. Ibid, 7.

16. Quoted in Bonnie S. Anderson and Judith P. Zinsser, *A History of Their Own: Women in Europe from Prehistory to the Present*, (New York: Harper & Row, 1988), vol. II, 253.

17. Evelyn Nakano Glenn, *Issei, Nisei, War Bride: Three Generations of Japanese American Women in Domestic Service* (Philadelphia: Temple University Press, 1986), 160.

18. Quoted in Rachel Salazar Parrenas, "Transgressing the Nation-State: The Partial Citizenship and 'Imagined (Global) Community' of Migrant Filipina Domestic Workers," *Signs* 26:4 (2001), 1148.

19. In 1990, under 1 percent of white and Asian American women workers and between 2 and 5 percent African American and Latina women workers in the United States engaged in paid private domestic help. Teresa Amott, *Caught in the Crisis: Women and the U.S. Economy Today* (New York: Monthly Review Press, 1993), 55, 74–75.

20. Quoted in Mary Romero, "Chicanas Modernize Domestic Service," *Qualitative Sociology* 11:4 (1988), 326, 328.

21. Quoted in Ruth Rosen, *The Lost Sisterhood: Prostitution in America, 1900–1918* (Baltimore: Johns Hopkins University Press, 1982), 5.

22. Ibid., 46.

23. Sanger in *Victorian Women*, 416.

24. Quoted in Rosen, *The Lost Sisterhood*, 31.

25. Aaron Sachs, "The Last Commodity: Child Prostitution in the Developing World," *World Watch* 7:4 (1994): 28.

26. Nicholas D. Kristof, "Tokyo Journal: A Sexy Economic Feud of No Interest to the I.M.F.," *New York Times*, 17 June 1999, A4.

-SEVEN-

1. Quoted in Jean Tepperman, *Not Servants, Not Machines* (Boston: Beacon, 1976), 17–20.

2. For another version of this song and its history, see Francis Tamburro, "A Tale of a Song: 'The Lowell Factory Girl,' " *Southern Exposure* (1974), 42.

3. Quoted in Joanna Hadjicostandi, "The Garment Industry in Greece," in *Women Workers and Global Restructuring*, ed. Kathryn Ward (Ithaca: Industrial and Labor Relations Press, 1990), 73, 79.

4. The ratio of women to men in the paid labor force changed between 1960 and 1990 as follows: Canada: .36 to .77; United Kingdom: .46 to .70; United States: .45 to .76; Sweden: .53 to .87. Daphne Spain and Suzanne M. Bianchi, *Balancing Act: Motherhood, Marriage and Employment Among American Women* (New York: Russell Sage Foundation, 1996), 101.

5. In 1995, 69.1 percent of married mothers and 67.7 percent of single mothers with children under age 18 participated in the paid labor force in the United States. Of those with children under age 2, 58.7 percent of married and 53.9 percent of single mothers earned wages. Joyce Jacobsen, *The Economics of Gender*, 2nd ed. (Oxford: Blackwell, 1998), Table 4.3, 112.

6. For example, from 1970 to 1990 (or 1992), the percentage of births to unmarried women increased in Australia from 8 to 24, in Canada from 10 to 23, in Denmark from 11 to 47, in the United Kingdom from 8 to 31, and in the United States from 11 to 28. In Japan the percentage fell slightly, from 2 to 1. From Table 1.7, "Percentage of Births to Unmarried Women for Selected Industrial Countries: 1970 and 1990/92," in Spain and Bianchi, *Balancing Act*, 22.

7. Quoted in Elizabeth Roberts, *Women and Families: An Oral History, 1940–1970* (Oxford: Blackwell, 1995), 126.

8. Barbara L.K. Pillsbury, Gisele Maynard-Tucker, and France Nguyen, *Women's Empowerment and Reproductive Health: Links Throughout the Life Cycle* (New York: United Nations Population Fund, 2000), 6.

9. Quoted in Roberts, *Women and Families*, 130.

10. In Great Britain, disapproval declined from 52 to 27 percent for men and 43 to 22 for women (Catherine Hill, Office of National Statistics, cited in Tracy Harrison, "Equality? What Equality? More Women Go Out to Work . . . Then Do Chores Too," *The Mirror* 22 October 1998, 6). In the United States, disapproval declined from 37 percent of men and 32 percent of women in 1972 to 21 percent for both sexes in 1989 (Floris Wood, ed., *An American Profile: Opinions and Behavior, 1972–1989* [Detroit: Gale Research, 1990], 544).

11. Quoted in Kalwant Bhopal, *Gender, Race and Patriarchy: A Study of South Asian Women* (Aldershot: Ashgate Publishing Limited, 1997), 111.

12. Three-fourths of men and women agreed that women could be successful and good mothers; 70 percent preferred that women stay home and take care of children. Kirsten Downey Grimsley, "Full-Time Moms Earn Respect, Poll Says," *Washington Post*, 22 March 1998, A16.

13. Arlie Hochschild, *The Time Bind: When Work Becomes Home and Home Becomes Work* (New York: Metropolitan Books, 1997), 37–38.

14. Quoted in Henrietta L. Moore, *Feminism and Anthropology* (Minneapolis: University of Minnesota Press, 1988), 111.

15. Naila Kabeer, *Reversed Realities: Gender Hierarchies in Development Thought* (New York: Verso, 1994), 150.

16. Malaysian government investment brochure, quoted in Annette Fuentes and Barbara Ehrenreich, *Women in the Global Factory* (Boston: South End Press, 1983), 16.

17. Rachael Kamel and Anya Hoffman, eds., *The Maquiladora Reader: Cross-Border Organizing Since NAFTA* (Philadelphia: American Friends Service Committee, 1999), 36.

18. Carla Freeman, *High Tech and High Heels in the Global Economy: Women, Work, and Pink-Collar Identities in the Caribbean* (Durham: Duke University Press, 2000), 200.

19. Fuentes and Ehrenreich, *Women in the Global Factory*, 22.

20. Quoted in Miriam Ching Louie, "Immigrant Asian Women in Bay Area Garment Sweatshops," *Amerasia Journal* 18:1 (1992), 10.

21. Quoted in Barbara Allen Babcock et al., *Sex Discrimination and the Law: History, Practice and Theory*, 2nd ed. (Boston: Little, Brown, 1996), 60.

22. Virginia Valian, *Why So Slow?: The Advancement of Women* (Cambridge: MIT Press, 1998), 241.

23. For example, men in the United States earn 5 percent more as registered nurses than women do. U.S. Dept. of Labor, Bureau of Labor Statistics, Report 943 (May 2000), Table 3, 9.

24. Quoted in Vicki Schultz, "Women 'Before' the Law: Judicial Stories About Women, Work, and Sex Segregation on the Job," in *Feminists Theorize the Political*, eds. Judith Butler and Joan W. Scott (New York: Routledge, 1992), 318 and "Pat Cull, Carpenter," in *Hard-Hatted Women*, ed. Molly Martin (Seattle: Seal Press, 1988), 51–52.

25. Fran Conley, *Walking Out on the Boys* (New York: Farrar, Straus, and Giroux, 1998), 47.

26. Ladka Bauerova, "Czech Poll: Harassment of Women is Common," *New York Times*, 9 January 2000, A7.

27. Quoted in Nancy MacLean, "The Hidden History of Affirmative Action: Working Women's Struggles in the 1970s and the Gender of Class," *Feminist Studies* 25:1 (1999), 56.

28. Karen J. Hossfeld, " 'Their Logic Against Them': Contradictions in Sex, Race, and Class in Silicon Valley," in *Women Workers and Global Restructuring*, ed. Kathryn Ward (Ithaca: Industrial and Labor Relations Press, 1990), 161.

29. Hossfeld, "Their Logic Against Them," 160–61, 171–72.

- EIGHT -

1. Quoted in Deborah Levenson-Estrada, "Working Class Feminism in Guatemala City, 1970s," in *The Gendered Worlds of Latin American Women Workers: From Household and Factory to the Union Hall and Ballot Box*, eds. John D. French and Daniel James (Durham, N.C.: Duke University Press, 1997), 215.

2. Dorothy Mokgalo, quoted in "Congress of South African Trade Unions," in *No Turning Back: Fighting for Gender Equality in the Unions*, ed. Lesley Lawson (Johannesburg: Lacom [Cosatu Wits Women's Forum], 1992), 4.

3. Quoted in Radha Kumar, *The History of Doing: An Illustrated Account of Movements for Women's Rights and Feminism in India, 1800–1990* (New York: Verso, 1993), 103.

4. Quoted in Paola Gianturco and Toby Tuttle, *In Her Hands: Craftswomen Changing the World* (New York: Monacelli Press, 2000), 232–33.

5. Barbara Allen Babcock et al., *Sex Discrimination and the Law: History, Practice and Theory* (Boston: Little, Brown, 1996), 101.

6. Quoted in Babcock et al., *Sex Discrimination*, 716–17.

7. Quoted in Vicki Schultz, "Women 'Before' the Law: Judicial Stories About Women, Work, and Sex Segregation on the Job," in *Feminists Theorize the Political*, eds. Judith Butler and Joan W. Scott (New York: Routledge, 1992), 317.

8. Quoted in Deborah Rhode, *Justice and Gender: Sex Discrimination and the Law* (Cambridge: Harvard University Press, 1989), 188.

9. Canadian Human Rights Act, 1985, Part I, Section 11 (1).

10. Deborah M. Figart and June Lapidus, "Will Comparable Worth Reduce Race-Based Wage Discrimination?" *Review of Radical Political Economics* 30:3 (1998), 15.

11. Betsy Brill, "Small Loans, Big Change," *San Francisco Examiner*, 2 May 1999, A12.

12. Quoted in Elora Shehabuddin, "Contesting the Illicit: Gender and the Politics of Fatwas in Bangladesh," *Signs* 24:4 (1999): 1036.

13. Power of Women Collective, *All Work and No Pay: Women, Housework, and the Wages Due*, eds. Wendy Edmond and Suzie Fleming (London: Falling Wall Press Ltd., 1975), 7; Wages for Housework, "Notice to All Governments," in *Dear Sisters: Dispatches from the Women's Liberation Movement*, eds. Rosalyn Baxandall and Linda Gordon (New York: Basic Books, 2000), 258.

14. Quoted in Sondra R. Herman, "Dialogue: Children, Feminism, and Power: Alva Myrdal and Swedish Reform, 1929–1956," *Journal of Women's History* 4:2 (1992), 98.

15. Roberta Spalter-Roth, Claudia Withers, and Sheila Gibbs, "Improving Employment Opportunities for Women Workers: An Assessment of the Ten Year Eco-

nomic and Legal Impact of the Pregnancy Discrimination Act of 1978," cited in Heidi Hartmann, "Improving Employment Opportunities for Women," *Testimony Concerning H.R.1, Civil Rights Act of 1991, Before the U.S. House of Representatives, Committee on Education and Labor, 27 February 1991* (Washington, D.C.: Institute for Women's Policy Research, 1991), 17.

16. Quoted in Tamar Lewin, "Father Awarded $375,000 in a Parental Leave Case," *New York Times*, 3 February 1999, A11.

17. Janneke Plantenga, "Welfare-State Reform and Equal Opportunities: The Case of the Netherlands," in *Women and Public Policy*, eds. Susan Baker and Anneke van Doorne-Huiskes (Aldershot UK: Ashgate, 1999), 161.

18. Alva Myrdal, *Nation and Family,* in Susan Groag Bell and Karen M. Offen, eds., *Women, Family, and Freedom* (Stanford: Stanford University Press, 1983), vol. II, 413.

19. Johnnie Tillmon, "Welfare," *Ms.* 6:1 (1995), 50.

20. Gwendolyn Mink, "The Lady and the Tramp (II): Feminist Welfare Politics, Poor Single Mothers, and the Challenge of Welfare Justice," *Feminist Studies* 24:1 (1998), 58–59.

21. Plantenga, "Welfare-State Reform," 159.

22. Katha Pollitt, "Subject to Debate," *The Nation*, 30 January 1995, 120.

23. Sheila Rowbotham, *A Century of Women: The History of Women in Britain and the United States in the Twentieth Century* (New York: Viking, 1997), 553.

24. Mink, "The Lady and the Tramp," 63.

-NINE-

1. Ruth Hubbard, "The Political Nature of 'Human Nature,' " in *Theoretical Perspectives on Sexual Difference* (New Haven: Yale University Press, 1990), 69.

2. Simone de Beauvoir, *The Second Sex*, trans. and ed. H. M. Parshley (New York: Knopf, 1953), p. 249.

3. Gerda Lerner, *The Creation of Patriarchy* (New York: Oxford University Press, 1986), 143, 148.

4. Quoted in Barbara Ehrenreich and Deirdre English, *For Her Own Good: 150 Years of the Experts' Advice to Women* (New York: Anchor Press, 1978), 110.

5. Charlotte Perkins Gilman, "Why I Wrote 'The Yellow Wallpaper'?" reprinted in *The Charlotte Perkins Gilman Reader*, ed. Ann J. Lane (New York: Pantheon, 1980), 20.

6. Quoted in Hazel V. Carby, " 'It Jus Be's Dat Way Sometime': The Sexual Politics of Women's Blues," in *Unequal Sisters: A Multicultural Reader in U.S. Women's History*, eds. Ellen Carol DuBois and Vicki L. Ruiz (New York: Routledge, 1990), 247.

7. "Brown Sugar," on *Sticky Fingers*, The Rolling Stones (EMD/Virgin Records, 1971).

8. Quoted in Elisabeth Rosenthal, "China's Chic Waistline: Convex to Concave," *New York Times*, 9 December 1999, A1.

9. Ibid., A4.

10. Quoted in Becky W. Thompson, *A Hunger So Wide and Deep: A Multiracial View of Women's Eating Problems* (Minneapolis: University of Minnesota Press, 1994), 114.

11. Nellie Wong, "When I Was Growing Up," in *This Bridge Called My Back*, eds. Cherríe Moraga and Gloria Anzaldúa (Watertown, Mass.: Persephone Press, 1981; repr., Brooklyn: Kitchen Table/Women of Color Press, 1983), 7–8.

12. Quoted in Joan Jacobs Brumberg, *The Body Project* (New York: Random House, 1997), xxxii.

13. Dr. Tielun, quoted in Judy Yung, "The Social Awakening of Chinese American Women," in DuBois and Ruiz, eds., *Unequal Sisters*, 197.

14. Carol Hanisch, "Two Letters from the Women's Liberation Movement," in *The Feminist Memoir Project: Voices from Women's Liberation*, eds. Rachel Blau duPlessis and Ann Snitow (New York: Three Rivers Press, 1998), 199.

15. Quoted in Bonnie S. Anderson and Judith P. Zinsser, *A History of Their Own: Women in Europe from Prehistory to the Present* (New York: Harper & Row, 1988), vol. II, 413.

16. Alice J. Wolfson, "Clenched Fist, Open Heart," in duPlessis and Snitow, *Feminist Memoir Project*, 269–70.

17. Boston Women's Health Book Collective, *The New Our Bodies, Ourselves* (New York: Simon & Schuster, 1992), 15.

18. Gloria Naylor, "Power: Rx for Good Health: Byllye Avery's Battle Cry for Black Women Is 'Sister I'm Here to Support You,' " *Ms.* 14:11 (1986), 56.

19. "National Latina Health Organization, Program Description" (flyer), 1, 5. See also National Latina Health Organization at http://clnet.ver.edu/women/nlho/.

20. "Body Image Summit," Women and Equality Unit (Cabinet Office), Minister of Women, Initiatives at http://www.womens-unit.gov.uk.

21. Although a range of terms appears in the literature, I use "female genital cutting" to avoid the sensationalistic implications of the term "mutilation" and the medically neutral implication of the term "circumcision."

22. Association of African Women for Research and Development, "A Statement on Genital Mutilation," in *Third World, Second Sex: Women's Struggle and National Liberation/Third World Women Speak Out*, ed. Miranda Davies (London: Zed Books, 1983), vol. 2, 217–19.

23. Quoted in Noor J. Kassamali, "When Modernity Confronts Traditional Practices: Female Genital Cutting in Northeast Africa," in *Women in Muslim Societies: Diversity within Unity*, ed. Herbert L. Bodman and Nayereh Tohidi (Boulder, Colo: Lynne Riener, 1998), 46.

24. Mimi Nguyen, "Revolutionary Glamour," *exoticize my fist* (ezine), accessed at http://members.aol.com/CritChicks/index.html, 15 June 1999.

25. Quoted in Skye Lavin, "Dissidence and Creativity, Wholeness and Censorship: A conversation with Egyptian Feminist Nawal El Saadawi," *Sojourner* 25:5 (2000), 21.

26. Jim Coffman, "Choosing the Veil," *Mother Jones* 16:6 (1991), 24; also see

the Revolutionary Association of the Women of Afghanistan Web site at http://www.rawa.org.

27. Lavin, "Dissidence and Creativity," 21.

28. Emily Honig and Gail Hershatter, *Personal Voices: Chinese Women in the 1980s* (Stanford: Stanford University Press, 1988), 50–51, 68, 72.

29. Carol Munter, "Fat and the Fantasy of Perfection," in *Pleasure and Danger: Exploring Female Sexuality*, ed. Carol S. Vance (Boston: Routledge and Kegan Paul, 1984), 228–29; Naomi Wolf, *The Beauty Myth: How Images of Beauty Are Used Against Women* (New York: William Morrow, 1991), 10.

30. Susan Bordo, *Unbearable Weight: Feminism, Western Culture, and the Body* (Berkeley: University of California Press, 1993), 179.

31. "What Is Nikegoddess," accessed at http://goddess.nike.com/nikegoddess/html/index.jsp, 21 August 2001.

32. *Sports Illustrated for Women* 2:5 (September 2000).

-TEN-

1. Margaret Sanger, "Birth Control—A Parents' Problem or Woman's" (1920), in *Women Imagine Change: A Global Anthology of Women's Resistance from 600 B.C.E. to Present* (New York: Routledge, 1997), 392; Ellen Chesler, *Woman of Valor: Margaret Sanger and the Birth Control Movement in America* (New York: Simon & Schuster, 1992), 216.

2. Aida Hayhoe, quoted in Bonnie S. Anderson and Judith P. Zinsser, *A History of Their Own: Women in Europe from Prehistory to the Present* (New York: Oxford University Press, 1988), vol. II, 286.

3. Quoted in Vicki Ruiz, *From Out of the Shadows: Mexican Women in Twentieth-Century America* (New York: Oxford University Press, 1998), 113.

4. By 2000, 16 percent of men in Britain, 11 percent in the Netherlands, but only 1 percent of Frenchmen (compared to 6 percent of French women sterilized) have had vasectomies. John Tagliabue, "British Vasectomy Offer Brings French Outrage," *New York Times*, 18 August 2000, A8.

5. Quoted in Lois Wessel, "Reproductive Rights in Nicaragua: From the Sandinistas to the Government of Violeta Chamorro," *Feminist Studies* 17:3 (1991), 546.

6. Gwendolyn Brooks, "The Mother," in *The World Split Open: Four Centuries of Women Poets in England and America, 1552–1950*, ed. Louise Bernikow (New York: Vintage Books, 1974), 328; Betty Friedan, "Feminism's Next Step," *New York Times*, 5 July 1981, sec. 6, p. 14.

7. Quoted in Wessel, "Reproductive Rights in Nicaragua," 547.

8. Barbara Gelpi, text of "Speech at Pro-Choice Rally," 24 April 1989, Stanford University, (emphasis in original).

9. Of the total voluntary sterilizations in China in the 1990s, 37 percent were tubal ligations for women and 12 percent vasectomies for men. IUDs account for 41

percent of birth control methods. In 1989 the abortion rate was 632 per 1,000 births, much higher than most industrialized nations. Center for Reproductive Law and Policy, *Women of the World: Laws and Policies Affecting Their Reproductive Lives* (New York: CRLP, 1995), accessed at http://www.crlp.org/ww_sbr_china.html, 25 August 2001.

10. Quoted in Family Health International, "China: Different Generations, Different Points of View," in *Women's Voices, Women's Lives: The Impact of Family Planning*, ed. Barbara Barnett (Research Triangle Park, N.C.: The Project, 1998), 55.

11. Quoted in Adriana Ortiz Ortega, Ana Amuchástegui, and Marta Rivas, " 'Because They Were Born from Me': Negotiating Women's Rights in Mexico," in *Negotiating Reproductive Rights: Women's Perspectives Across Countries and Cultures*, eds. Rosalind P. Petchesky and Karen Judd (London: Zed Books, 1998), 170–171.

12. Quoted in M. G. Fried, "Beyond Abortion: Transforming the Pro-Choice Movement," *Social Policy* 23:4 (1993), 26.

13. Quoted in Christine R. Riddiough, "UN Conferences Link Environment, Development and Women's Rights," *Not Far Enough* (Democratic Socialists of America Feminist Commission), fall 1994. Accessed at http://www.dsausa.org/archive/Fem/NFE949.html, 26 August 2001.

14. Paul Lewis, "Women's Groups Oppose Vatican on Family Planning," *New York Times*, 2 July 1999, A3.

15. UN Population Fund, *Lives Together, Worlds Apart: Men and Women in a Time of Change* (New York: UN Population Fund 2000), 2.

16. United Nations, *Final Act of the International Conference on Human Rights* (New York: United Nations, 1968).

-ELEVEN-

1. *Oxford English Dictionary,* second ed., 1989.

2. Quoted in Thomas Laqueur, "Orgasm, Generation, and the Politics of Reproductive Biology," *Representations* 14 (spring 1986), 1.

3. Fatima Mernissi, "Beyond the Veil: Male Female Dynamics in Modern Muslim Society," in *Women Imagine Change: A Global Anthology of Women's Resistance from 600 B.C.E. to Present*, eds. Eugenia DeLamotte, Natania Meeker, and Jean F. O'Barr (New York: Routledge, 1997), 82.

4. Dr. Johnson, quoted in Jeffery Weeks, *Sex, Politics, and Society: The Regulation of Sexuality Since 1800* (London: Longman, 1989), 29.

5. Clelia Duel Mosher, *The Mosher Survey: Sexual Attitudes of 45 Victorian Women*, eds. James MaHood and Kristine Wenburg (New York: Arno Press, 1980), 139, 416; Marie C. Stopes, *Married Love* (New York: Eugenics Publishing Co., 1931), 75–76.

6. Charlotte Wolff, quoted in Bonnie S. Anderson and Judith P. Zinsser, *A History of Their Own: Women in Europe from Prehistory to the Present* (New York: Harper & Row, 1988), vol. II, 222.

7. Quoted in Gerda Lerner, *Black Women in White America: A Documentary History* (New York: Vintage Books, 1973), 442–443.

8. Charlotte Perkins Gilman, *The Living of Charlotte Perkins Gilman: An Autobiography* (New York: Harper and Row, 1935), 331.

9. Quoted in Anderson and Zinsser, *A History of Their Own*, vol. II, 420.

10. Quoted in Mari Jo Buhle, *Feminism and Its Discontents: A Century of Struggle with Psychoanalysis* (Cambridge: Harvard University Press, 1998), 332.

11. Boston Women's Health Book Collective, *Our Bodies, Ourselves* (New York: Simon and Schuster, 1984), 178.

12. Charlotte Wolff, quoted in Anderson and Zinsser, *A History of Their Own*, vol. II, 424.

13. Quoted in Dianne Forte and Karen Judd, "The South Within the North: Reproductive Choice in Three U.S. Communities," in *Negotiating Reproductive Rights: Women's Perspectives Across Countries and Cultures*, eds. Rosalind P. Petchesky and Karen Judd (London: Zed Books, 1998), 287–88.

14. Camille Paglia, "Madonna I: Animality and Artifice," *New York Times*, 14 December 1990, reprinted in *Sex, Art, and American Culture: Essays* (New York: Vintage, 1992), 3–5; Naomi Wolf, *Promiscuities: An Ordinary American Girlhood* (New York: Random House, 1997), xvii.

15. Hortense Spillers, "Interstices: A Small Drama of Words," in *Pleasure and Danger: Exploring Female Sexuality*, ed. Carol S. Vance (Boston: Routledge and Kegan Paul, 1984), 78, 95.

16. Angela Davis, "Sex—Egypt," in *Women: A World Report* (New York: Oxford University Press, 1985), 330.

17. Evelyne Accad, "Sexuality and Sexual Politics: Conflicts and Contradictions for Contemporary Women in the Middle East," in *Third World Women and the Politics of Feminism*, eds. Chandra Talpade Mohanty, Ann Russo, and Lourdes Torres (Bloomington: Indiana University Press, 1991), 239–40.

18. Madhu Kishwar, "Women, Sex and Marriage: Restraint as a Feminine Strategy," *Manushi* 99 (March–April 1997), 24–25, 35–36.

19. Carmen Barroso and Cristina Bruschini, "Building Politics from Personal Lives: Discussions on Sexuality among Poor Women in Brazil," in Mohanty, Russo, and Torres, eds., *Third World Women*, 153–71.

20. Quoted in Tze-Ian Deborah Sang, "Feminism's Double: Lesbian Activism in the Mediated Public Sphere of Taiwan," in *Spaces of Their Own: Women's Public Sphere in Transnational China*, ed. Mayfair Mei-Hui Yang (Minneapolis: University of Minnesota Press, 1999), 144.

21. Quoted in Meredith Tax, "World Culture War," *The Nation*, 17 May 1999, 26–27.

22. Catharine A. MacKinnon, "Feminism, Marxism, Method, and the State: An Agenda for Theory," *Signs* 7:3 (1982), 515.

23. Andrea Dworkin, *Intercourse* (New York: The Free Press, 1987), 127–28.

24. Susan Brownmiller, *Against Our Will: Men, Women, and Rape* (New York: Simon and Schuster, 1975), 395.

25. Kuniko Funabashi, "Pornographic Culture and Sexual Violence," in *Japanese Women: New Feminist Perspectives on the Past, Present, and Future*, eds. Kumiko Fujimura-Fanselow and Atsuko Kameda (New York: The Feminist Press, 1995), 255.

26. Mandy Rose, quoted in Sheila Rowbotham, *A Century of Women* (New York: Viking Penguin, 1997), 508.

27. "Deepa Mehta's *Fire* Creates Controversy," South Asian Women's Network (SAWNET), http://www.umiacs.umd.edu/users/sawweb/sawnet/news/fire.html, September 2000; T. Padmanabha Rao, "S.C. Directive to State in 'Fire' Case," *The Hindu*, 16 December 1998, 10.

28. Cherríe Moraga, *Loving in the War Years/Lo Que Nunca Pasó Por Sus Labios* (Cambridge, MA: South End Press, 1983, 2nd ed., 2001), 119.

29. "Samara," quoted in "Triple Treat," by Rev. Kellie Everts, and Donna Marie Niles, "Confessions of a Prostitute," in *Sex Work: Writings by Women in the Sex Industry*, eds. Frédérique Delacoste and Priscilla Alexander (Pittsburgh: Cleis, 1987), 38, 148–49.

30. Femke Halsema, quoted in Suzanne Daley, "New Rights for Dutch Prostitutes, But No Gain," *New York Times*, 12 August 2001, A1.

-TWELVE-

1. International Council of Women, 1913, quoted in Leila J. Rupp, *Worlds of Women: The Making of an International Women's Movement* (Princeton, N.J.: Princeton University Press, 1997), 86–87.

2. Susan Brownmiller, *Against Our Will: Men, Women, and Rape* (New York: Simon and Schuster, 1975), 15.

3. Susan Griffin, "Politics, 1971" in *Rape: The Power of Consciousness* (New York: Harper & Row, 1979), 3.

4. Quoted in Donald G. McNeil Jr., "In a New South Africa, Old Anti-Gay Bias Persists," *New York Times*, 18 November 1997, A3.

5. "Living Without Fear: An Integrated Approach to Tackling Violence Against Women," Conference Report of the Home Office Special Conference on Violence Against Women, 24–25 November 1999 (London: Home Office/Women's Unit, 1999), accessed at http://www.womens-unit.gov.uk/living_without_fear/, 20 August 2001, chapter 4.

6. Quoted in Catherine MacPhail and Catherine Campbell, " 'I Think Condoms Are Good but, aai, I Hate Those Things': Condom Use Among Adolescents and Young People in a Southern African Township," *Social Science & Medicine* 52:11 (2001), 1623.

7. Nancy T. Miller, "Calling His Bluff," in *Her Wits About Her: Self-Defense Success Stories by Women*, eds. Denise Caignon and Gail Groves (New York: Harper & Row, 1987), 47–48.

8. "Interview with Jackson Katz," *Family Life Matters: A Newsletter for Health, Family Life and Sexuality Educators* 37 (spring 1999), 6; Tafadzwa Mumba, "Rape: An Expression of Manhood?" [interview with Jonah Gokova], *Woman Plus* 22 (1997), 17–18.

9. U.N. Vienna Declaration, quoted in Kazuko Watanabe, "Trafficking in Women's Bodies, Then and Now: The Issue of Military 'Comfort Women,'" *Women's Studies Quarterly* 27:1–2 (1999), 29; Beijing Platform of Action, *From Beijing: A Platform for Action and a Clear Mandate for Women's Progress* (New York: UN Department of Public Information, 1995), paragraph 112.

10. Sue Hill, "Police Handling of New Rape/New Rape Centers," in *Lifting the Lid on Sexual Violence*, conference report (London: Rape and Sexual Assault Support Center, 2000), http://www.gn.apc.org/womeninlondon/rasascrp.htm, August 2001.

11. Supreme Court of Appeals, Rome, quoted in Alessandra Stanley, "Ruling on Tight Jeans and Rape Sets Off Anger in Italy," *New York Times*, 16 February 1999, A6.

12. Camille Paglia, *Sex, Art, and American Culture: Essays* (New York: Vintage, 1992), 53, 63.

13. "Living Without Fear," chapter 4.

14. Michele Clossik, Caitlin Kelly, and Brenda Seery, "Responses to the *Ms.* Survey on Male Violence," *Ms.* 1:5 (1991), 38–40.

15. Quoted in Josephine Masimba, "Zimbabwe-Human Rights: Baring the Ugly Facts," InterPress News Service, 11 February 1997.

16. Women's Information Centre, "Shelter for Battered Women in Thailand," *Third World Second Sex*, ed. Miranda Davies (London: Zed Books, 1987), vol. II, 207.

17. Quoted in Lee Ann Hoff, *Battered Women as Survivors* (London: Routledge, 1990), 154.

18. bell hooks, *Feminist Theory: From Margin to Center* (Cambridge: South End Press, 1984; reprinted 2000), 132.

19. Dorothy Allison, *Skin* (Ithaca: Firebrand Books, 1994), 52.

20. Judith Herman, *Father-Daughter Incest* (Cambridge: Harvard University Press, 1981), 49.

21. Clossik, Kelly, and Seery, "Responses," 40.

22. Joy Harjo, "I Give You Back," (From "She Had Some Horses"), in *Making Face, Making Soul/Haciendo Caras: Creative and Critical Perspectives by Women of Color*, ed. Gloria Anzaldúa (San Francisco: Aunt Lute, 1990), 151–52.

-THIRTEEN-

1. Virginia Woolf, *Three Guineas* (New York: Harcourt, Brace & Co., 1938; reprinted 1966), 176.

2. Carol Seajay, "20 Years of Feminist Bookstores," *Ms.* 3:1 (1992), 60.

3. In two-thirds of the studies of formal speech and one-third of the studies of informal speech, men predominate. See Penelope Eckert and Sally McConnell-Ginet,

Language and Gender: The Construction of Meaning in Social Practice (Cambridge: Cambridge University Press, forthcoming), chapter 4.

4. Peggy Orenstein, *School Girls: Young Women, Self-Esteem, and the Confidence Gap* (New York: Doubleday, 1994), 11.

5. Emma Pérez, "Irigaray's Female Symbolic in the Making of Chicana Lesbian *Sitios y Lenguas*," in *Living Chicana Theory*, ed. Carla Trujillo (Berkeley: Third Woman Press, 1998), 98.

6. Quoted in Casey Miller, Kate Swift, and Rosalie Maggio, "Liberating Language," *Ms.* 8:2 (1997), 54.

7. Anne Bradsteet, "The Prologue," in *The Norton Anthology of Literature by Women: The Tradition in English*, eds. Sandra Gilbert and Susan Gubar (New York: W. W. Norton, 1985), 62; Southey, quoted in Françoise Basch, *Relative Creatures: Victorian Women in Society and the Novel* (New York: Schocken Books, 1974), 108.

8. Adrienne Rich, "When We Dead Awaken: Writing as Re-Vision" (1971), in *On Lies, Secrets and Silence: Selected Prose, 1966–1978* (New York: W.W. Norton, 1979), 44–45.

9. Marge Piercy, *To Be of Use: Poems by Marge Piercy* (New York: Doubleday, 1973), 8.

10. Ursula LeGuin, "Bryn Mawr Commencement Address," (1986) in *Dancing at the Edge of the World: Thoughts on Words, Women, Places* (New York: Grove Press, 1989), 151.

11. Gloria Anzaldúa, *Borderlands/La Frontera: The New Mestiza* (San Francisco: Aunt Lute Press, 1987), 58.

12. Gilbert and Gubar, eds., *Norton Anthology*, 1786.

13. Hélène Cixous, "The Laugh of the Medusa," trans. Keith Cohen and Paula Cohen, *Signs* 1:4 (1976), 877, 880.

14. Linda Nochlin, *Women, Art, and Power and Other Essays* (New York: Harper & Row, 1988), 150.

15. Dürer, quoted in Bonnie S. Anderson and Judith P. Zinsser, eds., *A History of Their Own: Women in Europe from Prehistory to the Present* (New York: Harper & Row, 1988), vol. I, 412; Mendelssohn, quoted in ibid., vol. II, 175.

16. Virginia Woolf, *A Room of One's Own* (New York: Harcourt, Brace and World, 1957), 48–50.

17. Quoted in Anderson and Zinsser, *A History of Their Own*, vol. II, 176.

18. Quoted in Jo Catling, ed., *A History of Women's Writing in Germany, Austria and Switzerland* (Cambridge: Cambridge University Press, 2000), 9.

19. Quoted in Angela Davis, *Blues Legacies and Black Feminism: Gertrude "Ma" Rainey, Bessie Smith, and Billie Holiday* (New York: Pantheon Books, 1998), 356–57.

20. Alice Walker, *In Search of Our Mothers' Gardens: Womanist Prose* (San Diego: Harcourt Brace Jovanovich, 1983), 239, 241–42.

21. http://www.guerillagirls.com/posters/whitey.html

22. Peggy Phelan, *Art and Feminism* (London: Phaidon Press, 2001), 23.

23. Catherine King, "Feminist Arts," in *Imagining Women: Cultural Representations and Gender*, eds. Frances Bonner and Lizbeth Goodman (Cambridge, UK: Polity Press, 1992), 181.

24. Griselda Pollock, "Tracing Figures of Presence, Naming Ciphers of Absence: Feminism, Imperialism, and Postmodernity in the Work of Sutapa Biswas," in *With Other Eyes: Looking at Race and Gender in Visual Culture*, ed. Lisa Bloom (Minneapolis: University of Minnesota Press, 1999), 237.

25. Lynn Gottlieb, *She Who Dwells Within: A Feminist Vision of a Renewed Judaism* (San Francisco: HarperCollins, 1995), quoted in Jody Elizabeth Myers, "The Myth of Matriarchy in Recent Writings on Jewish Women's Spirituality," *Jewish Social Studies* 4:1 (1997), 5.

26. Lindiwe Mabuza and Elaine Maria Upton, "Born to the Struggle, Learning to Write: An Interview with Lindiwe Mabuza, Poet and Chief Representative of the African National Congress (of South Africa) in the United States," *Feminist Studies* 21:3 (1995), 615–27.

27. Yvonne Ranier, "Skirting," in *The Feminist Memoir Project: Voices from Women's Liberation*, eds. Ann Snitow and Rachel Blau Duplessis, (New York: Crown Publishers, 1998), 447.

28. "Wendy Wasserstein," *Ms.* 8:2 (1997), 44–45.

29. Quoted in Upton, "Born to Struggle," 625.

30. Harriet A. Hirshorn, "Interview [with Trinh T. Minh-ha, filmmaker]," *Heresies* 22 (1987), 16.

31. Quoted in Noy Thrupkaew, "This Ain't Your Mama's Feminism," *Sojourner* 26:4 (2000), 23.

32. Jessica Rosenberg and Gitana Garofalo, "Riot Grrrl: Revolutions from Within," *Signs* 23:3 (1998), 812–13.

33. Laurel Gilbert and Crystal Kile, *Surfergrrrls: Look Ethel! An Internet Guide for Us* (Seattle: Seal Press, 1996), quoted in Ednie Kaeh Garrison, "U.S. Feminism—Grrrl Style! Youth (Sub)Culture and the Technologics of the Third Wave," *Feminist Studies* 26:1 (2000), 141.

34. Quoted in Barbara Fedders, "Watch Me Make Up My Mind Instead of My Face," *Sojourner* 25:11–12 (2000), 47.

35. Quoted in Paola Gianturco and Toby Tuttle, *In Her Hands: Craftswomen Changing the World* (New York: Monacelli Press, 2000), 83.

-FOURTEEN-

1. *New Shorter Oxford English Dictionary,* "Politics" definitions 3a, 2.

2. Susan Moller Okin, *Women in Western Political Thought* (Princeton, N.J.: Princeton University Press, 1979), 284–85.

3. Quoted in Vicki Ruiz, *From Out of the Shadow: Mexican Women in Twentieth-Century America* (New York: Oxford University Press, 1998), 143.

4. Quoted in Elizabeth Friedman, "Women's Human Rights: The Emergence of a

Movement," in *Women's Rights, Human Rights: International Feminist Perspectives*, eds. Julie Peters and Andrea Wolper (New York: Routledge, 1995), 22.

5. Quoted in Deborah Sontag, "Israel Honors Mothers of Lebanon Withdrawal," *New York Times*, 3 June 2000, A3.

6. Quoted in Marguerite Bouvard, "Revolutionary Mothers of Argentina," *Sojourner* 17:5 (1992), 21.

7. Tatyana Mamanova and Helen Caldicott quoted in *Women on War*, ed. Daniela Gioseffi (New York: Simon and Schuster, 1988), 55, 295.

8. "Simone de Beauvoir Talks About Sartre," *Ms.* 12:2 (1983), 90.

9. Quoted in Friedman, "Women's Human Rights," 123.

10. Amira El Azhary Sonbol, ed., *Women, the Family, and Divorce Laws in Islamic History* (Syracuse: Syracuse University Press, 1996), 9.

11. Quoted in Barbara Crossette, "Egyptian at Center on Rights of Women," *New York Times*, 8 June 2000, A7.

12. "Kuwait Narrowly Kills New Bill to Give Women Political Rights" *New York Times*, 1 December 1999, A5.

13. "Moroccans and Women: Two Rallies," *New York Times*, 3 March 2000, A8.

14. Joni Seager, *The State of Women in the World Atlas*, rev. edition (London: Penguin, 1997), 90. See also Map 30, 90–91.

15. Chetna Gala, "Empowering Women in Villages: All-Women Village Councils in Maharashtra, India," *Bulletin of Concerned Asian Scholars* 29:2 (1997), 35.

16. Ibid., 42.

17. Linda Racioppi and Katherine O'Sullivan See, "Organizing Women Before and After the Fall: Women's Politics in the Soviet Union and Post-Soviet Russia," *Signs* 20:4 (1995), 829.

18. Quoted in Virginia Cornue, "Practicing NGOness and Relating Women's Space Publicly: The Women's Hotline and the State," in *Spaces of Their Own: Women's Public Sphere in Transnational China*, ed. Mayfair Mei-Hui Yang (Minneapolis: University of Minnesota Press, 1999), 71.

19. Quoted in Meredith Tax, "World Culture War," *The Nation*, 17 May 1999, 27.

20. Sabine Lang, "The NGO-ization of Feminism: Institutionalization and Institution Building Within the German Women's Movements," in *Global Feminisms Since 1945*, ed. Bonnie Smith (London: Routledge, 2000), 296.

21. Quoted in *Ms.* 8:2 (1997), 49.

22. "Moving Beyond Rhetoric," in *Women: Looking Beyond 2000* (New York: United Nations, 1995), 121.

APPENDICES

A. YEAR WOMEN GRANTED RIGHT TO VOTE, 1890–2001

B. PERCENTAGE OF ADULT WOMEN IN U.S. PAID LABOR FORCE BY ETHNICITY/RACE, 1900–2000

C. PERCENTAGE OF ADULT WOMEN IN U.S. PAID LABOR FORCE BY MARITAL STATUS AND PRESENCE OF CHILDREN, 1970–1999

D. WOMEN IN THE WORLD LABOR FORCE, 1970–1997

E. FEMALE LIFE EXPECTANCY AND FERTILITY RATES FOR SELECTED COUNTRIES, 2000

F. PERCENTAGE OF WOMEN IN PARLIAMENTS, 1975, 1999

G. WOMEN IN POLITICAL OFFICE, UNITED STATES, 1980, 2001

APPENDIX A:

YEAR WOMEN GRANTED RIGHT TO VOTE, 1890–2001

(chronological within period)

1890–1910	1910–1940	1940–1960	1960–2001
New Zealand	USSR	France	Cyprus
Australia	Austria	Italy	Algeria
Finland	Canada	Japan	Congo
	UK	Vietnam	Iran
	Germany	Pakistan	Kenya
	Netherlands	Venezuela	Angola
	United States	Belgium	South Africa
	Thailand	Israel	Iraq
	Brazil	China	
	Cuba	India	
	Turkey	Nepal	
	Philippines	Bolivia	
		Mexico	
		Sudan	
		Nicaragua	
		Egypt	
		Zimbabwe	
		Korea	

APPENDIX B:

PERCENTAGE OF ADULT WOMEN IN U.S. PAID LABOR FORCE BY ETHNICITY/RACE, 1900–2000

	All Women	White	Black	Latina[1] MX	Latina[1] PR-US	Asian American[2] CH	Asian American[2] JP	Asian American[2] FL	Native American
1900	21.2	16.0	40.7	n/a*	n/a	10.4	30.1	n/a	13.8
1920	21.1	19.5	38.9	n/a	n/a	12.5	25.9	11.6	11.5
1950	29.1	28.1	37.4	21.9	38.9	33.7	41.6	28.0	17.0
1960	37.7	38.0	42.2	28.8	36.3	44.2	44.1	36.2	25.5
1970	43.3	43.0	47.5	36.4	31.6	49.5	49.4	55.2	35.3
1980	51.1	52.0	53.3	49.0	40.1	58.3	58.5	68.1	47.7
1990	56.8	56.4	59.5	52.8	42.8	59.2	55.5	72.3	55.1
1996	59.3	59.1	60.4	53.4	47.4[3]	n/a	58.6	n/a	n/a
2000	60.9	60.2	65.1	54.6	55.0[4]	n/a	n/a	n/a	n/a

*n/a = not available

[1] Not including Islander Puerto Rican. The first figure represents Mexican American women; the second figure represents U.S. Puerto Rican women. Available Islander Puerto Rican women's rates were 13.9% in 1900, 18.9% in 1920, 21.3% in 1950, 20.0% in 1960, 22.9% in 1970, 29.1% in 1980.

[2] The first figure represents Chinese Americans; the second figure represents Japanese Americans; the third figure represents Filipina Americans. Single figure for 1996 is a composite; ethnic-specific data is not available.

[3] Because figures were not available for Puerto Rican women in 1996, data is from 1995.

[4] Because figures were not yet available for 2000, data is from 1999. Available rates for Cuban-origin women were 55.9% in 1990, 50.8% in 1995, and 50.2% in 1999.

Sources: Teresa Amott and Julie Matthaei, *Race, Gender, and Work: A Multi-Cultural Economic History of Women in the United States* (Boston: South End Press, 1996), 307; Bureau of Labor Statistics News (Washington D.C.: U.S. Department of Labor, 2000), Tables No. A1 and A2; Joyce Jacobsen, *The Economics of Gender*, 2nd ed., Table 15.2 (Oxford: Blackwell Publishers, 1998), 459. See Amott and Matthaei for discussion of problems in data comparability.

APPENDIX C:

PERCENTAGE OF ADULT WOMEN IN U.S. PAID LABOR FORCE BY MARITAL STATUS AND PRESENCE OF CHILDREN, 1970–1999

All U.S. Women	Single	Married*	Other**	Single w/children	Married w/children	Other w/children
1970	53	40.8	39.1	Not available	39.7	60.7
1980	61.5	50.1	44	52	54.1	69.4
1985	65.2	54.2	45.6	51.6	60.8	71.9
1990	66.4	58.2	46.8	55.2	66.3	74.2
1995	65.5	61.1	47.3	57.5	70.2	75.3
1999	68.1	61.6	49.4	73.4	70.1	80.4

*Husband present
**Widowed, divorced, or separated

Source: Statistical Abstract of the United States (Washington, D.C.: U.S. Department of Commerce/U.S. Census Bureau, 2000), Table No. 653. Table reflects civilian noninstitutional women sixteen years and over.

APPENDIX D:

WOMEN IN THE WORLD LABOR FORCE, 1970–1997

Region and Country	Percentage of labor force that is female (age 15+)			Percentage of Adult Women Economically Active, 1997[1]
	1970	*1980*	*1997*	
Africa				
Northern	9	20	26	29
Sub-Saharan	39	42	43	62
Latin America				
Caribbean	32	38	43	53
Central	20[2]	27	33	39
South	20[2]	27	38	45
Europe				
Western	33[3]	36	42	49
Eastern	44	45	45	53
Other developed countries	33[3]	39	44	55
United States	38	42	46	60
Asia				
East & Southeast	37.5	41	43	61
Southern	20	31	33	45
Western	19	23	27	33
Central	45	47	46	59
Oceania[4]	31	35	38	57

[1]"Economic activity rate covers all production oriented to the market, some types of nonmarket production (including production and processing of primary products for own consumption), own-account construction and other production of fixed assets for own use. It excludes unpaid domestic activities and volunteer work." (*The World's Women 2000*, p. 111.)

[2]Central and South America calculated together in this source.

[3]Western Europe and other developed nations calculated together in this source.

[4]Sparse data for this subregion; average should be interpreted with caution.

Sources: The World's Women 2000: Trends and Statistics (New York: United Nations, 2000), Charts 5.1 and 5.2, 110; *The World's Women 1995: Trends and Statistics* (New York: United Nations, 1995), Chart 5.4A, 109.

APPENDIX E:

FEMALE LIFE EXPECTANCY AND FERTILITY RATES FOR SELECTED COUNTRIES, 2000

Country	Life Expectancy	Fertility Rate
Brazil	62.9	2.13
Canada	79.4	1.60
China	71.4	1.82
Egypt	63.3	3.15
France	78.8	1.75
India	62.5	3.11
Japan	80.7	1.41
Kenya	48.0	3.66
Mexico	71.5	2.67
Pakistan	61.1	4.56
Russia	67.2	1.25
South Africa	51.1	2.47
United Kingdom	77.7	1.73
United States	77.1	2.06
Zimbabwe	37.8	3.34

Source: Statistical Abstract of the United States (Washington, D.C.: U.S. Department of Commerce, Economics and Statistics Administration, U.S. Census Bureau, 2000), Table 1355.

APPENDIX F:

PERCENTAGE OF WOMEN IN PARLIAMENTS*
1975, 1999

	1975	1999
Developed regions		
Eastern Europe	25	10
Western Europe and other	7	18–21
Africa		
Northern	2	3
Sub-Saharan	4.5	10
Latin America and Caribbean	5	13
Asia and Pacific		
East/Southeast Asia	9.5	12–13
Southern	4.5	5
Western	2	5
Oceania	1	3

*Parliament = unicameral assembly or lower chamber of bicameral assembly

Sources: *The World's Women 1970–1990: Trends and Statistics* (New York: United Nations, 1991), 32; *The World's Women 2000: Trends and Statistics* (New York: United Nations, 2000), 164.

APPENDIX G:

WOMEN IN POLITICAL OFFICE, UNITED STATES, 1980, 2001

Women Elected Officials (of total)	1980 All women		2001 All Women		2001 Women of color	
	n	(%)	n	(%)	n	(%)
Congress (535)	20	(4.0)	73	(13.6)	22[1]	(4.1)
Senate (100)	1	(1.0)	13	(13.0)	0	(0.0)
House (435)	19	(4.0)	60	(13.8)	22	(5.1)
Statewide executive (322)	34	(10.5)	88	(27.3)	5	(1.6)
State legislatures (7,424)[2]	908	(12.2)	1,663	(22.4)	266	(3.6)
State senates (1,984)	138	(7.0)	396	(20.0)	73	(3.7)
State houses (5,440)	770	(14.2)	1,267	(23.3)	193	(3.5)
Mayors of U.S. cities with population over						
30,000 (975)	n/a	n/a	209	(21.4)	n/a	n/a
170,000 (100)	10	(10.0)	13	(13.0)	2	(2.0)

[1]Number reflects twenty women in Congress, and two delegates to the House from Washington, D.C., and the Virgin Islands.
[2]Number of legislators reflects 2001 totals (n=7424).

Source: Center for the American Woman and Politics (CAWP), National Information Bank on Women in Public Office, Eagleton Institute of Politics, Rutgers University. *U.S. Mayor Newspaper* 66:111 (June 28,1999).

BIBLIOGRAPHIC NOTES

In addition to the endnotes, which credit sources of quotations and selected data, the following works contributed significantly to each chapter.

CHAPTER ONE: THE HISTORICAL CASE FOR FEMINISM

On the origins of the term *feminism*, see Karen Offen, "Defining Feminism: A Comparative Historical Approach," *Signs* 14:1 (1988), 119–57, and Leila Rupp, "Feminist Movements," in *International Encyclopedia of the Social Sciences*, eds. Neil J. Smelser and Paul B. Bultes (New York: Elsevier Sciences, forthcoming) Nancy Cott, *The Grounding of Modern Feminism* (New Haven: Yale University Press, 1987) describes the U.S. struggles over terminology; see also her "What's in a Name: The Limits of Social Feminism," *Journal of American History* 76:3 (1989), 809–29. On international women's movements, see Leila Rupp, *Worlds of Women: The Making of an International Women's Movement* (Princeton: Princeton University Press, 1997) and Amrita Basu, ed., *The Challenge of Local Feminisms: Women's Movements in Global Perspective* (Boulder: Westview Press, 1995). Joni Seager, *The State of Women in the World Atlas* (London: Penguin, 1997) provides an excellent comparison of vital data across countries. On media coverage of feminism, see Susan Faludi, *Backlash: The Undeclared War Against American Women* (New York: Crown, 1991) and "Feminists Want to Know: Is the Media Dead?" in Jennifer Baumgardner and Amy Richards, eds., *Manifesta: Young Women, Feminism and the Future* (New York: Farrar, Straus, and Giroux, 2000), 87.

For overviews of Anglo-American feminist scholarship, see two collections edited by Juliet Mitchell and Ann Oakley: *What Is Feminism: A Re-Examination* (New York: Pantheon Books, 1986) and *Who's Afraid of Feminism* (New York: The New Press, 1997). On the growth of feminist scholarship in the United States, see Ellen Carol DuBois, Gail Paradise Kelly, Elizabeth Lapovsky Kennedy, Carolyn W. Lorsmeyer, and Lillian S. Robinson, *Feminist Scholarship: Kindling in the Groves of Academe* (Urbana: University of Illinois Press, 1987).

CHAPTER TWO: GENDER AND POWER

On the cross-cultural analysis of gender, see Michelle Zimbalist Rosaldo, "Woman, Culture, and Society: A Theoretical Overview," in *Woman, Culture, and Society*, eds. Michelle Zimbalist Rosaldo and Louise Lamphere (Stanford: Stanford University

Press, 1974), 17–42 (and other essays in this volume); Michelle Zimbalist Rosaldo, "The Use and Abuse of Anthropology," *Signs* 5:3 (1980), 389–417; Jane F. Collier and Michelle Zimbalist Rosaldo, "Politics and Gender in Simple Societies," in *Sexual Meanings: The Cultural Construction of Gender and Sexuality*, eds. Sherry B. Ortner and Harriet Whitehead (Cambridge: Cambridge University Press, 1981), 275–329 (and other essays in this volume); and Louise Lamphere, "The Domestic Sphere of Women and the Public World of Men: The Strengths and Limitations of an Anthropological Dichotomy," in *Gender in Cross-Cultural Perspective*, eds. Caroline B. Brettell and Carolyn F. Sargent (Upper Saddle River, N.J.: Prentice Hall, 1997), 82–92 (and other essays in this volume).

Origin stories, kinship, and the long historical view appear in Peggy Sanday, *Female Power and Male Dominance: On the Origins of Sexual Inequality* (Cambridge: Cambridge University Press, 1981); Eleanor Leacock, "Women's Status in Egalitarian Society: Implications for Social Evolution," *Current Anthropology* 19:2 (1978), 247–55; an important theoretical essay by Gayle Rubin, "The Traffic in Women: Notes on the 'Political Economy' of Sex," in *Toward an Anthropology of Women*, ed. Rayna Rapp (New York: Monthly Review Press, 1975), 157–210 (and other essays in this volume); Jane Fishburne Collier and Sylvia Junko Yanagisako, *Gender and Kinship: Essays Towards a Unified Analysis* (Stanford: Stanford University Press, 1987); and Gerda Lerner, *The Creation of Patriarchy* (New York: Oxford University Press, 1986). On Vanatinai Island, see Maria Lepowsky, *Fruit of the Motherland: Gender in an Egalitarian Society* (New York: Columbia University Press, 1993).

Studies of native gender relations in the Americas and the impact of Europeans include Joan Jensen, "Native American Women and Agriculture: A Seneca Case Study," in *Unequal Sisters: A Multi-Cultural Reader in U.S. Women's History*, eds. Ellen Carol DuBois and Vicki L. Ruiz, 1st ed. (New York: Routledge, 1990), 51–65; Irene Silverblatt, *Moon, Sun and Witches: Gender Ideologies and Class in Inca and Colonial Peru* (Princeton: Princeton University Press, 1987); and Elinor Burkett, "Indian Women and White Society: The Case of Sixteenth Century Peru," in *Latin American Women: Historical Perspectives*, ed. Asuncion Lavrin (Westport, Conn.: Greenwood Press, 1978).

For Africa, I draw especially on Ester Boserup, *Woman's Role in Economic Development* (New York: St. Martin's Press, 1970); Simi Afonja, "Changing Patterns of Gender Stratification in West Africa," in *Persistent Inequalities: Women and World Development*, ed. Irene Tinker (New York, Oxford University Press, 1990), 198–209; Richard Roberts, "Women's Work and Women's Property: Household Social Relations in the Maraka Textile Industry of the Nineteenth Century," *Comparative Studies in Society and History* 26:2 (1984), 229–50; Iris Berger and E. Frances White, *Women in Sub-Saharan Africa: Restoring Women to History* (Bloomington: Indiana University Press, 1999); and Jean Davison, *Agriculture, Women, and Land: The African Experience* (Boulder: Westview Press, 1988).

The following studies of gender relations in Chinese history proved extremely useful: Judith Stacey, "When Patriarchy Kowtows: The Significance of the Chinese Family Revolution for Feminist Theory," *Feminist Studies* 2:2–3 (1975), 64–112; Janice Stockard, *Daughters of the Canton Delta: Marriage Patterns and Economic Strategies in South China, 1860–1930* (Stanford: Stanford University Press, 1989); Francesca Bray, *Technology and Gender: Fabrics of Power in Late Imperial China* (Berkeley: University of California Press, 1997); Patricia Buckley Ebrey, *The Inner Quarter: Marriage and the Lives of Chinese Women in the Sung Period* (Berkeley: University of California Press, 1993); Hill Gates, *China's Motor: A Thousand Years of Petty Capitalism* (Ithaca: Cornell University Press, 1996); Dorothy Ko, *Teachers of the Inner Chambers: Women and Culture in Seventeenth Century China* (Stanford: Stanford University Press, 1994); Margery Wolf, *Women and the Family in Rural Taiwan* (Stanford: Stanford University Press, 1972) and *Revolution Postponed: Women in Contemporary China* (Stanford: Stanford University Press, 1985); Barbara N. Ramusack and Sharon Sievers, *Women in Asia: Restoring Women to History* (Bloomington: Indiana University Press, 1999); Susan Mann, *Precious Records: Women in China's Long Eighteenth Century* (Stanford: Stanford University Press, 1997); Emily Honig, *Sisters and Strangers: Women in the Shanghai Cotton Mills, 1919–1949* (Stanford: Stanford University Press, 1986).

For an excellent collection of essays on European women's history, see the various editions of *Becoming Visible*, eds. Renate Bridenthal and Claudia Koonz (Boston: Houghton Mifflin, 1977), including Joan Kelley, "Did Women Have a Renaissance?" 137–64. Throughout this book I draw heavily on the encyclopedic survey by Bonnie S. Anderson and Judith P. Zinsser, *A History of Their Own: Women in Europe from Prehistory to the Present*, 2 vols. (New York: Harper and Row, 1988). See also Judith Shaver Hughes and Brady Hughes, *Women in Ancient Civilizations* (Washington: American Historical Association, 1998); Judith M. Bennett, "Medieval Women, Modern Women: Across the Divide," in *Culture and History 1350–1600: Essays on English Communities, Identities and Writing*, ed. David Aers (London: Harvester Wheatsheaf, 1992), 147–75; Natalie Zemon Davis, *Women on the Margins: Three Seventeenth-Century Lives* (Cambridge: Harvard University Press, 1995); Susan Moller Okin, *Women in Western Political Thought* (Princeton: Princeton University Press, 1979); Gerda Lerner, *The Creation of Feminist Consciousness: From the Middle Ages to 1870* (New York: Oxford University Press, 1993); Erna Olafson Hellerstein, Leslie Parker Hume, and Karen M. Offen, eds., *Victorian Women: A Documentary Account of Women's Lives in Nineteenth-Century England, France and the United States*, assoc. eds. Estelle Freedman, Barbara Gelpi, and Marilyn Yalom (Stanford: Stanford University Press, 1981). On the colonial encounter, see Margaret Strobel, *Gender, Sex, and Empire* (Washington: American Historical Association, 1993), and Strobel and Nupur Chaudhuri, *Western Women and Imperialism: Complicity and Resistance* (Bloomington: University of Indiana Press, 1991); Ann Laura Stoler and Frederick Cooper, eds., *Tensions of Empire: Colonial Cultures in a Bourgeois World* (Berkeley: University of California Press, 1997), and see below, Chapter 6.

CHAPTER THREE: WOMEN'S RIGHTS, WOMEN'S WORK, AND WOMEN'S SPHERE

On European feminisms, see Bonnie S. Anderson and Judith P. Zinsser, *A History of Their Own: Women in Europe from Prehistory to the Present* (New York: Harper and Row, 1988), vol. II; Gerda Lerner, *Creation of Feminist Consciousness* (New York: Oxford University Press, 1993); Bonnie S. Anderson, *Joyous Greetings: The First International Women's Movement, 1830–1860* (Oxford: Oxford University Press, 2000); Joan Scott, *Only Paradoxes to Offer: French Feminists and the Rights of Man* (Cambridge: Harvard University Press, 1996); Karen Offen, *European Feminisms, 1700–1950: A Political History* (Stanford: Stanford University Press, 2000); Marion Kaplan, *The Jewish Feminist Movement in Germany: The Campaigns of the Jüdischer Frauenbund, 1904–1938* (Westport, Conn.: Greenwood Press, 1979); Ray Strachey, *The Cause: A Short History of the Women's Movement in Great Britain* (London: Virago, 1978 [1928]); Judith R. Walkowitz, *Prostitution in Victorian Society: Women, Class, and the State* (Cambridge: Cambridge University Press, 1980); Marilyn J. Boxer and Jean H. Quataert, *Socialist Women: European Socialist Feminism in the Nineteenth and Early Twentieth Centuries* (New York: Elsevier North-Holland, 1978); Barbara Engel, "Women as Revolutionaries: The Case of the Russian Populists," in *Becoming Visible: Women in European History*, eds. Renate Bridenthal and Claudia Koonz (Boston: Houghton Mifflin, 1977). On Scandinavia see Ida Blom, "Nation, Class, Gender: Scandinavia at the Turn of the Century," *Scandinavian Journal of History* 21:1 (1996), 1–16; Ingrid Aberg, "Revivalism, Philanthropy and Emancipation: Women's Liberation and Organization in the Early Nineteenth Century," *Scandinavian Journal of History* 13:4 (1988), 399–420.

On the United States see Linda Kerber, *Women of the Republic: Intellect and Ideology in Revolutionary America* (Chapel Hill: University of North Carolina Press, 1980); Alice Rossi, *The Feminist Papers: From Adams to de Beauvoir* (New York: Columbia University Press, 1973); Evelyn Brooks Higginbotham, *Righteous Discontent: The Women's Movement in the Black Baptist Church, 1880–1920* (Cambridge: Harvard University Press, 1993); Mary Ryan, *Cradle of the Middle Class: The Family in Oneida County, New York, 1790–1865* (Cambridge: Cambridge University Press, 1981); and Carroll Smith-Rosenberg, *Disorderly Conduct: Visions of Gender in Victorian America* (New York: Oxford University Press, 1986). On Charlotte Perkins Gilman, see Carl Degler's introduction to Gilman's *Women and Economics: A Study of the Economic Relation Between Men and Women* (New York: Harper and Row, 1966 [1898]); Louise Michelle Newman, *White Women's Rights: The Racial Origins of Feminism in the United States* (New York: Oxford University Press, 1999); and Gail Bederman, *Manliness and Civilization: A Cultural History of Gender and Race in the United States, 1880–1917* (Chicago: University of Chicago Press, 1995). Steven Buechler, *Women's Movements in the United States: Woman Suffrage, Equal Rights, and Beyond* (New Brunswick: Rutgers University Press, 1990) provides an overview, while Seth Koven and Sonya Michel's edited collection *Mothers of a New World: Maternalist Politics and the Origins of Welfare States* (New York: Routledge, 1993) offers comparative perspectives on maternalism. See also Daniel Horowitz, *Betty Friedan and the Making of the Feminine Mystique: The American Left, the Cold War, and Modern Feminism* (Amherst: University of Massachusetts Press, 1988).

On Latin America, see especially Nina M. Scott, " 'If You Are Not Pleased to Favor Me, Put Me Out of Your Mind . . .': Gender and Authority in Sor Juana Inés de la Cruz and the Translation of the Letter to the Reverend Father Maestro Antonio Núñez of the Society of Jesus," *Women's Studies International Forum* 11:5 (1988), 429–38, and "Sor Juana Inés de la Cruz: 'Let Your Women Keep Silence in the Churches . . .' " *Women's Studies International Forum* 8:5 (1985), 511–19; Francesca Miller, *Latin American Women and the Search for Social Justice* (Hanover, N.H.: University Press of New England, 1991); the special issue of the *Pacific Historical Review* 69:4 (2000) on suffrage in the Americas; June E. Hahner, *Emancipating the Female Sex: The Struggle for Women's Rights in Brazil, 1850–1940* (Durham: Duke University Press, 1990); Sylvia Arrom, *The Women of Mexico City, 1790–1857* (Stanford: Stanford University Press, 1985); and Evelyn Stevens, "Marianismo: The Other Face of Machismo in Latin America," in *Female and Male in Latin America: Essays*, ed. Ann Pescatello (Pittsburgh: University of Pittsburgh Press, 1977). On Japan, see Sharon Sievers, *Flowers in Salt: The Beginnings of Feminist Consciousness in Modern Japan* (Stanford: Stanford University Press, 1983).

CHAPTER FOUR: RACE AND THE POLITICS OF IDENTITY IN U.S. FEMINISM

Overviews of the early women's rights and feminist movements in the United States include Eleanor Flexner, *Century of Struggle: The Woman's Rights Movement in the United States* (Cambridge: Belknap Press of Harvard University Press, 1959, reprinted 1996) and Steven Buechler, *Women's Movements in the U.S.: Woman Suffrage, Equal Rights, and Beyond* (New Brunswick: Rutgers University Press, 1990). On racial conflicts in the nineteenth century, see Ellen Carol Dubois, *Feminism and Suffrage: The Emergence of An Independent Women's Movement in America, 1848–1869* (Ithaca: Cornell University Press, 1978), Louise Michelle Newman, *White Women's Rights: The Racial Origins of Feminism in the United States* (New York: Oxford University Press, 1999) and Aileen Kraditor, *The Ideas of the Woman Suffrage Movement, 1890–1920* (New York: W. W. Norton, 1965). On changing female consciousness see Nancy Cott, *The Bonds of Womanhood: "Woman's Sphere" in New England, 1780–1835*, (New Haven: Yale University Press, 1977), and *The Grounding of Modern Feminism* (New Haven: Yale University Press, 1987). In addition to Sara Evans' discussion of the origins of radical feminism in *Personal Politics: The Roots of Women's Liberation in the Civil Rights Movement and the New Left* (New York: Vintage Books, 1979), Ruth Rosen provides a thorough account of second-wave movements in *The World Split Open: How the Modern Women's Movement Changed America* (New York: Viking, 2000). Alice Echols, *Daring to Be Bad: Radical Feminism in America, 1967–1975* (Minneapolis: University of Minnesota Press, 1989) critiques cultural feminism.

Primary sources not otherwise cited in the text include Shulamith Firestone, *The Dialectic of Sex: The Case for Feminist Revolution* (New York: Morrow, 1970); Robin Morgan, ed., *Sisterhood Is Powerful: An Anthology of Writings from the Women's Liberation Movement* (New York: Random House, 1970); Anne Koedt, Ellen Levine, and Anita Rapone, eds., *Radical Feminism* (New York: Quadrangle, 1973). Several recent books collect sources from U.S. feminism: Karen Kahn, ed., *Frontline Feminism, 1975–1985: Essays from Sojourner's First 20 Years* (San Francisco: Aunt Lute, 1995); Barbara A. Crow, ed., *Radical Feminism: A Documentary Reader* (New York: New York University Press, 2000) and Rosalyn Baxandall and Linda Gordon, eds., *Dear Sisters: Dispatches From the Women's Liberation Movement* (New York: Basic Books, 2000).

On the relationship of women's movements to slavery, abolitionism, emancipation, and lynching, see Deborah Gray White, *Ar'n't I a Woman: Female Slaves in the Plantation South* (New York: W. W. Norton, 1985) and *Too Heavy a Load: Black Women in Defense of Themselves, 1894–1994* (New York: W. W. Norton, 1999); Shirley J. Lee, *Black Women Abolitionists: A Study in Activism, 1828–1860* (Knoxville: University of Tennessee Press, 1992); Lora Romero, *Home Fronts: Domesticity and its Critics in the Antebellum United States* (Durham: Duke University Press, 1997); Nell Irwin Painter, *Sojourner Truth: A Life, a Symbol* (New York: W. W. Norton, 1996); Gerda Lerner, *The Grimké Sisters from South Carolina: Pioneers for Woman's Rights and Abolition* (New York: Schocken Books, 1971); Jacquelyn Dowd Hall, *Revolt Against Chivalry: Jessie Daniel Ames and the Women's Campaign Against Lynching* (New York: Columbia University Press, 1979); and essays in Kimberly Springer, ed., *Still Lifting, Still Climbing: African American Women's Contemporary Activism* (New York: New York University Press, 1999).

Important contemporary works by African American feminists include bell hooks, *Ain't I a Woman: Black Women and Feminism* (Boston: South End Press, 1981) and *Feminist Theory: From Margins to Center* (Boston: South End Press, 1984, reprinted 2000); Angela Y. Davis, *Women, Race and Class* (New York: Random House, 1981); Gloria T. Hull, Patricia Bell Scott, and Barbara Smith, eds., *All the Women Are White, All the Men Are Black, but Some of Us Are Brave* (Old Westbury, N.Y.: Feminist Press, 1982); Audre Lorde, *Zami: A New Spelling of My Name* (Watertown, Mass.: Persephone Press, 1982); Barbara Smith, ed., *Home Girls: A Black Feminist Anthology* (New Brunswick: Rutgers University Press, 2000), and *The Truth That Never Hurts: Writings on Race, Gender, and Freedom* (New Brunswick: Rutgers University Press, 1998); Patricia Hill Collins, *Black Feminist Thought: Knowledge, Consciousness, and the Politics of Empowerment* (Boston: Unwin Hyman, 1990, reprinted 2000).

Organizing among women of color is discussed in Judy Yung, *Unbound Feet: A Social History of Chinese Women in San Francisco* (Berkeley: University of California Press, 1995); Karen Anderson, *Changing Woman: A History of Racial Ethnic Women in Modern America* (New York: Oxford University Press, 1996); and Vicki L. Ruiz, *From*

Out of the Shadows: Mexican Women in Twentieth-Century America (New York: Oxford University Press, 1998). On intercultural relations among women, see Peggy Pascoe, *Relations of Rescue: The Search for Female Moral Authority in the American West, 1874–1939* (New York: Oxford University Press, 1990). Paula Gunn Allen writes about Native American women's history and culture in *The Sacred Hoop: Recovering the Feminine in American Indian Traditions* (Boston: Beacon Press, 1992).

Contemporary Chicana feminism is the subject of Alma M. García, "The Development of Chicana Feminist Discourse, 1970–1980," in *Unequal Sisters: A Multicultural Reader in U.S. Women's History*, eds. Vicki L. Ruiz and Ellen Carol DuBois, 1st ed. (New York: Routledge, 1990), 418–31, and Alma M. García, ed., *Chicana Feminist Thought: The Basic Historical Writings* (New York: Routledge, 1997); Beatriz M. Pesquera and Denise A. Segura, "There Is No Going Back: Chicanas and Feminism," in *Chicana Critical Issues*, eds. Norma Alarcon et al. (Berkeley: Third Woman Press, 1993); Ramón Gutiérrez, "Community, Patriarchy, and Individualism: The Politics of Chicano History and the Dream of Equality," in *Unequal Sisters: A Multicultural Reader in U.S. Women's History*, eds. Vicki L. Ruiz and Ellen Carol DuBois, 3rd ed. (New York: Routledge, 2000), 587–606. Gloria Anzaldúa, *Borderlands/La Frontera: The New Mestiza* (San Francisco: Spinsters/Aunt Lute, 1987) and *Making Face, Making Soul/Haciendo Caras: Creative and Critical Perspectives by Feminists of Color* (San Francisco: Aunt Lute Books, 1990) document the politics of multiple identity since the 1970s, as does Anzaldúa and Cherríe Moraga, eds., *This Bridge Called My Back: Writings by Radical Women of Color* (Watertown, Mass.: Persephone Press, 1981). See also Cherríe Moraga, *Loving in the War Years: Lo Que Nunca Pasó Por Sus Labios* (Boston: South End Press, 1983) and M. Jacqui Alexander, ed., *Third Wave: Feminist Perspectives on Racism* (Brooklyn: Kitchen Table/Women of Color Press, 1994).

On women in labor, pacifist, and liberal movements, see Dorothy Sue Cobble, "Recapturing Working-Class Feminism: Union Women in the Postwar Era," in *Not June Cleaver: Women and Gender in Postwar America, 1945–1960*, ed. Joanne Meyerowitz (Philadelphia: Temple University Press, 1994), 56–83; Susan Lynn, *Progressive Women in Conservative Times: Racial Justice, Peace, and Feminism, 1945 to the 1960s* (New Brunswick: Rutgers University Press, 1992); Susan Hartmann, *The Other Feminists: Activists in the Liberal Establishment* (New Haven: Yale University Press, 1998); and Blanche Wiesen Cook, *Eleanor Roosevelt* (New York: Viking, 1992). On women's racist activities, see Kathleen M. Blee, *Women of the Klan: Racism and Gender in the 1920s* (Berkeley: University of California Press, 1991).

Important contemporary explorations of race, racism, and identities include Bettina Aptheker, "Race and Class: Patriarchal Politics and Women's Experience," *Women's Studies Quarterly* 10:4 (1982), 10–15; Ruth Frankenberg, *White Women, Race Matters: The Social Construction of Whiteness* (Minneapolis: University of Minnesota Press, 1993); Vron Ware, *Beyond the Pale: White Women, Racism, and History* (London: Verso, 1992); Elizabeth V. Spelman, *Inessential Woman: Problems of Exclusion in Femi-*

nist Thought (Boston: Beacon Press, 1988); Diana Fuss, *Essentially Speaking: Feminism, Nature and Difference* (New York: Routledge, 1989); Donna Haraway, "A Cyborg Manifesto: Science, Technology, and Socialist-Feminism in the Late Twentieth Century," in *Simians, Cyborgs, and Women: The Reinvention of Nature*, (New York: Routledge, 1991); Judith Butler, *Gender Trouble: Feminism and the Subversion of Identity* (New York: Routledge, 1990); Chela Sandoval, "U.S. Third World Feminism: The Theory and Method of Oppositional Consciousness in the Postmodern World," *Genders* 10 (1991), 1–24; Maria C. Lugones and Elizabeth V. Spelman, "Have We Got a Theory for You! Feminist Theory, Cultural Imperialism and the Demand for 'The Woman's Voice,' " *Women's Studies International Forum* 6:6 (1983), 573–81; Linda Martín Alcoff, "Cultural Feminism vs. Poststructuralism: The Identity Crisis in Feminist Theory," *Signs* 13:3 (1988), 405–36 and "Philosophy and Racial Identity," *Philosophy Today* (spring, 1997), 67–76; Paula M. L. Moya, "Chicana Feminism and Postmodernist Theory," *Signs* 26:2 (2001), 441–83, and *Reclaiming Identity: Realist Theory and the Predicament of Postmodernism*, eds. Paula M. L. Moya and Michael R. Hames-García (Berkeley: University of California Press, 2000); and essays in Teresa de Lauretis, ed., *Feminist Studies/Critical Studies* (Bloomington: Indiana University Press, 1986). On the use of experience in feminist theory, see, e.g., Patricia J. Williams, *The Alchemy of Race and Rights: Diary of a Law Professor* (Cambridge: Harvard University Press, 1991). For a critique, see Joan Scott, "The Evidence of Experience," *Critical Inquiry* 17:4 (1991), 773–97.

CHAPTER FIVE: THE GLOBAL STAGE AND THE POLITICS OF LOCATION

For overviews of the history of gender and colonialism, see Margaret Strobel, *Gender, Sex, and Empire* (Washington, D.C.: American Historical Association, 1993) and Strobel and Nupur Chaudhuri, eds., *Western Women and Imperialism: Complicity and Resistance* (Bloomington: Indiana University Press, 1992); and Clare Midgley, *Gender and Imperialism* (New York: Manchester University Press, 1998). Influential interpretations of women and empire appear in Ann L. Stoler, "Making Empire Respectable: The Politics of Race and Sexual Morality in Twentieth-Century Colonial Cultures," *American Ethnologist* 16:4 (1989), 634–60, and Anne McClintock, *Imperial Leather: Race, Gender and Sexuality in the Colonial Conquest* (New York: Routledge, 1994). Chandra Mohanty, "Under Western Eyes: Feminist Scholarship and Colonial Discourses," *Feminist Review* 30 (1988), 61–85, critiques early feminist studies of women outside the West. See also Jane Hunter, *The Gospel of Gentility: American Women Missionaries in Turn-of-the-Century China* (New Haven: Yale University Press, 1984); M. Jacqui Alexander and Chandra Talpade Mohanty, eds., *Feminist Genealogies, Colonial Legacies, Democratic Futures* (New York: Routledge, 1997); Aihwa Ong, "Colonialism and Modernity: Feminist Representations of Women in Non-Western Societies," in *Theorizing Feminism: Parallel Trends in the Humanities and Social Sciences*, eds. Anne C. Hermann and Abigail J. Stewart (Boulder: Westview

Press, 1994), 372–81; and Caren Kaplan, "The Politics of Location as Transnational Feminist Practice," in Inderpal Grewal and Caren Kaplan, eds., *Scattered Hegemonies: Postmodernity and Transnational Feminist Practices* (Minneapolis: University of Minnesota Press, 1994).

The literature on India includes Lata Mani, "Contentious Traditions: The Debate on *Sati* in Colonial India," in *Recasting Women: Essays in Colonial History*, eds. Kumkum Sangari and Sudesh Vaid (New Delhi: Kali for Women, 1989), 88–125; Antoinette M. Burton, *Burdens of History: British Feminists, Indian Women, and Imperial Culture, 1865–1915* (Chapel Hill: University of North Carolina Press, 1994); Mrinalini Sinha, "Introduction to Katherine Mayo," in *Mother India*, ed. Mrinalini Sinha (Ann Arbor: University of Michigan Press, 2000 [1927]). Radha Kumar provides a comprehensive history of women's movements in India in *The History of Doing: An Illustrated Account of Movements for Women's Rights and Feminism in India, 1800–1990* (London: Verso, 1993). See also Ivy George, "Shakti and Sati: Women, Religion and Development," in *Religion, Feminism, and the Family*, eds. Anne Carr and Mary Stewart Van Leeuwen (Louisville: Westminster John Knox Press, 1996); Shakuntala Rao, "Woman-as-Symbol: The Intersection of Identity Politics, Gender, and Indian Nationalism," *Women's Studies International Forum* 22:3 (May–June, 1999), 317–28; Aparna Basu, "Feminism and Nationalism in India, 1917–1947," *Journal of Women's History* 7:4 (1995), 95–107; and Amrita Basu, "Women's Activism and the Vicissitudes of Hindu Nationalism," *Journal of Women's History* 10:4 (1999), 104–24. Rokeya Sakhawat Hossain's *Sultana's Dream* has been reprinted as *Sultana's Dream and Selections from The Secluded Ones*, trans. and ed. Roushan Jahan (New York: Feminist Press, 1988 [1905]).

For historical overviews of gender and feminism in the Middle East, see Judith Tucker, *Gender and Islamic History* (Washington, D.C.: American Historical Association, 1993) and Beth Baron and Nikki Keddie, eds., *Women in Middle Eastern History* (New Haven: Yale University Press, 1991). Important regional and national studies include Deniz Kandiyoti, ed., *Gendering the Middle East: Emerging Perspectives* (London: I. B. Tauris, 1996) and *Women, Islam, and the State* (Philadelphia: Temple University Press, 1991); Margot Badran, *Feminists, Islam, and the Nation: Gender and the Making of Modern Egypt* (Princeton: Princeton University Press, 1995) and Badran and Miriam Cook, eds., *Opening the Gates: A Century of Arab Feminist Writing* (London: Virago, 1990); Maryam Poya, *Women, Work and Islamism: Ideology and Resistance in Iran* (London: Zed Books, 1999); Carol Delaney, "Father State, Motherland, and the Birth of Modern Turkey," in *Naturalizing Power: Essays in Feminist Cultural Analysis*, eds. Sylvia Yanagisako and Carol Delaney (New York: Routledge, 1995), 177–99. Key works by Nawal El Saadawi include *The Hidden Face of Eve: Women in the Arab World*, trans. and ed. Sherif Hetata (London: Zed Books, 1980) and Saadawi, ed., *The Nawal El Saadawi Reader* (London: Zed Books, 1997).

On international and regional feminist organizing see Leila Rupp, *Worlds of Women: The Making of an International Women's Movement* (Princeton: Princeton University Press, 1997) and Rupp and Verta Taylor, "Forging Feminist Identity in an International Movement: A Collective Identity Approach to Twentieth-Century Feminism," *Signs* 24:2 (1999), 374; Ellen Carol DuBois, "Woman Suffrage Around the World: Three Phases of Suffragist Internationalism," in *Suffrage and Beyond: International Feminist Perspectives*, eds. Caroline Daley and Melanie Nolan (New York: New York University Press, 1994), 252–74. For national political contexts see Barbara J. Nelson and Najma Chowdhury, eds., *Women and Politics Worldwide* (New Haven: Yale University Press, 1994) and Amrita Basu, ed., *The Challenge of Local Feminisms: Women's Movements in Global Perspective* (Boulder: Westview Press, 1995), as well as essays in *Global Feminisms Since 1945: Rewriting Histories*, ed. Bonnie G. Smith (London: Routledge, 2000) and *Scattered Hegemonies: Postmodernity and Transnational Feminist Practices*, eds. Inderpal Grewal and Caren Kaplan (Minneapolis: University of Minnesota Press, 1994). For current scholarship see the special issue on Globalization and Gender, *Signs* 26:4 (2001).

On the United Nations see Arvonne S. Fraser, *The U.N. Decade for Women: Documents and Dialogue* (Boulder: Westview Press, 1987) and "Images of Nairobi: Reflections and Follow-up," *Decade for Women Information Resources* 5 (New York: International Women's Tribune Center/United Nations, 1986). On development policies, see Lourdes Beneria and Gita Sen, "Accumulation, Reproduction, and Women's Role in Economic Development: Boserup Revisited," *Signs* 7:2 (1981), 279–98; Naila Kabeer, *Reversed Realities: Gender Hierarchies in Development Thought* (London: Verso, 1994); Helen Zweifel, "The Gendered Nature of Biodiversity Conservation," *NWSA Journal*, 9:3 (1997) 106–16; and Martha C. Nussbaum and Jonathan Glover, eds., *Women, Culture, and Development: A Study of Human Capabilities* (New York: Oxford University Press, 1995). See also Martha C. Nussbaum, *Women and Human Development: The Capabilities Approach* (Cambridge: Cambridge University Press, 2000).

For Latin American movements, see Jane Jaquette, ed., *The Women's Movement in Latin America: Participation and Democracy*, 2nd ed. (Boulder: Westview Press, 1994); Nancy Saporto Sternbach, Marysa Navarro-Arangurnen, Patricia Chuchryk, and Sonia Alvarez, "Feminisms in Latin America: From Bogota to San Bernardo," *Signs* 17:2 (1992), 393–434; June E. Hahner, *Emancipating the Female Sex: The Struggle for Women's Rights in Brazil, 1850–1940* (Durham: Duke University Press, 1990); Carmen Diana Deere and Magdalena León, *Rural Women and State Policy: Feminist Perspectives on Latin American Agricultural Development* (Boulder: Westview Press, 1987); and Sonia E. Alvarez, *Engendering Democracy in Brazil: Women's Movements in Transition Politics* (Princeton: Princeton University Press, 1990).

CHAPTER SIX: NEVER DONE: WOMEN'S DOMESTIC LABOR

On the ideology and labor of domesticity in the United States, see Kathryn Kish Sklar, *Catharine Beecher: A Study in Domesticity* (New Haven: Yale University Press,

1973); Nancy F. Cott, *The Bonds of Womanhood: "Woman's Sphere" in New England, 1780–1835*, (New Haven: Yale University Press, 1977); Jeanne Boydston, *Home and Work: Housework, Wages, and the Ideology of Labor in the Early Republic* (New York: Oxford University Press, 1990); and Glenna Matthews, *"Just a Housewife": The Rise and Fall of Domesticity in America* (New York: Oxford University Press, 1987). Ann Oakley, *Woman's Work: The Housewife Past and Present* (New York: Random House, 1976) first raised many feminist critiques. Calculations of the value of housework, based on U.S. Department of Labor statistics, appear in Hunter College Women's Studies Collective, *Women's Realities, Women's Choices: An Introduction to Women's Studies* (New York: Oxford University Press, 1995), Table 13.1, 459, and from the U.N. Development Programme, *The Human Development Report 1995* (New York: Oxford University Press, 1995), 6.

Data on time spent in housework come from: *The World's Women, 2000: Trends and Statistics* (New York: United Nations, 2000), 126; *The World's Women, 1995: Trends and Statistics* (New York: United Nations, 1995), 106, and *The World's Women 1970–1990: Trends and Statistics* (New York: United Nations, 1991); Frances K. Goldscheider and Linda J. Waite, *New Families, No Families* (Berkeley: University of California Press, 1991), 113; Arlie Russell Hochschild (with Anne Manchung), *The Second Shift: Working Parents and the Revolution at Home* (New York: Viking, 1989); Daphne Spain and Suzanne M. Bianchi, *Balancing Act: Motherhood, Marriage, and Employment Among American Women* (New York: Russell Sage Foundation, 1996); John P. Robinson, "Who's Doing the Housework?" *American Demographics* 10:12 (1988), 24–29; Janeen Baxter, "Gender Equality and Participation in Housework: A Cross-National Perspective," *Journal of Comparative Family Studies* 28:3 (1997), 220–47; Andrew J. Cherlin, "By the Numbers," *New York Times Magazine*, 5 April 1998, 39–41; Joseph Pleck, "Balancing Work and Family," *Scientific American Presents* 10:2 (1999), 38–43; and Jeevan Vasagar, *The Guardian* (London), 6 July 2001, reporting on Man Yee Kan study. On problems with self-reported housework studies, see Julie Press and Eleanor Townsley, "Wives' and Husbands' Housework Reporting: Gender, Class, and Social Desirability," *Gender and Society* 12:2 (1998), 188–218. Results of the California poll appeared in the "The New Attitudes of Men and Women," *San Francisco Chronicle*, 13 February 1986, A20. For the effects of labor-saving devices, see Ruth Schwartz Cowan, *More Work for Mother: The Ironies of Household Technology from the Open Hearth to the Microwave* (New York: Basic Books, 1983).

Sources for women's caring and emotional work include Marjorie L. DeVault, *Feeding the Family: The Social Organization of Caring as Gendered Work* (Chicago: University of Chicago Press, 1991); Elizabeth H. Pleck, *Celebrating the Family: Ethnicity, Consumer Culture, and Family Rituals* (Cambridge: Harvard University Press, 2000); Susan Krieger, *The Family Silver: Essays on Relationships Among Women* (Berkeley: University of California Press, 1996); Takako Sodei, "Care of the Elderly: A Women's Issue," in *Japanese Women: New Feminist Perspectives on the Past, Present, and*

Future, eds. Kumiko Fujimura-Fanselow and Atsuko Kameda (New York: The Feminist Press, 1995), 213–28; and Melba Sánchez-Ayéndez, "Puerto Rican Elderly Women: Shared Meanings and Informal Supportive Networks," in *All American Women: Lines That Divide, Ties That Bind*, ed. Johnetta Cole (New York: The Free Press, 1986).

Nancy Chodorow, *The Reproduction of Mothering: Psychoanalysis and the Sociology of Gender* (Berkeley: University of California Press, 1978), set the stage for much interdisciplinary literature on the meaning of motherhood. For critiques, see Judith Lorber et al., "On *The Reproduction of Mothering*: A Methodological Debate," *Signs* 6:3 (1981), 482–514. The importance of domestic identities is evident in Linda Kerber, *No Constitutional Right to Be Ladies: Women and the Obligations of Citizenship* (New York: Hill and Wang, 1998). See also Joan Williams, *Unbending Gender: Why Family and Work Conflict and What to Do About It* (New York: Oxford University Press, 2000).

For paid domestic workers, see David M. Katzman, *Seven Days a Week: Women and Domestic Service in Industrializing America* (New York: Oxford University Press, 1978); Evelyn Nakano Glenn, *Issei, Nisei, War Bride: Three Generations of Japanese American Women in Domestic Service* (Philadelphia: Temple University Press, 1986), 160, and Glenn, "From Servitude to Service Work: Historical Continuities in the Racial Division of Paid Reproductive Labor," in *Unequal Sisters: A Multi-Cultural Reader in U.S. Women's History*, eds. Ellen Carol DuBois and Vicki L. Ruiz, 2nd ed. (New York: Routledge, 1994), 405–35; Theresa M. McBride, *The Domestic Revolution: The Modernization of Household Service in England and France, 1820–1920* (New York: Holmes & Meier, 1976); Judith Rollins, *Between Women: Domestics and Their Employers* (Philadelphia: Temple University Press, 1985); Mary Romero, "Chicanas Modernize Domestic Service," *Qualitative Sociology* 11:4 (1988), 319–33, and Romero, *Maid in the U.S.A.* (New York: Routledge, 1992); Elizabeth Jelin, "Migration and Labor Force Participation of Latin American Women: The Domestic Servants in the Cities," *Signs* 3:1 (1977), 129–41; Grace Chang, *Disposable Domestics: Immigrant Women Workers in the Global Economy* (Cambridge: South End Press, 2000); Henrietta Moore, *Feminism and Anthropology* (Cambridge, UK: Polity, 1988); Rachel Salazar Parrenas, "Transgressing the Nation-State: The Partial Citizenship and 'Imagined (Global) Community' of Migrant Filipina Domestic Workers," *Signs* 26:4 (2001), 1129–54; and Raymond Bonner, "Report from Kuwait: A Woman's Place," *New Yorker*, 16 November 1992, 56–66. On the decline of paid domestic service jobs, see for the United States: Alice Kessler-Harris, *Out to Work: A History of America's Wage-Earning Women* (New York: Oxford University Press, 1982) and, for Brazil, June E. Hahner, *Emancipating the Female Sex: The Struggle for Women's Rights in Brazil, 1850–1940* (Durham: Duke University Press, 1990), 97.

On contemporary attitudes toward working women and working mothers, see Kirsten Downey Grimsley, "Full-Time Moms Earn Respect, Poll Says," *Washington Post*, 22 March 1998, A16; Kalwant Bhopal, *Gender, "Race" and Patriarchy: A Study of South Asian Women* (Aldershot, UK: Ashgate, 1997); Tracey Harrison, "Equality? What Equality? More Women Go Out to Work . . . Then Do Chores Too," *The Mirror* (London), 22 October 1998, 6; Howard W. French, "Women Win a Battle, but Job Bias Still Rules Japan," *New York Times*, 26 February 2000, A3; Tamar Lewin, "Study Says Little Has Changed in Views on Working Mothers," *New York Times*, 10 September 2001, A20.

On prostitution see John D'Emilio and Estelle B. Freedman, *Intimate Matters: A History of Sexuality in America*, rev. ed. (Chicago: University of Chicago Press, 1997); Lucy Cheng Hirata, "Free, Indentured, Enslaved: Chinese Prostitutes in Nineteenth-Century America," *Signs* 5:1 (1979), 3–29; Luise White, *The Comforts of Home: Prostitution in Colonial Nairobi* (Chicago: University of Chicago Press, 1990); Ruth Rosen, *The Lost Sisterhood: Prostitution in America, 1900–1918* (Baltimore: Johns Hopkins University Press, 1982), 5; and Gail Hershatter, *Dangerous Pleasures: Prostitution and Modernity in Twentieth Century Shanghai* (Berkeley: University of California Press, 1997).

On contemporary sexual commerce, see Cynthia H. Enloe, *Bananas, Beaches and Bases: Making Feminist Sense of International Politics* (London: Pandora, 1989, repr. Berkeley: University of California Press, 1990); Karim el-Gawhary, "Sex Tourism in Cairo," *Middle East Report*, September-October 1995, 26–27; Masum Momaya, "The Cost of Living: Taking Her Place in the Global Economy," honors thesis, Program in Feminist Studies, Stanford University, 1999; and Kamala Kempadoo, ed., *Sun, Sex, and Gold: Tourism and Sex Work in the Caribbean* (Lanham, Md.: Rowman and Littlefield, 1999). Pushpa Das' story appears in Celia W. Dugger, "Dead Zones: Fighting Back in India: Calcutta's Prostitutes Lead the Fight on AIDS," *New York Times*, 4 January, 1999, A4.

CHAPTER SEVEN: INDUSTRIALIZATION, WAGE LABOR, AND THE ECONOMIC GENDER GAP

The data used in this chapter come from the following sources: Joni Seager, *The State of Women in the World Atlas*, 2nd ed. (New York: Penguin, 1997); *The World's Women 1970–1990: Trends and Statistics* (New York: United Nations, 1991); "Employment Status of the Civilian Noninstitutional Population by Sex, Age, Race, and Hispanic Origin," Bureau of Labor Statistics, U.S. Department of Labor, *Employment and Earnings* 47:1 (2000), 172; Roderick Harrison and Claudette Bennett, "Racial and Ethnic Diversity," in *State of the Union: America in the 1990s*, ed. Reynolds Farley (New York: Russell Sage Foundation, 1995), Table 4.6; Irene Browne, "Latinas and African American Women in the U.S. Labor Market," in *Latinas and African American Women at Work: Race, Gender, and Economic Inequality*, ed. Irene Browne (New York: Russell Sage Foundation, 1999), 1–30; Daphne Spain and Suzanne M. Bianchi, *Balancing Act: Motherhood, Marriage, and Employment Among American Women* (New York: Russell Sage Foundation, 1996); Joyce P. Jacobsen, *The Economics of Gender*, 2nd ed. (Oxford: Blackwell, 1998); Rina Singh, *Gender Autonomy in Western Eu-*

rope: An Imprecise Revolution (New York: St. Martin's Press, 1998), 42–47; *ILO Yearbook of Labour Statistics* (Geneva: International Labour Office, 1999); *The World's Women, 2000: Trends and Statistics* (New York: United Nations, 2000); Janice Hamilton Outtz, "Are Mommies Dropping Out of the Labor Force?" in *Times Educational Supplement*, no. 4256, 23 January 1998, F22; "Women in the Global Economy," fact sheet 4, United Nations Fourth World Conference on Women, 4–15 September, 1995; Kumiko Fujimura-Fanselow, "Introduction," in *Japanese Women: New Feminist Perspectives on the Past, Present and Future*, eds. Kumiko Fujimura-Fanselow and Atsuko Kameda (New York: Feminist Press, 1995), xvii-xxxviii; Sun Shaoxian, "Reflections on Female Employment in China," Copenhagen Discussion Papers No. 21 (Copenhagen: Center for East and Southeast Asian Studies, 1993); and "Women and Work: Challenge and Opportunity," fact sheet (London: Women's Unit, UK Ministry of Women, 2001).

On the wage gap see Claudia Goldin, *Understanding the Gender Gap: An Economic History of American Women* (New York: Oxford University Press, 1990); Derek Robinson, "Differences in Occupational Earnings by Sex," *International Labour Review* 137:1 (1998), 3–31; "Wage Gap Widens for Women," *The Courier-Mail* (Australia), 28 March 2001, 9; "Earnings Differences Between Women and Men," Facts on Working Women (Washington, D.C.: Women's Bureau, Department of Labor, 1993); and "The Wage Gap: Women's and Men's Earnings" (February, 1995) and "The Male-Female Wage Gap: Lifetime Earnings Losses," research briefing paper (Washington, D.C.: The Institute for Women's Policy Research, 1988).

On the history of women's wage labor, see Goldin, *Understanding the Gender Gap;* Louise A. Tilly and Joan W. Scott, *Women, Work and Family* (New York: Routledge, 1987), and Tilly's review of historical scholarship for Europe, the United States, Japan, and China in *Industrialization and Gender Inequality* (Washington, D.C.: American Historical Association, 1993); Alice Kessler-Harris, *Out to Work: A History of Wage-Earning Women in the United States* (New York: Oxford University Press, 1982); Thomas Dublin, *Women at Work: The Transformation of Work and Community in Lowell, Massachusetts, 1826–1860* (New York: Columbia University Press, 1979); Emily Honig, *Sisters and Strangers: Women in the Shanghai Cotton Mills, 1919–1949* (Stanford: Stanford University Press, 1986); Bonnie S. Anderson and Judith P. Zinsser, *A History of Their Own: Women in Europe From Prehistory to the Present* (New York: Harper & Row, 1988), vol. II; Yoko Kawashima, "Female Workers: An Overview of Past and Current Trends," in *Japanese Women: New Feminist Perspectives on the Past, Present and Future*, eds. Kumiko Fujimura-Fanselow and Atsuko Kameda (New York: Feminist Press, 1995), 271–93; Myra H. Strober and Agnes Miling Kaneko Chan, *The Road Winds Uphill All the Way: Gender, Work, and Family in the United States and Japan* (Cambridge: MIT Press, 1999); Kathryn Ward, ed., *Women Workers and Global Restructuring* (Ithaca: ILR Press, 1990); Amrita Basu, ed., *The Challenge of Local Feminisms* (Boulder: Westview Press, 1995); and Annette Fuentes and Barbara Ehrenreich, *Women in the Global Factory* (Boston: South End

Press, 1983). I also found useful material throughout Henrietta L. Moore, *Feminism and Anthropology* (Minneapolis: University of Minnesota Press, 1988), especially Chapter 4. Studies of individual occupations and industries are numerous, e.g., Arlie Russell Hochschild, *The Managed Heart: Commercialization of Human Feelings* (Berkeley: University of California Press, 1983) (on flight attendants) and Patricia Zavella, *Women's Work and Chicano Families: Cannery Workers of the Santa Clara Valley* (Ithaca: Cornell University Press, 1987).

On white collar jobs and the professions, see Michael Carter and Susan Carter, "Women's Recent Progress in the Professions, or Women Get Ticket to Ride After the Gravy Train Leaves the Station," *Feminist Studies* 7:3 (1981), 477–504; Deborah Rhode, "Perspectives on Professional Women," *Stanford Law Review* 40:5 (1988), 1163–207; Myra H. Strober, "Toward a General Theory of Occupational Sex Segregation: The Case of Public School Teaching," in Barbara Reskin, ed., *Sex Segregation in the Workplace: Trends, Explanations, Remedies* (Washington, D.C.: National Academy Press, 1984); Virginia Valian, *Why So Slow? The Advancement of Women* (Cambridge: MIT Press, 1998); Christine L. Williams, "The Glass Escalator: Hidden Advantages for Men in the 'Female' Professions," *Social Problems* 39:3 (1992), 253–57; Cynthia Fuchs Epstein, *Woman's Place: Options and Limits in Professional Careers* (Berkeley: University of California Press, 1970) and *Women in Law*, 2nd ed. (Urbana: University of Illinois Press, 1993); Gail Warshofsky Lapidus, "Occupational Segregation and Public Policy: A Comparative Analysis of American and Soviet Patterns," *Signs* 1:3, part 2 (1976), 119–36; "How Are We Doing," *Ms.* 8:2 (1997), 22–23; Heidi Hartmann, "Improving Employment Opportunities for Women," *Testimony Concerning H.R.1, Civil Rights Act of 1991, Before the U.S. House of Representatives, Committee on Education and Labor, 27 February 1991* (Washington, D.C.: Institute for Women's Policy Research, 1991); Roberta M. Spalter-Roth and Heidi Hartmann, *Increasing Working Mothers' Earnings*, with Christina A. Andrews et al. (Washington, D.C.: Institute for Women's Policy Research, 1991); Jean Eaglesham, "Legal Eagles Get Time to Roost," *Financial Times* (London), 16 March 2000, 14; I. C. McManus and K.A. Sproston, "Women in Hospital Medicine in the United Kingdom: Glass Ceiling, Preference, Prejudice or Cohort Effect," *Journal of Epidemiology and Community Health* 54 (January 2000), 10; and Ian Murray, "Women Doctors Urged to Become Surgeons," *The Times* (London), 15 September 1999.

On blue-collar trades see Kay Deaux and Joseph C. Ullman, *Women of Steel: Female Blue-collar Workers in the Basic Steel Industry* (New York: Praeger, 1983); Trudie Ferguson with Madeline Sharples, *Blue Collar Women: Trailblazing Women Take on Men-Only Jobs* (Liberty Corner, N.J.: New Horizon Press, 1994); and Molly Martin, ed., *Hard-Hatted Women: Life on the Job*, 2nd ed. (Seattle: Seal Press, 1997).

On structures and ideologies that affect women workers, see Heidi I. Hartmann, "Capitalism, Patriarchy, and Job Segregation by Sex," *Signs* 1:3, part 2 (1976), 137–69; Cynthia Fuchs Epstein, *Deceptive Distinctions: Sex, Gender, and the Social Order* (New Haven: Yale University Press, 1988), especially Chapter 7, and

Epstein, "Workplace Boundaries: Conceptions and Creations," *Social Research* 56:3 (1989), 571–90; Sandra Lipsitz Bem, *The Lenses of Gender: Tranforming the Debate on Sexual Inequality* (New Haven: Yale University Press, 1993); Cecilia L. Ridgeway, "Gender, Status, and the Social Psychology of Expectations," in *Theory on Gender/Feminims on Theory*, ed. Paula England (New York: Aldine de Gruyter, 1993), 175–97; Vicki Schultz, "Telling Stories About Women and Work: Judicial Interpretations of Sex Segregation in the Workplace in Title VII Cases Raising the Lack of Interest Argument," *Harvard Law Review* 103:8 (1990), 1750–843; Karen J. Hossfeld, "Their Logic Against Them: Contradictions in Sex, Race, and Class in Silicon Valley," in *Women Workers and Global Restructuring*, ed. Kathryn Ward (Ithaca: ILR Press, 1990), 149–78; Barbara F. Reskin, "Bringing the Men Back In: Sex Differentiation and the Devaluation of Women's Work," in *Feminist Frontiers IV*, eds. Laurel Richardson, Verta Taylor, and Nancy Whittier (New York: McGraw-Hill, 1997), 215–28; Janet W. Salaff, *Working Daughters of Hong Kong: Filial Piety or Power in the Family?* (New York: Cambridge University Press, 1981); Naila Kabeer, "Cultural Dopes or Rational Fools? Women and Labour Supply in the Bangladesh Garment Industry," *European Journal of Development Research*, June 1991, 133–60; Margery Wolf, *Revolution Postponed: Women in Contemporary China* (Stanford: Stanford University Press, 1985), especially Chapter 3; and Ruth Milkman, "Women's History and the Sears Case," *Feminist Studies* 12:2 (1986), 375–400.

In addition to Catharine MacKinnon, *Sexual Harassment of Working Women: A Case of Sex Discrimination*, with Thomas I. Emerson (New Haven: Yale University Press, 1979), see "Equal Opportunities: Commission Proposes to Update Policies and Laws in Anti-Harassment Drive," *European Report*, section 2507, 10 June 2000; "EU Seeks Tougher Sex Harass Law," *United Press International*, 5 June 2000; and Joseph Kahn, "Morgan Stanley Is Target Sex Bias Inquiry," *New York Times*, 29 July 1999, C1. On Japan, see Howard W. French, "Women Win a Battle, but Job Bias Still Rules Japan," *New York Times*, 26 February 2000, A3.

The following anthologies on feminist economics contain classic essays on labor force theory and practice: Alice H. Amdsden, ed., *The Economics of Women and Work* (New York: St. Martin's Press, 1980); Mariann A. Feber and Julie A. Nelson, *Beyond Economic Man: Feminist Theory and Economics* (Chicago: University of Chicago Press, 1993); and Ann Helton Stromberg and Shirley Harkness, *Women Working: Theories and Facts in Perspective*, 2nd ed. (Mountain View, Calif.: Mayfield Publishing, 1988).

CHAPTER EIGHT: WORKERS AND MOTHERS: FEMINIST SOCIAL POLICIES

For the life of one of the founding mothers of welfare policy, see Sissela Bok, *Alva Myrdal: A Daughter's Memoir* (Reading, Mass.: Addison-Wesley, 1991). On women's workplace organizing and legal strategies, see Alice Kessler-Harris, *Out to Work: A History of America's Wage-Earning Women* (New York: Oxford University Press, 1982); Thomas Dublin, *Women at Work: The Transformation of Work and Community in Lowell,*

Massachusetts, 1826–1860, 2nd ed. (New York: Columbia University Press, 1993); Emily Honig, *Sisters and Strangers: Women in the Shanghai Cotton Mills, 1919–1949* (Stanford: Stanford University Press, 1986); Annelise Orleck, *Common Sense and a Little Fire: Women and Working-Class Politics in the United States, 1900-1965* (Chapel Hill, University of North Carolina Press, 1995); Roberta Goldberg, *Organizing Women Office Workers: Dissatisfaction, Consciousness, and Action* (New York: Praeger, 1993); Jean Tepperman, *Not Servants, Not Machines: Office Workers Speak Out!* (Boston: Beacon Press, 1976); Bonnie S. Anderson and Judith P. Zinsser, *A History of Their Own: Women in Europe From Prehistory to the Present,* (New York: Harper & Row, 1988), vol. II; Sheila Rowbotham, *A Century of Women: The History of Women in Britain and the United States* (New York: Viking, 1997); Radha Kumar, *A History of Doing: An Illustrated Account of Movements for Women's Rights and Feminism in India, 1800–1990* (New Delhi: Kali for Women, 1993); and Mary Goldsmith and Elsa Chaney, "From Bolivia to Beijing: Household Workers Organize at the Local, National, and International Levels," in V. E. Rodriguez et al., *Memorial of the Bi-National Conference: Women in Contemporary Mexican Politics II* (Austin: The Mexican Center of ILAS, University of Texas at Austin, 1996).

On union membership, see Rina Singh, *Gender Autonomy in Western Europe: An Imprecise Revolution* (New York: St. Martin's Press, 1998); Amrita Basu, ed., *The Challenge of Local Feminisms* (Boulder: Westview Press, 1995); Johanna Brenner, "The Best of Times, the Worst of Times: Feminism in the United States," in *Mapping the Women's Movement: Feminist Politics and Social Transformation in the North,* ed. Monica Threlfall (London: Verso, 1996), 17–72. The effect of unions on wages appears in Heidi Hartmann, Roberta Spalter-Roth, and Nancy Collins, "What Do Unions Do for Women?" *Challenge* 37:4 (1994), 11–18, and "Median weekly earnings of full-time wage and salary workers by union affiliation and selected characteristics (Table 41)," *Employment and Earnings,* Bureau of Labor Statistics, United States Department of Labor, January, 2001.

Overviews of United States workplace legal strategies appear in Barbara Allen Babcock et al., *Sex Discrimination and the Law: History, Practice, and Theory,* 2nd ed. (Boston: Little, Brown & Co., 1995), and Deborah L. Rhode, *Justice and Gender: Sex Discrimination and the Law* (Cambridge: Harvard University Press, 1989). For Europe see Mariagrazia Rossilli, "The European Community's Policy on the Equality of Women: From the Treaty of Rome to the Present," *The European Journal of Women's Studies* 4 (1997), 63–82; Linda Hantrais, "Women, Work and Welfare in France," in *Women and Social Policies in Europe: Work, Family and the State,* ed. Jane Lewis (Aldershot, UK: Edward Elgar Publishing, 1993); and the series *Equality in Law Between Men and Women in the European Community,* eds. Michel Verwilghen and Ferdinand von Prondzynski (Boston: Martinus Nijhoff Publishers, 1994–1998). On affirmative action, see Nancy MacLean, "The Hidden History of Affirmative Action: Working Women's Struggles in the 1970s and the Gender of Class," *Feminist Studies* 25:1 (1999), 43–78; and Edmund L. Andrews, "European Union Court Upholds Affirmative Action for Women," *New York Times*, 12 November 1997, A7. On comparable worth, see Janet A. Flammang, "Women Made a Difference: Comparable Worth in San Jose," in *The Women's Movements of the United States and Western Europe: Consciousness, Political Opportunity, and Public Policy*, eds. Mary Fainsod Katzenstein and Carol McClurg Mueller (Philadelphia: Temple University Press, 1987), 290–309; Laura Pincus and Bill Shaw, "Comparable Worth: An Economic and Ethical Analysis," *Journal of Business Ethics* 17:5 (1998), 455–70; and Elaine Sorenson, "Implementing Comparable Worth: A Survey of Recent Job Evaluation Studies," *American Economic Review* 76:2 (1986), 364–67. On microenterprise, see Rae Blumberg, "Gender, Microenterprise, Performance and Power," in *Women in the Latin American Development Process*, eds. Christine E. Bose and Edna Acosta-Belen (Philadelphia: Temple University Press, 1995), and Patricia B. Kelly, "The Real Profits of Village Banking," *Americas* 48:6 (1996), 38–43.

On policies relating to parents, see Joan Williams, *Unbending Gender: Why Family and Work Conflict and What to Do About It* (New York: Oxford University Press, 2000); Ann Crittenden, *The Price of Motherhood: Why the Most Important Job in the World Is Still the Least Valued* (New York: Metropolitan Books/Henry Holt, 2001); Betty Friedan, *The Second Stage* (New York: Summit Books, 1981); Anneke Van Doorne-Huiskes, "Work-Family Arrangements: The Role of the State Versus the Role of the Private Sector," in *Women and Public Policy: The Shifting Boundaries Between the Public and Private Spheres*, eds. Susan Baker and Anneke van Doorne-Huiskes (Aldershot, UK: Ashgate, 1999), 93–110; Christopher J. Ruhm and Jacqueline L. Teague, "Parental Leave Policies in Europe and North America," in *Gender and Family Issues in the Workplace*, eds. Francine D. Blau and Ronald G. Ehrenberg (New York: Russell Sage Foundation, 1997); Victor R. Fuchs, *Women's Quest for Economic Equality* (Cambridge: Harvard University Press, 1988); and Trudie Knijn and Monique Dremer, "Gender and the Caring Dimension of Welfare States: Toward Inclusive Citizenship," *Social Politics* 4:3 (1997), 328–61. A fact sheet on Sweden, "Equality Between Men and Women in Sweden," February 2000, can be accessed at http://www.si.se/docs/infosweden/engelska/fs82.pdf (9 September 2001).

Information on child care comes from Rina Singh, *Gender Autonomy in Western Europe: An Imprecise Revolution* (New York: St. Martin's Press, 1998); "Ministry of Education: Establish Child Care Rooms at Schools," *Korean Women Today* 42:5 (1994); "Women and Work: Challenge and Opportunity," fact sheet (London: Women's Unit, UK Ministry of Women, 2001); Vera Mackie, "Feminist Critiques of Modern Japanese Politics," in *Mapping the Women's Movement: Feminist Politics and Social Transformation in the North*, ed. Monica Threlfall (London: Verso, 1996). Socialist provisions are summarized in Henrietta L. Moore, *Feminism and Anthropology* (Minneapolis: University of Minnesota Press, 1988), and Myra Marx Feree, "The Rise and Fall of 'Mommy Politics': Feminism and Unification in (East) Germany," *Feminist Studies* 19:1 (1993): 89–116. See also Myra Marx Feree and Beth B. Hess, *Controversy and Coalition: The New Feminist Movement Across Three Decades of Change*, 3rd ed. (New York: Routledge, 2000).

Sources for changing fathers' roles include Arnlaug Leira, "Caring as Social Right: Cash for Child Care and Daddy Leave," *Social Politics* 5:3 (1998), 362–78; Warren Hoge, "Issue Aborning at No. 10: Will Daddy Stay Home?" *New York Times*, 29 March 2000, A4; Helen Froud, "Helping Working Mothers," *Women's International Net* 34 (2000), accessed at http://www.winmagazine.org/issues/issue34/win34c.htm (15 August 2001); "Divorced Housewives Gain More Alimony," *Die Welt*, 13 June 2001, 1; "How Much Can Child Support Provide? Welfare, Family Income and Child Support," (Washington, D.C.: Institute for Women's Policy Research, 1999), accessed at http://www.iwpr.org (1 September 2001).

Data on poverty come from Joni Seager, *The State of Women in the World Atlas* (London: Penguin, 1997) and Heidi Hartmann et al., "Poverty Alleviation and Single-Mother Families," *National Forum* 76:3 (1996), 24–27. On welfare state policies, see Susan Pedersen, *Family, Dependence, and the Origins of the Welfare State: Britain and France, 1914–1945* (New York: Cambridge University Press, 1993); Gisela Bock and Pat Thane, eds., *Maternity and Gender Policies: Women and the Rise of the European Welfare States, 1880–1950s* (New York: Routledge, 1991); Nancy Fraser, *Justice Interruptus: Critical Reflections on the "Postsocialist" Condition* (New York: Routledge, 1997); Theda Skocpol, *Protecting Soldiers and Mothers: The Political Origins of Social Policy in the United States* (Cambridge: Harvard University Press, 1992); Linda Gordon, *Pitied but Not Entitled: Single Mothers and the History of Welfare, 1890–1935* (New York: Free Press, 1994), and Gordon, ed., *Women, the State, and Welfare* (Madison: University of Wisconsin Press, 1990); and Gwendolyn Mink, *Wages of Motherhood: Inequality in the Welfare State, 1917–1942* (Ithaca: Cornell University Press, 1995). For contemporary activism, see "Welfare Beat," *Sojourner*, January 1999, 22–28. On structural adjustment, see Pamela Sparr, ed., *Mortgaging Women's Lives: Feminist Critiques of Structural Adjustment* (London: Zed Books, 1994).

CHAPTER NINE: MEDICINE, MARKETS, AND THE FEMALE BODY

Important feminist critiques of biological determinism include Ann Fausto-Sterling, *Myths of Gender: Biological Theories About Women and Men* (New York: Basic Books, 1985) and *Sexing the Body: Gender Politics and the Construction of Sexuality* (New York: Basic Books, 2000); Ruth Bleier, *Science and Gender: A Critique of Biology and Its Theories on Women* (New York: Pergamon Press, 1984); and essays in Mary Jacobus, Evelyn Fox Keller, and Sally Shuttleworth, eds., *Body/Politics: Women and the Discourses of Science* (New York: Routledge, 1990). For feminist uses of biological thinking, see Alice S. Rossi, "Equality Between the Sexes: An Immodest Proposal," *Daedalus* 117:3 (1988), 25–71. On scientific and cultural ideas about the female body, see Carolyn Merchant, *The Death of Nature: Women, Ecology, and the Scientific Revolution* (New York: Harper & Row, 1980); Carolyn Walker Bynum, *Holy Feast and Holy Fast: The Religious Significance of Food to Medieval Women* (Berkeley: University of California Press, 1987); Thomas Laqueur, *Making Sex: Body and Gender from the Greeks to Freud* (Cambridge: Harvard University Press, 1990); Joan Jacob Brumberg, *Fasting Girls: The Emergence of Anorexia Nervosa as a Modern Disease* (Cambridge: Harvard University Press, 1988) and *The Body Project: An Intimate History of American Girls* (New York: Random House, 1997); Lois W. Banner, *American Beauty* (New York: Knopf, 1983); Wendy Doniger O'Flaherty, *Women, Androgynes, and Other Mythical Beasts* (Chicago: University of Chicago Press, 1980); Sander Gilman, *Making the Body Beautiful: A Cultural History of Aesthetic Surgery* (Princeton: Princeton University Press, 1999); Emily Martin, *The Woman in the Body: A Cultural Analysis of Reproduction* (Boston: Beacon Press, 1987); Susan Suleiman, ed., *The Female Body in Western Culture* (Cambridge: Harvard University Press, 1986); and Susan Bordo, *Unbearable Weight: Feminism, Western Culture, and the Body* (Berkeley: University of California Press, 1993). Lynn S. Chancer, *Reconcilable Differences: Confronting Beauty, Pornography and the Future of Feminism* (Berkeley: University of California Press, 1998) is a thoughtful survey of feminist politics concerning the body.

Barbara Ehrenreich and Deirde English, *For Her Own Good: 150 Years of Experts' Advice to Women* (Garden City, N.Y.: Anchor Press, 1978) first raised many of the questions addressed in later feminist scholarship. On U.S. medical treatment of women see Carroll Smith-Rosenberg, *Disorderly Conduct: Visions of Gender in Victorian America* (New York: Oxford University Press, 1986). On women as doctors, see Regina Morantz-Sanchez, *Sympathy and Science: Women Physicians in American Medicine* (Chapel Hill: University of North Carolina Press, 2000), and on women social scientists and the critique of Darwinian views, see Rosalind Rosenberg, *Beyond Separate Spheres: Intellectual Roots of Modern Feminism* (New Haven: Yale University Press, 1982). See also Rachel P. Maines, *The Technology of Orgasm: "Hysteria," the Vibrator, and Women's Sexual Satisfaction* (Baltimore: Johns Hopkins University Press, 1999). Philippine shamans are mentioned in Barbara N. Ramusack and Sharon Sievers, *Women in Asia: Restoring Women to History* (Bloomington: Indiana University Press, 1999).

Studies of consumer culture and the body include Wendy Chapkis, *Beauty Secrets* (Boston: South End Press, 1986); Elizabeth Wilson, *Adorned in Dreams: Fashion and Modernity* (London: Virago, 1985); and Kathy Peiss, *Hope in a Jar: The Making of America's Beauty Culture* (New York: Metropolitan Books, 1998). For Japan, see Midori Fukunishi Suzuki, "Women and Television: Portrayal of Women in the Mass Media," in *Japanese Women: New Feminist Perspectives on the Past, Present, and Future*, eds. Kumiko Fujimura-Fanselow and Atsuko Kameda (New York: The Feminist Press, 1995); the Fiji study is described in Erica Goode, "Study Finds TV Trims Fiji Girls' Body Image and Eating Habits," *New York Times*, 20 May 1999, A13. For two views of race and popular culture see Hazel Carby, "It Jus Be's Dat Way Sometime': The Sexual Politics of Women's Blues," in *Unequal Sisters: A Multicultural Reader in U.S. Women's History*, eds., Ellen Carol DuBois and Vicki L. Ruiz, 1st ed. (New York: Routledge, 1990), 238–49, and Ann duCille, "Blues Notes on Black Sexuality: Sex and the Texts of Jessie Fauset and Nella Larsen," in *American Sexual Politics: Sex,*

Gender, and Race Since the Civil War, eds. John C. Fout and Maura Shaw Tantillo (Chicago: University of Chicago Press, 1993). On femme style, see Joan Nestle, ed., *The Persistent Desire: A Femme-Butch Reader* (Boston: Alyson, 1992).

Classic feminist treatments of body size include Kim Chernin, *The Obsession: Reflections on the Tyranny of Slenderness* (New York: Harper and Row, 1981) and Susie Orbach, *Fat Is a Feminist Issue: The Anti-Diet Guide to Permanent Weight Loss* (New York: Paddington Press, 1978) and *Hunger Strike: The Anorectic's Struggle as a Metaphor for Our Age* (New York: W. W. Norton, 1986). See also Naomi Wolf, *The Beauty Myth: How Images of Beauty Are Used Against Women* (New York: William Morrow, 1991), and Jane Hirshmann and Carol Munter, *When Women Stop Hating Their Bodies* (New York: Fawcett Columbine, 1995). On disability, see Nancy Mairs, *Waist High in the World: A Life Among the Nondisabled* (Thorndike, ME.: G. K. Hall, 1997) and Barbara Hillyer, *Feminism and Disability* (Norman, Okla.: University of Oklahoma Press, 1993).

The sections on weight and dieting draw on the following scholarship: Esther D. Rothblum, "Women and Weight: Fad and Fiction," *Journal of Psychology* 124:1 (1990), 5–24, "The Stigma of Women's Weight: Social and Economic Realities," *Feminism and Psychology* 2:1 (1992), 61–73, and "I'll Die for the Revolution But Don't Ask Me Not to Diet: Feminism and the Continuing Stigmatization of Obesity," in *Feminist Perspective on Eating Disorders*, eds. Patricia Fallon, Melanie A. Katzman, and Susan C. Wooley (New York: Guilford Press, 1994), 53–76; Andrew J. Hill and Razia Bhatti, "Body Shape Perception and Dieting in Preadolescent British Asian Girls: Links with Eating Disorders," *International Journal of Eating Disorders* 17:2 (1995), 175; Pamela J. Brink, "The Fattening Room Among the Annang of Nigeria," *Medical Anthropology* 12:1 (1989), 131–43; and Becky W. Thompson, *A Hunger So Wide and Deep: A Multiracial View of Women's Eating Problems* (Minneapolis: University of Minnesota Press, 1994). On the costs and profits of weight, see S. L. Gortmaker et al., "Social and Economic Consequences of Overweight in Adolescence and Young Adulthood," *New England Journal of Medicine* 329:14 (1993), 1008–12, and Laura Fraser, *Losing It: America's Obsession with Weight and the Industry That Feeds on It* (New York: Dutton, 1997). Data on cosmetic surgery come from "2000 Gender Distribution, Cosmetic Surgery," American Society of Plastic Surgeons, accessed at http://www.plasticsurgery.org (1 August 2001), and Lucien Chauvin et al., "Bodies à la Carte: Passionate for Pulchritude, Latin American Women are Reshaping Their Form Through Plastic Surgery," *Time International*, 9 July 2001.

Data on women in medicine appear in a special issue of the *Journal of the American Medical Women's Association* 55:1 (2000) titled "The Woman Physician in the Year 2000," including Janet Bickel, "Women in Academic Medicine" (10–19); Felicia Knaul et al., "The Gender Composition of the Medical Profession in Mexico: Implications for Employment Patterns and Physician Labor Supply" (32–35); and Shafika Nasser and Randa Baligh, "Egyptian Medical Women, Past and Present" (36–44). For women's health centers, see Francine Nichols, "History of the

Women's Health Movement in the 20th Century," *Journal of Obstetric, Gynecologic, and Neonatal Nursing* 29:1 (2000), 56–65, and Karen de Souza, "Our Network Is a Point of Reference," *Women's Health Journal*, January-March 1999, 21–23. Information on national health movements appear in Amrita Basu, ed., *The Challenge of Local Feminisms: Women's Movements in Global Perspective* (Boulder: Westview Press, 1995) and Mayfair Mei-hui Yang, *Spaces of Their Own: Women's Public Sphere in Transnational China* (Minneapolis: University of Minnesota Press, 1999).

On the self-help movement, see Verta A. Taylor, *Rock-a-by Baby: Feminism, Self Help, and Postpartum Depression* (New York: Routledge, 1996), and on feminist responses to AIDS see Beth E. Schneider and Nancy E. Stoller, eds., *Women Resisting AIDS: Feminist Strategies of Empowerment* (Philadelphia: Temple University Press, 1995) and Nancy E. Stoller, *Lessons from the Damned: Queers, Whores, and Junkies Respond to AIDS* (New York: Routledge, 1998). Cancer rates based on an 85-year life span appear in Joni Seager, *The State of Women in the World Atlas*, 2nd ed. (London: Penguin, 1997). Sources for female genital cutting include AAWORD, "A Statement on Genital Mutilation," in *Third World, Second Sex: Women's Struggle and National Liberation/Third World Women Speak Out*, ed. Miranda Davies (London: Zed Books, 1983); Nawal El Saadawi, *The Hidden Face of Eve* (London: Zed Books, 1980); Noy Thrupkaew, "Senegalese Women Win Ban on Female Genital Cutting," *Sojourner* (March 1999), 25–27; Cheryl Johnson-Odim, "Common Themes, Different Contexts: Third World Women and Feminism," in *Third World Women and the Politics of Feminism*, eds. Chandra Talpade Mohanty, Ann Russo, and Lourdes Torres (Bloomington: University of Indiana Press, 1991); and Gerry Mackie, "Female Genital Cutting: The Beginning of the End," *Female Circumcision in Africa: Culture, Controversy, and Change*, eds. Bettina Shell-Duncan and Ylva Hernlund (Boulder: Lynne Rienner Publishers, 2000), 253–281. For the history of women and sports in the U.S., see Susan Cahn, *Coming on Strong: Gender and Sexuality in Twentieth-Century Women's Sport* (New York: The Free Press, 1994).

CHAPTER TEN: REPRODUCTION: THE POLITICS OF CHOICE

Margaret Atwood, *The Handmaid's Tale* (Boston: Houghton Mifflin, 1986). On the history of fertility control in the United States see Linda Gordon, *Woman's Body, Woman's Right: Birth Control in America* (New York: Grossman, 1976); James Mohr, *Abortion in America: The Origins and Evolution of National Policy, 1800–1900* (New York: Oxford University Press, 1978); and John D'Emilio and Estelle B. Freedman, *Intimate Matters: A History of Sexuality in America*, rev. ed. (Chicago: University of Chicago Press, 1997). Two important accounts of race and reproduction appear in Angela Davis, *Women, Race, and Class* (New York: Random House, 1981) and Dorothy E. Roberts, *Killing the Black Body: Race, Reproduction, and the Meaning of Liberty* (New York: Pantheon Books, 1997). Elaine Tyler May, *Barren in the Promised Land: Childless Americans and the Pursuit of Happiness* (New York: Basic Books, 1995) discusses eugenics and sterilization as well as infertility in the United States. On Great Britain, see Anna Davin, "Imperialism and Motherhood," *History Workshop* 5 (1978), 9–65. Bonnie S. Anderson and Judith P. Zinsser, eds., *A History of Their Own: Women in Europe from Prehistory to the Present* (New York: Harper & Row, 1988), vol. II, describes fertility control and reproductive politics in Europe. See also Leslie J. Reagan, *When Abortion Was a Crime: Women, Medicine, and Law in the United States, 1867–1973* (Berkeley: University of California Press, 1997); Janet Farrell Brodie, *Contraception and Abortion in Nineteenth-Century America* (Ithaca: Cornell University Press, 1994); Andrea Tone, *Devices and Desires: A History of Contraceptives in America* (New York: Hill and Wang, 2001); and Rickie Solinger, ed., *Abortion Wars: A Half Century of Struggle, 1950–2000* (Berkeley: University of California Press, 1998). On the Jane Collective see "Heather Booth Speaks," in *The Feminist Memoir Project: Voices from Women's Liberation*, eds. Rachel Blau duPlessis and Ann Snitow (New York: Three Rivers Press, 1998) and Laura Kaplan, *The Story of Jane: The Legendary Underground Feminist Abortion Service* (New York: Pantheon Books, 1995).

Worldwide contraceptive use is documented in Joni Seager, *The State of Women in the World Atlas* (London: Penguin, 1997); Rosalind Petchesky, "Cross-Country Comparisons and Political Visions," in *Negotiating Reproductive Rights: Women's Perspectives Across Countries and Cultures*, eds. Rosalind Petchesky and Karen Judd (London: Zed Books, 1998); and Colin Francome, *Abortion Freedom: A Worldwide Movement* (London: Allen and Unwin, 1984). Other data come from Stanley K. Henshaw, Susheela Singh, and Taylor Haas, "The Incidence of Abortion Worldwide," *International Family Planning Perspectives* 25, supplement (1999), 30–38 and *Hopes and Realities: Closing the Gap Between Women's Aspirations and Their Reproductive Experiences* (New York: Alan Guttmacher Institute, 1995); and *The World's Women, 2000: Trends and Statistics*, (New York: United Nations, 2000). Vasectomy rates appear in John Tagliabue, "British Vasectomy Offer Brings French Outrage," *New York Times*, 18 August 2000, A8.

World opinion on abortion appears in Rita James Simon, *Abortion: Statutes, Policies, and Public Attitudes the World Over* (Westport, Conn.: Praeger, 1998) and for the United States, see Fox News poll, conducted 24–25 January 2001 and 12–13 July 2001, archived at Roper Center for Public Opinion Research Online, http://www.ropercenter.uconn.edu/data_index.html. In addition to Kristen Luker, *Abortion and the Politics of Motherhood* (Berkeley: University of California Press, 1984), see Faye Ginsburg, *Contested Lives: The Abortion Debate in an American Community* (Berkeley: University of California Press, 1989). Overlapping values among pro-life and pro-choice appear in Bill Rolston and Anna Eggert, *Abortion in the New Europe: A Comparative Handbook* (Westport, Conn.: Greenwood Press, 1994) and Laurie Shrage, *Moral Dilemmas of Feminism: Prostitution, Adultery, and Abortion* (New York: Routledge, 1994). See also Marlene Gerber Fried, "Beyond Abortion: Transforming the Pro-Choice Movement," *Social Policy* 23:4 (1993), 22–28. On abortion laws, see Center for Reproductive Law and Policy, "The Facts: The World's Abortion Laws"

(February, 1999), accessed at http://www.crlp.org/pub_fac_abor11cpd.html (8 September 2001); and Anika Rahman, L. Katzive, and S.K. Henshaw, "A Global Review of Laws on Induced Abortion, 1985–1997," *International Family Planning Perspectives* 24:2 (1998), 56–64.

For policies and politics in individual countries, see entries in *Women and Politics Worldwide*, eds. Barbara J. Nelson and Najma Chowdhury (New Haven: Yale University Press, 1994), especially (for Mexico) Eli Barta, "The Struggle for Life, or Pulling Off the Mask of Infamy" (448–60) and Yue Daiyun and Li Jin, "Women's Life in New China" (162–73); and Amrita Basu, ed., *The Challenge of Local Feminisms: Women's Movements in Global Perspective* (Boulder: Westview Press, 1995). In addition, on Polish reproductive politics, see United Nations Committee on Economic, Social and Cultural Rights, "Federation for Women and Family Planning & International Planned Parenthood Federation Report," European Network, April 1998, accessed at http://www.waw.pdi.net/~polfedwo/english/english1.htm (16 November 2000); and on China, Margery Wolf, *Revolution Postponed: Women in Contemporary China* (Stanford: Stanford University Press, 1985), Chapter 10; and Emily Honig and Gail Hershatter, *Personal Voices: Chinese Women in the 1980s* (Stanford: Stanford University Press, 1988).

Other sources used for reproductive politics include Susan Yanow, "Puerto Rican Feminist Battles Barriers to Abortion Access" (interview with Yamila Azize-Vargas), *Sojourner*, October 2000, 19; Lorraine E. Ferris, Margot McMain-Klein, and Kary Iron, "Factors Influencing the Delivery of Abortion Services in Ontario: A Descriptive Study," *Family Planning Perspectives* 30:3 (1998), 134–38; Diana Khor, "Organizing for Change: Women's Grass Roots Activism in Japan," *Feminist Studies* 25:3 (1999), 633–61; Jean Schroedel, *Is the Fetus a Person: A Comparison of Fetal Policies Across the 50 States* (Ithaca: Cornell University Press, 2000); Rosalind Petchesky, "Spiraling Discourse of Reproductive and Sexual Rights: A Post-Beijing Assessment of International Feminist Politics," in *Women Transforming Politics*, eds. Cathy J. Cohen, Kathleen B. Jones, and Joan C. Tronto (New York: New York University Press, 1997), 569–87; International Reproductive Rights Research Action Group, *Catalysts and Messengers: The Story of the International Reproductive Rights Research Action Group* (New York: IRRRAG, 1999); Gigi Santow, "Social Roles and Physical Health: The Case of Female Disadvantage in Poor Countries," *Social Science and Medicine* 40:2 (1995), 158; Barbara Winslow, "Primary and Secondary Contradictions in Seattle: 1967–1969" (225–48), and Meredith Tax, "For the People Hear Us Singing, 'Bread and Roses! Bread and Roses!'" (311–23), in *The Feminist Memoir Project: Voices from Women's Liberation*, eds. Rachel Blau duPlessis and Ann Snitow (New York: Three Rivers Press, 1998); and Amartya Sen, *Development as Freedom* (New York: Knopf, 2000), Chapter 8.

On reproductive technologies, see Rita Arditti, "Reproductive Engineering and The Social Control of Women," *Radical America* 19:6 (1985), 9–26, and "The Surrogacy Business," *Social Policy* (fall 1987), 42–46; Patricia Boling, ed., *Expecting*

Trouble: Surrogacy, Fetal Abuse, and New Reproductive Technologies (Boulder: Westview Press, 1995); Debra Satz, "Markets in Women's Reproductive Labor," *Philosophy & Public Affairs* 21:2 (1992), 107–23; Susan Shiu and Cynthia Wan, "New Law Bans Most Surrogacy," *South China Morning Post*, 23 June 2000, 6; and Rebecca Mead, "Eggs for Sale," *The New Yorker*, 9 August 1999, 56–65.

CHAPTER ELEVEN: SEXUALITIES, IDENTITIES, AND SELF-DETERMINATION

For the United States, I draw heavily on John D'Emilio and Estelle B. Freedman, *Intimate Matters: A History of Sexuality in America*, 2nd ed. (Chicago: University of Chicago Press, 1997). Important European studies include Peter Gay, *The Bourgeois Experience, Victoria to Freud*, vol. I: *Education of the Senses* (New York: Oxford University Press, 1984), and vol. II: *The Tender Passion* (New York: Oxford University Press, 1986); Michel Foucault, *The History of Sexuality*, trans. Robert Hurley (New York: Pantheon, 1978); Jeffrey Weeks, *Sex, Politics and Society: The Regulation of Sexuality Since 1800* (London: Longman, 1981); Thomas Laqueur, *Making Sex: Body and Gender from the Greeks to Freud* (Cambridge: Harvard University Press, 1990); and Lesley Hall and Roy Porter, *The Facts of Life: The Creation of Sexual Knowledge in Britain, 1650–1950* (New Haven: Yale University Press, 1995). Two helpful collections of essays explore the relationship of sexuality, race, and nationalism: Andrew Parker, Mary Russo, Doris Sommer, and Patricia Yaeger, eds., *Nationalisms and Sexualities* (New York: Routledge, 1992), and Lenore Manderson and Margaret Jolly, eds., *Sites of Desire, Economics of Pleasure: Sexualities in Asia and the Pacific* (Chicago: University of Chicago Press, 1997). On China see Gail Hershatter, *Dangerous Pleasures: Prostitution and Modernity in Twentieth-Century Shanghai* (Berkeley: University of California Press, 1997).

On sex and empire, in addition to Edward W. Said, *Orientalism* (New York: Pantheon, 1978), see Sander Gilman, "Black Bodies, White Bodies: Towards an Iconography of Female Sexuality in Late-Nineteenth-Century Art, Medicine and Literature," in *"Race," Writing and Difference*, ed. Henry Louis Gates (Chicago: University of Chicago Press, 1986), 223–26; Ann L. Stoler, "Making Empire Respectable: The Politics of Race and Sexual Morality in Twentieth-Century Colonial Cultures," *American Ethnologist* 16:4 (1989), 634–60, and *Race and the Education of Desire: Foucault's History of Sexuality and the Colonial Order of Things* (Durham: Duke University Press, 1995); Anne McClintock, *Imperial Leather: Race, Gender and Sexuality in the Colonial Conquest* (New York: Routledge, 1994); and Barbara Watson Andaya, "From Temporary Wife to Prostitute: Sexuality and Economic Change in Early Modern Southeast Asia," *Journal of Women's History* 9:4 (1998), 11–35.

On homosexuality, the cross-cultural literature includes essays in Sherry B. Ortner and Harriet Whitehead, eds., *Sexual Meanings: The Cultural Construction of Gender and Sexuality* (Cambridge: Cambridge University Press, 1981); Gilbert H. Herdt, ed., *Rituals of Manhood: Male Initiation in Papua New Guinea* (Berkeley: University of

California Press, 1982); Gloria Wekker, " 'What's Identity Got to Do with It?' Re-thinking Identity in Light of the *Mati* Work in Suriname" (119–38), and Kendall, "Women in Lesotho and the (Western) Construction of Homophobia" (157–78) in *Female Desires: Same-Sex Relations and Transgender Practices Across Cultures*, eds. Evelyn Blackwood and Saskia E. Wieringa (New York: Columbia University Press, 1999). See also Matthew H. Sommer, *Sex, Law, and Society in Late Imperial China* (Stanford: Stanford University Press, 2000). For the United States, Jonathan Ned Katz provides historical documents and commentary in *Gay American History: Lesbians and Gay Men in the U.S.A.* (New York: Crowell, 1976) and *Gay/Lesbian Almanac: A New Documentary in Which Is Contained, in Chronological Order, Evidence of the True and Fantastical History of Those Persons Now Called Lesbians and Gay Men . . .* (New York: Harper and Row, 1983), and an interpretation in *The Invention of Heterosexuality* (New York: Dutton, 1995). See also John D'Emilio, *Sexual Politics, Sexual Communities: The Making of a Homosexual Minority in the United States, 1940–1970* (Chicago: University of Chicago Press, 1983) and George Chauncey, *Gay New York: Gender, Urban Culture, and the Makings of the Gay Male World, 1890–1940* (New York: Basic Books, 1994). For lesbian history, see Carroll Smith Rosenberg, *Disorderly Conduct: Visions of Gender in Victorian America* (New York: Oxford University Press, 1986); Lillian Faderman, *Surpassing the Love of Men: Romantic Friendship and Love Between Women from the Renaissance to the Present* (New York: Morrow, 1981), and *Odd Girls and Twilight Lovers: A History of Lesbian Life in Twentieth-Century America* (New York: Columbia University Press, 1991). On the sexualized culture and its limits, see Kathy Peiss, *Cheap Amusements: Working Women and Leisure in New York City* (Philadelphia: Temple University Press, 1985); Christina Simmons, "Companionate Marriage and the Lesbian Threat," *Frontiers* 4:3 (1979), 54–59; Elizabeth Lunbeck, " 'A New Generation of Women': Progressive Psychiatrists and the Hypersexual Female," *Feminist Studies* 13 (1987), 513–43; and Carol Groneman, *Nymphomania: A History* (New York: W. W. Norton, 2000). Studies of lesbian communities include Susan Krieger, *The Mirror Dance: Identity in a Women's Community* (Philadelphia: Temple University Press, 1983); Shane Phelan, *Identity Politics: Lesbian Feminism and the Limits of Community* (Philadelphia: Temple University Press, 1989); and Elizabeth Lapovsky Kennedy and Madeline D. Davis, *Boots of Leather, Slippers of Gold: The History of a Lesbian Community* (New York: Routledge, 1993).

Second-wave feminist analysis of sexuality appear in Kate Millett, *Sexual Politics* (New York: Avon-Doubleday, 1970); Germaine Greer, *The Female Eunuch* (London: MacGibbon & Kee, 1970); Anne Koedt, "The Myth of the Vaginal Orgasm," in *Radical Feminism*, eds., Anne Koedt, Ellen Levine, and Anita Rapone (New York: Quadrangle Books, 1973); Shere Hite, *The Hite Report: A Nationwide Study on Female Sexuality* (New York: Macmillan, 1976); Rose Marie Muraro, *Sexualidade da Mulher Brasileira: Corpo e Classe Social no Brazil* (Petropolis: Vozes, 1983); Adrienne Rich, "Compulsory Heterosexuality and Lesbian Existence," in Rich, *Blood, Bread, and Poetry: Selected Prose, 1979–1985* (New York: W. W. Norton, 1986), 23–75; and

Carol S. Vance, ed., *Pleasure and Danger: Exploring Female Sexuality* (New York: Routledge, 1984). An example of the many anthologies refining sexual identity is Evelyn Torton Beck, ed., *Nice Jewish Girls: A Lesbian Anthology* (Watertown, Mass.: Persephone Press, 1982). See also Dana Y. Takagi, "Maiden Voyage: Excursion into Sexuality and Identity Politics in Asian America," *Amerasia Journal* 20:1 (1994), 1–17.

On the 1990s, for queer identity see, e.g., Lisa Duggan, "Making It Perfectly Queer," and other essays in *Sex Wars: Sexual Dissent and Political Culture*, eds. Lisa Duggan and Nan D. Hunter (New York: Routledge, 1995); Amber Hollibaugh, *My Dangerous Desires: A Queer Girl Dreaming Her Way Home* (Durham: Duke University Press, 2000); Judith Butler, *Bodies That Matter: On the Discursive Limits of "Sex"* (New York: Routledge, 1993); and Teresa de Lauretis, *The Practice of Love: Lesbian Sexuality and Perverse Desire* (Bloomington: Indiana University Press, 1994). On dilemmas of heterosexual youth, see Naomi Wolf, *Promiscuities: The Secret Struggle for Womanhood* (New York: Random House, 1997); and for a study of feminist sexual commerce, see Meika Loe, "Feminism for Sale: Case Study of a Pro-Sex Feminist Business," *Gender and Society* 13:6 (1999), 705–32.

Outside the West, see Carmen Barroso and Cristina Brushcini, "Building Politics from Personal Lives: Discussions on Sexuality Among Poor Women in Brazil," in *Third World Women and the Politics of Feminism*, eds. Chandra Talpade Mohanty, Ann Russo, and Lourdes Torres (Bloomington: Indiana University Press, 1991), 153–72; Evelyne Accad, "Sexuality and Sexual Politics: Conflicts and Contradictions for Contemporary Women in the Middle East," also in *Third World Women*, 237–50; and Rosalind Petchesky, "Spiraling Discourses of Reproductive and Sexual Rights: A Post-Beijing Assessment of International Feminist Politics," in *Women Transforming Politics: An Alternative Reader*, eds. Cathy J. Cohen, Kathleen B. Jones, and Joan C. Tronto (New York: New York University Press, 1997), 569–87.

On the history of prostitution in the West, see Ruth Rosen, *The Lost Sisterhood: Prostitution in America, 1900–1918* (Baltimore: Johns Hopkins University Press, 1982), and Judith Walkowitz, *Prostitution and Victorian Society: Women, Class, and the State* (New York: Cambridge University Press, 1980). Useful accounts of the debates over pornography appear in Lynne Segal and Mary McIntosh, eds., *Sex Exposed: Sexuality and the Pornography Debate* (New Brunswick: Rutgers University Press, 1993). See also Catharine MacKinnon and Andrea Dworkin, *Pornography and Civil Rights: A New Day for Women's Equality* (Minneapolis: Organizing Against Pornography, 1988); Andrea Dworkin, *Intercourse* (New York: The Free Press, 1987); and Ellen Willis, "Feminism, Moralism, and Pornography," in *Powers of Desire: The Politics of Sexuality*, eds. Ann Snitow, Christine Stansell, and Sharon Thompson, 460–67; Kathleen Barry, *Female Sexual Slavery*, 2nd ed. (New York: New York University Press, 1984), 471–76; Gail Pheterson, *A Vindication of the Rights of Whores* (Seattle: Seal Press, 1989); and Gillian Rodgerson and Linda Semple, "Who Watches the Watchwomen?: Feminists Against Censorship," in *Imagining Women: Cultural Repre-*

sentations and Gender, eds. Frances Bonner, Lizbeth Goodman, and Richard Allen (Cambridge: Polity Press/Open University, 1992), 268–72.

CHAPTER TWELVE: GENDER AND VIOLENCE

On the effort to criminalize wartime rape, see Barbara Bedont and Katherine Hall Martinez, "Ending Impunity for Gender Crimes under the International Criminal Court," *The Brown Journal of World Affairs* 6:1 (1999), 65–85. For the impact on women, see Alexandra Stiglmayer, ed., *Mass Rape: The War against Women in Bosnia-Herzegovina*, trans. Marion Faber (Lincoln: University of Nebraska Press, 1994); Beverly Allen, *Rape Warfare: The Hidden Genocide in Bosnia-Herzegovina and Croatia* (Minneapolis: University of Minnesota Press, 1996); and Elisabeth Bumiller, "Deny Rape or Be Hated: Kosovo Victims' Choice," *New York Times*, 22 June 1999.

I draw on the following sources on the history of rape: Ruth Kittel, "Rape in Thirteenth-Century England: A Study of the Common-Law Courts," in *Women and the Law*, ed. D. Kelly Weisberg (Cambridge: Shenkman, 1982), vol. 2, 101–15; Roy Porter, "Rape—Does It Have a Historical Meaning?" in *Rape*, eds. Sylvana Tomaselli and Roy Porter (Oxford: Blackwell, 1986), 216–79; and Vivien W. Ng, "Sexual Abuse of Daughters-in-Law in Qing China: Cases from the Zing'an Huilan," *Feminist Studies* 20:2 (1994), 373–91. Elizabeth Hafkin Pleck, *Domestic Tyranny: The Making of Social Policy Against Family Violence from Colonial Times to the Present* (New York: Oxford University Press, 1987) describes early feminist responses to rape and domestic violence in the United States and England. Susan Brownmiller, *Against Our Will: Men, Women, and Rape* (New York: Simon and Schuster, 1975) includes historical and contemporary examples of rape. Susan Griffin's works include "Rape: The All-American Crime," *Ramparts* 10 (1971), 26–35, and *Rape: The Politics of Consciousness* (San Francisco: Harper & Row, 1979). Angela Davis's essay "The Myth of the Black Rapist" appears in *Women, Race and Class* (New York: Random House, 1981), 172–201. See also Susan Estrich, *Real Rape* (Cambridge: Harvard University Press, 1987). On the Glen Ridge case, see Bernard Lefkowitz, *Our Guys: The Glen Ridge Rape and the Secret Life of the Perfect Suburb* (Berkeley: University of California Press, 1997). A recent sociobiological account appears in Randy Thornhill and Craig Palmer, *A Natural History of Rape: Biological Bases of Sexual Coercion* (Cambridge: MIT Press, 2000); for an alternative view, see Frans De Waal and Frans Lanting, *Bonobo: The Forgotten Ape* (Berkeley: University of California Press, 1997).

On "comfort women" see Miriam Ching Yoon Louise, "*Minjung* Feminism: Korean Women's Movement for Gender and Class Liberation," in *Global Feminisms Since 1945*, ed. Bonnie G. Smith (London: Routledge, 2000), 119–38; David E. Sanger, "Historian Exposes a Brutal Chapter," *New York Times*, 27 January 1992, A4; and Seth Mydans, "Inside a Wartime Brothel: The Avenger's Story," *New York Times*, 12 November 1996.

Data on reported rape rates appear in Diana Russell and Nancy Howell, "The

Prevalence of Rape in the U.S. Revisited," *Signs* 8:4 (1983), 688–95, and Diana Russell, *Sexual Exploitation: Rape, Child Sexual Abuse, and Workplace Harassment* (Beverly Hills: Sage Publications, 1984); "Living Without Fear: An Integrated Approach to Tackling Violence Against Women," Conference Report of the Home Office Special Conference on Violence against Women, 24–25 November 1999 (London: Home Office/Women's Unit, 1999) at http://www.womensunit.gov.uk/ living_without_fear/; Josephine Masimba, "Zimbabwe-Human Rights: Baring the Ugly Facts," *InterPress News Service*, 11 February 1997, www.aegis.com/nes/ips/ 1997/IP970201.html; U.S. Bureau of Justice Statistics, *Sex Offenses and Offenders: An Analysis of Data on Rape and Sexual Assault* (Washington, D.C.: U.S. Department of Justice, 1996), and Bureau of Justice Statistics, *Violence Against Women: Estimates from the Redesigned Survey* (Washington, D.C.: U.S. Department of Justice, 1995), accessed at http://www.ojp.usdoj.gov/bjs/pub/ascii/femvied.txt (9 September 2001). See also Joni Seager, *The State of Women in the World Atlas* (London: Penguin, 1997); Judith Mackay, *The Penguin Atlas of Human Sexual Behavior* (New York: Penguin Group, 2000); and "Violence Against Women," Fact Sheet 5, United Nations Fourth World Conference on Women, 4–15 September 1995. Data on known assailants appears in "Study Finds Half of Victims Know Attackers," *New York Times*, 25 August 1997, A16; and *Women of the World—Laws and Policies Affecting their Reproductive Lives—Latin America and the Caribbean* (New York: Center for Reproductive Law and Policy, 1997), 195–204.

Information on legal reform and antiviolence movements comes from Amrita Basu, ed., *The Challenge of Local Feminisms: Women's Movements in Global Perspective* (Boulder: Westview Press, 1995); Johanna Brenner, "The Best of Times, the Worst of Times: Feminism in the United States," in *Mapping the Women's Movement: Feminist Politics and Social Transformation in the North*, ed. Monica Threlfall (London: Verso, 1996), 17–72; Sonia E. Alvarez, "Translating the Global: Effects of Transnational Organizing on Local Feminist Discourses and Practices in Latin America," *Meridians* 1:1 (2000), 29–67. On individual and cultural strategies, see, e.g., Pauline B. Bart and Patricia H. O'Brien, *Stopping Rape: Successful Survival Strategies* (New York: Pergamon, 1985); Timothy Beneke, *Men on Rape* (New York: St. Martin's Press, 1982); and Emilie Buchwald, Pamela R. Fletcher, and Martha Roth, eds., *Transforming a Rape Culture* (Minneapolis: Milkweed Editions, 1993). The critique of date rape appears in Katie Roiphe, *The Morning After: Sex, Fear, and Feminism on Campus* (Boston: Little, Brown & Co., 1993). On the "tight jeans" defense, see Alessandra Stanley, "Ruling on Tight Jeans and Rape Sets Off Anger in Italy," *New York Times*, 16 February 1999, A6.

In addition to Catharine MacKinnon, *The Sexual Harassment of Working Women: A Case of Sex Discrimination* (New Haven: Yale University Press, 1979), see Cheryl Benard and Edit Schlaffler, " 'The Man on the Street': Why He Harasses," in *Feminist Frontiers IV*, eds. Laurel Richardson, Verta Taylor, and Nancy Whittier (New York: McGraw-Hill, 1997), 395–98. The Indian Supreme Court is mentioned in

Rina Singh, *Gender Autonomy in Western Europe: An Imprecise Revolution* (Basingstoke: Macmillan, 1998), 80. For commentaries on Anita Hill and the Clarence Thomas hearings, see Toni Morrison, ed., *Race-ing Justice, En-Gendering Power*, (New York: Pantheon Books, 1992).

The histories of domestic violence and social responses in the United States are detailed in Pleck, *Domestic Tyranny,* and Linda Gordon, *Heroes of Their Own Lives: The Politics and History of Family Violence* (New York: Viking, 1988). Data on spousal abuse and marital rape come from: "Sweden: Country Report on Human Rights Practices for 1997," United States Congress, Committee on International Relations (Hearing Before the Subcommittee on International Operations and Human Rights, House of Representatives, 105th Congress, second session, February 3, 1998); "Violence Against Women: An Issue of Human Rights," *genderaction* 4:4 (summer, 1997), 11-12; and Partha Benerjee, "Bride Burning and Dowry Deaths in India: Gruesome and Escalating Violence on Women," *Manavi Newsletter* 8-1 (1996), 1-5.

On responses to domestic violence see Radha Kumar, *The History of Doing: An Illustrated Account of Movements for Women's Rights and Feminism in India, 1800–1990* (London: Verso, 1993); Women's Information Center, "Shelter for Battered Women in Thailand," in *Third World, Second Sex: Women's Struggle and National Liberation/ Third World Women Speak Out*, comp. Miranda Davies (London: Zed Books, 1987), vol. 2, 205–10; Pauline W. Gee, "Ensuring Police Protection for Battered Women: The Scott v. Hart Suit," *Signs* 8:3 (1983), 554–67; "The Netherlands Country Report on Human Rights Practices for 1997," United States Congress, Committee on International Relations (Hearing Before the Subcommittee on International Operations and Human Rights, House of Representatives, 105th Congress, second session, February 3, 1998); Basu, *Challenge of Local Feminisms*; Sandyha Shukla, "Feminisms of the Diaspora Both Local and Global: The Politics of South Asian Women Against Domestic Violence," in *Women Transforming Politics*, eds. Cathy Cohen, Kathleen B. Jones, and Joan C. Tronto (New York: New York University Press, 1997), 269–83. The British response appears in "Lifting the Lid on Sexual Violence," Conference Report (London: Rape and Sexual Assault Support Center, 2000), accessed at http://www.gn.apc.org/womeninlondon/rasascrp.htm (August 2001); and "Living Without Fear: An Integrated Approach to Tackling Violence Against Women," Conference Report of the Home Office Special Conference on Violence Against Women, 24–25 November 1999 (London: Home Office/Women's Unit, 1999), accessed at http://www.womens-unit.gov.uk/living_without_fear/ (20 August 2001). Data on shelters appear in Albert R. Roberts, "Introduction: Myths and Realities Regarding Battered Women," in *Helping Battered Women: New Perspectives and Remedies*, ed. Albert R. Roberts (New York: Oxford University Press, 1996) and Albert R. Roberts, *Crisis Intervention and Time-Limited Cognitive Treatment* (Thousand Oaks: Sage, 1995). The legal response is discussed in Barbara Allen Babcock et al., *Sex Discrimination and the Law: History, Practice and Theory*, 2nd ed. (Boston: Little, Brown & Co., 1996).

Early feminist works on child sexual abuse include Florence Rush, *The Best Kept Secret: Sexual Abuse of Children* (Englewood Cliffs, N.J.: Prentice-Hall, 1980) and Judith Herman, *Father Daughter Incest* (Cambridge: Harvard University Press, 1981). Estimated world rates appeared in Charles W. Henderson, "Public Health: WHO Calls Child Abuse a Major Health Threat," *World Disease Weekly Plus*, 19 April 1999. See also Diana E. H. Russell, *Sexual Exploitation: Rape, Child Sexual Abuse, and Workplace Harassment* (Beverly Hills: Sage Publications, 1984) and the Commonwealth Fund study reported in Tamar Lewin, "Sexual Abuse Tied to 1 in 4 Girls in Teens," *New York Times*, 1 October 1997, A24. The association of abuse with later imprisonment appears in Jason deParle, "Early Sex Abuse Hinders Many Women on Welfare," *New York Times*, 28 Nov 1999, A1, and "Sexual Abuse: When Men Are Victims," *New York Times*, 30 March 1999, F8. For an example of personal memory, see Annie G. Rogers, *A Shining Affliction: A Study of Harm and Healing in Psychotherapy* (New York: Penguin USA, 1996), and on the complexities of memory, see Janice Haaken, *Pillar of Salt: Gender, Memory and the Perils of Looking Back* (New Brunswick: Rutgers University Press, 1998). Deaths from violence appears in "Report of the Special Rapporteur on violence against women, its causes and consequences, Ms. Radhika Coomaraswamy, submitted in accordance with Commission on Human Rights resolution 1995/85," Commission on Human Rights, United Nations Social and Economic Council, 5 February 1996, accessed at http://www. unhcr.ch/refworld/un/chr/chr96/thematic/53-wom.htm (1 September 2001).

Examples of feminist reconsiderations of violence can be found in Nancy C. M. Hartsock, "Political Change: Two Perspectives on Power," in *Building Feminist Theory: Essays from Quest: A Feminist Quarterly*, eds. Charlotte Bunch et al. (New York: Longman, 1981), 3–19, and Hartsock, "Community/Sexuality/Gender: Rethinking Power," in Nancy J. Hirschmann and Christine Di Stefano, eds., *Revisioning the Political: Feminist Reconstructions of Traditional Concepts in Western Political Theory* (Boulder: Westview Press, 1996), and bell hooks, *Feminist Theory: From Margin to Center* (Cambridge: South End Press, 1984).

CHAPTER THIRTEEN: NEW WORDS AND IMAGES: WOMEN'S CREATIVITY AS FEMINIST PRACTICE

The scholarship on gender and language is surveyed in Barrie Thorne, Cheris Kramarae, and Nancy Henley, eds., *Language, Gender and Society* (Rowley, Mass.: Newbury House, 1983) and in Penelope Eckert and Sally McConnell-Ginet, *Language and Gender: The Construction of Meaning in Social Practice* (Cambridge University Press, forthcoming). For Japanese see Orie Endo, "Aspects of Sexism in Language," in *Japanese Women: New Feminist Perspectives on the Past, Present, and Future*, eds. Kumiko Fujimura-Fanselow and Atsuko Kameda (New York: The Feminist Press, 1995), 29–42. The differential treatment of girls and boys in classrooms appears in American Association of University Women, *Shortchanging Girls, Shortchanging America* (Washington, D.C.: AAUW, 1991) and Peggy Orenstein, *Schoolgirls: Young*

Women, Self-Esteem, and the Confidence Gap (New York: Doubleday, 1994). For a complex analysis of gender socialization in schools, see Barrie Thorne, *Gender Play: Girls and Boys in School* (New Brunswick: Rutgers University Press, 1993).

The tradition of women's poems and songs can be found in Lila Abu-Lughod, *Veiled Sentiments: Honor and Poetry in a Bedouin Society* (Berkeley: University of California Press, 1986); Susan Mann, *Precious Records: Women in China's Long Eighteenth Century* (Stanford: Stanford University Press, 1997); Elaine Showalter, *A Literature of Their Own: British Women Novelists from Bronte to Lessing* (Princeton: Princeton University Press, 1977, reprinted 1999) and *The Norton Anthology of Literature by Women*, eds. Sandra M. Gilbert and Susan Gubar (New York: W. W. Norton, 1985). See also *Opening the Gates: A Century of Arab Feminist Writing*, eds. Margot Badran and Miriam Cooke (London: Virago, 1990). For the impact of English women writers on national literature, see Jennifer Summit, *Lost Property: The Woman Writer and English Literary History, 1380–1589* (Chicago: University of Chicago Press, 2000). Feminist utopian tales include Charlotte Perkins Gilman, *Herland* (New York: Pantheon Books, 1979); Rokeya Sakhawat Hossain, *Sultanas Dream*, ed. and trans. Roushan Jahan (New York: The Feminist Press, 1988). Feminist science fiction writing in the U.S. includes Ursula LeGuin, *The Left Hand of Darkness* (New York: Walker, 1969); Joanna Russ, *The Female Man* (Boston: Beacon Press, 1975); and Marge Piercy, *Woman on the Edge of Time* (New York: Knopf, 1976). Adrienne Rich has written extensively on women's consciousness, including essays collected in *On Lies, Secrets, and Silences: Selected Prose, 1966–78* (New York: W. W. Norton, 1979) and *Blood, Bread and Poetry: Selected Prose, 1979–1985* (New York: W. W. Norton, 1986).

Feminist literary criticism is a vast field. For an overview see Mary Eagleton, ed., *Feminist Literary Theory: A Reader*, 2nd ed. (Oxford: Blackwell, 1996). On French feminist theory, see, for example, Carolyn Burke, Naomi Schor, and Margaret Whitford, eds., *Engaging with Irigaray: Feminist Philosophy and Modern European Thought* (New York: Columbia University Press, 1994). Influential works include Toril Moi, *Sexual/Textual Politics: Feminist Literary Theory* (London: Routledge, 1995) and Barbara Johnson, *The Feminist Difference: Literature, Psychoanalysis, Race, and Gender* (Cambridge: Harvard University Press, 1998). On second-wave feminist novels see Lisa Hogeland, *Feminism and Its Fictions: The Consciousness-Raising Novel and the Women's Liberation Movement* (Philadelphia: University of Pennsylvania Press, 1998). Francine Prose explored the limits of women's gains in U.S. literature in "Scent of a Woman's Ink: Are Women Writers Really Inferior?" *Harper's*, June 1998, 61–70.

Tillie Olsen, *Silences* (New York: Delacorte, 1978) surveyed a century of women's writing. For recoveries of women's texts, see, for example, Margaret Littler, ed, *Gendering German Studies* (Oxford: Blackwell, 1997) and Jo Catling, ed., *A History of Women's Writing in Germany, Austria and Switzerland* (Cambridge: Cambridge University Press, 2000). In addition to Linda Nochlin, *Women, Art, and Power and Other Essays* (New York: Harper & Row, 1988), important reconsiderations of women's relationship to culture include Patricia Mainardi, "Quilts: The Great American Art," in *Feminism and Art History: Questioning the Litany*, eds. Norma Broude and Mary D. Garrard (New York: Harper & Row, 1982), 331–46; Janice Radway, *Reading the Romance: Women, Patriarchy, and Popular Literature* (Chapel Hill: University of North Carolina Press, 1991); and Purnima Mankekar, *Screening Culture, Viewing Politics: An Ethnography of Television, Womanhood, and Nation in Postcolonial India* (Durham: Duke University Press, 1999). On film see Laura Mulvey, *Visual and Other Pleasures* (Bloomington: Indiana University Press, 1989); E. Ann Kaplan, *Women and Film: Both Sides of the Camera* (New York: Methuen, 1983) and *Feminism and Film* (Oxford: Oxford University Press, 2000); and B. Ruby Rich, *Chick Flicks: Theories and Memories of the Feminist Film Movement* (Durham, NC: Duke University Press, 1998). For critiques of gender and race in U.S. popular culture, see the works of bell hooks, especially *Art on My Mind: Visual Politics* (New York: W. W. Norton, 1995) and *Outlaw Culture: Resisting Representation* (New York: Routledge, 1994).

My discussion of women and art draws on the following sources: Frances Bonner, Lizbeth Goodman, and Richard Allen, eds., *Imagining Women: Cultural Representations and Gender* (Cambridge: Polity Press/Open University, 1992), especially the introduction and essays by Elaine Showalter, Michelle Cliff, and Catherine King; Katy Deepwell, *New Feminist Art Criticism* (Manchester, UK: Manchester University Press/St. Martin's, 1995); Jill Dolan, *The Feminist Spectator as Critic* (Ann Arbor, Mich.: UMI Research Press, 1988); Dinah Dysart and Hannah Fink, *Asian Women Artists* (Roseville East, Australia: Craftsman House/G+B Arts International, 1996); Rita Felski, *Beyond Feminist Aesthetics: Feminist Literature and Social Change* (Cambridge: Harvard University Press, 1989); "The Female Gaze," in *Sexual Politics: Judy Chicago's Dinner Party in Feminist Art History*, ed. Amelia Jones (Los Angeles: Armand Hammer Museum, and Berkeley: University of California Press, 1996); Alicia Gaspar de Alba, *Chicano Art: Inside/Outside the Master's House* (Austin: University of Texas Press, 1998); Mary Kelly, *Imaging Desire* (Cambridge: MIT Press, 1996); Terence Maloon, "Interview with Mary Kelley," in *Visibly Female: Feminism and Art*, ed. and intro. Hilary Robinson (New York: Universe Books, 1987), 72–79; Rozsika Parker and Griselda Pollock, *Old Mistresses: Women, Art and Ideology* (New York: Pantheon Books, 1981); Peggy Phelan, *Art and Feminism* (London: Phaidon Press, 2001); Griselda Pollock, *Differencing the Canon: Feminist Desire and the Writing of Art's Histories* (London: Routledge, 1999) and Pollock "Tracing Figures of Presence," in *With Other Eyes: Looking at Race and Gender in Visual Culture* (Minneapolis: University of Minnesota Press, 1999); Ella Shohat, *Talking Visions: Multicultural Feminism in a Transnational Age* (Cambridge: MIT Press, 1998); Mira Schor, *WET: On Painting, Feminism, and Art Culture* (Durham: Duke University Press, 1997); Nancy Spero, "The Art of Getting to Equal," in *The Feminist Memoir Project: Voices from Women's Liberations*, eds. Rachel Blau duPlessis and Ann Snitow (New York: Three Rivers Press, 1998), 362–70, and Michelle Wallace, "To Hell and Back: On the Road with Black Feminism in the 1960's and 1970's," in *The Feminist Memoir Project*, 437–47.

For examples of feminist political theater, see Diana Taylor and Juan Villegas, eds. *Negotiating Performance: Gender, Sexuality, and Theatricality in Latin/o America* (Durham: Duke University Press, 1994). On feminist theater see Elaine Aston, *Feminist Theatre Practice: A Handbook* (London: Routledge, 1999). The literature on revisions of myths includes Adelaida R. Del Castillo, "Malintzin Tenépal: A Preliminary Look into a New Perspective," in *Essays on La Mujer* (Los Angeles: UCLA Chicano Studies Center, 1977), Anthology 1, 124–49; Norma Alarcón, "Traddutora, Traditora: A Paradigmatic Figure in Chicana Feminism," *Cultural Critique* 13 (1989); Mary Louise Pratt, "Yo Soy La Malinche': Chicana Writers and the Poetics of Ethnonationalism," *Callaloo* 16:4 (1993), 859–74; and Enid Dame, Lilly Rivlin, and Henny Wenkart, *Which Lilith?: Feminist Writers Re-create the World's First Woman* (Northvale, N.J.: Jason Aronson, 1998).

Third-wave feminist youth culture is discussed in Ednie Kaeh Garrison, "U.S. Feminism-Grrrl Style! Youth (Sub)Culture and the Technologics of the Third Wave," *Feminist Studies* 26:1 (2000), 141, and the special issue of *Signs* 23:3 (1998) on youth cultures. On "riot grrrls" and feminist 'zines, see Jennifer Baumgardener and Amy Richards, *Manifesta: Young Women, Feminism and the Future* (New York: Farrar, Straus, and Giroux, 2000), Chapter 3. See also Michelle Wallace, "Women Rap Back," *Ms.* 1:3 (1990), 61. On queer theater see Sue-Ellen Case, ed., *Split Britches: Lesbian Practice/Feminist Performance* (New York: Routledge, 1996). Women's folk art revivals are discussed in Sandra Gunning, "Re-Crafting Contemporary Female Voices: The Revival of Quilt-Making Among Rural Hindu Women of Eastern India," *Feminist Studies* 23:3 (2000), 719–26, and Paolo Gianturco and Toby Tuttle, *In Her Hands: Craftswomen Changing the World* (New York: Monacelli Press, 2000).

CHAPTER FOURTEEN: NO TURNING BACK: WOMEN AND POLITICS

For the redefinition of politics, in addition to Carole Pateman, *The Sexual Contract* (Stanford: Stanford University Press, 1988), Pateman, *The Disorder of Women: Democracy, Feminism, and Political Theory* (Stanford: Stanford University Press, 1989), and Susan Moller Okin, *Women in Western Political Thought* (Princeton: Princeton University Press, 1979), see Nancy J. Hirschman and Christine Di Stefano, eds., *Revisioning the Political: Feminist Reconstructions of Traditional Concepts in Western Political Theory* (Boulder: Westview Press, 1996), and Najma Chowdhury and Barbara J. Nelson with Kathryn A. Carver, Nancy J. Johnson, and Paula L. O'Loughlin, "Redefining Politics: Patterns of Women's Political Engagement from a Global Perspective," in *Women and Politics Worldwide*, eds. Barbara J. Nelson and Najma Chowdhury (New Haven: Yale University Press, 1994).

Conceptual frameworks for women's politics also appear in Maxine Molyneux, "Mobilization Without Emancipation? Women's Interests, State, and Evolution," in Richard R. Fagen, Carmen Diana Deere, and Jose Luis Coraggio, eds., *Transition and Development: Problems of Third World Socialism* (Boston: Monthly Review Press, 1986), 280–302; and Janet Saltzman Chafetz and Anthony Gary Dworkin, *Female Revolt:*

Women's Movements in World and Historical Perspective (Totowa, N.J.: Rowland and Allanheld, 1986).

Female consciousness is discussed in Temma Kaplan, *Crazy for Democracy: Women in Grassroots Movements* (New York: Routledge, 1997). The term "relational feminism" is used by Karen Offen, "Defining Feminism," *Signs* 14:1 (1988), 119–57. See also Sonia E. Alvarez, *Engendering Democracy in Brazil: Women's Movements in Transition Politics* (Princeton, N.J.: Princeton University Press, 1990). Maternalist themes also appear in Sara Ruddick, *Maternal Thinking: Toward a Politics of Peace* (Boston: Beacon Press, 1989), and Carole Gilligan, *In a Different Voice: Psychological Theory and Women's Development* (Cambridge: Harvard University Press, 1982). For women's involvement in pacifism in the United States, see Linda Schott, *Reconstructing Women's Thoughts: The International League for Peace and Freedom Before World War II* (Stanford: Stanford University Press, 1997), and Sue Lynn, *Progressive Women in Conservative Times: Racial Justice, Peace, and Feminism, 1945 to the 1960s* (New Brunswick, N.J.: Rutgers University Press, 1992). On Latin America, see Nikki Craske, *Women and Politics in Latin America* (New Brunswick N.J.: Rutgers University Press, 1999), and Elizabeth Friedman, "Paradoxes of Gendered Political Opportunity in the Venezuelan Transition to Democracy," *Latin American Research Review* 33:3 (1998), 87–135.

On feminist consciousness see Mary Fainsod Katzenstein, "Comparing the Feminist Movements of the United States and Western Europe: An Overview," in Katzenstein and Carol McClurg Mueller, eds., *The Women's Movements of the United States and Western Europe: Consciousness, Political Opportunity, and Public Policy* (Philadelphia: Temple University Press, 1987), 3–20. For examples of women in democratization movements, see Alicia Frohmann and Teresa Valdés, "Democracy in the Country and in the Home: The Women's Movement in Chile," in *The Challenge of Local Feminisms: Women's Movements in Global Perspective*, ed. Amrita Basu (Boulder: Westview Press, 1995), 276–301.

Islamic women's movements are discussed in Afsaneh Najmabadi, "Feminism in an Islamic Republic: 'Years of Hardship, Years of Growth,' " in *Islam, Gender, and Social Change*, eds. Yvonne Yazbeck Haddad and John L. Esposito (New York: Oxford University Press, 1998); Shahnaz Khan, "Muslim Women: Negotiations in the Third Space," *Signs* 23:2 (1998), 463–94; Deniz Kandiyoti, "Contemporary Feminist Scholarship and Middle East Studies," in *Gendering the Middle East: Emerging Perspectives*, ed. Kandiyoti (London: I.B. Tauris, 1996), 1–28; Margot Badran, "Competing Agenda: Feminists, Islam and the State in Nineteenth- and Twentieth-Century Egypt," in *Women, Islam, and the State*, ed. Deniz Kandiyoti (Philadelphia: Temple University Press, 1991), 201–36; Nikki R. Keddie, "The New Religious Politics and Women Worldwide: A Comparative Study," *Journal of Women's History* 10:4 (1999), 11–24; and interview with Hina Jilani, "Submission Is Not an Option," *Amnesty Now*, spring 2000, 14–15. On recent events see "Kuwait Narrowly Kills New Bill to Give Women Political Rights," *New York Times*, 1 December

1999, A5; Susan Sachs, "Egypt's Women Win Equal Rights to Divorce," *New York Times*, 1 March 2000, A1.

Women's human rights are discussed by Marguerite Guzman Bouvard, *Women Reshaping Human Rights: How Extraordinary Activists Are Changing the World* (Wilmington, Del.: Scholarly Resources, 1996); *Human Rights Are Women's Right* (New York: Amnesty International USA, 1995); Saba Bahar, "Human Rights Are Women's Right: Amnesty International and the Family," in *Global Feminisms Since 1945*, ed. Bonnie G. Smith (London: Routledge, 2000), 265–89; and Elizabeth Friedman, "Women's Human Rights: The Emergence of a Movement," in *Women's Rights, Human Rights: International Feminist Perspectives*, eds. Julie Peters and Andrea Wolper (New York: Routledge, 1995), 22. International funds for human rights work are described in the newsletter of the Global Fund for Women, *Raising Our Voices*, July 1999, and the fund's annual report for 1998–99. The asylum cases appear in Patrick J. McDonnell, "Change Planned in Asylum Rules on Domestic Abuse," *Los Angeles Times*, 7 December 2000; Brenda Sandburg, "Civil Rights Group Assists Asylum Seekers," *The Recorder* (American Lawyer Media), 3 January 2000, 4; Christopher Nugent and Lavi Soloway, "Racing the Asylum Deadline: Keeping Gays and Lesbians from Falling in the Cracks," *New York Law Journal*, 9 February 1998, 2; and Amy Waldman, "Woman Fearful of Mutilation Wins Long Battle for Asylum," *The New York Times*, 18 August 1999, B3.

Electoral data come from the Center for American Women and Politics, Eagleton Institute of Politics (Rutgers: State University of New Jersey), accessed at http://www.cawp.rutgers.edu (3 September 2001); *The World's Women, 2000: Trends and Statistics* (New York: United Nations, 2000); and Joni Seager, *The State of Women in the World Atlas* (London: Penguin Books, 1997). Women's campaigns in the United States are discussed in Linda Witt, Karen M. Paget, and Glenna Matthews, *Running as a Woman: Gender and Power in American Politics* (New York: The Free Press, 1994). On WIN WIN see Mary Jordan, "Women in Japan Want More Female Politicians," *San Francisco Chronicle*, 9 May 1999, A7, and "Wake-Up Call," *Ms.* 9:6 (1999), 25. On European politics, see M. Grazia Rossilli, "The European Union's Policy on the Equality of Women," *Feminist Studies* 25:1 (1999), 171–81, and Mary Nash, "Diverse Identities: Constructing European Feminisms," Global Forum Series, Center for International Studies, Duke University, April 1996. Annette Lu is described in Marcos Calo Medina, "New Vice President-elect Taiwan's Premier Feminist" (AP), *San Francisco Examiner and Chronicle*, 19 March 2000, A23. For women's political views see Sam Howe Verhovek, "Record for Women in Washington Legislature," *New York Times*, 4 February 1999, A18; "Connecting Women in the U.S. and Global Issues," survey report for A Women's Lens on Global Issues/ Aspen Institute, May 2000, accessed at http://www.ccmc.org/women2000/poll.pdf (8 September 2001); and Barbara Crossette, "Women's Global Views Examined by Survey," *New York Times*, 7 June 2000, A14.

On electoral procedures to ensure equal representation of women, see Francoise

Gaspard, *Au Pouvoir, Citoyennes! Liberté, Egalité, Parité* (Paris: Editions du Seuil, 1992); Jane Kramer, "Liberty, Equality, Sorority," *The New Yorker*, 29 May 2000, 112–23; "Halving It All," *Ms.* 11:4 (2001), 18; Chetna Gala, "Empowering Women in Villages: All Women Village Councils in Maharashtra, India," *Bulletin of Concerned Asian Scholars* 29:2 (1997), 31–45; Mary Anne Weaver, "Gandhi's Daughters," *The New Yorker*, 10 January 2000, 50–61; and Celia W. Dugger, "Lower-Caste Women Turn Village Rule Upside Down," *New York Times*, 3 May 1999, A1.

Communist and postcommunist feminist politics are discussed in Naihua Zhang with Wu Xu, "Discovering the Positive Within the Negative: The Women's Movement in a Changing China," in Amrita Basu, *Challenge of Local Feminisms*, 25–57; Virginia Cornue, "Practicing NGOness and Relating Women's Space Publicly: The Women's Hotline and the State," in *Spaces of Their Own: Women's Public Sphere in Transnational China*, ed. Mayfair Mei-Hui Yang (Minneapolis: University of Minnesota Press, 1999), 68–91; Maxine Molyneux, "Women's Rights and the International Context in the Post-Communist States," in *Mapping the Women's Movement: Feminist Politics and Social Transformation in the North*, ed. Monica Threlfall (London: Verso, 1996), 232–59; Susan Gal and Gail Kligman, "Introduction," *The Politics of Gender After Socialism: A Comparative-Historical Essay* (Princeton: Princeton University Press, 2000); Linda Racioppi and Katherine O'Sullivan See, *Women's Activism in Contemporary Russia* (Philadelphia: Temple University Press, 1997); and Laura Grunbert, "Women's NGOs in Romania," in *Reproducing Gender: Politics, Publics, and Everyday Life After Socialism*, eds. Susan Gal and Gail Kligman (Princeton: Princeton University Press, 2000), 307–36.

For other discussions of transnational feminist organizing, see Sonia E. Alvarez, "Translating the Global: Effects of Transnational Organizing on Local Feminist Discourses and Practices in Latin America," *Meridians* 1:1 (2000), 29–67, and Inderpal Grewal and Caren Kaplan, eds. *Scattered Hegemonies: Postmodernity and Transnational Feminist Practices* (Minneapolis: University of Minnesota, 1994).

INDEX

ABOUT THE AUTHOR

For the past twenty-five years, **Estelle B. Freedman**, a founder of the Program in Feminist Studies at Stanford University, has written about the history of women in the United States. Freedman is the author of two award-winning studies: *Their Sisters' Keepers: Women's Prison Reform in America, 1830–1930* and *Maternal Justice: Miriam Van Waters and the Female Reform Tradition.* Freedman coauthored *Intimate Matters: A History of Sexuality in America*, which was a *New York Times* Notable Book. Professor Freedman lives in San Francisco.

Visit the author online at http://noturningback.stanford.edu